Lecture Notes in Computer Science 8471

Commenced Publication in 1973
Founding and Former Series Editors:
Gerhard Goos, Juris Hartmanis, and Jan van Leeuwen

Editorial Board

More information about this series at http://www.springer.com/series/7408

Dimitra Giannakopoulou · Daniel Kroening (Eds.)

Verified Software: Theories, Tools and Experiments

6th International Conference, VSTTE 2014
Vienna, Austria, July 17–18, 2014
Revised Selected Papers

 Springer

Editors
Dimitra Giannakopoulou
NASA Ames Research Center
Mountain View
USA

Daniel Kroening
University of Oxford
Oxford
UK

ISSN 0302-9743
ISBN 978-3-319-12153-6
DOI 10.1007/978-3-319-12154-3

ISSN 1611-3349 (electronic)
ISBN 978-3-319-12154-3 (eBook)

Library of Congress Control Number: 2014953213

Springer Cham Heidelberg New York Dordrecht London

Printed on acid-free paper

Springer is part of Springer Science+Business Media (www.springer.com)

Preface

This volume contains the papers presented at the Sixth International Conference on Verified Software: Theories, Tool and Experiments (VSTTE), which was held in Vienna, Austria, during July 17–18, 2014, as part of the Vienna Summer of Logic. The final version of the papers was prepared by the authors after the event took place, which has permitted them to take feedback received at the meeting into account.

VSTTE has originated from the Verified Software Initiative (VSI), which is an international initiative directed at the scientific challenges of large-scale software verification. The inaugural VSTTE conference was held at ETH Zurich in October 2005, and was followed by VSTTE 2008 in Toronto, VSTTE 2010 in Edinburgh, VSTTE 2012 in Philadelphia, and VSTTE 2013 in Menlo Park. The goal of the VSTTE conference is to advance the state of the art through the interaction of theory development, tool evolution, and experimental validation.

The call for papers for VSTTE 2014 has solicited submissions describing significant advances in the production of verified software, i.e., software that has been proved to meet its functional specifications. We are especially interested in submissions describing large-scale verification efforts that involve collaboration, theory unification, tool integration, and formalized domain knowledge. We welcome papers describing novel experiments and case studies evaluating verification techniques and technologies.

There were 34 submissions. Each submission was reviewed by at least two, and on average 3.3, members of the Program Committee. The committee decided to accept 17 papers. The program has also included two invited talks, given by Orna Grumberg (Technion) and Michael Whalen (University of Minnesota), and a presentation on the 2014 Verified Software Competition organized by Ernie Cohen, Marcelo Frias, Peter Mueller, and Natarajan Shankar.

We would like to thank the invited speakers and all submitting authors for their contributions to the program. We owe a lot to Natarajan Shankar, who took care of all organization, Elizabeth Polgreen for managing the website and the proceedings, Leo Freitas (Publicity Chair), and Martina Seidl (CAV Workshop Chair). Finally, we would like to thank the external reviewers and the Program Committee for their reviews and for selecting the papers that appear in this volume.

July 2014

Dimitra Giannakopoulou
Daniel Kroening

Organization

Program Committee

Elvira Albert	Complutense University of Madrid, Spain
Domagoj Babic	Google, USA
Sandrine Blazy	IRISA – Université Rennes 1, France
Alessandro Cimatti	FBK-irst, Italy
Ernie Cohen	University of Pennsylvania, USA
Dimitra Giannakopoulou	NASA Ames Research Center, USA
Arie Gurfinkel	Software Engineering Institute, Carnegie Mellon University, USA
Klaus Havelund	Jet Propulsion Laboratory, California Institute of Technology, USA
Mats Heimdahl	University of Minnesota, USA
Andrew Ireland	Heriot-Watt University, UK
Bart Jacobs	Katholieke Universiteit Leuven, Belgium
Rajeev Joshi	Laboratory for Reliable Software, Jet Propulsion Laboratory, USA
Temesghen Kahsai	NASA Ames Research Center, USA
Moonzoo Kim	KAIST, South Korea
Daniel Kroening	University of Oxford, UK
Francesco Logozzo	Microsoft Research, USA
Tiziana Margaria	University of Potsdam, Germany
Peter Müller	ETH Zurich, Switzerland
Shiva Nejati	University of Luxembourg, Luxembourg
Shaz Qadeer	Microsoft, USA
Zvonimir Rakamaric	University of Utah, USA
Natarajan Shankar	SRI, USA
Nishant Sinha	IBM Research Labs, India
Cesare Tinelli	The University of Iowa, USA
Arnaud Venet	CMU/NASA Ames Research Center, USA
Jim Woodcock	University of York, UK
Karen Yorav	IBM Haifa Research Lab, Israel

Additional Reviewers

Aananthakrishnan, Sriram	Brain, Martin
Abate, Alessandro	Bubel, Richard
Balakrishnan, Gogul	Cattaruzza, Dario
Besson, Frédéric	Chaki, Sagar
Bingham, Jesse	Chiang, Wei-Fan

Deharbe, David
Dimjasevic, Marko
Duggirala, Parasara Sridhar
Gascon, Adria
Hadarean, Liana
Hong, Shin
Isberner, Malte
Ivancic, Franjo
Juhasz, Uri
Kannan, Jayanthkumar
Kesseli, Pascal
Kim, Yunho
Komuravelli, Anvesh
Landsberg, David

Lopez-Garcia, Pedro
Montenegro, Manuel
Navas, Jorge A.
Neubauer, Johannes
Parker, David
Rüthing, Oliver
Schaef, Martin
Schanda, Florian
Segura, Clara
Sezgin, Ali
Sousa, Marcelo
Summers, Alexander J.
Venet, Arnaud
Whalen, Michael

Contents

Analysis: Understanding
and Explanation

A Logical Analysis of Framing for Specifications with Pure Method Calls

Anindya Banerjee[1] and David A. Naumann[2]([⊠])

[1] IMDEA Software Institute, Madrid, Spain
anindya.banerjee@imdea.org
[2] Stevens Institute of Technology, Hoboken, USA
naumann@cs.stevens.edu

Abstract. For specifying and reasoning about object-based programs it is often attractive for contracts to be expressed using calls to pure methods. It is useful for pure methods to have contracts, including read effects to support local reasoning based on frame conditions. This leads to puzzles such as the use of a pure method in its own contract. These ideas have been explored in connection with verification tools based on axiomatic semantics, guided by the need to avoid logical inconsistency, and focusing on encodings that cater for first order automated provers. This paper adds pure methods and read effects to region logic, a first-order program logic that features frame-based local reasoning and a proof rule for linking of clients with modules to achieve end-to-end correctness by modular reasoning. Soundness is proved with respect to a conventional operational semantics and using the extensional (i.e., relational) interpretation of read effects.

1 Introduction

In reasoning about programs, a frame condition is the part of a method's contract that says what part of the state may be changed by an invocation of the method. Frame conditions make it possible to retain a global picture while reasoning locally: If predicate Q can be asserted at some point in a program where method m is called, Q still holds after the call provided that the locations on which Q depends are disjoint from the locations that may be written according to m's frame condition. This obvious and familiar idea is remarkably hard to formalize in a way that is useful for sound reasoning about programs acting on dynamically allocated mutable objects (even sequential programs, to which we confine attention here). One challenge is to precisely describe the writable state in case it involves heap allocated objects. Another challenge is to determine what part of such state may be read by Q (its 'footprint'). For reasons of abstraction, Q may be expressed in terms of named functions. To hide information about

---

A. Banerjee – Currently on leave at the US National Science Foundation.
D.A. Naumann – Partially supported by US NSF award CNS-1228930.

D. Giannakopoulou and D. Kroening (Eds.): VSTTE 2014, LNCS 8471, pp. 3–20, 2014.
DOI: 10.1007/978-3-319-12154-3_1

data representation, the function definitions may not be visible in the client program where m is called. This paper provides a foundational theory addressing these and related challenges.

Consider a class Cell with instances holding an integer value, used in the following client code.

method get(): **int**
method set(v: **int**) **ensures self**.get() = v
var c, d: Cell; c:= new Cell; d:= new Cell; c.set(5); d.set(6); **assert** c.get() = 5;

class Cell { **private** val: **int**; **ghost** footp: **rgn**;
  pure method get(): **int ensures self**.get() = **result**
                reads self.footp'**any**
  method set(v: **int**) **ensures self**.get() = v
              writes self.footp'**any** //(we elide read effects for impure methods)
              ensures ∀o: Cell . o ≠ **self** ⇒ o.footp # **self**.footp }

Fig. 1. Example: Cell. Type **rgn** (for 'region') means sets of object references and footp'**any** denotes a set of locations, namely all fields of objects in footp.

The goal is to prove the assertion by reasoning that the state read by c.get() is disjoint from the state written by d.set(6). Suppose the internal representation of Cell objects consists of an integer field val. The specifications could say set writes **self**.val and get reads **self**.val. Then the frame condition of d.set(6) would allow the postcondition of the call c.set(5), i.e., the predicate c.get()= 5, to be framed over the call d.set(6), yielding the assertion. But such specifications expose the internal representation. It would preclude, for example, an alternative implementation that uses, instead of integer field val, a pointer to a character string that represents the number using 0s and 1s.

Better specifications appear in Fig. 1, using ghost state to describe the 'footprint' of each cell, and postconditions from which the client can deduce disjointness of the representations of c and d. Use of ghost state for footprints is a key part of the 'dynamic frames' approach [8], and in addition to explicit disjointness conditions it supports separation reasoning based on freshness.

The example illustrates another challenging issue: one method (get) is used in the specification of others (get, set). Here is an example of calling a pure method in a frame condition: Instead of the ghost field footp one might choose to define a region-valued method footpm. If footpm is only used in specifications, one may argue it should be defined as part of the mathematical theory in which reasoning is carried out (though its read effect would still be useful). But there are practical benefits to using programmed methods in specifications, which can be justified provided that they are *pure* in the sense of having no effects other than reading.

Use of pure methods, especially ones in the program rather than part of the ambient mathematical theory, poses challenges. One is how to model such specifications without inconsistency. For example, care must be taken for sound treatment of specifications like **method** f(x: **int**): **int ensures result** = f(x)+1. Recursion aside, one may also wonder about soundness of using a pure method in its own postcondition, e.g., get in Fig. 1, or in its own frame condition: e.g., the read effect of footpm might be footpm()'**any** (making it 'self-framing'). Another issue is that the specifications of get and set are abstract, in the sense that they are consistent with many interpretations of the function get (e.g., get could return **self**.val+7). Client code should respect the abstraction, i.e., be correct with respect to any interpretation, whereas the expected implementations of get and set are only correct with respect to the interpretation that returns **self**.val.

The issues discussed so far have been addressed in prior work, especially in the context of verification-condition generation (VC-gen); see Sect. 7. However, most of the VC-gen work takes axiomatic semantics for granted rather than defining and proving soundness with respect to operationally grounded program semantics; the focus is on methodological considerations and on encodings that work effectively with SMT-based theorem provers. In these works, hypotheses are encoded as axioms, and linking of separately verified methods is implicit in the implementation of the VC-gen. The intricacies of dealing with heap structure, framing, purity, and self-framing frame conditions have led to soundness bugs in implemented verification systems (see [6]).

This paper provides a foundational account, by way of a conventional logic of programs that caters for SMT-provers by reasoning about framing using ghost state and FOL, and that is proved sound with respect to a standard operational semantics. Our account focuses on a *proof rule for linking* the implementation of an interface (i.e., collection of method specifications) with a client that relies on that interface.

The approach we take is motivated by two additional challenges. The first is information hiding, in the sense that implementations rely on invariants on module-internal data structures, but these invariants do not appear in the interface specification [7]. As a contrived example, representing the integer cell using a string might have the invariant that only 0 and 1 characters appear, without leading zeros. The invariant might be exploited by a method getAsString, but it has no place in the interface specification of method get which returns an integer. An alternative to hiding is to rely on abstraction: a predicate whose definition is opaque in the interface can be defined internally to be the invariant [9,11,15].

The second additional challenge arises from the practical need to use programmed methods that are only ***observationally pure*** in the sense that they do have side effects but these effects are benevolent [7] and not observable to clients. There are many examples, including memoization, lazy initialization, and path compression in Union-Find structures. These may involve allocation of fresh objects and mutation of existing ones.

Strong encapsulation is critical both for hiding of invariants [1,7,14] and for observational purity [13]. Both involve linking a client with the implementation of a module, where that implementation is verified against specifications different from those used by clients of the module—hiding invariants and hiding effects. In prior work we developed ***region logic*** (RL), a Hoare logic for sequential object-based programs, using standard FOL for assertions. By contrast with separation logic and permission-based systems, in RL separation is expressed as disjointness of explicit footprints, following the approach of dynamic frames. A benefit is that the verifier does not need to support separating conjunction; it comes at the cost of more verbose specifications. The language features expressions that denote **regions**, i.e., sets of object references. The logic provides a frame rule for local reasoning, based on frame conditions of methods and a subsidiary judgment for framing of formulas (Fig. 10). In addition to ordinary frame conditions, the logic formalizes encapsulation boundaries for modules, again in the manner of dynamic frames. This supports a second-order frame rule for linking method implementations to clients, hiding invariants [7,14].

In ongoing work, we have extended RL to a relational version, akin to [3,12, 20] but featuring a proof rule for representation independence. We plan to use this as basis for a proof system that allows use of observationally pure methods in specifications, which relies on relational consequences of encapsulation [7,13]. The problem is that general relational reasoning depends on read effects in frame conditions, a non-trivial if not earthshaking extension of RL. It deserves to be studied and presented in isolation from the complications needed for encapsulation and information hiding.

This paper builds on RLI [2] and RLII [1], extending RL with pure method calls in specifications and read effects in frame conditions. This involves adding read effects to frame conditions for commands and for pure and impure methods.

Outline and Contributions. Section 2 introduces the programming language and specifications, as well as the judgment of correctness under hypotheses. The latter is written $\Delta \vdash C : P \rightsquigarrow Q \, [\varepsilon]$. It says that under precondition P command C does not fault; if it terminates its final state satisfies Q and the computation's effects are allowed by ε. Moreover this conclusion is under hypothesis Δ, a list of method specifications. What's new in this paper is read effects in ε and Δ, and pure methods used in $\Delta, P, C, Q, \varepsilon$, specified in Δ. Section 3 takes the first step towards defining semantics, sketching two ways to interpret the hypotheses and pointing out a potential circularity. To dodge this circularity, semantics of expressions and formulas is parameterized on the interpretation of pure methods. Section 4 formalizes an extensional semantics of read effects; this is used to define correct interpretations of pure method specifications and to define the denotation of impure method specifications. The latter is like a specification statement, and is used in the operational semantics of programs; its first order semantics is justified by a closure property that is our first technical result. Section 5 completes the semantics of the correctness judgment, suitably instantiating the interpretation of pure methods as motivated by the rule for linking. For C verified under hypothesis Δ that specifies pure method p called in C and/or used in the specification of C, linking discharges the hypothesis. If the specification of p is unsatisfiable, it is not possible to instantiate the interpretation as required by the linking rule. This shows that a separate satisfiability check is not needed in a tool that correctly verifies the linked program, though the check maybe be helpful to flag problems early.

Section 6 gives selected proof rules and states the main result, soundness of the rules. Proofs and technical details that we gloss over can be found in the full version of the paper. The proofs are intricate because we work directly with small-step operational semantics, yet this is essential for the use of dynamic frames to provide flexible encapsulation of modules in RLII. But the proofs are elementary and do not involve fixpoints.

Section 7 briefly discusses related work. For future work, the next steps towards observational purity are (a) to extend the logic with second order framing, as in RLII but with hiding of effects, and (b) to add weak purity which allows allocation though not other effects (this is not hard but does add a few complications). Another step is to add read effects and pure methods to our prototype SMT-based verifier for RL [16,17], which already provides limited support for pure function definitions with framing, based on a version of Leino's Dafny. As a first step, we have successfully checked versions of the Cell example by manual encoding in Why3, using SMT-provers only.

2   Programs, Specifications, and Correctness Judgments

Figure 2 illustrates features of our programming and specification notations, by way of the Composite pattern, a well-known verification challenge problem [4,16]. A Comp is the root of a tree, nodes of which are accessible to clients. Here is an example client:

```
class Comp {
    private children: listOf(Comp);
    specpublic parent: Comp; // (private but visible in specifications)
    specpublic size: int := 1; // number of descendants
    ghost desc: rgn; // set of descendants

    method addChild(x: Comp)
        requires x ≠ null ∧ x.parent = null ∧ ...
        ensures // x is added as a child self
        writes children, x.parent, ancestors(self)'size, ancestors(self)'desc
    pure method getSize(): int
        reads size ensures result = size
    pure method ancestors(p: Comp): rgn
        reads ancestors(p)'desc, ancestors(p)'parent
        ensures result = { o ∈ alloc | type(o,Comp) ∧ p ∈ o.desc } }
```

Fig. 2. Composite example, adapted from RLI. Ghost code maintains the invariant that desc is the set of descendants.

var b, c, d: Comp; **var** i: int; ... i := d.getSize(); b.add(c); **assert** i = d.getSize();

To prove the assertion we want to frame the formula i = d.getSize() over the call b.add(c). The frame condition of addChild says it is allowed to write **self**.children,

$m, p \in MethName \quad x, y \in VarName \quad f, g \in FieldName \quad K \in DeclaredClassNames$

(Types) $T ::= \mathsf{int} \mid \mathsf{rgn} \mid \mathsf{Obj} \mid K$

(Program Expressions) $E ::= x \mid c \mid \mathsf{null} \mid E \oplus E \mid m(E)$ where c is in $\mathbb{Z}$, $\oplus$ is in $\{=, +, \ldots\}$

(Region Expressions) $G ::= \varnothing \mid x \mid \{E\} \mid G {}^{`}f \mid G \otimes G \mid m(F) \quad$ where $\otimes$ is in $\{\cup, \cap, \backslash\}$

(Expressions) $F ::= E \mid G$

(Commands) $C ::= \mathsf{skip} \mid x := F \mid x := \mathsf{new}\ K \mid x := x.f \mid x.f := F$
$\mid \mathsf{if}\ E\ \mathsf{then}\ C\ \mathsf{else}\ C \mid \mathsf{while}\ E\ \mathsf{do}\ C \mid C\ ; C \mid \mathsf{var}\ x{:}T\ \mathsf{in}\ C$
$\mid m(x) \mid \mathsf{let}\ m(x{:}T) = C\ \mathsf{in}\ C \mid \mathsf{let}\ m(x{:}T, \mathsf{res}{:}U) = C\ \mathsf{in}\ C$

Fig. 3. Programming language, highlighting additions to RLII [1].

x.parent, and the size and desc fields of the ancestors of **self**. In method set (Fig. 1) we use `**any** to abstract from field names, but here both size and desc are appropriate to make visible in the interface. (See RLI for more discussion of this facet of information hiding.) The frame condition would be less precise using ancestors(**self**)`**any**.

In order to reason using the frame rule (Fig. 10), we establish a subsidiary judgment written $\vdash \mathsf{rd}\, i, d, d.size$ frm $i = d.getSize()$ which says the formula $i = d.getSize()$ depends only on the values of i, d, and $d.size$. The rules let us establish this judgment based on the specification of $getSize$. The frame rule also requires us to establish validity of a so-called **separator formula**. This formula is determined from the frame of the formula and from the write effect of addChild. The function $\cdot/.$ generates the separator formula and is defined by recursion on syntax.[1] In the example, we compute $\varepsilon \cdot/. (\mathsf{rd}\, i, d, d.size)$, where ε is the write effect of addChild. The formula is the disjointness $\{d\}\ \#\ \mathsf{ancestors}(b)$, which says the singleton region $\{d\}$ is disjoint from the set of ancestors. It needs to hold following the elided part of the example client. In general, $\eta \cdot/. \varepsilon$ is a formula which implies that the locations writable according to ε are disjoint from the locations readable according to η.

Figure 3 gives the grammar of programs, revised from RLII to allow method calls in expressions. We assume given a fixed collection of classes. A class has a name and some typed fields. We do not formalize dynamic dispatch or even associate methods with classes; so the term 'method' is just short for procedure. For expository clarity methods have exactly one parameter (plus res for pure methods).

The linking construct $\mathsf{let}\ m(x{:}T, \mathsf{res}{:}U) = C\ \mathsf{in}\ C'$ designates that m is pure, with return type U, as indicated by the distinguished variable name res. It binds x, res, and m in C, and m in C'. Calls of m are expressions and pass a single argument. The body C is executed in a state with both x and res, the latter initialized to the default value for type U. The final value of res is the value of the call expression. The linking construct $\mathsf{let}\ m(x{:}T) = C\ \mathsf{in}\ C'$ designates that m is impure; command $m(y)$ depicts its call.

---

[1] Please note that $\cdot/.$ is not syntax in the logic; it's a function in the metalanguage that is used to obtain formulas from effects; see Sect. 6.

$$\begin{aligned}
df(m(F),\Delta) &= df(P_F^x,\Delta) \wedge df(F,\Delta) \wedge P_F^x \text{ where } \Delta(m) = (x:T,\mathsf{res}:U)P \rightsquigarrow Q\,[\varepsilon]\\
df(x.f = E,\Delta) &= x \neq \mathsf{null} \Rightarrow df(E,\Delta)\\
df(G_1 \subseteq G_2,\Delta) &= df(G_1,\Delta) \wedge df(G_2,\Delta)\\
df(\forall x:K \in G.\,P,\Delta) &= df(G,\Delta) \wedge \forall x:K \in G.\,df(P,\Delta)\\
df(P_1 \wedge P_2,\Delta) &= df(P_1,\Delta) \wedge (P_1 \Rightarrow df(P_2,\Delta))
\end{aligned}$$

Fig. 4. Definedness formulas for expressions and formulas (selected), for swf method context Δ.

Typing contexts, ranged over by Γ, are finite maps, written in conventional form. The judgment $\Gamma \vdash E : T$ means that E is well-formed and has type T. The typing rules straightforward. A command C is **well-formed in context Γ** provided that it is typable, i.e., $\Gamma \vdash C$, and in addition method call expressions $m(F)$ occur only in assignments $x := m(F)$ to a simple variable and with F free of method calls.

Values of type K are references to objects of class K (including the improper reference **null**). Value of type rgn are sets of references of any type. If $\Gamma \vdash G : \mathsf{rgn}$ then $\Gamma \vdash G`f : \mathsf{rgn}$ for any field name $f$ of region or reference type. In case $f : K$, the value of $G`f$ is the set of f-values of objects in G. In case $f : \mathsf{rgn}$, the value of $G`f$ is the union of the f-values. Aside from allocation and dereference (in the command forms $x := y.f$ and $y.f := F$), the only operation on references is equality test.

The syntax of formulas is standard and unchanged from RLI (Sect. 4.2), except that now the expressions include method calls, as in the points-to predicate $x.f = E$ and region containment $G \subseteq G'$.

$$P ::= E = E \mid x.f = E \mid G \subseteq G \mid (\forall x:K \in G.P) \mid P \wedge P \mid \neg P$$

The formula $\forall x : K \in G.P$ quantifies over all non-null references of type K in G. For disjointness of regions it is convenient to write $G \,\#\, H$ for $G \cap H \subseteq \{\mathsf{null}\}$.

Specifications. **Effects** are given by $\varepsilon ::= \mathsf{rd}\,x \mid \mathsf{rd}\,G`f \mid \mathsf{wr}\,x \mid \mathsf{wr}\,G`f \mid \mathsf{fr}\,G \mid \varepsilon,\varepsilon \mid (empty)$. Effects must be **syntactically well-formed (swf)** for the context Γ in which they occur: $\mathsf{rd}\,x$ and $\mathsf{wr}\,x$ are swf if $x \in dom(\Gamma)$; $\mathsf{rd}\,G`f$, $\mathsf{wr}\,G`f$, and $\mathsf{fr}\,G$ are swf if G is swf in Γ. In particular, if G is a call $m(F)$ to a pure method, then it must be that $\Gamma \vdash m(F) : \mathsf{rgn}$. The freshness effect $\mathsf{fr}\,G$ says the value of G in the final state contains only (but not necessarily all) references that were not allocated in the initial state. Later we use the term 'well-formed', without qualification, to mean in addition that the expressions do not depend on pure methods invoked outside their preconditions.

Specifications for impure methods take the form $(x{:}T)R \rightsquigarrow S\,[\eta]$ and for pure methods the form $(x{:}T,\mathsf{res}{:}U)R \rightsquigarrow S\,[\eta]$: x is the parameter (passed by value), R the precondition, S the postcondition, and η the effects. For these specifications to be swf in context Γ, η must not include $\mathsf{wr}\,x$. (This is standard in Hoare logic; postconditions refer to initial parameter values.) Moreover, R must be typable in $\Gamma, x{:}T$. Both S and η must be typable in $\Gamma, x{:}T$, for the impure form or $\Gamma, x{:}T, \mathsf{res}{:}U$, for the pure form. Finally, for the pure method there can be no write effects in η. Although the body of a pure method will write res, the semantics is a return value, not an observable mutation of state. In this paper, there's no need for impure methods to have read effects, but they will be needed for reasoning about data abstraction and observational purity. In any context Γ, there is a read effect that imposes no restriction: $\mathsf{rd}\ vars(\Gamma), \mathsf{rd}\ \mathsf{alloc'any}$.

A **method context** Δ is a finite map from method names to specifications. We are interested in specifications that may refer to global variables declared in some typing context Γ. Moreover, specifications in Δ are allowed to refer to any of the pure methods in Δ; the specification of p may have calls to p in its post-condition and effect, or p and m may refer mutually to each other—subject to the restriction that calls in preconditions must exhibit acyclic dependency. To make this restriction precise, we define a relation $\prec_\Delta$ on method names: $m \prec_\Delta m'$ iff m' occurs in the precondition of $\Delta(m)$. Now we can define what it means for a context Δ to be swf in Γ. First, the transitive closure, $\prec_\Delta^+$, is irreflexive. Second, the domains of Γ and Δ are disjoint and each specification is swf in the context $vars(\Gamma), sigs(\Delta)$. Here $sigs$ extracts the types of methods. For example, let Δ_0 be $m : (x{:}T)R \rightsquigarrow S\ [\eta],\ p : (y{:}V, \mathsf{res}{:}U)P \rightsquigarrow Q\ [\varepsilon]$. Then $sigs(\Delta_0)$ is $m : (x{:}T),\ p : (y{:}V, \mathsf{res}{:}U)$. Also $vars$ discards method declarations.

A **correctness judgment** takes the form $\Delta \vdash^\Gamma C :\ P \rightsquigarrow Q\ [\varepsilon]$. It is swf iff Δ is swf in Γ and C, P, Q, ε are all swf in $vars(\Gamma), sigs(\Delta)$. We often elide Γ.

Sound proof rules for correctness judgments prevent a pure method from being applied outside its precondition, to avoid the need to reason about undefined or faulty values. As is common in VC-generation, we use **definedness formulas**, see Fig. 4. The idea is that in states where $df(P, \Delta)$ holds, evaluation of P does not depend on values of pure methods outside their preconditions. Although the clause for $df(m(F), \Delta)$ refers to a method specification that may refer to another pure method in its precondition, df is well-defined, owing to the requirement that $\prec_\Delta^+$ is irreflexive (and $dom\,\Delta$ is finite).

An expression or formula will be considered well-formed if its definedness formula is valid, in addition to it being swf. To define validity, we proceed to semantics.

3   Semantics of Expressions and Formulas

There are two approaches to semantics of a judgment $\Delta \vdash C :\ P \rightsquigarrow Q\ [\varepsilon]$. The first goes by quantifying over all correct implementations of the procedures specified by Δ. The second goes by using nondeterminacy to represent a 'worst implementation' of each procedure, akin to the 'specification statement' used in axiomatic semantics. The second avoids a quantification and has been found to be quite effective [1,14]; we use it for impure methods (and in so doing show how the specification statement can include read effects). However, for pure method calls in formulas conventional semantics requires determinate values, so we use the first approach for pure methods.[2]

The transition semantics uses an environment for let-bound methods. A call to such m results in execution of the body found in the method environment. By contrast, if m is declared in Δ then its call is a single step in accord with its specification. If m is impure, the step goes to any state allowed by the specification $\Delta(m)$; we describe this by a relation $[\![\Delta(m)]\!]$ (Definition 2). If m is pure, we need a determinate result value but no change of state. So we use a function $\theta(m)$ to provide this value. The semantics of a correctness judgment (Definition 5) quantifies over all θ such that $\theta(m)$ conforms to the specification $\Delta(m)$ for each m in $dom\,\Delta$ (Definition 3). This is similar to an axiomatic semantics where $\theta(m)$ is an uninterpreted function constrained by $\Delta(m)$.

To define what it means for $\theta(m)$ to conform, and to define $[\![\Delta(m)]\!]$, we need semantics of expressions, formulas, and effects—and these depend on the meaning of pure method calls. To break this circularity, we define in this section a notion of candidate interpretation, and define the semantics of formulas and expressions with respect to any candidate interpretation θ.

We assume given an infinite set *Ref* of reference values including a distinguished 'improper reference' *null*. A **Γ-state** is comprised of a global heap and a store. The store is a type-respecting assignment of values to the variables in Γ and to the variable alloc : rgn which is special. Updates of alloc are built into the program semantics so that alloc holds the set of all allocated references. We write $\sigma(x)$ for the value of variable x in state σ, $\sigma(o.f)$ to look up field f of object o in the heap, $Dom(\sigma)$ for the variables of σ, and $[\![\Gamma]\!]$ for the set of Γ-states. We write $[\![T]\!]\sigma$ for the set of values of type T in state σ. Thus $[\![int]\!]\sigma = \mathbb{Z}$ and $[\![K]\!]\sigma = \{null\}\cup\{o|o \in \sigma(\text{alloc}) \wedge Type(o,\sigma) = K\}$. Besides states, we use the faulting outcome ⨳ for runtime errors (null-dereference), and also to signal precondition violations as described later.

For a typing context Γ, a **candidate Γ-interpretation** θ is a mapping from the pure method names in Γ such that if $\Gamma(m) = (x : T, res : U)$ then $\theta(m)$ is a function such that for any T-value t and state σ, $\theta(\sigma,t)$ is a U-value or ⨳. To be precise, $\theta(m)$ has the dependent type $(\sigma \in [\![\Gamma]\!]) \times [\![T]\!]\sigma \to ([\![U]\!]\sigma\cup\{⨳\})$. A **candidate Δ-interpretation** is just a candidate $sigs(\Delta)$-interpretation.

The denotation of an expression F in candidate Γ-interpretation θ and state σ is written $[\![F]\!]_\theta\sigma$ and defined straightforwardly, see Fig. 5. The second line in the figure is for application $m(F)$ of a pure method: evaluate F to get a value v, then apply the function $\theta(m)$ to the pair (σ,v). Using the semantics for expressions we define the 3-valued semantics of formulas in Fig 6. We also define $\sigma \models_\theta^\Gamma P$ iff $[\![P]\!]_\theta\sigma = $ true. Figure 7 shows that when the definedness formulas hold, the usual 2-valued clauses hold.

---

[2] This does not preclude nondeterminacy modulo an equivalence relation, which is especially important for 'weakly pure' methods that return freshly allocated references [13]. For VCs this is explored in [10].

$\llbracket E_1 + E_2 \rrbracket_\theta \sigma = \text{let } v_1 = \llbracket E_1 \rrbracket_\theta \sigma \text{ in let } v_2 = \llbracket E_2 \rrbracket_\theta \sigma \text{ in } v_1 + v_2$

$\llbracket m(F) \rrbracket_\theta \sigma \quad = \text{let } v = \llbracket F \rrbracket_\theta \sigma \text{ in } \theta(m)(\sigma, v)$

$\llbracket \{E\} \rrbracket_\theta \sigma \quad = \text{let } v = \llbracket E \rrbracket_\theta \sigma \text{ in } \{v\}$

$\llbracket G\text{`}f \rrbracket_\theta \sigma \quad = \text{let } X = \llbracket G \rrbracket_\theta \sigma \text{ in } \{\sigma(o.f) \mid o \in X \wedge o \neq \text{null} \wedge \text{Type}(o, \sigma) = \text{DeclClass}(f)\}$
$\qquad\qquad\qquad \text{if } f : K \text{ for some } K$

$\qquad\qquad = \text{let } X = \llbracket G \rrbracket_\theta \sigma \text{ in } \bigcup \{\sigma(o.f) \mid o \in X \wedge o \neq \text{null} \wedge \text{Type}(o, \sigma) = \text{DeclClass}(f)\}$
$\qquad\qquad\qquad \text{if } f : \text{rgn}$

Fig. 5. Semantics of selected program and region expressions, for state σ and candidate interpretation θ. We use the $\frac{1}{2}$-strict let-binder, i.e., '*let* $v = X$ *in* Y' denotes $\frac{1}{2}$ if X denotes $\frac{1}{2}$.

$\llbracket E_1 = E_2 \rrbracket_\theta \sigma \qquad = \text{let } v_1 = \llbracket E_1 \rrbracket_\theta \sigma \text{ in let } v_2 = \llbracket E_2 \rrbracket_\theta \sigma \text{ in if } v_1 = v_2 \text{ then } \textit{true} \text{ else } \textit{false}$

$\llbracket x.f = E \rrbracket_\theta \sigma \qquad = \text{if } \sigma(x) = \text{null then } \textit{false} \text{ else let } v = \llbracket E \rrbracket_\theta \sigma \text{ in}$
$\qquad\qquad\qquad\qquad \text{if } \sigma(x.f) = v \text{ then } \textit{true} \text{ else } \textit{false}$

$\llbracket x.f = E \rrbracket_\theta \sigma \qquad = \text{let } v = \llbracket E \rrbracket_\theta \sigma \text{ in if } \sigma(x) \neq \text{null and } \sigma(x.f) = v \text{ then } \textit{true} \text{ else } \textit{false}$

$\llbracket G_1 \subseteq G_2 \rrbracket_\theta \sigma \qquad = \text{let } X_1 = \llbracket G_1 \rrbracket_\theta \sigma \text{ in let } X_2 = \llbracket G_2 \rrbracket_\theta \sigma \text{ in if } X_1 \subseteq X_2 \text{ then } \textit{true} \text{ else } \textit{false}$

$\llbracket \Gamma \vdash \forall x : K \in G. P \rrbracket_\theta \sigma = \frac{1}{2} \text{ if } \llbracket G \rrbracket_\theta \sigma = \frac{1}{2} \text{ or } \llbracket \Gamma, x : K \vdash P \rrbracket_\theta \text{Extend}(\sigma, x, o) = \frac{1}{2}$
$\qquad\qquad\qquad\qquad \text{for some } o \text{ in } (\llbracket G \rrbracket_\theta \sigma) \backslash \{\text{null}\} \text{ with } \text{Type}(o, \sigma) = K$

$\qquad\qquad = \textit{true} \text{ if } \llbracket \Gamma, x : K \vdash P \rrbracket_\theta \text{Extend}(\sigma, x, o) = \textit{true}$
$\qquad\qquad\qquad \text{for all } o \text{ in } (\llbracket G \rrbracket_\theta \sigma) \backslash \{\text{null}\} \text{ with } \text{Type}(o, \sigma) = K$

$\qquad\qquad = \textit{false} \text{ otherwise}$

Fig. 6. Formulas: three-valued semantics, $\llbracket \Gamma \vdash P \rrbracket_\theta \sigma \in \{\textit{true}, \textit{false}, \frac{1}{2}\}$. Typing context is elided in most cases.

4   Semantics of Effects and Programs

Effects. A **location** is either a variable name x or a heap location comprised of a reference o and field name f. We write $o.f$ for such pairs. Define $rlocs(\sigma, \theta, \varepsilon)$, the locations designated by read effects of ε, in σ, by $rlocs(\sigma, \theta, \varepsilon) = \{x \mid \varepsilon \text{ contains rd } x\} \cup \{o.f \mid \varepsilon \text{ contains rd } G\text{`}f \text{ with } o \in \llbracket G \rrbracket_\theta \sigma\}$. Define *wlocs* similarly, for write effects.

Write effects constrain what locations are allowed to change between one state and another. We say ε **allows change from σ to τ under θ**, written $\sigma \rightarrow \tau \models_\theta \varepsilon$, provided (a) if y changed value (i.e., $\tau(y) \neq \sigma(y)$) then wr y is in ε; (b) if $o.f$ changed value then there is wr $G\text{`}f$ in ε such that $o \in \llbracket G \rrbracket_\theta \sigma$; and (c) if fr G is in ε then elements of G in τ are fresh. Reads are ignored, so $\sigma \rightarrow \tau \models_\theta \varepsilon$ iff $\sigma \rightarrow \tau \models_\theta writes(\varepsilon)$. In (b), region expressions G are interpreted in the initial state because frame conditions need only report writes to fields of pre-existing objects and not freshly allocated objects.

Read effects constrain what locations an outcome can depend on. Dependency is expressed by considering two initial states that agree on the locations deemed readable. Agreement needs to take into account variation in allocation, as two states may have isomorphic pointer structure but differently chosen references.

$$\sigma \models_\theta E_1 = E_2 \qquad \text{iff } [\![E_1]\!]_\theta \sigma = [\![E_2]\!]_\theta \sigma$$

$$\sigma \models_\theta x.f = E \qquad \text{iff } \sigma(x) \neq null \text{ and } \sigma(x.f) = [\![E]\!]_\theta \sigma$$

$$\sigma \models_\theta G_1 \subseteq G_2 \qquad \text{iff } [\![G_1]\!]_\theta \sigma \subseteq [\![G_2]\!]_\theta \sigma$$

$$\sigma \models_\theta^\Gamma \forall x : K \in G. P \quad \text{iff } \textit{Extend}(\sigma, x, o) \models_\theta^{\Gamma, x:K} P$$
$$\text{for all } o \text{ in } ([\![G]\!]_\theta \sigma) \backslash \{null\} \text{ with } \textit{Type}(o, \sigma) = K$$

$$\sigma \models_\theta P_1 \wedge P_2 \qquad \text{iff } \sigma \models_\theta P_1 \text{ and } \sigma \models_\theta P_2$$

$$\sigma \models_\theta \neg P \qquad \text{iff } \sigma \not\models_\theta P$$

Fig. 7. Two-valued semantics. These clauses hold when $\sigma \models_\theta df(P, \Delta)$ (Lemma 6).

Let π range over **partial bijections** on Ref. We write $\pi(p) = p'$ to express that π is defined on p and has value p'. A **refperm** from σ to σ' is partial bijection π such that

- $dom(\pi) \subseteq \sigma(\text{alloc}) \cup \{null\}$ and $rng(\pi) \subseteq \sigma'(\text{alloc}) \cup \{null\}$
- $\pi(null) = null$
- $\pi(p) = p'$ implies $\textit{Type}(p, \sigma) = \textit{Type}(p', \sigma')$ for all proper references p, p'

Define $p \overset{\pi}{\sim} p'$ to mean $\pi(p) = p'$. We extend $\overset{\pi}{\sim}$ to a relation on integers by $i \overset{\pi}{\sim} j$ iff $i = j$. For reference sets X, Y we define $X \overset{\pi}{\sim} Y$ iff $\pi(X) \supseteq Y$ and $X \subseteq \pi^{-1}(Y)$ (where $\pi(X)$ is the direct image of X). That is, π forms a bijection between X and Y.

Define $freshLocs(\sigma, \tau) = \{p.f \mid p \in freshRefs(\sigma, \tau) \wedge f \in Fields(\textit{Type}(p, \tau))\}$ where $freshRefs(\sigma, \tau) = \tau(\text{alloc}) \backslash \sigma(\text{alloc})$. For a set W of variables and heap locations, define $Lagree(\sigma, \sigma', W, \pi)$ iff $\forall x \in W.\sigma(x) \overset{\pi}{\sim} \sigma'(x)$ and $\forall (o.f) \in W.o \in dom(\pi) \wedge \sigma(o.f) \overset{\pi}{\sim} \sigma'(\pi(o).f)$.

Definition 1 (agreement on read effects). Let ε be an effect that is swf in Γ. Consider states σ, σ'. Let π be a partial bijection. Let θ be a candidate interpretation (for some Δ that is swf in Γ). Say that σ and σ' **agree on ε modulo π**, written $Agree(\sigma, \sigma', \varepsilon, \pi, \theta)$, iff $Lagree(\sigma, \sigma', rlocs(\sigma, \theta, \varepsilon), \pi)$. Define $Agree(\sigma, \sigma', \varepsilon, \theta) = Agree(\sigma, \sigma', \varepsilon, \pi, \theta)$ where π is the identity on $\sigma(\text{alloc}) \cap \sigma'(\text{alloc})$.

Programs. In the following we consider a method context Δ that is well-formed in some typing context Γ (often elided). For substitution we use the notation P_e^x. For clarity we use substitution notation in satisfaction statements, even though strictly speaking the syntax does not (and should not) include reference literals. If $\Gamma, x : T \vdash P$ and $\sigma \in [\![\Gamma]\!]$ and $v \in [\![T]\!]\sigma$, we may write $\sigma \models_\theta^\Gamma P_v^x$ to abbreviate $Extend(\sigma, x, v) \models_\theta^{\Gamma, x:T} P$.

The transition relation depends on a method context Δ. Configurations take the form $\langle C, \sigma, \mu \rangle$ where μ is a method environment. The call of a let-bound method m executes the body $\mu(m)$ with variables renamed to avoid clashes with the calling context. In case of a pure method the call takes the form $y := m(F)$ and there is some extra bookkeeping to assign the final value of res (or rather, a fresh instance thereof) to y.

$$\frac{[\![\Delta(m)]\!](\theta,z)\,\sigma\,\tau}{\langle m(z), \sigma, \mu \rangle \stackrel{\Delta,\theta}{\longmapsto} \langle \text{skip}, \tau, \mu \rangle} \qquad \frac{[\![\Delta(m)]\!](\theta,z)\,\sigma\,\mathbf{\xi}}{\langle m(z), \sigma, \mu \rangle \stackrel{\Delta,\theta}{\longmapsto} \mathbf{\xi}}$$

$$\frac{[\![m(F)]\!]_\theta\sigma \neq \mathbf{\xi} \quad \tau = [\sigma \mid x : [\![m(F)]\!]_\theta\sigma]}{\langle x := m(F), \sigma, \mu \rangle \stackrel{\Delta,\theta}{\longmapsto} \langle \text{skip}, \tau, \mu \rangle} \qquad \frac{[\![m(F)]\!]_\theta\sigma = \mathbf{\xi}}{\langle x := m(F), \sigma, \mu \rangle \stackrel{\Delta,\theta}{\longmapsto} \mathbf{\xi}}$$

Fig. 8. Transition rules for calls of impure and pure procedures in context Δ.

The transition semantics for pure method call $y := m(F)$ takes a step that assigns to y the value $[\![m(F)]\!]_\theta\sigma$ (defined in Fig. 5). The transition semantics of a call $m(z)$, for impure m in Δ, takes a single step to a final state (or $\mathbf{\xi}$) that satisfies the specification $\Delta(m)$. Such states are described by the denotation $[\![\Delta(m)]\!]$ of the specification.

Definition 2 (Denotation of impure method spec). Let Δ be swf and let $(x{:}T)R \rightsquigarrow S\,[\eta]$ be in Δ. Let θ be a candidate interpretation of Δ and z a variable name. Then $[\![(x{:}T)R \rightsquigarrow S\,[\eta]]\!](\theta, z)$ is defined as follows, for any $\Gamma_1 \supseteq \Gamma$ and Γ_1-states σ, τ:

(i) $[\![(x{:}T)R \rightsquigarrow S\,[\eta]]\!](\theta, z)\sigma\mathbf{\xi}$ iff $\sigma \not\models R^x_z$
(ii) $[\![(x{:}T)R \rightsquigarrow S\,[\eta]]\!](\theta, z)\sigma\tau$ iff
 (a) $\sigma \models^{\Gamma_1}_\theta R^x_z$ and $\tau \models^{\Gamma_1}_\theta S^x_z$ and $\sigma \to \tau \models_\theta \eta^x_z$ and
 (b) for all σ', π, if $Agree(\sigma, \sigma', \eta^x_z, \pi, \theta)$ and $\sigma' \models^{\Gamma_1}_\theta R^x_z$ then there are τ', ρ with
  – $\tau' \models^{\Gamma_1}_\theta S^x_z$ and – $\sigma' \to \tau' \models_\theta \eta^x_z$
  – $\rho \supseteq \pi$ and $freshRefs(\sigma', \tau') \subseteq \rho(freshRefs(\sigma, \tau))$
  – $Lagree(\tau, \tau', X, \rho)$ where $X = freshLocs(\sigma, \tau) \cup wlocs(\sigma, \theta, \eta^x_z)$

It is item (ii)(b) that is new in this paper; the rest is from RLII. Note that X is defined by interpreting η in the initial state.

A state σ may have no successor because the specification is unsatisfiable at σ. Unsatisfiability may be due to the postcondition, but it can also happen that τ satisfies the postcondition but not the read effect. The specification $(x{:}\text{Cell})true \rightsquigarrow y = x.val\,[\text{wr}\,y]$ is unsatisfiable: y cannot be set to $x.val$ without reading $\{x\}\text{`}val$ or having a stronger precondition like $y = x.val$.

Although specifications include read effects—a relational property—the denotation of a specification need not be defined as an extreme solution to constraints including that relational property. The elementary definition above has the property that any τ' that satisfies the conditions in (ii) is a possible successor of σ', i.e., the denotation is closed in the sense that it includes the pair σ', τ'. This is made precise in Theorem 9. The condition $freshRefs(\sigma', \tau') \subseteq \rho(freshRefs(\sigma, \tau))$ in (ii)(b) was not immediately obvious but is crucial for Theorem 9.

With all the ingredients in hand, the transition semantics can be defined; see Fig. 8.

5 Semantics of Correctness Judgments

To link a client C with implementation B of a method m used by C we want C to be correct for all interpretations of the method context. But reasoning about B can use a particular interpretation for m. Such an interpretation might be provided directly, as a mathematical definition provided by the programmer, or it might be derived from the code as it is in work on VC generation for pure methods [5]. Here we treat such interpretations semantically. To that end, we generalize the correctness judgment form to $\Delta; \theta \vdash^\Gamma C : P \leadsto Q\,[\varepsilon]$. For this to be swf, θ should be a candidate interpretation of some subset of Δ, and $\Delta \vdash^\Gamma C : P \leadsto Q\,[\varepsilon]$ should be swf as defined in Sect. 2. The original form is essentially the special case where θ is the empty function. The generalized correctness judgment is important for the linking rule, which we introduce here in abridged form. We consider a single method specification $\Theta \equiv m : (x{:}T, \mathsf{res}{:}U)Q \leadsto Q'$, we elide effects, and the partial interpretation of the ambient library Δ is empty.

$$\frac{\Delta, \Theta; \varnothing \vdash C : P \leadsto P' \quad \Delta, \Theta; \theta \vdash B : Q \leadsto Q' \quad \mathrm{dom}\,\theta = \{m\} \quad \theta \models \Delta, \Theta}{\Delta; \varnothing \vdash \mathsf{let}\ m(x{:}T, \mathsf{res}{:}U) = B\ \mathsf{in}\ C : P \leadsto P'} \quad (1)$$

A client C is linked with the implementation B of a pure procedure m. The verification condition for C is under the hypothesis of some specifications Δ, Θ which include the specification Θ of m. The rule may only be instantiated with swf judgments, so Δ is swf (as it appears in the conclusion) and the larger method context Δ, Θ is also swf.

According to the semantics to follow, the judgment for C means that it is correct with respect to any interpretation φ of all the pure procedures in Δ, Θ. The verification condition for B also has hypothesis Δ, Θ for procedures that may be called in B or used in its specification, and B must be correct with respect to any interpretation of the pure procedures in Δ, but fixed interpretation θ of m. The rule requires that in fact θ is an interpretation of Θ, meaning that $\theta(m)$ satisfies the specification of m. Because this specification may refer to pure methods in the ambient context Δ, satisfaction is expressed as $\theta \models \Delta, \Theta$. This is defined in terms of the following.

Definition 3 (context interpretation). Let Δ be swf in Γ and let θ be a candidate Δ-interpretation. (Note that $\mathrm{dom}\,\theta = \mathrm{dom}\,\Delta$.) Say θ is a **Δ-interpretation** iff the following holds for each $m : (x{:}T, \mathsf{res}{:}U)P \leadsto Q\,[\varepsilon]$ in Δ. For any $\sigma \in [\![\Gamma]\!]$ and $v \in [\![T]\!]\sigma$,

(a) $\theta(m)(\sigma, v) = \frac{1}{2}$ iff $\sigma \not\models_\theta P_v^x$

Furthermore, if $\sigma \models_\theta P_v^x$ then letting $w = \theta(m)(\sigma, v)$ we have

(b) $\sigma \models_\theta Q_{v,w}^{x,\mathsf{res}}$
(c) for any $\sigma' \in [\![\Gamma]\!]$, $v' \in [\![T]\!]\sigma'$ with $\sigma' \models_\theta P_{v'}^x$, and any refperm π from σ to σ', if $v \overset{\pi}{\sim} v'$ and $\mathit{Agree}(\sigma, \sigma', \varepsilon, \pi, \theta)$ then $w \overset{\pi}{\sim} w'$ where $w' = \theta(m)(\sigma', v')$

Definition 4 (partial context interpretation). Let Δ be swf and Δ, Θ be swf. Let θ be a candidate interpretation of Θ. We say θ is a ***partial interpretation*** of Δ, Θ, written $\theta \models \Delta, \Theta$, provided that for any Δ-interpretation δ, the candidate $\delta \cup \theta$ is a (Δ, Θ)-interpretation.[3]

Definition 5 (valid judgment). A swf correctness judgment $\Delta; \theta \vdash^{\Gamma} C : P \rightsquigarrow Q [\varepsilon]$ is ***valid*** iff the following conditions hold for all Γ-environments μ, all Δ-interpretations δ such that $\theta \subseteq \delta$, and all states σ such that $\sigma \models_{\delta}^{\Gamma, sigs(\Delta)} P$.

    (Safety) It is not the case that $\langle C, \sigma, \mu \rangle \overset{\Delta, \delta}{\longmapsto}^* \lightning$.

    (Post) $\tau \models_{\delta} Q$ for every τ with $\langle C, \sigma, \mu \rangle \overset{\Delta, \delta}{\longmapsto}^* \langle \mathsf{skip}, \tau, \mu \rangle$

    (Effect) $\sigma \rightarrow \tau \models_{\delta} \varepsilon$ for every τ with $\langle C, \sigma, \mu \rangle \overset{\Delta, \delta}{\longmapsto}^* \langle \mathsf{skip}, \tau, \mu \rangle$

    (Read Effect) for any τ such that $\langle C, \sigma, \mu \rangle \overset{\Delta, \delta}{\longmapsto}^* \langle \mathsf{skip}, \tau, \mu \rangle$, and any σ', π, τ such that $Agree(\sigma, \sigma', \varepsilon, \pi, \delta)$ and $\sigma' \models_{\delta}^{\Gamma} P$, there are τ', ρ such that

    $\langle C, \sigma', \mu \rangle \overset{\Delta, \delta}{\longmapsto}^* \langle \mathsf{skip}, \tau', \mu \rangle$ and $\rho \supseteq \pi$ and $freshLocs(\sigma', \tau') \subseteq \rho(freshLocs(\sigma, \tau))$ and $Lagree(\tau, \tau', X, \rho)$ where $X = freshLocs(\sigma, \tau) \cup wlocs(\sigma, \delta, \varepsilon)$.

In case $\Delta(m)$ is unsatisfiable (except possibly by divergence), no Δ-interpretation exists. Then the judgment holds but the hypotheses cannot be discharged by linking because there is no way to instantiate θ in rule (1).

    The definitions up to this point apply even if pure methods are called outside their precondition. For understandable proof rules, and to stay within FOL for assertions, we will disallow such specifications and correctness judgments.

Lemma 6 (two-valued semantics of formulas). If θ is a Δ-interpretation and $\sigma \models_{\theta} df(P, \Delta)$ then $[\![P]\!]_{\theta}\sigma$ is not $\lightning$. And for any σ and any Δ-interpretation θ, if $\sigma \models_{\theta} df(P, \Delta)$ then $\sigma \models_{\theta} P$ satisfies the usual defining clause, see Fig. 7.

Definition 7. Let Γ be a typing context and let Δ be a specification context that is swf in Γ. Let P be a formula that is swf in $vars(\Gamma), sigs(\Delta)$. Then P is ***Δ-valid***, written $\Delta \models P$, if and only if $\sigma \models_{\theta} P$ for all Δ-interpretations θ and all states σ.

Definition 8 (healthy, well-formed). Let Γ and Δ satisfy the conditions of Definition 7. A formula P that is swf is ***healthy*** iff $df(P, \Delta)$ is valid. A swf specification $P \rightsquigarrow Q [\eta]$ is ***healthy*** (with respect to Γ, Δ) iff the three formulas $df(P, \Delta)$, $P \Rightarrow df(Q, \Delta)$, and $P \Rightarrow df(\eta, \Delta)$ are Δ-valid. A swf correctness judgment $\Delta; \theta \vdash^{\Gamma} C : P \rightsquigarrow Q [\eta]$ is ***healthy*** iff the three formulas $df(P, \Delta)$, $P \Rightarrow df(Q, \Delta)$, and $P \Rightarrow df(\eta, \Delta)$ are Δ-valid. The term ***well-formed*** means swf and healthy.

    The definitions to this point are intricate but elementary; in particular, there are no fixpoints. But by contrast with axiomatic semantics, correctness is directly

---

[3] Under these conditions, if the specifications in Θ refer to methods in Δ, Θ is not swf on its own, and then it is not meaningful to call θ a Θ-interpretation.

grounded in a conventional operational semantics. The one unconventional element is that transition semantics depends on method context. The ultimate confirmation that we *are* reasoning about program behavior is soundness of the linking rule, which can be used to discharge all hypotheses.

6   Proof System

The *framing judgment* has the form $P; \Delta \vdash \eta$ frm Q and is swf under evident conditions. It means that in P-states, Q reads within the read effect η. The judgment is *healthy* iff the formulas $df(P, \Delta)$, $P \Rightarrow df(\eta, \Delta)$, and $P \Rightarrow df(Q, \Delta)$ are all Δ-valid. The judgment is *valid*, written $P; \Delta \models^\Gamma \eta$ frm Q, iff for all Γ-states σ, σ', refperms π, and Δ-interpretations θ, if $Agree(\sigma, \sigma', \eta, \pi, \theta)$, and $\sigma \models_\theta^\Gamma P \wedge Q$, then $\sigma' \models_\theta^\Gamma Q$.

A verifier can check framing judgments in terms of the validity property, but our logic includes rules to derive framing judgments. A basic rule allows to infer, for atomic formula P, the judgment $true; \Delta \vdash ftpt(P, \Delta)$ frm P concerning a precise footprint computed by function $ftpt$ which is defined in Fig. 9. For non-atomic formulas there are syntax-directed rules, e.g., the rule for conjunction allows to infer $P; \Delta \vdash \varepsilon$ frm $Q_1 \wedge Q_2$ from $P; \Delta \vdash \varepsilon$ frm Q_1 and $P \wedge Q_1; \Delta \vdash \varepsilon$ frm Q_2. There are also subsidiary rules for subsumption of effects and for logical manipulation of P. These rules are adapted in a straightforward way from RLI (Sect. 6.1).

The point of establishing $P; \Delta \vdash \eta$ frm Q is that code that writes outside η cannot falsify Q. This is expressed in the frame rule by computing, from the frame η of Q and the frame condition ε of the code, a *separator formula* which is a conjunction of region disjointness formulas describing states in which writes allowed by ε cannot affect the value of a formula with read effect η. We define the separator formula as $\eta \, ./ \, \varepsilon$, using function $./$ which recurses on syntax (see RLI Sect. 6.2). For example, rd $G' f \, ./ \,$ wr $H' g$ is *true*, and rd $G' f \, ./ \,$ wr $H' f$ is the disjointness formula $G \# H$. Also, rd $x \, ./ \,$ wr y is simply *false*, if x and y are the same variable, and *true* otherwise. Writes on the left and reads on the right are ignored, so $\eta \, ./ \, \varepsilon$ is the same as $reads(\eta) \, ./ \, writes(\varepsilon)$.

The key property of a separator is to establish the agreement to which frame validity refers. To be precise, suppose $\sigma \rightarrow \tau \models_\theta \varepsilon$ and $\sigma \models_\theta \eta \, ./ \, \varepsilon$. Then $Agree(\sigma, \tau, \eta, id, \theta)$, where id is the identity on $\sigma(\text{alloc})$.

An effect ε is called *self-framing* in method context Δ provided that for every rd $G' f$ or wr $G' f$ in ε, $ftpt(G, \Delta)$ is in ε. Such effects arise, for example, in case a method refers to itself in its frame condition. So are effects obtained

$$
\begin{aligned}
ftpt(x, \Delta) &= \text{rd } x & ftpt(E = E', \Delta) &= ftpt(E, \Delta), ftpt(E', \Delta) \\
ftpt(G' f, \Delta) &= \text{rd } G' f, ftpt(G, \Delta) & ftpt(G_1 \subseteq G_2, \Delta) &= ftpt(G_1, \Delta), ftpt(G_2, \Delta) \\
ftpt(\varnothing, \Delta) &= \varnothing & ftpt(x.f = F, \Delta) &= \text{rd } x, x.f, ftpt(F, \Delta) \\
ftpt(m(F), \Delta) &= reads(\varepsilon_F^x), ftpt(F, \Delta) & \multicolumn{2}{l}{\text{for } \Delta(m) = (x : T, \text{res} : U)P \rightsquigarrow Q\,[\varepsilon]}
\end{aligned}
$$

Fig. 9. Footprints of region expressions and atomic assertions well-formed in Δ.

$$\Delta; \varnothing \vdash x.f := F : x \neq \text{null} \land y = F \rightsquigarrow x.f = y \, [\text{wr}\, x.f, \text{rd}\, x, \mathit{ftpt}(F, \Delta)]$$

$$\text{FRAME} \quad \frac{\Delta; \theta \vdash C : P \rightsquigarrow Q\,[\varepsilon] \qquad P; \Delta \vdash \eta \text{ frm } R \qquad \Delta; \theta \models P \land R \Rightarrow \eta \cdot /. \, \varepsilon}{\Delta; \theta \vdash C : P \land R \rightsquigarrow Q \land R\,[\varepsilon]}$$

$$\frac{\Delta; \theta \vdash C : P \rightsquigarrow Q\,[\varepsilon]}{\Delta; \theta \cup \theta' \vdash C : P \rightsquigarrow Q\,[\varepsilon]} \qquad \qquad \frac{\varepsilon \text{ is self-framing}}{m : (x{:}T)P \rightsquigarrow Q\,[\varepsilon]; \varnothing \vdash m(z) : P_z^x \rightsquigarrow Q_z^x\,[\varepsilon_z^x]}$$

$$\frac{x \notin \mathit{Vars}(H) \cup FV(Q)}{m : (y{:}T, \text{res}{:}U)P \rightsquigarrow Q\,[\varepsilon]; \varnothing \vdash x := m(H) : P_H^y \rightsquigarrow Q_{H,x}^{y,\text{res}}\,[\text{wr}\, x, \mathit{ftpt}(H, \Delta), \varepsilon_H^y]}$$

$$\frac{\begin{array}{c} \Theta \text{ is } m : (x{:}T, \text{res}{:}U)Q \rightsquigarrow Q'\,[\eta] \qquad \text{dom}\,\theta = \text{dom}\,\Theta \qquad \theta \models \Delta, \Theta \\ \Delta, \Theta; \delta \vdash^\Gamma C : P \rightsquigarrow P'\,[\varepsilon] \qquad \Delta, \Theta; \delta \cup \theta \vdash^{\Gamma, x{:}T, \text{res}{:}U} B : Q \rightsquigarrow Q'\,[\text{wr}\,\text{res}, \text{rd}\,x, \eta] \\ \eta \text{ is wr-free and self-framing} \qquad \mathit{terminates}(Q, B) \end{array}}{\Delta; \delta \vdash^\Gamma \text{let } m(x{:}T, \text{res}{:}U) = B \text{ in } C : P \rightsquigarrow P'\,[\varepsilon]}$$

Fig. 10. Proof rules for field update, framing, interpreting, pure/impure calls, and linking.

using the *ftpt* function and most of the framing rules. For self-framing ε, if $\mathit{Agree}(\sigma, \sigma', \varepsilon, \pi, \theta)$ then $[\![G]\!]_\theta \sigma \overset{\pi}{\sim} [\![G]\!]_\theta \sigma'$ for any $\text{rd}\, G^\epsilon f$ or $\text{wr}\, G^\epsilon f$ in ε.

Theorem 9 (denotation closure). Suppose η is self-framing and θ is a Δ-interpretation. If $[\![(x{:}T)R \rightsquigarrow S\,[\eta]]\!](\theta, z)\sigma\tau$ then $[\![(x{:}T)R \rightsquigarrow S\,[\eta]]\!](\theta, z)\sigma'\tau'$, provided that σ', τ' satisfy the conditions in Definition 2(ii).

Proof Rules for Correctness Judgments. Figure 10 presents a few proof rules. They are to be instantiated only with well-formed premises and conclusions (Definition 8). The first, for field update, is a 'local axiom' that precisely describes the effect; it shows how read effects can easily be incorporated into the rules from RLI (Sect. 7.1) and RLII (Sect. 7.1). Next is the frame rule, adapted from RLI/II by adding Δ to the side conditions. Then come rules for impure and pure method calls. For reasons of parsimony we make self-framing an explicit premise where needed for soundness. It turns out that in non-trivial provable judgements the frame conditions in the method context will be self-framing.

We give an illustrative rule for linking a client with a method implementation. The general rule allows several pure and impure methods that may refer to each other in their specifications and code (of course, subject to the proviso concerning $\prec_\Delta^+$ in the definition of swf method context in Sect. 2). Predicate $\mathit{terminates}(Q, B)$ says that from any Q-state, B terminates (normally or abnormally). One premise is that partial (Δ, Θ)-interpretation θ is provided; it gives the *chosen* interpretation for m, to be used in verifying the body B. By contrast, the premise for C requires correctness with respect to *all* interpretations of m.

Theorem 10. Any derivable correctness judgment is valid.

7   Related Work

We take the Cell example from the most closely related work, [18], where read effects of pure methods are specified using dynamic frames and methods may be self-framing. They define (and implement) a VC-generator including VCs that encode the semantics of read effects, albeit only for a pair of states in succession. (That avoids the need for refperms, and suffices for framing but not relational reasoning for data abstraction and encapsulation.) They give a detailed proof of soundness with respect to transition semantics, by showing that the VCs ensure a small-step invariant that implies correctness and fault-avoidance. Axioms are included (and proved sound) to exploit read effects for framing. Different from our work, the body of a pure method is required to be a single 'return E' statement and E is visible to clients; and pure methods do not have postconditions. (Their implementation does include such postconditions.) Although VCs are generated modularly, we do not discern an explicit account of linking, or an easy adaptation to cater for hiding a pure method body or invariants from clients. As usual in practical systems, the syntax embeds specifications in programs, as opposed to judgments that ascribe properties to programs.

A number of earlier works point out the importance of read effects for pure methods and explore VC-generation, e.g. [5], explore weak purity which allows allocation, and shows consistency of a system of VCs (but not operational soundness). The analog of consistency, in our setting, is being able to discharge hypotheses in the linking rule.

Framing in separation logic encompasses read and write effects, implicitly in syntax but explicitly in the semantics (safety monotonicity, frame property [14]). Whereas self-framing is a property of effects, in our setting, it is a property of formulas in other settings. In separation logic, all assertions are effectively self-framing. The abstract predicates approach [15] to data abstraction has inspired several works that cater for SMT provers by using ghost instrumentation to encode intensional semantics of effects in terms of permissions. One provides a VC generator and sketches an argument for its operational soundness [6]. Another gives a detailed semantics and soundness proof for VCs that provide effective reasoning about recursively defined abstract predicates and abstraction functions [19]. The latter works have extensive pointers to related work.

References

1. Banerjee, A., Naumann, D.A.: Local reasoning for global invariants. Part II: Dynamic boundaries. J. ACM **60**(3), 19:1–19:73 (2013)
2. Banerjee, A., Naumann, D.A., Rosenberg, S.: Local reasoning for global invariants. Part I: Region logic. J. ACM **60**(3), 18:1–18:56 (2013)
3. Benton, N.: Simple relational correctness proofs for static analyses and program transformations. In: POPL (2004)
4. Bobot, F., Filliâtre, J.-C.: Separation predicates: a taste of separation logic in first-order logic. In: Aoki, T., Taguchi, K. (eds.) ICFEM 2012. LNCS, vol. 7635, pp. 167–181. Springer, Heidelberg (2012)

5. Darvas, A., Müller, P.: Reasoning about method calls in interface specifications. J. Object Technol. **5**, 59–85 (2006)
6. Heule, S., Kassios, I.T., Müller, P., Summers, A.J.: Verification condition generation for permission logics with abstract predicates and abstraction functions. In: Castagna, G. (ed.) ECOOP 2013. LNCS, vol. 7920, pp. 451–476. Springer, Heidelberg (2013)
7. Hoare, C.A.R.: Proofs of correctness of data representations. Acta Inf. **1**, 271–281 (1972)
8. Kassios, I.T.: The dynamic frames theory. Formal Aspects Comput. **23**(3), 267–288 (2011)
9. Krishnaswami, N.R., Aldrich, J., Birkedal, L.: Verifying event-driven programs using Ramified frame properties. In: TLDI (2010)
10. Leino, K.R.M., Müller, P.: Verification of equivalent-results methods. In: Drossopoulou, S. (ed.) ESOP 2008. LNCS, vol. 4960, pp. 307–321. Springer, Heidelberg (2008)
11. Nanevski, A., Ahmed, A., Morrisett, G., Birkedal, L.: Abstract predicates and mutable ADTs in Hoare type theory. In: De Nicola, R. (ed.) ESOP 2007. LNCS, vol. 4421, pp. 189–204. Springer, Heidelberg (2007)
12. Nanevski, A., Banerjee, A., Garg, D.: Dependent type theory for verification of information flow and access control policies. ACM Trans. Program. Lang. Syst. **35**(2), 6 (2013)
13. Naumann, D.A.: Observational purity and encapsulation. Theor. Comput. Sci. **376**(3), 205–224 (2007)
14. O'Hearn, P.W., Yang, H., Reynolds, J.C.: Separation and information hiding. ACM Trans. Prog. Lang. Syst. **31**(3), 1–50 (2009)
15. Parkinson, M.J., Bierman, G.M.: Separation logic and abstraction. In: POPL (2005)
16. Rosenberg, S., Banerjee, A., Naumann, D.A.: Local reasoning and dynamic framing for the composite pattern and its clients. In: Leavens, G.T., O'Hearn, P., Rajamani, S.K. (eds.) VSTTE 2010. LNCS, vol. 6217, pp. 183–198. Springer, Heidelberg (2010)
17. Rosenberg, S., Banerjee, A., Naumann, D.A.: Decision procedures for region logic. In: Kuncak, V., Rybalchenko, A. (eds.) VMCAI 2012. LNCS, vol. 7148, pp. 379–395. Springer, Heidelberg (2012)
18. Smans, J., Jacobs, B., Piessens, F., Schulte, W.: Automatic verification of Java programs with dynamic frames. Formal Aspects Comput. **22**(3–4), 423–457 (2010)
19. Summers, A.J., Drossopoulou, S.: A formal semantics for isorecursive and equirecursive state abstractions. In: Castagna, G. (ed.) ECOOP 2013. LNCS, vol. 7920, pp. 129–153. Springer, Heidelberg (2013)
20. Yang, H.: Relational separation logic. Theor. Comput. Sci. **375**(1–3), 308–334 (2007)

Efficient Refinement Checking in VCC

Sumesh Divakaran[1]([⊠]), Deepak D'Souza[1], and Nigamanth Sridhar[2]

[1] Indian Institute of Science, Bangalore, India
{sumeshd,deepakd}@csa.iisc.ernet.in
[2] Cleveland State University, Cleveland, OH, USA
n.sridhar1@csuohio.edu

Abstract. We propose a methodology for carrying out refinement proofs
across declarative abstract models and concrete implementations in C,
using the VCC verification tool. The main idea is to first perform a systematic translation from the top-level abstract model to a ghost implementation in VCC. Subsequent refinement proofs between successively refined
abstract models and between abstract and concrete implementations are
carried out in VCC. We propose an efficient technique to carry out these
refinement checks in VCC. We illustrate our methodology with a case study
in which we verify a simplified C implementation of an RTOS scheduler,
with respect to its abstract Z specification. Overall, our methodology leads
to efficient and automatic refinement proofs for complex systems that
would typically be beyond the capability of tools such as Z/Eves or Rodin.

1 Introduction

Refinement-based techniques are a well-developed approach to proving functional correctness of software systems. In a correct-by-construction approach
using step-wise refinement, one begins with an abstract specification of the system's functionality, say $\mathcal{M}_1$, and successively refines it via some intermediate
models, to a concrete implementation, say $\mathcal{P}_2$ in an imperative language. Similarly, in a post-facto proof of correctness, one begins with a concrete implementation $\mathcal{P}_2$, specifies its functionality abstractly in $\mathcal{M}_1$, and comes up with the
intermediate models by simultaneously refining $\mathcal{M}_1$ towards $\mathcal{P}_2$ and abstracting
$\mathcal{P}_2$ towards $\mathcal{M}_1$. This is depicted in Fig.1(a). We note that it is convenient to have
$\mathcal{M}_1$ specified in an abstract modelling language such as Z [16] or Event-B [1],
since this gives us a concise yet readable, and mathematically precise specification of the system's behaviour, which serves as a specification of functional
behaviour for users and clients of the system.

Refinement-based proofs of functional correctness have several advantages
over an approach of directly phrasing and proving pre and post conditions on
methods. To begin with, refinement-based approaches help to break down assertions on complex programs using successive refinement steps, leading to more
modular and transparent proofs. Secondly, they provide a useful framework for

This work was partially supported by the Robert Bosch Center at IISc, Bangalore.

D. Giannakopoulou and D. Kroening (Eds.): VSTTE 2014, LNCS 8471, pp. 21–36, 2014.
DOI: 10.1007/978-3-319-12154-3_2

verifying *clients* of a library more efficiently. In principle, one could reason about assertions in a client program $\mathcal{C}$ that uses a concrete implementation of a library $\mathcal{P}_2$, by showing that $\mathcal{C}$ with a more abstract library $\mathcal{M}_1$ satisfies the same assertions. This could lead to considerable reductions in the verification effort as reported in [9]. In a similar way, if one replaces a library implementation by a more efficient one, one does not have to reprove certain properties of its possibly numerous clients if one has shown that the new implementation refines the old one.

There are nevertheless a couple of key difficulties faced in carrying out refinement proofs between the successive models in a refinement-based approach, in our experience. The first is that performing a refinement proof between the abstract models (such as a proof that $\mathcal{M}_1$ is refined by $\mathcal{M}_2$), is challenging because the level of automation in tools such as Z/Eves [14] and Rodin [2] is inadequate, and requires non-trivial human effort and expertise in theorem proving to get the prover to discharge the proof obligations. The second hurdle we encounter is in showing the refinement between the abstract model $\mathcal{M}_2$ and the imperative language model $\mathcal{P}_1$. The problem here is that there is no tool which understands *both* the modelling languages of $\mathcal{M}_2$ and $\mathcal{P}_1$. One way of getting around this is to "import" the before-after-predicates (BAP's) from $\mathcal{M}_2$ to $\mathcal{P}_1$, by using requires and ensures clauses that are equivalent to formulas in which the abstract state is existentially quantified away. But there are some disadvantages to this approach: (i) existential quantifications are difficult to handle for the theorem prover and can lead to excessive time requirement or can even cause the prover to run out of resources, and (ii) can be error-prone, and the equivalence should ideally be checked using a general-purpose theorem prover like Isabelle/HOL or PVS.

In this paper we propose a method of performing step-wise refinement and proving the ensuing refinement conditions, fully within the VCC toolset [6], with the aim of overcoming some of the hurdles described above. Continuing the example above, the idea is to first translate the high-level specification $\mathcal{M}_1$ into a model $\mathcal{G}_1$ in VCC's "ghost" modelling language. Next we refine $\mathcal{G}_1$ to another ghost implementation $\mathcal{G}_2$ in VCC, which will play the role of $\mathcal{M}_2$ subsequently. How does this help us to get around the problems mentioned above? The first problem of proving refinement between the abstract models is alleviated as VCC is typically able to check the refinement between ghost models like $\mathcal{G}_1$ and $\mathcal{G}_2$ efficiently and automatically. The second problem of moving from an abstract model to an imperative implementation is also addressed because we now have both $\mathcal{G}_2$ and $\mathcal{P}_1$ in a language that VCC understands, and we can then proceed to phrase and check the refinement conditions (for instance by using a joint version of $\mathcal{G}_2$ and $\mathcal{P}_1$ together) within VCC.

Our contributions in this paper are the following. First, we provide a systematic and mechanizable translation procedure to translate specifications written in a subset of the Z modelling language to a ghost specification in VCC. The fragment of Z we target is chosen to cover the case study we describe next, and essentially comprises finite sequences and operations on them. There is an

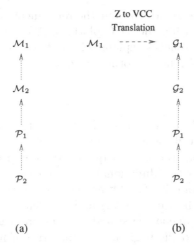

Fig. 1. (a) A typical refinement chain, with $\mathcal{M}_1$ and $\mathcal{M}_2$ being abstract models in a language like Z, and $\mathcal{P}_1$ and $\mathcal{P}_2$ being programs in a language like C. (b) The proposed translation and refinement chain, with $\mathcal{G}_1$ and $\mathcal{G}_2$ being "ghost" implementations in VCC. Dotted arrows denote the "refines" relationship.

inevitable blow-up of around 10x in the number of specification lines while going from Z to VCC, as VCC does not support many data-types (such as sequences) and operators that Z supports. While refining one ghost model to another ($\mathcal{G}_1$ to $\mathcal{G}_2$), the size of the model is not a problem: typically only a few aspects of the models change in each refinement step.

Secondly, we propose a two-step technique of phrasing the refinement check between ghost models and C programs in VCC that improves VCC's efficiency considerably. A naïve encoding of the refinement conditions can cause VCC to run out of memory due to the size of the model and complexity of the verification conditions. Using our two-step refinement check, VCC always terminates and leads to a reduction of over 90 % in the total time taken by a naïve check, when evaluated on our case-study.

The notion of refinement, theory and methodology for coming up with intermediate models used in this paper, are all based on the work in [7], where the functional correctness of a complex existing system—the FreeRTOS open-source real-time operating system [12]—was specified and verified. Experience with that case study, where we encountered the problems mentioned above, prompted us to explore these issues in a simpler setting. In this paper we use a simpler version of the FreeRTOS scheduler, which we built ourselves for this verification exercise. This scheduler, which we call Simp-Sched provides the same task-related API's as FreeRTOS (like vtaskCreate and vtaskDelay), but uses a task id (a number) instead of a full Task Control Block (TCB), and an array-based list library instead of the more complex circular doubly-linked xList library used in FreeRTOS. We begin with the Z specification of the scheduler API's that we used in [7], and apply the techniques described above to translate the initial model to VCC, and then carry out the refinement checks between successive models completely within the VCC platform. We carry out the refinement checks using different approaches explained in Sect. 4 and report on the comparative improvements we obtain over other approaches.

2   Preliminaries

In this section we introduce the notion of refinement we will use in this paper and a running example to illustrate some of the techniques we propose.

Consider a C implementation of a queue Abstract Data Type (ADT) (or library) shown in Fig. 2, whose functional correctness we want to reason about. This example is taken from [7]. The library uses an integer array A to store the elements of the queue. The variables beg and end denote positions in the array and the elements of the queue are stored starting from beg to end - 1 in the array, wrapping around to the beginning of the array if necessary. The library provides the operations *init*, *enq* and *deq* to respectively initialize, enqueue, and dequeue elements from the list. The *enq* operation inserts the given element into the position end in the array, and the *deq* operation returns the element at the position beg in the array. Both operations update the len variable and increment the beg/end pointer modulo MAXLEN.

In a refinement-based approach we would begin by specifying the functionality of the queue abstractly. We could do this in the Z specification language for instance, as shown in Fig. 3. The model specifies the state of the ADT and how the operations update the state, using the convention that primed variables denote the post-state of the operation.

We now want to show that the queue implementation *refines* the abstract Z specification. Refinement notions are typically specified in terms of a *simulation* between the concrete and abstract models. The simulation is witnessed by an *abstraction relation*. In this case, a possible abstraction relation ρ we could use is roughly as follows:

$$\begin{aligned}
&\text{len} = \#\text{content} \wedge \\
&(\text{beg} < \text{end}) \implies \forall i \in \mathbb{N}.((i < \text{end} - \text{beg}) \implies A[\text{beg} + i] = \text{content}(i)) \wedge \\
&(\text{beg} > \text{end} \vee (\text{beg} = \text{end} \wedge \text{len} > 0)) \implies \\
&\quad \forall i \in \mathbb{N}.((i < \text{MAXLEN} - \text{beg}) \implies A[\text{beg} + i] = \text{content}(i)) \wedge \\
&\quad \forall i \in \mathbb{N}.((i < \text{end}) \implies A[i] = \text{content}(\text{MAXLEN} - \text{beg} + i)).
\end{aligned}$$

```
1: int A[MAXLEN];              11: void enq(int t) {
2: unsigned beg, end, len;     12:    if (len == MAXLEN)
3:                             13:       assert(0); /* exception */
4: void init() {               14:    A[end] = t;
5:    beg = 0;                 15:    if (end < MAXLEN-1)
6:    end = 0;                 16:       end++;
7:    len = 0;                 17:    else
8: }                           18:       end = 0;
9:                             19:    len++;
10 int deq() { ... }           20: }
```

Fig. 2. c-queue: a C implementation of a Queue library.

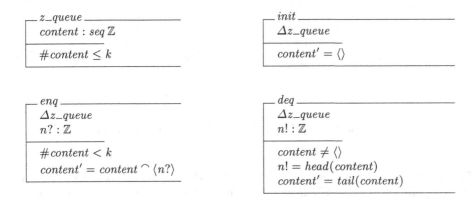

Fig. 3. A Z specification, z_queue_k, of a queue library which allows a maximum of k elements in the Queue. The notation ΔS for a Z schema S expands to the definition of S with an additional definition S' representing the post state with *primed* field names.

The direction of simulation varies: a common notion of refinement used in the literature (for example in Event-B [1], and tools like Resolve [8], Dafny [11], and Jahob [17]), is to require the abstract to simulate the concrete. In this paper we use the notion from [7] where we require the *concrete* to simulate the *abstract*. We choose to use this notion as it gives us stronger verification guarantees. Nonetheless, the results we show in this paper are independent of the direction of simulation used, and apply for refinement notions with the other direction of simulation as well. We now briefly outline the notion of refinement used, and point the reader to [7] for more details.

An *ADT type* is a finite set N of *operation names*. Each operation name n in N has an associated *input type* I_n and an *output type* O_n, each of which is simply a set of values. We require that there is a special *exceptional value* denoted by e, which belongs to each output type O_n; and that the set of operations N includes a designated *initialization operation* called *init*. A (deterministic) *ADT* of type N is a structure of the form $\mathcal{A} = (Q, U, E, \{op_n\}_{n \in N})$ where Q is the set of states of the ADT, $U \in Q$ is an arbitrary state in Q used as an *uninitialized* state, and $E \in Q$ is an *exceptional* state. Each op_n is a *realisation* of the operation n given by $op_n : Q \times I_n \to Q \times O_n$ such that $op_n(E, -) = (E, e)$ and $op_n(p, a) = (q, e) \implies q = E$.

Let $\mathcal{A} = (Q, U, E, \{op_n\}_{n \in N})$ and $\mathcal{A}' = (Q', U', E', \{op_n\}_{n \in N})$ be ADT's of type N. We say $\mathcal{A}'$ *refines* $\mathcal{A}$ (written $\mathcal{A}' \preceq A$), if there exists a relation $\rho \subseteq Q' \times Q$ such that:

(init) Let $a \in I_{init}$ and let (q_a, b) and (q'_a, b') be the resultant states and outputs after an $init(a)$ operation in $\mathcal{A}$ and $\mathcal{A}'$ respectively, with $b \neq e$. Then we require that $b = b'$ and $(q'_a, q_a) \in \rho$.

(sim) For each $n \in N$, $a \in I_n$, $b \in O_n$, and $p' \in Q'$, with $(p', p) \in \rho$, whenever $p \xrightarrow{(n,a,b)} q$ with $b \neq e$, then there exists $q' \in Q'$ such that $p' \xrightarrow{(n,a,b)} q'$ with $(q', q) \in \rho$. This is visualized in Fig. 4.

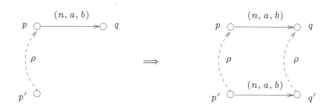

Fig. 4. Illustrating the condition (RC-sim) for refinement.

The notation $p \xrightarrow{(n,a,b)} q$ denotes the fact that the ADT in state p can allow a call to operation n with argument a, return a value b, and transition to state q. We call this condition (RC).

In the rest of the paper we describe our contributions with this background in mind. Our aim is to carry out the refinement checks across abstract models and C implementations, fully within the VCC tool, in a way that gets around some of the problems with checking refinements outlined in the introduction. In Sect. 3 we explain how we can systematically translate a Z model to a ghost implementation in VCC. In Sect. 4 we explain different techniques for carrying out refinement checking in VCC, beginning with the natural approaches, followed by our more efficient two-step approach. We evaluate our techniques in a case study involving a simple RTOS scheduler called `Simp-Sched`, which we introduce in Sect. 5, and discuss the performance comparison in Sect. 6. Finally we conclude with some pointers to related work in Sect. 7.

3   Translating Z to VCC

The objective here is to translate an abstract Z model $\mathcal{M}$ into a ghost implementation $\mathcal{G}$ in VCC such that $\mathcal{G} \preceq \mathcal{M}$. The idea is to translate the state schema like that of z_queue in Fig. 3, comprising fields and invariants, into a structure in VCC with corresponding fields and invariants. Similarly, for the operations as well.

We translate each operation schema $\mathcal{S}_{op}^{\mathcal{M}}$ of $\mathcal{M}$, corresponding to an operation op in the library, into *function contracts* (in terms of `requires` and `ensures` clauses) for the corresponding implementation of the function in VCC, say $func_{op}^{\mathcal{G}}$. In this translation we classify the set of predicates in $\mathcal{S}_{op}^{\mathcal{M}}$ into $pre_{op}^{\mathcal{M}}$ (*precondition*) and $BAP_{op}^{\mathcal{M}}$ (*before-after predicates*). Here $pre_{op}^{\mathcal{M}}$ is the set of predicates defined over the pre-state and input of $\mathcal{S}_{op}^{\mathcal{M}}$, and the remaining predicates relating the post-state to the pre-state are denoted by $BAP_{op}^{\mathcal{M}}$.

Table 1 presents a look-up procedure for encoding various Z objects in VCC. If X is a set then the notation A_X denotes an arbitrary subset of X. The Z objects are encoded in VCC in a way that facilitates easy proofs for the required verification conditions. This is crucial for scalability.

Figure 5 shows excerpts from the VCC code obtained by translating the Z schema of Fig. 3.

Table 1. Table showing the translation of Z objects to VCC objects. It gives a *suitable* encoding of Z objects in VCC which enables fast verification. If X is a set then the notation A_X denotes an arbitrary subset of X.

	Requirement	Possible Z spec.	Equivalent VCC spec.
Set	Set of elements of type T.	A_T : ℙ T	_(ghost \bool A_T[T])
	Set membership.	e ∈ A_T	A_T[e]==\true
	Set Complement.	AComp_T = T \ A_T	\forall T t; AComp_T[t]<==>!A_T[t]
	Set Union.	C_T = A_T ∪ B_T	\forall T t;C_T[t]<==>A_T[t]||B_T[t]
Map	Partial function from X to Y	pMap : X ⇸ Y	_(ghost Y pMap[X]) _(ghost \bool pMapDom[X])
	Domain restriction for maps	g = A_X ◁ f	\forall gDom x;(g[x]==f[x])∧ \forall X x; gDom[x]<==>(fDom[x] && A_X[x])
	Domain subtraction for maps.	g = A_X ⩤ f	\forall gDom x; g[x]==f[x])∧ \forall X x;(gDom[x]<==>(fDom[x] && !A_X[x])
	Range restriction for maps.	g = f ▷ B_Y	\forall gDom x; g[x]==f[x])∧ \forall X x;(gDom[x]<==>(fDom[x] && B_Y[f[x]])
	Range subtraction for maps.	g = f ⩥ B_Y	\forall gDom x; g[x]==f[x])∧ \forall X x;(gDom[x]<==>(fDom[x] && !B_Y[f[x]])
	Relational overriding for maps (f:X⇸Y, g:X⇸Y)	h = f ⊕ g	\forall hDom x;((gDom[x]==>(h[x]==g[x]))∧(!gDom[x]==> (h[x]==f[x]))∧\forall X x;(hDom[x]<==>(fDom[x]||gDom[x]))
	Containment of relational image (f:X⇸Y).	f⦇ A_X ⦈ ⊆ A_Y	\forall X x;A_X[x]==>A_Y[f[x]]
Seq	Injective sequence of elements of type T	s : iseq T	_(ghost T sElmnts[\natural]) _(ghost \natural sIndex[T]) _(ghost \natural sLength) _(invariant \forall \natural i;(i<sLength)==> (sIndex[sElmnts[i]]==i)) _(invariant \forall T e;(sIndex[e]<sLength)==> (sElmnts[sIndex[e]]==e))
	Membership in sequence.	e ∈ ran s	sIndex[e] < sLength
	Disjoint sequences.	ran s ∩ ran t = ∅	\forall T e; ((sIndex[e]<sLength==>tIndex[e]>=tLength)∧ (tIndex[e]<tLength==>sIndex[e]>=sLength))
	Sequence - containment.	ran s ⊆ ran t	\forall T e; sIndex[e]<sLength==>tIndex[e]<tLength
	Concatenation for injective sequences of the same type (s, t be disjoint sequences of type T).	u = s ⌢ t	\forall \natural i;(i<sLength)==>(uElmnts[i]==sElmnts[i]) \forall \natural i;(i<tLength)==>(uElmnts[i+sLength]==tElmnts[i]) \forall T e;(sIndex[e]<sLength)==>(uIndex[e]==sIndex[e]) \forall T e;(tIndex[e]<tLength)==>(uIndex[e]==tIndex[e]+sLength) \forall T e;((sIndex[e]>=sLength)&&(tIndex[e]>=tLength))==> (uIndex[e]==sLength+tLength) uLength==sLength+tLength
	Filter operation for sequence of type T.	t = s ↾ A_T	tLength<=sLength \forall \natural i;(i<tLength)==> ((sIndex[tElmnts[i]]<sLength)&&(A_T[tElmnts[i]])) \forall T e;((sIndex[t]<sLength)&&A_T[e])==>(tIndex[e]<tLength) \forall \natural i,j;((i<j)&&(j<tLength))==> (sIndex[tElmnts[i]]<sIndex[tElmnts[j]])
	Ectract operation for sequence of type T.	t = s ↿ A_T	tLength<=sLength \forall \natural i;(i<tLength)==> ((sIndex[tElmnts[i]]<sLength)&&(!A_T[tElmnts[i]])) \forall T e;((sIndex[t]<sLength)&&!A_T[e])==>(tIndex[e]<tLength) \forall \natural i,j;((i<j)&&(j<tLength))==> (sIndex[tElmnts[i]]<sIndex[tElmnts[j]])

```
_(ghost int content[\natural])          void enq(int a)
_(ghost \natural contentLen)            _(requires contentLen < MAXLEN)
_(invariant contentLen <= MAXLEN)       ...
...                                     _(ensures contentLen == \old(contentLen)+1)
void init(void)                         _(ensures \forall \natural n; (n < \old(contentLen))
...                                        => content[n] == \old(content[n])))
_(ensures contentLen == 0)              {
{                                         _(ghost content[contentLen] = a)
  _(ghost contentLen = 0)                 _(ghost contentLen = contentLen + 1)
}                                       }
```

Fig. 5. Part of the translation of the Z specification *z_queue* to a ghost version in VCC.

In this paper we present only those Z constructs that are used in the Z model of our case study in Sect. 5. Nevertheless other mathematical objects in Z can be handled in a similar way.

4   Phrasing Refinement Conditions in VCC

In this section we describe three ways to phrase the refinement condition (RC) of Sect. 2 as annotations in VCC. The first approach—which we call the "Direct-Import" approach—is useful when the abstract library is *not* available as a ghost model in VCC. Here one directly *imports* the abstract library as code level annotations in VCC. The second is the so-called "Combined" approach, which can be applied when the abstract library is available as a ghost implementation in VCC. Finally we describe our proposed "Two-Step" approach, which can again be applied when the abstract library is available as a ghost implementation, but which VCC discharges far more efficiently.

In each of these approaches we consider the case when the abstract model $\mathcal{M}$ is specified either as a Z specification or as a VCC ghost model, and the concrete model is given as an implementation in C, say $\mathcal{P}$. For clarity, we focus here only on the (sim) condition of (RC).

4.1   Direct-Import Approach

This approach is applicable when the abstract model $\mathcal{M}$ is specified in a specification language like Z. The idea is to existentially quantify away the abstract state from a glued joint (abstract and concrete) state, and phrase this as pre/post conditions on the concrete methods. The resulting **requires** and **ensures** conditions are independent of the abstract state.

Figure 6 shows a schematic for how one can apply the direct-import method in VCC. We use s and s' to denote respectively the pre and post states of the abstract model, and t and t' to represent the pre and post states of the concrete model. For an operation op, $pre_{op}^{\mathcal{M}}$ represents the precondition of op in library $\mathcal{M}$. We use inv_ρ to represent the abstraction relation which relates concrete and abstract states, and BAP to represent the predicates on pre and post states describing the transitions in the respective models.

Unfortunately this approach is not feasible in VCC as it is difficult for the theorem prover to handle the existential quantification. A possible way out is to transform the annotations to remove the existential quantification, and get an equivalent condition on the concrete state. For instance, for the queue example of Sect. 2, we could phrase the directly imported annotations by eliminating the existential quantification, as shown in Fig. 7 for the *deq* operation. The before-after predicates from the *z_queue* model of Fig. 3 are phrased as annotations over data structures in the C implementation.

This approach has two disadvantages. Firstly, the manual transformation can be error prone and the equivalence should ideally be checked in a theorem prover like PVS or Isabelle/HOL. Secondly, the invariants and preconditions need to

$op(\mathrm{X}_{op}\ \mathrm{x})$
_(requires $\exists\,s:\ pre_{op}^{\mathcal{M}}(s) \wedge inv_{\rho}(t,s))$
_(ensures $\exists\,s,s':\ BAP_{op}^{\mathcal{M}}(s,s') \wedge inv_{\rho}(s,t)$
$\qquad \wedge inv_{\rho}(s',t'))$
_(ensures $\backslash result = s'.y)$ {
    // function body
}

```
int deq()
 _(requires len != 0)
 _(ensures \result == \old(A[\old(beg)]))
 _(ensures len == \old(len) - 1)
 _(ensures \forall unsigned i; (i < len)
    ==> ((\old(beg) < end) =>
    A[beg+i] == \old(A[beg+i])))
    ...
{
    // function body
}
```

Fig. 6. Directly importing abstract library ($\mathcal{M}$) using code level annotations in VCC.

Fig. 7. Manually transforming the directly-imported before-after-predicates from the Z specification of Fig. 3 into the queue implementation of Fig. 2.

```
struct {
 _(ghost int lContent[\natural])
 _(ghost \natural lLen)
 -(invariant lLen <= 1)

 _(ghost int kContent[\natural])
 _(ghost \natural kLen)
 // gluing invariant
 _(invariant (lLen == kLen) &&
    (\forall \natural i;(i < lLen)
    ==> (lContent[i] == kContent[i])))
} LK;
```

```
void deqCombined()
 _(requires LK.lLen != 0)
 _(requires (LK.lLen == LK.kLen) &&
    (\forall \natural i;(i < LK.lLen)
    ==> (LK.lContent[i] == LK.kContent[i])))
 _(ensures (LK.lLen == LK.kLen) &&
    (\forall \natural i; (i < lLen)
    ==> (LK.lContent[i] == LK.kContent[i])))
 _(ensures lOut == kOut) {
    // function body of lDeq
    // function body of kDeq
}
```

Fig. 8. Joint structure combining the states of $\mathcal{G}_l$ and $\mathcal{G}_k$.

Fig. 9. Combined function to check refinement condition.

be specified *directly* on the concrete state. This can be quite complex for both the human and the tool, especially in the presence of potentially aliased data structures.

4.2 Combined Approach

A second technique can be used to prove the refinement between two libraries when both are available as ghost or concrete implementations in VCC. The refinement condition (RC) of Sect. 2 can be phrased in VCC by using a *combined function* to update the instance of a *joint structure* which combines the fields of abstract and concrete libraries. The abstraction relation ρ can be specified as an invariant in the joint structure which we call a *gluing invariant*. To illustrate this on a simple example, consider an abstract ghost implementation $\mathcal{G}_l$ of the queue library (Sect. 2) and another ghost implementation $\mathcal{G}_k$ such that $k \geq l$, where the subscript represents the maximum size of the queue. Figure 8 shows the joint structure to phrase the refinement condition between $\mathcal{G}_l$ and $\mathcal{G}_k$ and Fig. 9 shows the combined function to check the refinement between the abstract and concrete implementation of the *deq* operation.

Unfortunately when the concrete model is a C program, this approach could cause the prover to take lot of time or even run out of resources. In our opinion this is mainly due to the fact that a large number of extra annotations are required when reasoning about a joint (abstract and concrete) state that are both mutable. These annotations are required as loop invariants and as function contracts, to specify that each ghost object in the system is kept unmodified by a loop or function to modify the concrete data object. For instance, there should be a loop invariant in the combined function for updating the array A in the queue example of Fig. 2, which essentially says that each element in the abstract map (like *lContent* above) is kept unchanged. Similar predicates are required in the function contract if functions are used to update the concrete state. In our case study (Sect. 5), the number of such annotations required in a loop or function contract is about twice the number of annotations required in the proposed Two-Step approach to prove refinement conditions.

4.3   Two-Step Approach

We now propose an efficient approach, which we call the *Two-Step* approach, which overcomes some of the difficulties of the previous two approaches. The idea is to divide the refinement check into two steps. The first step is to prove the *BAP*s for the abstract and concrete functions separately by manually supplying the *BAP*s. The second step is to prove that the output states as defined by the *BAP*s satisfies the gluing invariant. The problem with the combined approach is avoided as in Step 1, we are interested in proving *only* the concrete *BAP* as the post condition of the concrete function and hence there is no need to specify the extra set of predicates in loops and concrete function contract to specify preservation of the abstract state.

Figure 10 illustrates the two steps of our approach. Figure 11 shows the skeleton of the function in VCC to prove the abstract *BAP* for an library operation *op*. Here $\mathcal{A}$ and $\mathcal{B}$ represent the abstract and concrete libraries respectively, $pre^{\mathcal{A}}$ represents the abstract precondition (like $lLen \neq 0$ for *deq*) and inv_ρ

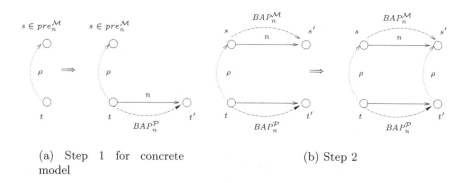

(a) Step 1 for concrete   (b) Step 2
model

Fig. 10. Illustrating the conditions checked in the two-step approach.

```
opᴬ( )
  _(requires preᴬ)
  _(ensures BAPᴬₒₚ)
{
    // body of opᴬ
}
```

```
op( )
  _(requires preᴬ ∧ invₚ)
  _(decreases 0)
  _(ensures BAPᴮₒₚ)
{
    // body of opᴮ
}
```

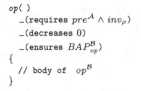

Fig. 11. Step 1 of the two-step app-roach for proving the *abstract BAP*.

Fig. 12. Step 1 of the two-step app-roach for proving the *concrete BAP*.

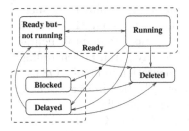

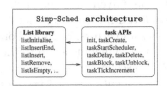

Fig. 13. Task states in FreeR-TOS/Simp-Sched

Fig. 14. Components in the scheduler implementation

represents the gluing invariant. For instance, the BAP of the deq operation is $(ret = \text{\\old}(content[0]) \land (len = old(len) - 1) \land (0 \le i < len \mid content[i] = \text{\\old}(content[i+1]))$. Figure 12 shows the skeleton of the function in VCC to prove the concrete BAP. The annotation _(**decreases** 0) says that the function *terminates*.

The second step of the Two-Step approach is checking the validity of the following implication and one can use a dummy function in VCC to check its validity.

$$pre^{\mathcal{A}}_{op} \land inv_\rho \land BAP^{\mathcal{A}}_{op} \land BAP^{\mathcal{B}}_{op} \implies inv'_\rho \land ret^{\mathcal{A}} = ret^{\mathcal{B}}.$$

5 Case Study: Simp-Sched

Here we describe our experiences with building specifications and a correct-by-construction implementation of a software system. The system we chose to work with is the scheduler component of FreeRTOS, which is a popular real-time operating system (RTOS) that is widely used in the embedded systems community both in academic settings as well as in industry [3].

The FreeRTOS scheduler API provides operations to create, schedule, and remove tasks, as well as to delay and resume task operation (see Fig. 13 for a summary of task states). Application programmers can use these operations to implement application functionality using these tasks as units of behaviour. For our case study, we create a simplified version of the FreeRTOS scheduler, called `Simp-Sched`. Our new implementation maintains all key aspects of timing and scheduling. The simplification is based on two things:

1. Tasks in the FreeRTOS scheduler are maintained in a struct called a *task control block*, which includes pointers to function behaviour. In `Simp-Sched`, we simply use an integer *task ID* to represent the TCB of a task.
2. All task lists (ready, delayed, etc.) are maintained in a data structure called `xlist`, which is implemented as a circular doubly-linked list. In `Simp-Sched`, we replace this data structure with array implementations of the task lists.

All other aspects of the scheduler implementation are maintained. As such, the stock FreeRTOS scheduler implementation is a refinement of our `Simp-Sched` implementation. Given this, one of the key uses of our `Simp-Sched` implementation is use in a runtime monitor that can be used to identify potential scheduling inconsistencies and errors. Each API operation implementation in FreeRTOS can be instrumented to include a call to the corresponding operation in `Simp-Sched`, so that the two scheduler implementations are running in parallel.

The C implementation of `Simp-Sched` includes 769 lines of C code and 106 lines of comments [15]. The task lists are implemented as a separate library in which list is implemented using arrays in C. Figure 14 shows the components in the `Simp-Sched` implementation with interface operations.

5.1   Refinement Strategy for `Simp-Sched`

We now describe our methodology for constructing a *correct* C program from a mathematical specification of `Simp-Sched` by applying the refinement theory from [7]. The methodology involves five stages.

1. We start with a mathematical model in Z which we call $\mathcal{M}_1$ capturing the high-level functionality of `Simp-Sched`.
2. We apply our mechanizable procedure explained in Sect. 3 to translate $\mathcal{M}_1$ to a declarative model in VCC, which we call $\mathcal{G}_1$. Note that the translation guarantees that $\mathcal{G}_1 \preceq \mathcal{M}_1$.
3. We then refine $\mathcal{G}_1$ to a more concrete model $\mathcal{G}_2$ in VCC to capture some machine level requirements. For example, the system clock is unbounded in $\mathcal{G}_1$, which is not directly realizable in the C language. In $\mathcal{G}_2$ the clock value cycles in the interval $[0, \text{maxNumVal}]$ where `maxNumVal` is the maximum value that an `unsigned int` in C can take. This change has another effect: the *delayed* tasks are maintained in a single delayed list in $\mathcal{G}_1$, which has to be broken into two lists in $\mathcal{G}_2$ to cope with the bounding of the clock value. The refinement between $\mathcal{G}_2$ and $\mathcal{G}_1$ is verified using the *combined* approach explained in Sect. 4.2.
4. Next, we refine $\mathcal{G}_2$ to $\mathcal{P}_1$ where every data object except task lists in $\mathcal{G}_2$ is implemented using executable objects and functions in C. The refinement between $\mathcal{P}_1$ and $\mathcal{G}_2$ is verified using the *Two-Step* approach explained in Sect. 4.3.

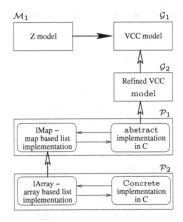

Fig. 15. Overview of the construction of `Simp-Sched`.

Model	LOA	LOC	Model	LOA	LOC
$\mathcal{M}_1$	222	-	$\mathcal{G}_2 \preceq \mathcal{G}_1$	741	3271
$\mathcal{G}_1$	1580	1317	$\mathcal{P}_1 \preceq \mathcal{G}_2$	7639	24
$\mathcal{G}_2$	2287	1954	$\mathcal{L}_1 \preceq \mathcal{L}_2$	837	20
$\mathcal{P}_1$	293	609	$\mathcal{L}_1$	602	240
$\mathcal{P}_2$	-	769	$\mathcal{L}_2$	56	104

Fig. 16. Code metrics and human effort involved. Here LOA and LOC respectively represent the number of Lines Of Annotations and number of Lines Of Code without comments and blank lines, $\mathcal{L}_1$ and $\mathcal{L}_2$ represent *lMap* and *lArray* respectively.

5. Finally we refine $\mathcal{P}_1$ to $\mathcal{P}_2$ where the map-based abstract implementation of the list library (`lMap`) is replaced with an array-based list implementation (`lArray`). The refinement between $\mathcal{P}_2$ and $\mathcal{P}_1$ is verified using the *Two-Step* approach explained in Sect. 4.3.

$\mathcal{P}_2$ is a C program and we conclude using the transitivity and substitutability theorems from [7] that $\mathcal{P}_2 \preceq \mathcal{M}_1$. The verification artifacts from this case study are available at [15] (Fig. 15).

5.2 Code Metrics and Human Effort Involved

We spent two human-months to complete this work. The code metrics are presented in the table in Fig. 16. Even though there are around 22,500 lines of code/annotations there is only a small modification required in successive refinements and hence the size of the initial model $\mathcal{G}_1$ and $\mathcal{L}_1$ model extracted from $\mathcal{G}_2$ are the important parts deciding the human effort required. The models $\mathcal{G}_1$ and $\mathcal{L}_1$ contain 2,422 lines of annotation in VCC, which is about 3 times the size of the executable code in $\mathcal{P}_2$.

6 Performance Comparison

We report the time taken by VCC to prove the refinement conditions between different models in the case study. Table 2 shows the time taken under the three different approaches, namely the *Direct-Import*, *Combined*, and *Two-Step* approaches described in Sect. 4. Our *Two-Step* approach takes only 7.4 % of the total time taken by the *Direct-Import* approach. The time taken by the *Combined* approach is much longer than the time taken by the *Direct-Import* approach.

Table 2. Time taken by VCC to prove refinement conditions with the different techniques.

Sl.No.	API	Time taken by VCC (in seconds)				
		Direct import	Combined	Two-step		
				Step1	Step2	Total
1.	*init*	**257.56**	**89.63**	231.01	3.52	**234.53**
2.	*taskCreate*	**357.09**	**780.88**	9.41	4.28	**13.69**
3.	*taskStartScheduler*	**10.36**	**13.95**	5.13	4.55	**9.68**
4.	*taskDelay*	**285.09**	**18773.61**	22.19	8.47	**30.66**
5.	*taskDelete*	**436**	**18391.04**	68.23	7.86	**76.09**
6.	*taskBlock*	**422.7**	**20699.25**	21.64	5.28	**26.92**
7.	*taskUnblock*	**227.06**	**16838.05**	27.44	6.02	**33.46**
8.	*listInitialise*	**2.11**	**2.7**	2.34	1.88	**4.22**
9.	*listGetNumberOfElements*	**2.02**	**2.19**	2.06	1.89	**3.95**
10.	*listIsEmpty*	**1.97**	**2.34**	3.86	2.14	**6.00**
11.	*listIsContainedIn*	**2.31**	**2.19**	2.83	4.44	**7.27**
12.	*listGetIDofFirstFIFOtask*	**3.05**	**2.3**	2.26	2.97	**5.23**
13.	*listGetIDofFirstPQtask*	**1.69**	**2.59**	2.52	4.39	**6.91**
14.	*listGetKeyOfFirstPQtask*	**1.83**	**3.08**	2.36	1.97	**4.33**
15.	*listInsertEnd*	**2.49**	**2.69**	2.19	4.52	**6.71**
16.	*listInsert*	**31.77**	**8.89**	2.77	2.22	**4.99**
17.	*listRemove*	**4447.67**	**42.7**	3.7	2.23	**5.39**
Total time taken by each technique		**6492.77**	**75658.08**			**489.94**

This is because of the presence of the abstract objects, abstract invariants, gluing relation and abstract function body in addition to the overhead involved in the *Direct-Import* approach.

7   Related Work and Conclusion

As already mentioned, the work in this paper uses the foundation laid in [7], in terms of the theory of refinement and methodology used. There again, VCC is the main tool used for refinement checking: first for checking the refinement conditions between abstract Z models by translating them to VCC, and secondly for checking the refinements between the refined Z model and the concrete implementation. However the Z to VCC translation was *partial*, as they only needed to check the refinement between the *changed* API's. As a result the approach used for phrasing the refinement conditions for the abstract to imperative implementation step was the "Direct-Import" technique described in Sect. 4.1. In contrast, in this paper we have (a) given a systematic translation from Z to VCC and (b) proposed a two-step refinement check to phrase the refinement conditions in VCC that we show leads to significant improvements in our case study.

VCC was used extensively in the Verisoft XT project [5] at Microsoft, where the goal was verification of Hyper-V hypervisor [10] and PikeOS [4] operating systems.

The methodology used there appears to have been to define an abstract specification as a ghost model in VCC, and to prove conformance of the C implementation to this abstract model. However it is not clear if these works make use of a formal theory of refinement and if so, how the refinement conditions are checked in VCC.

In future work, we plan to automate the Z to VCC translation and expand the subset of the language we handle. We would also like to explore the further translation of the VCC ghost model to a simple executable implementation in C, with the aim of acting as a simulator for the model along the lines of ProZ animator [13].

References

1. Abrial, J.R.: Modeling in Event-B - System and Software Engineering. Cambridge University Press, Cambridge (2010)
2. Abrial, J.R., Butler, M., Hallerstede, S., Hoang, T.S., Mehta, F., Voisin, L.: Rodin: an open toolset for modelling and reasoning in Event-B. Int. J. Softw. Tools Technol. Transf. **12**(6), 447–466 (2010). http://dx.doi.org/10.1007/s10009-010-0145-y
3. Barry, R.: Using the FreeRTOS Real Time Kernel - A Practical Guide. Real Time Engineers Ltd., Bristol (2010)
4. Baumann, C., Beckert, B., Blasum, H., Bormer, T.: Lessons learned from microkernel verification - specification is the new bottleneck. In: Cassez, F., Huuck, R., Klein, G., Schlich, B. (eds.) SSV, EPTCS, vol. 102, pp. 18–32 (2012)
5. Beckert, B., Moskal, M.: Deductive verification of system software in the verisoft XT project. KI **24**(1), 57–61 (2010)
6. Cohen, E., Dahlweid, M., Hillebrand, M., Leinenbach, D., Moskal, M., Santen, T., Schulte, W., Tobies, S.: VCC: a practical system for verifying concurrent C. In: Berghofer, S., Nipkow, T., Urban, C., Wenzel, M. (eds.) TPHOLs 2009. LNCS, vol. 5674, pp. 23–42. Springer, Heidelberg (2009)
7. Divakaran, S., D'Souza, D., Kushwah, A., Sampath, P., Sridhar, N., Woodcock, J.: A theory of refinement with strong verification guarantees. Technical Report TR-520, Department of Computer Science and Automation, Indian Institute of Science, June 2014
8. Edwards, S.H., Heym, W.D., Long, T.J., Sitaraman, M., Weide, B.W.: Part II: specifying components in resolve. SIGSOFT Softw. Eng. Notes **19**(4), 29–39 (1994). http://doi.acm.org/10.1145/190679.190682
9. Klein, G., Andronick, J., Elphinstone, K., Murray, T.C., Sewell, T., Kolanski, R., Heiser, G.: Comprehensive formal verification of an os microkernel. ACM Trans. Comput. Syst. **32**(1), 2 (2014)
10. Leinenbach, D., Santen, T.: Verifying the Microsoft Hyper-V Hypervisor with VCC. In: Cavalcanti, A., Dams, D.R. (eds.) FM 2009. LNCS, vol. 5850, pp. 806–809. Springer, Heidelberg (2009)
11. Leino, K.R.M.: Dafny: an automatic program verifier for functional correctness. In: Clarke, E.M., Voronkov, A. (eds.) LPAR-16 2010. LNCS, vol. 6355, pp. 348–370. Springer, Heidelberg (2010)
12. Real Time Engineers Ltd.: The FreeRTOS Real Time Operating System (2014). www.freertos.org
13. Plagge, D., Leuschel, M.: Validating Z specifications using the PROB animator and model checker. In: Davies, J., Gibbons, J. (eds.) IFM 2007. LNCS, vol. 4591, pp. 480–500. Springer, Heidelberg (2007)

14. Saaltink, M.: The Z/Eves system. In: Till, D., Bowen, Jonathan P., Hinchey, Michael G. (eds.) ZUM 1997. LNCS, vol. 1212, pp. 72–85. Springer, Heidelberg (1997)
15. Efficient refinement check in VCC: Project artifacts (2014). www.csa.iisc.ernet.in/~deepakd/SimpSched
16. Woodcock, J., Davies, J.: Using Z: Specification, Refinement, and Proof. Prentice-Hall, Englewood Cliffs (1996)
17. Zee, K., Kuncak, V., Rinard, M.C.: Full functional verification of linked data structures. In: Gupta, R., Amarasinghe, S.P. (eds.) PLDI, pp. 349–361. ACM (2008)

Formalizing Semantics with an Automatic Program Verifier

Martin Clochard[1,2,3], Jean-Christophe Filliâtre[2,3], Claude Marché[2,3], and Andrei Paskevich[2,3 (✉)]

[1] Ecole Normale Supérieure, 75005 Paris, France
[2] Lab. de Recherche En Informatique, Univ. Paris-Sud, CNRS, 91405 Orsay, France
andrei.paskevich@lri.fr
[3] INRIA Saclay – Île-de-France, 91893 Orsay, France

Abstract. A common belief is that formalizing semantics of programming languages requires the use of a *proof assistant* providing (1) a specification language with advanced features such as higher-order logic, inductive definitions, type polymorphism, and (2) a corresponding proof environment where higher-order and inductive reasoning can be performed, typically with user interaction.

In this paper we show that such a formalization is nowadays possible inside a mostly-automatic program verification environment. We substantiate this claim by formalizing several semantics for a simple language, and proving their equivalence, inside the Why3 environment.

1 Introduction

Interactive proof environments, also known as *proof assistants*, are tools of choice to formalize the semantics of programming languages and, more generally, to handle abstract syntax. For example, the project CompCert [1], formalizes in Coq [2] the semantics of a very large subset of the C programming language and verifies an optimizing compiler. Similarly, the L4.verified project [3] develops a verified operating system on top of a formalization of C in Isabelle/HOL [4], ACL2 [5] is used to formalize a Java virtual machine [6], and a complete semantics of JavaScript is formalized using Coq [7].

Typically, the formalization of a programming language makes heavy use of advanced logic constructs such as algebraic data types (e.g. to represent abstract syntax trees), inductive definition of predicates (e.g. to encode inference rules for typing or evaluation judgments), higher-order functions, dependent types, etc. Proving results on such a formalization (e.g. type soundness) thus typically involves complex reasoning steps, making use of the interactive tactics that a proof assistant provides for induction, case analysis, etc.

Work partly supported by the Bware project (ANR-12-INSE-0010, http://bware.lri.fr/) and the Joint Laboratory ProofInUse (ANR-13-LAB3-0007, http://www.spark-2014.org/proofinuse) of the French national research organization.

© Springer International Publishing Switzerland 2014
D. Giannakopoulou and D. Kroening (Eds.): VSTTE 2014, LNCS 8471, pp. 37–51, 2014.
DOI: 10.1007/978-3-319-12154-3_3

Automatic program verifiers aim at providing dedicated environments to verify behavioral properties of programs written in some specific programming language. Examples are Dafny [8], VeriFast [9], Frama-C [10], or SPARK [11]. They differ from proof assistants in two ways. First, they allow one to verify programs written in some imperative language whereas proof assistants rely on purely functional programming. Second, the main technique for proving properties is via the use of automatic theorem provers, such as SMT solvers. The high level of proof automation in such environments is possible because the specification languages they propose are less expressive than those of proof assistants. They are typically limited to some flavor of first-order logic.

Why3 is a program verifier developed since 2011 [12] that proposes a rich specification language, which extends first-order logic with type polymorphism, algebraic data types, and inductive predicates [13]. Recently, it was augmented with some support for higher-order logic. It is thus a good candidate for experimenting in formalizing semantics using fully automated theorem proving. In this paper, we report on such an experiment. We consider exercises related to defunctionalization [14] proposed by O. Danvy at the JFLA'2014 conference. Along the presentation of our solution, we expose the techniques used inside Why3 to encode complex logic constructs into the logic of SMT solvers.

This paper is organized as follows. Section 2 defines a direct, big-step style semantics of a minimal arithmetic language; meanwhile we explain how we deal with algebraic data types, recursive functions, and pattern matching. Then Sect. 3 introduces another definition in continuation-passing style (CPS) and proves it equivalent to the first one; meanwhile we explain how we encode higher-order logic. Section 4 defunctionalizes the CPS code to get a first-order interpreter; meanwhile we explain how we deal with inductive predicates and complex termination proofs.

The complete solution in Why3, including the full source code and a dump of the proof results, is available at http://toccata.lri.fr/gallery/defunctionalization.en.html.

2 Direct Semantics

Our running example is a very simple toy language of arithmetic expressions, limited to literals and subtraction. The grammar for this language is as follows.

$$
\begin{aligned}
n &\;:\; int && \text{integer constants} \\
e &\;:\; expr && \text{expressions} \\
e &::= n \mid e - e \\
p &\;:\; prog && \text{programs} \\
p &::= e
\end{aligned}
$$

Such abstract syntax trees are formalized with recursive algebraic data types. In Why3 such types are declared using an ML-like syntax:

```
type expr = Cte int | Sub expr expr
type prog = expr
```

```
1  function eval_0 (e: expr) : int =
2    match e with
3    | Cte n → n
4    | Sub e1 e2 → eval_0 e1 - eval_0 e2
5    end
```

Fig. 1. Direct, big-step semantics

Constructors `Cte` and `Sub` are used as regular function symbols. For instance, we can define an abstract syntax tree `p3` for the expression $(7 - 2) - (10 - 6)$ as follows:

    constant p3: prog = Sub (Sub (Cte 7) (Cte 2)) (Sub (Cte 10) (Cte 6))

This language is given a big-step operational semantics, with inference rules defining a judgment $e \Rightarrow n$ meaning that expression e evaluates to the value n.

$$\frac{}{n \Rightarrow n} \qquad \frac{e_1 \Rightarrow n_1 \quad e_2 \Rightarrow n_2 \quad n_1 - n_2 = n_3}{e_1 - e_2 \Rightarrow n_3}$$

Since this semantics is deterministic and total, the simplest way is to encode it in Why3 as a logic function, as shown on Fig 1. This definition is recursive and makes use of pattern matching on its argument `e` . It is worth pointing out that, for any logic function definition, Why3 statically checks that it defines a total function: recursion must be on structurally smaller arguments and pattern matching must be exhaustive [13].

2.1 Interpreting and Proving

Before doing any proof, we can make some quick tests to check our definitions. For instance, we can define `v3` as the application of `eval_0` to `p3`

    constant v3: int = eval_0 p3

and then ask Why3 to evaluate its value:

```
> why3 defunctionalization.mlw --eval v3
Evaluation of v3: 1
```

Of course, we can also *prove* that the value of `p3` is 1. We first state it:

    goal eval_p3: v3 = 1

Then we ask Why3 to run the Alt-Ergo SMT solver [15] on this goal:

```
> why3 -P alt-ergo defunctionalization.mlw
defunctionalization.mlw eval_p3 : Valid (0.02s)
```

It is discharged in no time.

2.2   Encoding Algebraic Data Types and Pattern Matching

Proving such a lemma with the external provers available within Why3 requires encoding the constructs of algebraic data types and pattern matching into the logic of those provers.

The encoding is quite simple: the algebraic type is treated as an abstract type, and constructor symbols are treated as uninterpreted functions whose semantics is established via a number of axioms. Let us see how the `expr` type is transformed. First come the type and the constructors:

```
type expr
function Cte (n: int) : expr
function Sub (e1 e2: expr) : expr
```

Then Why3 defines a polymorphic selector function, which will later help us to encode pattern-matching constructions inside terms:

```
function match_expr (e: expr) (b1 b2: 'a) : 'a

axiom match_expr_Cte : forall b1 b2: 'a, n: int.
  match_expr (Cte n) b1 b2 = b1

axiom match_expr_Sub : forall b1 b2: 'a, e1 e2: expr.
  match_expr (Sub e1 e2) b1 b2 = b2
```

Here, `'a` denotes a type variable which can be instantiated with any type. Why3 natively supports ML-style prenex polymorphism and employs monomorphic instantiation with symbol discrimination, preservation of interpreted types, and lightweight polymorphism encodings [16,17] to efficiently translate polymorphic formulas for provers supporting only multi-sorted or mono-sorted logic.

The definition of `match_expr` suffices to prove that the ranges of `Cte` and `Sub` are disjoint. However, most SMT solvers will not deduce this fact automatically, which is why we also define an index function:

```
function index_expr (e: expr) : int

axiom index_expr_Cte : forall n: int [Cte n].
  index_expr (Cte n) = 0

axiom index_expr_Sub : forall e1 e2: expr [Sub e1 e2].
  index_expr (Sub e1 e2) = 1
```

The terms in square brackets that appear before the quantified expressions in these axioms are *instantiation patterns*, also known as *triggers*. First-order SMT solvers accept triggers as hints to control instantiation of universally quantified premises. A trigger prescribes to an SMT solver to produce a new instance whenever a term that matches the trigger occurs in the set of currently assumed facts. The precise semantics of triggers varies among solvers; in particular, a solver may ignore the patterns given by a user, invent its own triggers, or use an instantiation method not based on triggers, e.g. paramodulation.

In the definition of `index_expr`, the triggers are given to force the index calculation for every occurrence of a constructor, which is enough to deduce that no application of `Cte` can be equal to an application of `Sub`, provided that the prover supports integers and knows that 0 is not equal to 1. If we target a prover that has no support for integer arithmetic, Why3 does not generate the `index_expr` function and produces instead the axioms of pairwise dis-equality of constructors:

```
axiom Cte_Sub : forall n: int [Cte n]. forall e1 e2: expr [Sub e1 e2].
  Cte n ≠ Sub e1 e2
```

The index function is preferable, however, because an axiom like `Cte_Sub` would be instantiated for any two occurrences of constructors, producing a quadratic number of instances.

Then we introduce constructor elimination functions, or *projections*:

```
function Cte_proj_1 (e: expr) : int
function Sub_proj_1 (e: expr) : expr
function Sub_proj_2 (e: expr) : expr


axiom Cte_proj_1_def : forall n: int. Cte_proj_1 (Cte n) = n
axiom Sub_proj_1_def : forall e1 e2: expr. Sub_proj_1 (Sub e1 e2) = e1
axiom Sub_proj_2_def : forall e1 e2: expr. Sub_proj_2 (Sub e1 e2) = e2
```

And finally, we close the `expr` type with the inversion axiom:

```
axiom expr_inversion : forall e: expr.
  e = Cte (Cte_proj_1 e)  ∨  e = Sub (Sub_proj_1 e) (Sub_proj_2 e)
```

Notice that this translation is not complete. Indeed, we do not state (nor can we in a first-order language) that `expr` is the least fixed point of constructor application: our translation could be applied to a co-inductive type just as well. This is not an important shortcoming, since the automated provers we target do not perform reasoning by induction, and therefore do not need this property. We will see below how proofs by induction can be constructed directly in Why3.

Now, let us show how pattern-matching expressions are translated. In simple cases, such as function definition by pattern matching, Why3 just splits the premise into several instances. Thus, the definition of `eval_0` turns into the following conjunction:

```
function eval_0 (e: expr) : int


axiom eval_0_def :
  (forall n: int. eval_0 (Cte n) = n) ∧
  (forall e1 e2: expr. eval_0 (Sub e1 e2) = eval_0 e1 - eval_0 e2)
```

In the general case, a `match-with` expression in a formula is translated as a conjunction of implications. For example, a Why3 formula

```
match e with
| Cte n → n > 0
| Sub e1 e2 → eval_0 e1 > eval_0 e2
end
```

```
1  function eval_1 (e: expr) (k: int → 'a) : 'a =
2    match e with
3    | Cte n → k n
4    | Sub e1 e2 →
5        eval_1 e1 (\ v1. eval_1 e2 (\ v2. k (v1 - v2)))
6    end
7
8  function interpret_1 (p : prog) : int = eval_1 p (\ n. n)
```

Fig. 2. Semantics encoded in CPS form

becomes

```
(forall n: int. e = Cte n → n > 0) ∧
(forall e1 e2: expr. e = Sub e1 e2 → eval_0 e1 > eval_0 e2)
```

When pattern matching happens in a term, we resort to the selector function. Here is how the match-with expression in the definition of eval_0 is translated:

```
match_expr e (Cte_proj_1 e)
  (eval_0 (Sub_proj_1 e) - eval_0 (Sub_proj_2 e))
```

Like ML or Coq, Why3 admits complex patterns, containing wildcards and or-patterns. These are compiled internally into nested match-with expressions over simple patterns [18].

3   Continuation-Passing Style

The next exercise is to CPS-transform the function eval_0. It amounts to adding a second argument, the *continuation*, which is a function k to be applied to the result. This trick allows us to replace any recursive call in the body of a program f by a tail call: $C[f\ x]$ becomes $f\ x\ (\lambda v.\ C\ v)$. Of course, this can be done only if the language supports higher-order functions. Such a support was added to Why3 recently.

For the function eval_0, we obtain the function eval_1 in Fig. 2. The new interpreter, interpret_1, calls eval_1 with the identity continuation.

3.1   Soundness Lemma

The soundness of our CPS-transformed interpreter can be expressed by two lemmas relating the CPS-based semantics with the direct big-step semantics, one for eval_1 and one for interpreter_1. The first lemma must naturally be generalized: for any continuation k, eval_1 e k returns the same result as the application of k to the direct value of e.

```
lemma cps_correct_expr:
  forall e: expr, k: int → 'a. eval_1 e k = k (eval_0 e)
```

The second lemma is an easy consequence of the first one, applied to the identity continuation.

```
lemma cps_correct: forall p. interpret_1 p = interpret_0 p
```

Proving the first lemma is not easy. It cannot be proved as such by SMT solvers, since it requires induction on e. Why3 provides two ways to perform such an induction.

Structural induction by a dedicated transformation. The first way is to apply a *Why3 transformation*, that is a kind of proof tactic directly coded in Why3's kernel, that reduces a given goal into one or several sub-goals that, all together, imply the original goal. Resulting sub-goals can in turn be solved by external provers, or subject to another transformation, etc.

A Why3 transformation is devoted to structural inductive reasoning on algebraic data-types, producing one sub-goal for each constructor of the considered data type. For our particular lemma, a heuristics selects structural induction on e, as the goal involves a function defined recursively over e, namely `eval_1`. Then the proof is easily completed using SMT solvers on the sub-goals. Using such a dedicated transformation to add support for induction in an automated verifier is originally due to Leino [19].

General induction via lemma functions. The second way to perform reasoning by induction, that would work for general recursion, is to use *lemma functions*. This concept, that should be classified as folklore, was first emphasized in the VeriFast verifier [9], where some inductive reasoning is required in the context of representations in separation logic. Such a notion also exists in Dafny [8], and now in Why3. It is based on the idea that a recursive program can be used to simulate induction, as soon as it is terminating and side-effect free. In Why3, such a lemma function is written as follows:

```
let rec lemma cps_correct_expr (e: expr) : unit
  variant { e }
  ensures { forall k: int → 'a. eval_1 e k = k (eval_0 e) }
= match e with
  | Cte _ → ()
  | Sub e1 e2 → cps_correct_expr e1; cps_correct_expr e2
  end
```

Here we are defining a *program*, using `let` instead of `function`. As for any program, we have to prove it correct, i.e., a verification condition is generated. When such a program is given the extra attribute `lemma`, its contract is then turned into a logical statement, which is added to the logical context. The statement is exactly that of lemma `cps_correct_expr` above. For that to be sound, a termination proof is mandatory, hence the `variant` clause. In this case, it means that recursive calls are made on arguments that are structurally smaller than e. (More details on variants and termination proofs are given in the next section.) The VC for this lemma function is easily proved by SMT solvers.

3.2   Encoding Higher-Order Functions

Why3 is essentially a first-order system. It treats the *mapping type* 'a → 'b as an ordinary abstract type whose inhabitants are lambda-abstractions. Why3 desugars functional applications like (k (eval_0 e)) using a binary "mapping application" operation: k @ eval_0 e. Partial applications of function and predicate symbols are replaced with suitable lambda-abstractions.

Why3 does not implement higher-order unification and provides no means of construction of new mappings beyond what can be derived from the user axioms using first-order logic. Thus, the only construction that requires special treatment is lambda-abstraction.

Why3 translates abstractions to first-order logic using lambda-lifting. This amounts to representing every lambda-term in the problem as a fresh top-level function which takes the free variables of that lambda-term as arguments. For example, here is how the definition of eval_1 in Fig. 2 is translated:

```
function lam1 (k: int → 'a) (v1: int) : int → 'a

function lam2 (k: int → 'a) (e2: expr) : int → 'a

function eval_1 (e: expr) (k: int → 'a) : 'a =
  match e with
  | Cte n → k @ n
  | Sub e1 e2 → eval_1 e1 (lam2 k e2)
  end

axiom lam1_def : forall k: int → 'a, v1 v2: int.
  lam1 k v1 @ v2 = k @ (v1 - v2)

axiom lam2_def : forall k: int → 'a, e2: expr, v1:int.
  lam2 k e2 @ v1 = eval_1 e2 (lam1 k v1)
```

Here, lam1 represents the inner lambda-term \ v2. k (v1 - v2). The function lam2 represents the outer term \ v1. eval_1 e2 (\ v2. k (v1 - v2)). Since eval_1 and the introduced functions lam1 and lam2 are mutually recursive, Why3 puts the translated definition of eval_1 between the declarations of uninterpreted symbols lam1 and lam2 and the axioms that define their semantics.

Why3 assumes extensional equality of mappings, even though it does not include the corresponding axiom in the translation (this may change in future versions). Because of this, lambda-terms that occur under equality are not lifted, but inlined. For example, an equality id = \ n: int. n is rewritten into forall n: int. id @ n = n. Then the axiom of extensionality can be directly proved in Why3.

The current implementation does not detect when two lambda-terms are instances of one common pattern. In particular, this makes it not robust with respect to inlining: if the definition of a function symbol contains a lambda-term and is inlined, then every occurrence of that term will be lifted separately, which may affect the provability of the task. We intend to alleviate this shortcoming in future versions of Why3.

4   Defunctionalization

The next step of our case study is to "defunctionalize" the code of the previous section. The general idea of defunctionalization is to replace the functions used as continuations by some first-order algebraic data type, having as many constructors as the various lambdas in the CPS code. For our example, this data type is

```
type cont = A1 expr cont | A2 int cont | I
```

It has three constructors, corresponding to the three continuations of the code on Fig. 2, two on line 5 and one on line 8. The second continuation on line 5 is (\ v2. k (v1 - v2)). It has two free variables: v1 of type int and k which is itself a continuation. The constructor A2 associated to this continuation is thus given parameters of type int and cont (hence the algebraic data type is recursive). Similarly, the first continuation has both e2 and k as free variables, so the corresponding constructor A1 is given parameters of type expr and cont. Finally, the third continuation has no free variables. It is associated to the constant constructor I.

To derive a new interpreter interpret_2, we introduce an extra function continue_2, defined mutually recursively with function eval_2 (Fig. 3). It takes as arguments a continuation c and a value v, and evaluates c applied to v. Notice that we now define *programs*, introduced with let, instead of logic functions introduced with function. The reason is technological: the mutual recursion above cannot be statically checked terminating by Why3, the termination argument being not structural. The termination has to be proved by theorem proving, as shown in Sect. 4.3 below.

It is worth pointing out that the code of eval_2 and continue_2 only make tail calls. Thus it can be seen as a small-step semantics for our language or, equivalently, as an abstract machine for interpreting programs in this language.

4.1   Soundness

Since we wrote a program and not a logic definition, the soundness of our defunctionalized interpreter is not expressed by a pure logical lemma but with a contract for the interpret_2 program, where the post-condition tells that the result coincides with the big-step semantics.

```
let interpret_2 (p: prog) : int
  ensures { result = eval_0 p }
```

To achieve the proof that the interpreter satisfies this contract, we need to find appropriate contracts for the auxiliary programs eval_2 and continue_2.

```
1   let rec continue_2 (c: cont) (v: int) : int =
2     match c with
3     | A1 e2 k → eval_2 e2 (A2 v k)
4     | A2 v1 k → continue_2 k (v1 - v)
5     | I → v
6     end
7
8   with eval_2 (e: expr) (c: cont) : int =
9     match e with
10    | Cte n → continue_2 c n
11    | Sub e1 e2 → eval_2 e1 (A1 e2 c)
12    end
13
14  let interpret_2 (p: prog) : int = eval_2 p I
```

Fig. 3. De-functionalized interpreter

For that purpose, a first idea would be to define a logic function `eval_cont` (`c:cont`) (`v:int`) returning the evaluation of `c` on `v`. Such a function would be a non-structurally recursive function, and would be rejected by Why3: logic functions and predicates must be guaranteed to terminate (see Sect. 5 for a discussion about this limitation of Why3). However, instead of a logic function, we can define a ternary predicate `eval_cont` (`c:cont`) (`v:int`) (`r:int`) expressing that `r` is the result of the evaluation of `c` on `v`. Such a predicate can be defined inductively as follows.

```
inductive eval_cont cont int int =
| a1 : forall e: expr, k: cont, v r: int.
         eval_cont (A2 v k) (eval_0 e) r → eval_cont (A1 e k) v r
| a2 : forall n: int, k: cont, v r: int.
         eval_cont k (n - v) r → eval_cont (A2 n k) v r
| i  : forall v: int. eval_cont I v v
```

Such a definition corresponds to a set of inference rules for an evaluation judgment $c\ v \Rightarrow r$ that means "the application of continuation c to the value v evaluates to r". To ensure the consistency of the definition, Why3 checks for the standard positivity conditions of occurrences of `eval_cont` in each clause. The contracts for our auxiliary programs can then be stated as follows.

```
let rec continue_2 (c: cont) (v: int) : int
  ensures { eval_cont c v result }

with eval_2 (e: expr) (c: cont) : int
  ensures { eval_cont c (eval_0 e) result }
```

Annotated as such, those programs are easily proved correct by automated provers. For example, Alt-Ergo, CVC3, and Z3 all discharge the VCs in no time.

4.2 Encoding of Inductive Predicates

Translation of inductive predicates for first-order provers is similar to that of algebraic types: Why3 declares an uninterpreted predicate symbol and then adds one axiom per clause of the inductive definition plus the axiom of inversion. Here is the translation of the eval_cont predicate.

```
predicate eval_cont (e: cont) (v r: int)

axiom a1 : forall e: expr, k: cont, v r: int.
  eval_cont (A2 v k) (eval_0 e) r → eval_cont (A1 e k) v r

axiom a2 : forall n: int, k: cont, v r: int.
  eval_cont k (n - v) r → eval_cont (A2 n k) v r

axiom a3 : forall v: int. eval_cont I v v

axiom eval_cont_inversion : forall k0: cont, v0 r0: int.
  eval_cont k0 v0 r0 →
    ((exists e: expr, k: cont.
        eval_cont (A2 v0 k) (eval_0 e) r0 ∧ k0 = A1 e k)   ∨
     (exists n: int, k: cont, v0 r0: int.
        eval_cont k (n - v0) r0 ∧ k0 = A2 n k)   ∨
     (k0 = I ∧ v0 = r0))
```

Just like in the case of algebraic types, this translation is incomplete, because we are unable to express in first-order logic that eval_cont is the least relation satisfying the axioms. If we declared eval_cont as a coinductive predicate (which is also supported by Why3), the translation for first-order provers would be exactly the same. This does not present a problem, since these provers do not perform reasoning by induction or by coinduction. However, it is desirable to be able to make proofs by induction over an inductive predicate inside Why3, using dedicated transformations and/or ghost lemmas, similarly to what we do for algebraic types (Sect. 3.1). This is one of the directions of our future work.

4.3 Termination

So far, we have proved the partial correctness of our interpreter. This is not fully satisfactory since an implementation that would loop forever would also satisfy the same contract. We thus aim at proving termination as well.

Because the two auxiliary programs are mutually recursive in a quite intricate way, it is not completely trivial to find a termination measure that decreases on each recursive call. One adequate measure is given by the following ad-hoc size functions:

```
function size_e (e: expr) : int =
  match e with
  | Cte _ → 1
  | Sub e1 e2 → 3 + size_e e1 + size_e e2
  end
```

```
function size_c (c: cont) : int =
  match c with
  | I → 0
  | A1 e2 k → 2 + size_e e2 + size_c k
  | A2 _ k → 1 + size_c k
  end
```

The contracts of our auxiliary functions are then augmented with the following variants:

```
let rec continue_2 (c: cont) (v: int) : int
  variant { size_c c }
  ...
```

```
with eval_2 (e: expr) (c: cont) : int
  variant { size_c c + size_e e }
  ...
```

Generally speaking, a set of mutually recursive programs can be annotated as

let rec f_1 x_1
    variant $\{ v_{1,1}(x_1)$ [with R_1], ..., $v_{1,m}(x_1)$ [with R_m] $\}$
$\vdots$
with f_n x_n
    variant $\{ v_{n,1}(x_n)$ [with R_1], ..., $v_{n,m}(x_n)$ [with R_m] $\}$

where each $v_{i,j}$ returns a value on some type τ_j and R_j is a binary relation on τ_j. The verification conditions are then:

1. Each relation R_j must be well-founded.
2. For each call $f_i(e)$ in the body of the program f_j, the vector $(v_{i,1}(e), \ldots, v_{i,m}(e))$ must be strictly less than the vector $(v_{j_1}(x_j), \ldots, v_{j,m}(x_j))$ with respect to the lexicographic combination of order relations $R_1, \ldots, R_m$.

These verification conditions ensure termination because if there were an infinite sequence of program calls, there would be an infinite decreasing sequence for $R_1, \ldots, R_m$.

Why3 assumes default relations for the variant clauses so that, most of the time, the user does not need to provide the relation. If the type τ_j is int, the default relation is

$$R_{int}\ y\ x := x > y \wedge x \geq 0.$$

If τ_j is an algebraic data type, then R_j is the immediate sub-term relation.

For our interpreter, the default relation R_{int} is used. The VCs related to termination cannot be proved automatically, since SMT solvers lack the information that sizes are non-negative. So we first state this as two lemmas:

```
lemma size_e_pos: forall e: expr. size_e e ≥ 1
lemma size_c_pos: forall c: cont. size_c c ≥ 0
```

Both require induction to be proved. As we did earlier in Sect. 3.1, we can either use Why3's transformation for structural induction or turn these lemmas into recursive lemma functions. The former is simpler. Once these two lemmas are proved, termination of `eval_2` and `continue_2` is proved automatically by SMT solvers.

5   Conclusions

Using the automatic program verifier Why3, we solved a student exercise aiming at illustrating, on a simple language, the relations between various semantics that were described in a research paper [14]. Unlike the students, we did not only *code* the interpreters and tested them, but also *proved them correct*. We formalized the big-step semantics of that language and proved correct its compilation, first into a CPS-style semantics and then into a small-step one, close to an abstract interpreter. The complete example available at http:// toccata.lri.fr/gallery/defunctionalization.en.html also contains another variant of that language, forbidding negative numbers and possibly raising an "Underflow" exception. It also formalizes another semantics based on rewriting, making an analogy between reduction contexts and continuations, and an explicit abstract machine for executing the language. Even if the specifications and the proofs require advanced features such as algebraic data types, inductive predicates, and higher-order functions, we were able to prove our interpreters formally using only automated theorem provers.

Related Tools and Experiments. Why3 is not the only software verification tool where this kind of formalization can be done. For instance, the second Verified Software Competition [20] featured a challenge related to the semantics of S and K combinators and this challenge was successfully tackled by systems such as ACL2, Dafny, VCC [21], or VeriFast. Some features, such as algebraic data types and pattern matching, can be encoded without too much difficulty if a given system does not have a native support for them. Other features, such as type polymorphism, are much more difficult to simulate. Fortunately, polymorphism (parametric or ad-hoc) gained much traction in the mainstream programming languages (Java generics, C++ templates) and the verification tools follow the trail. For instance, both Dafny and VeriFast support generic types.

Perspectives. The question behind this experiment is whether an automatic program verifier can be a reasonable replacement for an interactive proof assistant for formalizing a programming language, its semantics, and its compilation. More generally, any program performing symbolic computation is a potential use case for the proposed techniques. Recently, we developed a generic approach for data types with binders in Why3. On top of it, we built a verified interpreter for lambda-calculus and a verified tableaux-based first-order theorem prover [22]. A couple of years ago, we formalized in Why3 a simple imperative while-language [23], with an operational semantics, some Hoare-style rules proved correct with respect to the operational semantics, and (partially) a weakest precondition calculus. This former case study was involving a few Coq proofs and was missing support for higher-order logic, hence it would deserve to be revisited with the current Why3 environment.

Along these lines, we intend to improve Why3 in the following ways. In short term, we want to add support for non-structural recursion in pure functions, as it is done for programming functions. We also intend to allow lambda-expressions to be used in programs, provided they are terminating and side-effect free. A key challenge to apprehend large programs and large proofs is the ability to control the logical context. Indeed, automated provers are extremely sensitive to the number, size, and shape of logical premises. Why3 already provides a module system that allows the user to split specification and implementation into small interlinked components [13]. We are currently working on the principles of refinement for this module system (both for specification and program code). The idea is to verify program components in a most abstract and minimal context, and then to reuse them in a complex and refined development. Another way to minimize the context before invoking automated provers is to provide some limited interaction where the user filters out irrelevant concepts, e.g. everything which is related to the properties of sorted arrays if the conclusion under consideration does not require it.

Acknowledgments. We thank Olivier Danvy for proposing these exercises.

References

1. Leroy, X.: A formally verified compiler back-end. J. Autom. Reason. **43**(4), 363–446 (2009)
2. Bertot, Y., Castéran, P.: Interactive Theorem Proving and Program Development. Coq'Art: The Calculus of Inductive Constructions. Springer, Heidelberg (2004)
3. Klein, G., Andronick, J., Elphinstone, K., Heiser, G., Cock, D., Derrin, P., Elkaduwe, D., Engelhardt, K., Kolanski, R., Norrish, M., Sewell, T., Tuch, H., Winwood, S.: seL4: formal verification of an OS kernel. Commun. ACM **53**(6), 107–115 (2010)
4. Nipkow, Tobias, Paulson, Larry C., Wenzel, Markus: Isabelle/HOL. LNCS, vol. 2283. Springer, Heidelberg (2002)
5. Kaufmann, M., Moore, J.S., Manolios, P.: Computer-Aided Reasoning: An Approach. Kluwer Academic Publishers, Norwell (2000)
6. Liu, H., Moore, J.S.: Java program verification via a JVM deep embedding in ACL2. In: Slind, K., Bunker, A., Gopalakrishnan, G.C. (eds.) TPHOLs 2004. LNCS, vol. 3223, pp. 184–200. Springer, Heidelberg (2004)
7. Bodin, M., Charguéraud, A., Filaretti, D., Gardner, P., Maffeis, S., Naudziuniene, D., Schmitt, A., Smith, G.: A trusted mechanised JavaScript specification. In: Proceedings of the 41st ACM SIGPLAN-SIGACT Symposium on Principles of Programming Languages, San Diego, USA, January 2014. ACM Press (2014)
8. Leino, K.R.M.: Dafny: an automatic program verifier for functional correctness. In: Clarke, E.M., Voronkov, A. (eds.) LPAR-16 2010. LNCS, vol. 6355, pp. 348–370. Springer, Heidelberg (2010)

9. Jacobs, B., Smans, J., Philippaerts, P., Vogels, F., Penninckx, W., Piessens, F.: VeriFast: a powerful, sound, predictable, fast verifier for C and Java. In: Bobaru, M., Havelund, K., Holzmann, G.J., Joshi, R. (eds.) NFM 2011. LNCS, vol. 6617, pp. 41–55. Springer, Heidelberg (2011)

10. Cuoq, P., Kirchner, F., Kosmatov, N., Prevosto, V., Signoles, J., Yakobowski, B.: Frama-C: a software analysis perspective. In: Eleftherakis, G., Hinchey, M., Holcombe, M. (eds.) SEFM 2012. LNCS, vol. 7504, pp. 233–247. Springer, Heidelberg (2012)

11. Guitton, J., Kanig, J., Moy, Y.: Why Hi-Lite Ada? In: Boogie 2011: First International Workshop on Intermediate Verification Languages, Wrocław, Poland, August 2011, pp. 27–39 (2011)

12. Filliâtre, J.-C., Paskevich, A.: Why3 — where programs meet provers. In: Felleisen, M., Gardner, P. (eds.) Programming Languages and Systems. LNCS, vol. 7792, pp. 125–128. Springer, Heidelberg (2013)

13. Bobot, F., Filliâtre, J.C., Marché, C., Paskevich, A.: Why3: shepherd your herd of provers. In: Boogie 2011: First International Workshop on Intermediate Verification Languages, Wrocław, Poland, August 2011, pp. 53–64 (2011)

14. Danvy, O., Nielsen, L.R.: Defunctionalization at work. In: Proceedings of the 3rd ACM SIGPLAN International Conference on Principles and Practice of Declarative Programming, PPDP '01, pp. 162–174. ACM Press (2001)

15. Bobot, F., Conchon, S., Contejean, E., Iguernelala, M., Lescuyer, S., Mebsout, A.: The Alt-Ergo automated theorem prover (2008). http://alt-ergo.lri.fr/

16. Bobot, F., Paskevich, A.: Expressing polymorphic types in a many-sorted language. In: Tinelli, C., Sofronie-Stokkermans, V. (eds.) FroCoS 2011. LNCS, vol. 6989, pp. 87–102. Springer, Heidelberg (2011)

17. Blanchette, J.C., Böhme, S., Popescu, A., Smallbone, N.: Encoding monomorphic and polymorphic types. In: Piterman, N., Smolka, S.A. (eds.) TACAS 2013 (ETAPS 2013). LNCS, vol. 7795, pp. 493–507. Springer, Heidelberg (2013)

18. Augustsson, L.: Compiling pattern matching. In: Jouannaud, J.-P. (ed.) FPLCA 1985. LNCS, vol. 201, pp. 368–381. Springer, Heidelberg (1985)

19. Leino, K.R.M.: Automating induction with an SMT solver. In: Kuncak, V., Rybalchenko, A. (eds.) VMCAI 2012. LNCS, vol. 7148, pp. 315–331. Springer, Heidelberg (2012)

20. Filliâtre, J.C., Paskevich, A., Stump, A.: The 2nd verified software competition: experience report. In: Klebanov, V., Grebing, S. (eds.) COMPARE2012: 1st International Workshop on Comparative Empirical Evaluation of Reasoning Systems, Manchester, UK, EasyChair, June 2012

21. Cohen, E., Dahlweid, M., Hillebrand, M., Leinenbach, D., Moskal, M., Santen, T., Schulte, W., Tobies, S.: VCC: a practical system for verifying concurrent C. In: Berghofer, S., Nipkow, T., Urban, C., Wenzel, M. (eds.) TPHOLs 2009. LNCS, vol. 5674, pp. 23–42. Springer, Heidelberg (2009)

22. Clochard, M., Marché, C., Paskevich, A.: Verified programs with binders. In: Programming Languages Meets Program Verification (PLPV). ACM Press (2014)

23. Marché, C., Tafat, A.: Weakest precondition calculus, revisited using Why3. Research report RR-8185, INRIA, December 2012

Verification Frameworks
and Applications

The KeY Platform for Verification and Analysis of Java Programs

Wolfgang Ahrendt[1], Bernhard Beckert[2], Daniel Bruns[2(✉)], Richard Bubel[3], Christoph Gladisch[2], Sarah Grebing[2], Reiner Hähnle[3], Martin Hentschel[3], Mihai Herda[2], Vladimir Klebanov[2], Wojciech Mostowski[4], Christoph Scheben[2], Peter H. Schmitt[2], and Mattias Ulbrich[2]

[1] Chalmers University of Technology, Gothenburg, Sweden
[2] Karlsruhe Institute of Technology, Karlsruhe, Germany
bruns@kit.edu
[3] Technische Universität Darmstadt, Darmstadt, Germany
[4] University of Twente, Enschede, The Netherlands

Abstract. The KeY system offers a platform of software analysis tools for sequential Java. Foremost, this includes full functional verification against contracts written in the Java Modeling Language. But the approach is general enough to provide a basis for other methods and purposes: (i) complementary validation techniques to formal verification such as testing and debugging, (ii) methods that reduce the complexity of verification such as modularization and abstract interpretation, (iii) analyses of non-functional properties such as information flow security, and (iv) sound program transformation and code generation. We show that deductive technology that has been developed for full functional verification can be used as a basis and framework for other purposes than pure functional verification. We use the current release of the KeY system as an example to explain and prove this claim.

1 Overview

Motivation. Over the last decades the reach and power of verification methods and tools has increased considerably, and there has been tremendous progress in the verification of real world systems. The basic technologies of deductive program verification have matured. State of the art verification systems can prove functional correctness at the source code level for programs written in industrial languages such as Java.

The authors gratefully acknowledge support by the German National Science Foundation (DFG) under projects http://www.key-project.org/DeduSec/DeduSec and http://www.se.tu-darmstadt.de/research/projects/albia/ALBIA both within http://www.spp-rs3.de/SPP 1496 "Reliably Secure Software Systems – RS³" and under project IMPROVE within SPP 1593 "Design For Future – Managed Software Evolution", as well as by the European Research Council (ERC) grant 258405 for the http://fmt.cs.utwente.nl/research/projects/VerCors/VerCors project.

© Springer International Publishing Switzerland 2014
D. Giannakopoulou and D. Kroening (Eds.): VSTTE 2014, LNCS 8471, pp. 55–71, 2014.
DOI: 10.1007/978-3-319-12154-3_4

While for many years the term *formal verification* had been almost synonymous with *functional verification*, in the last decade it became more and more clear that full functional verification is an elusive goal for almost all application scenarios. Ironically, this happened through the advances of verification technology: with the advent of verifiers that fully cover and precisely model industrial languages and that can handle realistic systems, it finally became obvious just how difficult and time-consuming the specification and verification of real systems is. Because of this, 'simpler' verification scenarios are often used in practice, relaxing the claim to universality of the verified properties.

Using deductive verification as core technology. In this paper, we show that deductive technology that has been developed for full functional verification (of Java programs) can be used as a basis and framework for other methods and purposes than pure functional verification:

- complimentary validation techniques such as testing and debugging,
- methods tackling the complexity of verification such as modularization and abstract interpretation,
- analyses of non-functional properties such as information flow security,
- sound program transformation and code generation.

We claim that for such an extended usage scenario, much of the work that went into the development of deductive verification systems can be reused. This includes the program logics and verification calculi that capture the semantics of the target programing language as well as the specification language, proof search mechanisms, user interfaces of semi-automatic verification systems that support proof construction and understanding proof states, interfaces to SMT (satisfiability modulo theories) solvers, as well as data structures for programs, specifications, and formulas, and associated parsers and pretty printers.

The KeY system. We use the current release of the KeY system [1] (KeY 2.2) to explain and prove the claim that deductive verifications methodology can serve as a platform for various verification and analysis methods, though other examples of this phenomenon, such as Boogie [2] and Why [3] verification frameworks, can be given. The KeY system is developed by the KeY project, a joint effort between the Karlsruhe Institute of Technology, Technical University of Darmstadt, and Chalmers University of Technology in Gothenburg, ongoing since 1999. KeY is free/libre/open source software and can be downloaded from http://key-project.org/download/.

Contents of this paper. In the following two sections, we describe the core technology for functional verification implemented in KeY: its program logic for Java and its sequent calculus, that provides symbolic execution for Java (Sect. 2), and its user interface (Sect. 3). Java is not a modular language. The specification of Java programs must support an appropriate mechanism that permits to decompose the verification target into components of manageable size that can be verified separately. In Sect. 4 we show that such a technology can be seamlessly integrated into the core verification technology. In Sect. 5 we describe how symbolic execution calculi can be reused for abstract interpretation based verification. Verification methods such as symbolic execution can be used to generate tests from the specification and the source code (glass box testing) or only the specification (black box testing) of the verification target. As shown in Sect. 6, using reasoning techniques, one can generate tests that exercise particular program paths, satisfy various code coverage criteria, or cover all disjunctive case distinctions in the specification. A further use of verification for bug finding is to enhance the debugging process by using verification technology that is based on symbolic execution to implement symbolic debuggers (Sect. 7). Symbolic debugging covers all possible execution paths, and there is no need to initialize input values. Besides functional verification, the verification of non-functional properties, e.g., security properties, is of growing importance. In Sect. 8, we show that information flow properties can be verified by using functional verification methods as a basis. Finally, in Sect. 9, we show that a deductive calculus is a good basis for covering additional mechanisms of the programing language in a modular way (no need to build a new calculus or system). This is exemplified with Java Card's transaction mechanism that is not part of standard Java.

2 A Prover Performing Symbolic Execution

The core of the KeY system consists of a theorem prover for a program logic that combines a variety of automated reasoning techniques. The KeY prover differs from many other deductive verification systems in that symbolic execution of programs, first order reasoning, arithmetic simplification, external decision procedures, and symbolic state simplification are interleaved.[1] For loop and recursion free programs, symbolic execution is performed in a fully automated manner.

The program logic supported by KeY is *Dynamic Logic* (DL) [5], a first order multi-modal logic. DL extends first order logic (FOL) with two families of modal operators: $\langle p \rangle$ ('diamond') and $[p]$ ('box') where p is a program fragment. The formula $\langle p \rangle \phi$ expresses that the program p terminates in a state in which ϕ holds, while $[p]\phi$ does not demand termination and expresses that *if p terminates, then ϕ holds in the final state.*[2] Typically, ϕ is a FOL formula; in this case, $\langle p \rangle \phi$ corresponds to the weakest precondition of p w.r.t. ϕ. Another frequent pattern of DL is $\phi \rightarrow [p]\psi$, which corresponds to $\{\phi\}\,p\,\{\psi\}$ in Hoare logic [6]. DL is closed under all logical connectives. For instance, the formula $\exists v.\,([p](\mathbf{x} \doteq v) \wedge [q](\mathbf{x} \doteq v))$ states that the final value of $\mathbf{x}$ is the same, whether we execute p or q.

To enable formal arguments about soundness and completeness, the KeY prover employs a *sequent calculus* for reasoning about Java DL formulas. Each

---

[1] The prover closest to KeY in this regard is KIV [4].

[2] This formulation assumes a deterministic programming language, like sequential Java in the context of KeY.

proof node is a sequent of the form $\Gamma \Rightarrow \Delta$, where Γ and Δ are sets of formulas, with the intuitive meaning that the conjunction of the assumptions Γ implies at least one of the formulas in Δ.

A proof in KeY consists of logical rule applications on DL sequents, using a proof strategy called *symbolic execution*. It is exactly this principle which makes the KeY prover an excellent basis for the various techniques described in this paper. We exemplify the principle of KeY style symbolic execution: consider the sequent (1), with precondition $x > y$ and postcondition $y > x$. The program in the modality swaps the values stored in x and y, using arithmetic.

$$x > y \Rightarrow \langle \texttt{x=x+y; y=x-y; x=x-y} \rangle \, y > x \tag{1}$$

To prove this formula, KeY symbolically executes one statement at a time, turning Java code into a compact representation of its effect.4 This representation is called *update*, essentially an explicit substitution, to be applied at some later point. In our example, symbolic execution of x=x+y; y=x-y; x=x-y; results in

$$x > y \Rightarrow \{x := y \| y := x\} \langle \rangle \, y > x \tag{2}$$

The expression $x := y \| y := x$ is an update. The symbol $\|$ indicates its *parallel* nature. Once the modality is empty, it is discarded, and the accumulated update is applied to the postcondition $y > x$, leading to the proof goal $x > y \Rightarrow x > y$, that can be closed immediately. The update application has swapped x and y, translating the condition on the intermediate state into a condition on the initial state. The interleaving of collecting and applying updates very much facilitates *forward* symbolic execution. This is exploited not only for giving the proving process an intuitive direction, but also as a basis for realizing the other features of the KeY platform outlined in this paper.

To reason efficiently in a rich program logic for a target language like Java, a large number of sequent calculus rules are needed (over 1500 in the standard configuration). To implement these efficiently and to permit external validation of the rules, we use so-called *taclets*, described in [1, Chap. 4]. Unbounded loops cannot be handled by symbolic execution alone. KeY has invariant and induction rules for this purpose [1, Sect. 3.6], see also Sect. 5 below. Method calls can be handled either by inlining the method body or by replacing a method invocation by the method's specification, see Sect. 4 for an example.

3   User Interface

The KeY verification system uses a graphical user interface (GUI) that is designed to make the interactive construction of formal verification proofs intuitive and efficient. During formal verification a vast amount of technical information is generated. The GUI helps the proof engineer to access relevant information.

Figure 1 shows KeY's GUI with a loaded and partly performed proof task. Problem files containing Java code and specifications as well as (partial) proofs

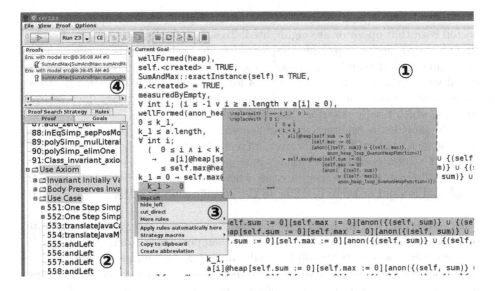

Fig. 1. The main window of the KeY GUI

can be loaded into the KeY system by selecting 'File → Load' or using the button ![icon]. A new 'Proof Management' window appears and the user can choose the proof obligation to verify. Complete and partly finished proofs are also listed. If code or specifications that were used in a proof have changed, this is indicated as well.

After choosing a proof obligation, the corresponding sequent formula is constructed and shown in the right pane of the main window, see Fig. 1 (1). Then the user can start the proof construction. In the upper left pane of the main window the opened proofs are listed. Clicking allows to switch between different proofs. The icon next to the proofs indicates whether a proof is complete (![icon]) or it contains open goals (![icon]). Below is a pane with different tabs to display the open goals, the proof tree, strategy settings for the proof search and information about the calculus rules. In Fig. 1 (2) the proof tree pane is shown. Each node of the proof tree is annotated either with the applied proof rule (e.g., impLeft) or with information about the proof step (case distinction, invariant, etc.). A right click on the proof tree or a node in it produces a context menu with possible actions on proof trees. The ability to prune, collapse, or unfold (parts of) the proof tree are indispensable for navigation and understanding in larger proofs. The user may also annotate proof nodes with free textual comments.

On the right pane ('Current Goal') of the of the main window the sequent of the selected proof node is shown. Pointing and right-clicking on parts of the sequent produces a context menu with a list of applicable proof rules for the highlighted formula, see Fig. 1 (3). Hovering over the rules shows a tooltip with the result that each rule gives when applied.

Hovering over operators in the 'Current Goal' pane, the subexpressions connected with that operator are highlighted. To search for formulas or proof nodes there are two mechanisms, one that searches for (sub)formulas in the sequent view and one that searches for proof nodes in the proof tree. These searches are useful when trying to understand how a formula has changed during the proof process. All buttons and menu entries as well as strategy settings have related tooltips, which briefly describe their functionality.

KeY provides a counter example generator (button ❷) that transforms a proof goal to an SMT formula over bitvector types and feeds it to an SMT solver. If a counterexample is found, it is presented to the user for inspection. This feature can help the user in cases where it is unclear whether the current proof goal is valid or there is a flaw in the specification or code.

User interaction during proof search. The KeY prover attempts to automate proof search as much as possible, but it also supports user interaction to guide the proof process. Proofs for valid formulas are often, but not always found automatically. For example, if complex quantifier instantiations are required, proof search may fail. When automated proof search fails, the user can apply inference rules interactively in a stepwise manner, as described above. The problem is that after a failed automated verification attempt, the user may be confronted with an intermediate proof object that is difficult to understand, because the automatic proof strategy tends to produce normal forms that are hard to read. This led us to pursue a semi-automated proof style where the user does not apply every step manually, but interacts with the automated strategy only at certain points of interest. KeY provides composite interaction steps, so-called *strategy macros*, that combine the application of basic deduction steps to achieve a specific purpose. The available strategy macros in KeY include: *Finish symbolic execution* symbolically executes Java programs in modalities. *Propositional expansion* applies only propositional rules. *Close provable goals* closes any open goal that is automatically provable, but does not touch goals where no automatic proof is found. The strategy macro *Autopilot* applies these three substrategies in this order. It divides the proof obligation into small subcases and thus guides the user to those points of the specification for which the automated proof failed.

4   Modular Specification and Verification

A crucial goal for any formal verification system is the ability to modularize a larger target program into manageable subtasks. In the context of KeY this concerns the program written in Java and the Java Modeling Language (JML) [7] for its specification. We have extended JML with concepts that support abstraction and modular verification to a language called JML* [8]. In the recent verification events in which KeY participated (VSTTE 2010, FoVeOOS 2011, VSTTE 2012, and FM 2012; cf. [9]), these concepts have proven to be effective.

Abstraction in JML specifications is provided through model fields, model methods, and ghost fields. When specifying object-oriented code modularly, it is generally important that an abstraction of the state of an object exists and can be used in other parts of the specification. This way, details of the object's implementation need not be revealed, which lets the verification both scale better and become more modular. In KeY we follow this general principle.

While similar in appearance to fields in Java, *model fields* are declared for specification and verification only, which allows the specifier to use JML* features beyond Java expressions for their definition (including quantification). The value of a model field is computed from the system state to which it is coupled through a **represents** clause that is understood as a logical axiom. *Ghost fields*, too, are only visible during verification. Unlike model fields, however, their value does not depend on the state but is part of it (like a Java field). Both abstraction techniques (ghost and model) can be used within the same specification in KeY.

Going beyond original JML, specification-only program elements in JML* allow the use of *abstract data types* (ADTs). When reasoning about concrete, mutable data structures, e.g., linked lists or trees, we are usually only interested in properties regarding the payload within these structures. ADTs provide an abstraction from the implementation, concealing details about the linked data structure that resides on the heap. JML* provides the two built-in ADTs \seq (finite sequences) and \locset (sets of memory locations; see below).

Modularity of verification is provided through the concept of design by contract [10]. Every method implementation is verified against its contract. Since method invocations are abstracted by their contracts, contracts proved correct remain valid even in case that new code has been added to the program. Method contracts do not only contain pre- and postconditions (to describe their intended behavior), but also *frame conditions* (to describe what must be *preserved*). In JML*, a frame is a set of heap locations to which a method may write at most.

In some cases, the locations of a frame are known beforehand and can be simply enumerated (static framing). For rich heap data structures, however, there is a need to describe all locations that 'belong to' the data structure; a set that may change during a run of the program. Such a set of locations is called a *footprint*. The technique to specify frames and footprints in JML* and to reason about them in KeY is the *dynamic frames* approach [8,11], that introduces a type \locset for location sets. Frames and footprints can be given in an abstract, possibly recursive, manner.

```
1   public interface List {
2   //@ public model instance \seq conts;
3   //@ accessible contents: footp;
4
5   //@ public model instance \locset footp;
6   //@ accessible footp: footp;
7
8   /*@ public normal_behavior
9     @ ensures \result == conts.length;
10    @ accessible footp;                    @*/
11  public /*@pure@*/ int size();
12
13  /*@ public normal_behavior
14    @ ensures conts == \seq_concat(
15    @      \old(conts), \seq_singleton(x));
16    @ ensures \new_elems_fresh(footp);
17    @ assignable footp;                     @*/
18  public void append(int x);    }
```

Fig. 2. List specified with model fields

For instance, the footprint of a linked list is the union of its head node's locations (for its local data) and the footprint of its tail (if not `null`).

Figure 2 shows an example of a list interface, that is specified using two model fields: `conts` for its contents and `footp` for its footprint. The mutator `append()` *changes only* the footprint of this instance (L. 17, `assignable` clause), while the pure method `size()` *depends only on* this footprint (L. 10, `accessible` clause). If for two lists `a` and `b` the footprints, `a.footp` and `b.footp` denote disjoint sets, we can conclude—without any knowledge about implementation—that a call to `a.append()` does not have an influence to the result of `b.size()`. Otherwise, `a` and `b` could be *aliased deeply*, for instance, `a` could be a tail of `b`. The predicate in L. 16 expresses that only fresh object references may be added to the footprint ensuring that sets are still disjoint after the method call if they were before.

Other verification frameworks have similar concepts of modularization: Dafny [12] uses less fine-grained dynamic frames, ghost state, and pure functions, and allows for user-defined ADTs. An alternative approach to the framing challenge is separation logic. VeriFast [13] allows the modular specification of Java and C code based on separation logic together with user defined ADTs and lemmas. VCC [14] uses ownership to deal with that challenge.

5   Abstract Interpretation

Achieving a high degree of automation is still a challenge in program verification. The nature of user interactions is either direct with the underlying theorem prover (cf. Sect. 3) or it is implicit in the need to provide specifications such as method contracts, loop invariants or induction hypotheses. SMT solvers and automated theorem provers have improved considerably during the previous decade such that writing and finding specifications is now the main bottleneck for program verification. In this section, we briefly sketch our approach to achieve higher automation by generating loop invariants automatically, using abstract interpretation techniques [15]. More details on the approach are given in [16] which, however, was only implemented recently and is available at http://www. se.tu-darmstadt.de/research/projects/albia/download/.

In a nutshell, our approach works as follows: the verification process starts as usual with a DL formula that represents a proof obligation, for instance, that a method `m()` satisfies its contract. The automated proof search executes `m()` symbolically. As Java DL models the semantics of sequential Java faithfully and precisely, we do not lose any precision until we reach a loop. In general, the user would now have to provide a loop invariant either annotated in the source code as a JML loop invariant specification or entered interactively when the loop is encountered during the proof. Instead, we use abstraction to avoid the need for a user-supplied invariant. But unlike in abstract interpretation, we avoid to abstract the symbolically executed program. Instead, we abstract only part of the symbolic state when the loop is encountered, namely that part which is possibly modified by the loop. The (automatically proven) soundness condition is that the abstract symbolic state represents at least all concrete states that are reachable by exiting the loop. For the part of the symbolic state that has not been abstracted, no precision is lost.

We illustrate the process with a small example: the loop in Fig. 3 increases the program variable i until n is reached. For ease of presentation we choose exemplarily a trivial abstract domain for integers, namely, the sign domain $\{0, \leq, \geq, <, >, \top\}$ which classifies integers into zero, non-positive, non-negative, negative, positive, or any integer.

```
i = 0;
while (i < n)
    i = i + 1;
```

Fig. 3. Loop example for symbolic state abstraction

On reaching the loop, the symbolic state looks as follows: n: n_0, i: 0 where n_0 is a symbolic value representing an unknown but concrete value. Note, both values are not abstract and no precision has been lost until this point. Abstraction of the symbolic state begins by unwinding the loop and analyzing which values have been changed, that is, one compares the state before entering the loop with the state after the first loop iteration. The only changed value is that of i. The most precise abstract value that we can give to i and that is valid before and after executing the body is $\geq$. Unwinding the loop once more and re-computing the abstract value for i gives no change. We found a fixed point and the abstracted symbolic state is n: n_0, i: $\geq$, which is used to continue symbolic execution after the loop.

In contrast to approaches like CEGAR [17], which use a counterexample guided refinement loop approach (i.e., a coarse abstraction is stepwise refined in case of a spurious counterexample), we start with a fully precise modeling and loose precision only when needed and only for a localized (and often small) part of the symbolic state. As is true for all abstraction based approaches, we loose some precision, and thus completeness, in exchange for higher automation. However, the trade off is more than justifiable when targeting specific program properties like secure information flow (see Sect. 8), absence of null pointer exceptions, etc.

Combining deductive verification and abstract interpretation has also been pursued by Leino and Logozzo [18]. They use a theorem prover from within an abstract interpretation system to compute loop invariants on demand. However, the abstract interpretation system and the theorem prover remain separate systems. Deep integration of abstract interpretation into deductive verification based on dynamic logic has also been proposed by [8] using the technique of predicate abstraction [19].

6   Test Case Generation

Even though the area of deductive verification made tremendous progress and provided powerful tools, deductive methods still require expert level knowledge. As a lightweight technique, KeY offers a verification based test case generation facility [20,21], where deductive verification is used as a base technology. From source code augmented with JML specifications, KeY generates proof obligations in dynamic logic. During verification with the prover, the proof branches over the necessary case distinctions, largely triggered by boolean decisions in the source

```
1  final class List { /*@ nullable */ public List nxt;
2
3  public /*@ pure nullable */ List get(int i){
4    return i==0?this:((nxt==null || i<0)?null:nxt.get(i-1));
5  }
6  /*@ public normal_behaviour
7    requires a.length>0 && l!=null;
8    ensures (\forall int i;0<=i&&i<a.length;a[i]==l.get(i));*/
9  public void L2A(/*@nullable */List l, List[] a){
10   for(int i=0; i<a.length; i++){ a[i]=l;
11     if(l==null) break; l=l.nxt;
12  } } }
```

Fig. 4. Method L2A violates its contract

Step 1. Create a proof tree

Step 2. Press the ⟳ button

Fig. 5. Test generation steps

code, as explained in Sect. 2. On each proof branch, a certain path through the program is executed symbolically. KeY TestGen uses the same machinery for a different purpose, namely generating JUnit test cases. The idea is to let the prover construct an unfinished proof tree (with a bounded number of loop unwindings), then to read off a *path constraint* from each branch, i.e., a constraint on the input parameters and initial state for this path. We generate concrete test input data satisfying each of these constraints, thereby achieving strong code coverage criteria, in particular MCDC (Modified Condition/Decision Criterion), by construction.

In addition to the source code, KeY's test generation facility requires formal specifications, for two purposes. First, specifications are needed to complete the test cases with *oracles* to check the test's pass/fail status. The second role of specifications is to allow symbolic execution of method calls within the code under test. The prover can use the specification, rather than implementation, of called methods to continue symbolic execution. In particular, frequently used library methods need to be specified.

As an example, Fig. 4 shows a class List (representing a list node). Method get returns the i-th list node starting from this and following the nxt field. The intended behavior of method L2A is to copy list elements starting from l into the array a—as many as fit into the array. The user may not see the mistake in the code and spend valuable time with failed verification attempts. However, the problem can be quickly detected using KeY's test generation functionality.

The first step is to create a proof tree. For example, to execute all program paths with a bound on loop unwindings, the user may choose the strategy macro 'TestGen' (Fig. 5, Step 1). By pressing the ⟳ button (Step 2), a test suite is generated which constructs different method arguments and creates various list shapes by initializing the nxt field, such that every case distinction in the proof tree (and hence in the program) is satisfied and executed. To detect the fault in method L2A, a test case is needed that executes the loop at least two times, i.e. a.length ≥ 2. To fix the method L2A, Line 11 must be replaced with if(l!=null)l=l.nxt; which ensures that the rest of the array is initialized with null if the end of the list is reached.

Besides generating test cases in order to find out why a proof cannot be closed, we can generate them out of a closed proof tree. In this case a test suite covering all feasible paths is created. This suite can be used for regression testing the software.

The usefulness of combining proofs and tests has been recognized in the last decade, leading to the conference series Tests and Proofs. A recent extension of a deductive verification tool with test generation capabilities is based on Frama-C [22]. A set of popular test generation tools that are based on symbolic execution and its variants is described in [23].

7 Debugging and Visualization

The Symbolic Execution Debugger (SED) [24,25] is an Eclipse extension that executes Java methods symbolically. It is implemented on top of KeY and offers interactive execution control just like a traditional debugger, including stepwise execution and suspension at breakpoints.

Symbolic execution makes it possible to explore *all* concrete execution paths of a program (up to a finite depth) in the symbolic states of a single symbolic execution run. The result is a *symbolic execution tree* (SET). In this sense, performing a proof in KeY realizes a sound, fully automatic, general purpose symbolic execution engine for Java. A specific proof search strategy guarantees that symbolic execution reflects the actual evaluation sequence defined by Java semantics. JML specifications are not required, but can be used during symbolic execution. Specifically, loop invariants ensure finite symbolic execution trees in presence of loops; method contracts permit to handle methods for which the source code is not available and guarantee finite symbolic execution trees in presence of recursive method calls.

Debugging by symbolic execution is interesting for various reasons. Most importantly, symbolic execution can start at any method or any other statement in a program, no fixture is required. The initial state can be specified partially or not at all. As all execution paths are covered, it is not necessary to set up a concrete initial program state leading to an execution where a targeted bug occurs. Because symbolic execution can be started 'close' to the suspected location of a bug and the symbolic states contain only program variables accessed during execution, the intermediate states of symbolic execution tend to be small and simple. This makes it easy for the bug hunter to comprehend intermediate states and the actions performed on them to find the origin of a bug. Finally, the intended behavior of a program is correctly reflected in its symbolic execution, which, therefore, will not cause a program error that disappears while debugging. The underlying reason is that classical debuggers interact and influence the execution of the analyzed program.

Figure 6 shows a debugging session where method eq() is inspected. Its full SET is displayed in the view on the left. Different icons emphasize the role of each node. The root is a start node representing the program fragment under execution. After the call to eq() the if-guard this.value == n.value is evaluated, which involves an access to the instance variable value of parameter n. As we know nothing about n—it might well be null—symbolic execution branches. The tree

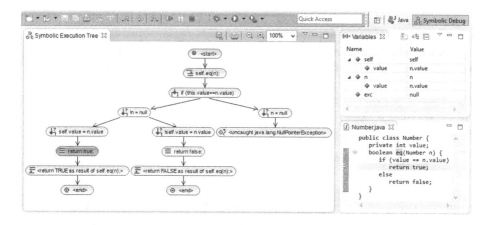

Fig. 6. Symbolic Execution Debugger: debugging method `eq` symbolically

branches are labelled with the condition under which each path is taken: if `n` is `null` then execution terminates with an uncaught `NullPointerException`, which may or may not be intended behavior. In the latter case, it directly points to a bug. Otherwise, the guard can be evaluated to either true or false. In each case a return statement is executed next.

The symbolic program state of a selected node is shown in the *Variables* view. The `value` fields of instance variables `self` and `n` have an identical symbolic value. So either `self.value` and `n.value` have the same value or `self` and `n` refer to the same object. Aliasing is a common source of bugs and SED helps to find them by visualizing all nonisomorphic memory layouts fulfilling a symbolic state.

EFFIGY [26] was the first system that allowed to interactively execute a program symbolically in the context of debugging. It did not support specifications or visualization. Behavior trees [27] are an abstract visual notation to specify the behavior of software systems. These are derived from a requirements analysis rather than from source code and they do not represent symbolic states.

8   Information Flow Analysis

Programs with publicly accessible interfaces (like web applications) are increasingly used to process confidential data. This raises the importance of information flow control within such applications: confidential information must not leak to public outputs. *Information flow* is the degree to which the initial values of variables containing confidential data ('high' variables) interfere with the final values of publicly observable ('low') variables. Formal techniques for information flow analysis and control are concerned with showing that information flow is absent or limited in a program. A survey is available in [28], though many advances have occurred since its publication. Three approaches for analyzing information flow have been implemented using KeY.

The first approach is based on *self-composition* [29, 30], which is appealing because it is semantically precise, supports semantic declassification (i.e., accepting that specific parts or properties of confidential information does become public), and can be realized on top of a software verification systems like KeY in a direct manner. The implementation in KeY [31] (which can be seen as a direct formulation of information flow in Java DL) symbolically executes a program p twice with equal symbolic values for the low variables but possibly different values for high variables. Absence of information flow is shown by proving that the symbolic values for the low variables are equal in the respective final states.

Beyond this basic idea, the approach and its implementation feature several optional refinements. First, it is possible to execute p symbolically only once and combine the obtained verification conditions. Second, if p is decomposable into individual parts, each without information flow, then these parts can be considered independently reducing the number of code paths that need to be reasoned about. Third, the analysis supports not only primitive types but also object references as secret and publicly observable values [32]. Finally, modular contracts used for functional verification (Sect. 4) can be used when proving absence of information flow as well.

Specifying information flow policies that programs must adhere to happens with an extension of JML [33]. The language allows a convenient and fine-grained specification of declassification and erasure by assigning security levels (high/low) to terms instead of variables and fields.

Another approach is to track information flow with ghost states [34]. It aims at a higher degree of automation and higher efficiency by trading precision. Declassification is supported. The approach can be combined with abstract interpretation (Sect. 5) and thus holds the potential for increasing automation by inference of suitable invariants. In this approach, we complement each program variable with a ghost variable that overapproximates the set of locations the actual variable depends on. When a program variable is assigned a new value t, its corresponding ghost variable is automatically updated too. The new value of the ghost variable is the union of the dependencies of all variables occurring in t (plus implicit dependencies caused by control flow). A program is secure if the set of calculated dependencies is a subset of those allowed by the specification.

The third approach combines KeY with external tools for projection computation and model counting in a tool chain for *quantitative* information flow analysis of imperative programs [35]. The user does not specify what information is acceptable to declassify, but instead the tool chain computes a number of information-theoretical measures (e.g., Shannon entropy or min-entropy) reflecting the amount of confidential information in bit disclosed by the program.

9   Verification of Java Card Applets

One of the specific strengths of KeY is its complete support for verification of programs written in Java Card [36], a dialect of Java for smart cards. This includes support for all features specific to the Java Card platform. These are

```
a[0] = 0;                              a[0] = 0;
JCSystem.beginTransaction();           JCSystem.beginTransaction();
Util.arrayFillNonAtomic(a,0,1,1);      a[0] = 2;
a[0] = 2;                              Util.arrayFillNonAtomic(a,0,1,1);
JCSystem.abortTransaction();           JCSystem.abortTransaction();
//@ assert a[0] == 1;                  //@ assert a[0] == 0;
```

Fig. 7. Two programs exhibiting subtleties of the Java Card memory management

the memory model that distinguishes between persistent and transient data as well as a transaction mechanism that ensures atomic updates of the persistent memory of the device [37, Chap. 7]. Each Java Card device is equipped with two types of memory: (i) persistent memory that keeps its contents between card power-ups (i.e., sessions), (ii) transient (scratch pad) memory that is reset on every power-up. Consequently, the semantics of a primitive assignment to an array element[3] depends on the kind of memory that the array is allocated to. Moreover, the transaction mechanism allows to group several assignments into atomic blocks and to collectively undo several assignments in one system API call.

On top of this, there is a specific interplay between special system API calls and regular assignments that involve the same persistent data. We illustrate this with the two programs in Fig. 7 that are both correct relative to their stated `assert` annotations. The call to the `arrayFillNonAtomic` method assigns value 1 to the array element `a[0]`. In principle, it should bypass any rollback effects of `abortTransaction` (which is what indeed happens in the program on the left), however, an earlier regular assignment to `a[0]` inside the same transaction disables this bypass effect of `arrayFillNonAtomic`.

A correct treatment of situations like the one in Fig. 7 in the underlying program logic may be expected to be difficult. Indeed, previous formalizations of Java Card were quite complex [38,39]. In KeY 2.2 we use the explicit heap model to our advantage: with an additional heap variable the Java Card memory model is formalized in a completely modular manner. This is achieved by adding a handful of carefully crafted rules for entering and exiting transactions, and assigning array elements in transaction contexts [40]. The introduction of an additional heap variable also involves a slight, yet fully transparent, extension of the JML* specification language to enable sound and complete modular verification also of programs involving Java Card transactions.

References

1. Ahrendt, W.: Using KeY. In: Beckert, B., Hähnle, R., Schmitt, P.H. (eds.) Verification of Object-Oriented Software. LNCS (LNAI), vol. 4334, pp. 409–451. Springer, Heidelberg (2007)

---

[3] Objects other than arrays are not subject to the described mechanisms.

2. Barnett, M., Chang, B.-Y.E., DeLine, R., Jacobs, B., M. Leino, K.R.: Boogie: a modular reusable verifier for object-oriented programs. In: de Boer, F.S., Bonsangue, M.M., Graf, S., de Roever, W.-P. (eds.) FMCO 2005. LNCS, vol. 4111, pp. 364–387. Springer, Heidelberg (2006)
3. Filliâtre, J.-C., Marché, C.: The Why/Krakatoa/Caduceus platform for deductive program verification. In: Damm, W., Hermanns, H. (eds.) CAV 2007. LNCS, vol. 4590, pp. 173–177. Springer, Heidelberg (2007)
4. Stenzel, K.: A formally verified calculus for full Java Card. In: Rattray, C., Maharaj, S., Shankland, C. (eds.) AMAST 2004. LNCS, vol. 3116, pp. 491–505. Springer, Heidelberg (2004)
5. Harel, D., Kozen, D., Tiuryn, J.: Dynamic Logic. MIT Press, Cambridge (2000)
6. Hoare, C.A.R.: An axiomatic basis for computer programming. Commun. ACM 12(10), 576–580, 583 (1969)
7. Leavens, G.T., Baker, A.L., Ruby, C.: Preliminary design of JML: A behavioral interface specification language for Java. SIGSOFT 31(3), 1–38 (2006)
8. Weiß, B.: Deductive verification of object-oriented software: dynamic frames, dynamic logic and predicate abstraction. Ph.D. Thesis, Karlsruhe Institute of Technology (2011)
9. Bruns, D., Mostowski, W., Ulbrich M.: Implementation-level verification of algorithms with KeY. Softw. Tools Technol. Transf. (Springer, Heidelberg) to appear. DOI:10.1007/s10009-013-0293-y
10. Meyer, B.: Applying "design by contract". IEEE Comput. 25(10), 40–51 (1992)
11. Kassios, I.T.: The dynamic frames theory. Form. Asp. Comput. 23(3), 267–288 (2011)
12. Leino, K.R.M.: Dafny: an automatic program verifier for functional correctness. In: Clarke, E.M., Voronkov, A. (eds.) LPAR-16 2010. LNCS, vol. 6355, pp. 348–370. Springer, Heidelberg (2010)
13. Jacobs, B., Smans, J., Philippaerts, P., Vogels, F., Penninckx, W., Piessens, F.: VeriFast: a powerful, sound, predictable, fast verifier for C and Java. In: Bobaru, M., Havelund, K., Holzmann, G.J., Joshi, R. (eds.) NFM 2011. LNCS, vol. 6617, pp. 41–55. Springer, Heidelberg (2011)
14. Schulte, W., Songtao, X., Smans, J., Piessens, F.: A glimpse of a verifying C compiler. In: C/C++ Verification Workshop (2007)
15. Cousot, P., Cousot, R.: Abstract interpretation: A unified lattice model for static analysis of programs by construction or approximation of fixpoints. In: Fourth ACM Symposium on Principles of Programming Language, Los Angeles, pp. 238–252. ACM Press, New York (1977)
16. Bubel, R., Hähnle, R., Weiß, B.: Abstract interpretation of symbolic execution with explicit state updates. In: de Boer, F.S., Bonsangue, M.M., Madelaine, E. (eds.) FMCO 2008. LNCS, vol. 5751, pp. 247–277. Springer, Heidelberg (2009)
17. Clarke, E., Grumberg, O., Jha, S., Lu, Y., Veith, H.: Counterexample-guided abstraction refinement. In: Emerson, E.A., Sistla, A.P. (eds.) CAV 2000. LNCS, vol. 1855, pp. 154–169. Springer, Heidelberg (2000)
18. M. Leino, K.R., Logozzo, F.: Loop invariants on demand. In: Yi, K. (ed.) APLAS 2005. LNCS, vol. 3780, pp. 119–134. Springer, Heidelberg (2005)
19. Graf, S., Saïdi, H.: Construction of abstract state graphs with PVS. In: Grumberg, O. (ed.) CAV 1997. LNCS, vol. 1254, pp. 72–83. Springer, Heidelberg (1997)
20. Engel, C., Hähnle, R.: Generating unit tests from formal proofs. In: Gurevich, Y., Meyer, B. (eds.) TAP 2007. LNCS, vol. 4454, pp. 169–188. Springer, Heidelberg (2007)

21. Beckert, B., Gladisch, C.: White-box testing by combining deduction-based specification extraction and black-box testing. In: Gurevich, Y., Meyer, B. (eds.) TAP 2007. LNCS, vol. 4454, pp. 207–216. Springer, Heidelberg (2007)

22. Petiot, G., Kosmatov, N., Giorgetti, A., Julliand, J.: How test generation helps software specification and deductive verification in Frama-C. In: Seidl, M., Tillmann, N. (eds.) TAP 2014. LNCS, vol. 8570, pp. 204–211. Springer, Heidelberg (2014)

23. Cadar, C., Godefroid, P., Khurshid, S., Pasareanu, C.S., Sen, K., Tillmann, N., Visser, W.: Symbolic execution for software testing in practice: preliminary assessment. In: Taylor, R.N., Gall, H., Medvidovic, N. (eds.) ICSE, pp. 1066–1071. ACM (2011)

24. Hentschel, M., Bubel, R., Hähnle, R.: Symbolic execution debugger (SED). In: Bonakdarpour, B., Smolka, S.A. (eds.) RV 2014. LNCS, vol. 8734, pp. 255–262. Springer, Heidelberg (2014)

25. Hentschel, M., Hähnle, R., Bubel, R.: Visualizing unbounded symbolic execution. In: Seidl, M., Tillmann, N. (eds.) TAP 2014. LNCS, vol. 8570, pp. 82–98. Springer, Heidelberg (2014)

26. King, J.C.: Symbolic execution and program testing. Commun. ACM **19**(7), 385–394 (1976)

27. Dromey, R.G.: From requirements to design: Formalizing the key steps. In: 1st International Conference on Software Engineering and Formal Methods, SEFM, IEEE (2003)

28. Sabelfeld, A., Myers, A.C.: Language-based information-flow security. IEEE J. Sel. Areas Commun. **21**(1), 5–19 (2003)

29. Barthe, G., D'Argenio, P.R., Rezk, T.: Secure information flow by self-composition. In: Proceedings of the 17th IEEE workshop on Computer Security Foundations, CSFW '04, Washington, USA, pp. 100–115. IEEE CS (2004)

30. Darvas, Á., Hähnle, R., Sands, D.: A theorem proving approach to analysis of secure information flow. In: Hutter, D., Ullmann, M. (eds.) SPC 2005. LNCS, vol. 3450, pp. 193–209. Springer, Heidelberg (2005)

31. Scheben, C., Schmitt, P.H.: Efficient Self-composition for weakest precondition calculi. In: Jones, C., Pihlajasaari, P., Sun, J. (eds.) FM 2014. LNCS, vol. 8442, pp. 579–594. Springer, Heidelberg (2014)

32. Beckert, B., Bruns, D., Klebanov, V., Scheben, C., Schmitt, P.H., Ulbrich, M.: Information flow in object-oriented software. In: Gupta, G., Peña, R. (eds.) Logic-Based Program Synthesis and Transformation, pp.15–32 (2013)

33. Scheben, C., Schmitt, P.H.: Verification of information flow properties of JAVA programs without approximations. In: Beckert, B., Damiani, F., Gurov, D. (eds.) FoVeOOS 2011. LNCS, vol. 7421, pp. 232–249. Springer, Heidelberg (2012)

34. van Delft, B.: Abstraction, objects and information flow analysis. Master's Thesis, Institute for Computing and Information Science, Radboud Uni Nijmegen (2011)

35. Klebanov, V.: Precise quantitative information flow analysis: A symbolic approach. Theor. Comput. Sci. **538**, 124–139 (2014). (to appear)

36. Chen, Z.: Java Card Technology for Smart Cards: Architecture and Programmer's Guide. Addison-Wesley, Boston (2000)

37. Oracle: Java Card 3 Platform Runtime Environment Specification, Classic Edition, Version 3.0.4., September 2012

38. Mostowski, W.: Formal reasoning about non-atomic JAVA CARD methods in dynamic logic. In: Misra, J., Nipkow, T., Sekerinski, E. (eds.) FM 2006. LNCS, vol. 4085, pp. 444–459. Springer, Heidelberg (2006)

39. Marché, C., Rousset, N.: Verification of Java Card applets behavior with respect to transactions and card tears. In: Proceedings of Software Engineering and Formal Methods (SEFM), Pune, India. IEEE CS Press (2006)
40. Mostowski, W.: A case study in formal verification using multiple explicit heaps. In: Beyer, D., Boreale, M. (eds.) FORTE 2013 and FMOODS 2013. LNCS, vol. 7892, pp. 20–34. Springer, Heidelberg (2013)

A Verification Condition Visualizer

Madiha Jami and Andrew Ireland$^{(\boxtimes)}$

School of Mathematical and Computer Sciences, Heriot-Watt University,
Edinburgh EH14 4AS, UK
a.ireland@hw.ac.uk

Abstract. When first encountering data structures such as arrays, records and pointers programmers are often presented with pictorial representations. The use of pictures to describe data structures and their manipulation can help establish basic programming intuitions. The same is true of program proving where pictures are frequently used within the literature to describe program properties such as loop invariants. Here we report on an experimental prototype of a visualization tool that translates verification conditions arising from array based code into pictures. While initially aimed at supporting teaching, we have received positive feedback from users of program proving tools within industry.

1 Introduction

The manifesto of the Verified Software Initiative [9] set out a fifteen year programme of research with the aim of demonstrating the viability of formal verification technologies in the development large-scale bug-free software systems. Central in this endeavor are the complementary strands of theory, tools and experiments. Here we focus on *tools* and the need for tools that increase the accessible formal verification techniques. Specifically we are interested in tools that support the teaching of assertion based program proving techniques and which will help win the hearts-and-minds of the next generation of formal methods researchers and practitioners.

While the basic notion of program proof via verification condition generation (VCG) is relatively simple for a toy programming language [4], the approach quickly becomes much harder to teach when working with an industrial-scale programming language and applications. Our language of choice is SPARK[1] [1], a programming language derived from Ada and which is supported by a range of static analysis techniques including formal verification. SPARK has been used extensively within the development of high-integrity software systems, including safety-critical applications such as railway signaling and avionics as well as security-critical application such as smartcard technologies. We have found that the high-profile nature of its applications makes SPARK relatively easy to motivate and is attractive to students. However, when introducing program proving, students find it hard to relate to verification conditions (VCs). Our aim is to use

---

[1] The version based upon Ada 95.

© Springer International Publishing Switzerland 2014
D. Giannakopoulou and D. Kroening (Eds.): VSTTE 2014, LNCS 8471, pp. 72–86, 2014.
DOI: 10.1007/978-3-319-12154-3_5

pictures where appropriate to help programmers gain insight as to the validity of VCs.

As a starting point we have focused on VCs arising from code that manipulates arrays. Whether learning how to construct algorithms that manipulate arrays [3,13] or how to the reason about the correction of such algorithms [6,8,12], authors typically use pictures in order to initially engage their readers. John Reynolds' use of so called *partition diagrams* [12] for reasoning about array based programs is may be the best example. And to a degree it is Reynolds' vision of "making program logics intelligible" that motivates our work.

Here we present an experimental tool that dynamically generates pictures from SPARK VCs. We believe that the generated pictures serve three purposes:

- A picture can more immediately help to identify whether or not a VC is provable.
- If provable then a picture may give guidance as to how a proof of the VC might proceed.
- If a VC is unprovable then the picture may give guidance as to where the bug lies.

While we have emphasized the role of pictures as an aid to teaching, we believe that the power of pictures is more general. For instance, within an industrial context verification engineers will be called upon to deal with the VCs that are not automatically discharged by the proof tools. Deciding whether or not a VC is provable can be a time consuming process, may be even involve wasted interactive proof attempts. If by turning the undischarged VCs into pictures such decisions can be made more quickly then the productivity gains could be significant.

In Sect. 2 we provide a brief overview of the SPARK programming language. Our overall approach is motivated in Sect. 3 while Sect. 4 describes our experimental tool. Related and future work is described in Sect. 5 with our conclusions in Sect. 6.

2   Background on SPARK

As mentioned above, the focus of our initial experiments has been the visualization of VCs arising from SPARK programs that manipulate arrays. Here we give a brief introduction to the structure of SPARK VCs in general and how arrays are handled specifically. For a more complete description the reader is directed to [1]. SPARK includes an annotation language that supports flow analysis and formal proof. In the case of formal proof the annotations capture the program specification, asserting properties that must be true at particular program points. The annotations are supplied within regular Ada comments, allowing a SPARK compliant program to be compiled using any Ada compiler. Within the work presented here we focus on three proof annotations, namely preconditions (--# pre), postconditions (--# post) and loop invariants (--# assert). When specifying properties of array based programs quantification is important. SPARK supports both universal (for all) and existential (for some) quantification.

Compliance to the SPARK language is enforced by a static analyser called the Examiner. In addition, the Examiner performs data flow and information flow analysis [2]. The Examiner supports formal verification by building directly upon the Floyd/Hoare style of reasoning. VCs can be generated for proofs of both partial correctness and exception freedom. In the conventional way, arrays are modelled as functions in the programming logic of SPARK, where:

- accessing the Ith element of array A is denoted by *element(A, [I])*, while
- updating the Ith element with the value V is denoted by *update(A, [I], V)*.

3   Our Basic Approach

Our pictures of array related VCs are based upon boxes for individual elements and rectangles containing ellipses for arbitrary sequences of elements, which we will refer to as *segments*. In terms of referencing elements, we place indexes above the array pictures while properties and relations are depicted using braces below. By way of illustration, Fig. 1 gives two pictures. The upper picture shows an array A where all the elements from f to $i - 1$ are strictly less than the ith element. The lower picture depicts the swapping of elements within an array. We also have pictorial representations for updating an element with an arbitrary value as well as updating with a value from another element within the array, but space precludes us from presenting them here.

In order to illustrate our basic approach we consider a simple teaching example - the *Polish Flag Problem*. The general idea is to partition a mixture of coloured objects into distinct colours. In the case of the Polish Flag Problem, there are two distinct colours, *i.e.* red and white, corresponding to the colours of the Polish National Flag[2]. A solution to the problem, written in SPARK, is given in Fig. 2. Note that an array Flag is used to represent the mixture of colours. It is assumed that all the elements of Flag are either Red or White. This assumption is expressed by the following precondition:

```
--# pre (for all I in IndexRange => (Flag(I)=Red or Flag(I)=White));
```

where IndexRange defines the range of valid indices for the array Flag. The required postcondition takes the following form:

```
--# post for some P in Integer range (Flag'First) .. (Flag'Last+1) =>
--#   ((for all Q in Integer range Flag'First..(P-1) => (Flag(Q)=Red)) and
--#    (for all R in Integer range P..Flag'Last => (Flag(R)=White)));
```

---

[2] This is a simplification of Dijkstra's *Dutch National Flag Problem* which requires three colours.

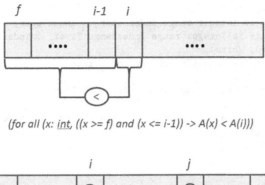

(for all (x: int, ((x >= f) and (x <= i-1)) -> A(x) < A(i)))

t:= A(i); A(i):=A(j); A(j):= t

Fig. 1. Arrays as pictures

This asserts that on termination all the **Red** elements within **Flag** will proceed the **White** elements, where the existential variable P is used to indicate the lower bound of the **White** elements. Note that to accommodate the situation where **Flag** contains no **White** elements, the upper bound of P is defined to be **Flag'Last+1**. The basic idea behind the algorithm is that a lower segment of **Red** elements and an upper segment of **White** elements are maintained during the computation. Two local variables, I and J are used in defining the upper and lower bounds of each segment respectively during this computation. Sandwiched between the lower and upper segments (I..J-1 inclusive) is a mixture of coloured elements. This "basic idea" is expressed formally by the loop invariant corresponding to the assert statement in Fig. 2. Note that on termination I=J and the consequently mixed colours segment (I..J-1) will be empty.

Here we focus on the VCs associated with the loop invariant and the postcondition. With regards to the loop we consider specifically the else-branch, where the corresponding VC is shown in Fig. 3. Note that both hypotheses and conclusions are identified using labels prefixed with H and C respectively. Note also that only those parts that are required in order to draw pictures of the array are given. In some sense this is more interesting than the then-branch since the conclusion formulas C4 and C5 involve nested updates, making it harder to decide whether or not the VC is provable. In contrast, we believe that the validity of the VC is more immediate if presented with the pictorial representation as provided in Fig. 4. Moreover, we would argue that the picture also provides a strong hint as to how a proof should proceed. That is, it tells you which parts of the

```
...
IndexUpper: constant := 4;
IndexLower: constant := 1;
subtype IndexRange is Integer range IndexLower .. IndexUpper;
subtype PointerRange is Integer range IndexRange'First .. IndexRange'Last+1;
type Colour is (Red, White);
type ArrayOfColours is array (IndexRange) of Colour;
...
procedure Partition_Section(Flag: in out ArrayOfColours)
is
  subtype JustBiggerRange is Integer range Flag'First .. Flag'Last+1;
  I: JustBiggerRange;
  J: JustBiggerRange;
  T: Colour;
  begin
    I:=Flag'First;
    J:=Flag'Last+1;
    loop
      --# assert Flag'First<=I and
      --#         J<=(Flag'Last+1) and
      --#         I<=J and
      --# (for all Q in Integer range Flag'First..(I-1) => (Flag(Q)=Red)) and
      --# (for all R in Integer range J..Flag'Last => (Flag(R)=White));
      exit when I=J;
      if Flag(I)=Red then
        I:=I+1;
      else
        J:=J-1;
        T:=Flag(I);
        Flag(I):=Flag(J);
        Flag(J):=T;
      end if;
    end loop;
end Partition_Section;
```

Fig. 2. Solution to Polish Flag problem written in SPARK

goal follow directly from the given, and which parts of the goal must first be decomposed, i.e. the white segment from $j-1$ to l must be decomposed into the $(j-1)^{th}$ element and the segment from j to l.

Now consider the post-loop VC which is given in Fig. 5 and the corresponding pictures shown in Fig. 6. Again we argue that the validity of the VC is more immediate when considering the pictorial representation. In addition, the pictures strongly suggest how to complete the proof, i.e. instantiate the existential variable p within the goal to be i (or j since $i = j$).

The real value of pictures, as hinted in the introduction, is in identifying when a VC is not provable or where inconsistencies have arisen between the code and the specification. By way of illustration, consider Fig. 7 which gives a revised version of the loop associated with our Polish Flag solution. Here we focus on the

```
procedure_partition_section_5.
...
H3:     i <= j .
...
H4:     for_all(q_: integer, ((q_ >= indexrange__first) and (
            q_ <= i - 1)) -> (element(flag, [q_]) = red)) .
H5:     for_all(r_: integer, ((r_ >= j) and (r_ <=
            indexrange__last)) -> (element(flag, [r_]) =
            white)) .
...
H12:    not (i = j) .
...
H17:    not (element(flag, [i]) = red) .
...

        ->

...
C4:     for_all(q_: integer, ((q_ >= indexrange__first) and (
            q_ <= i - 1)) -> (element(update(update(flag, [i], element(
            flag, [j - 1])), [j - 1], element(flag, [i])), [
            q_]) = red)) .
C5:     for_all(r_: integer, ((r_ >= j - 1) and (r_ <=
            indexrange__last)) -> (element(update(update(
            flag, [i], element(flag, [j - 1])), [j - 1], element(
            flag, [i])), [r_]) = white)) .
...
```

Fig. 3. Polish Flag: Loop invariant VC - else branch

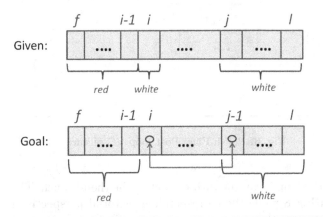

Fig. 4. Polish Flag: Loop invariant VC picture - else branch

```
procedure_partition_section_12.
H1:    indexrange__first <= i .
H2:    j <= indexrange__last + 1 .
...
H4:    for_all(q_: integer, ((q_ >= indexrange__first) and (
           q_ <= i - 1)) -> (element(flag, [q_]) = red)) .
H5:    for_all(r_: integer, ((r_ >= j) and (r_ <=
           indexrange__last)) -> (element(flag, [r_]) =
           white)) .
...
H12:   i = j .
       ->
C1:    for_some(p_: integer, ((p_ >= indexrange__first) and (
           p_ <= indexrange__last + 1)) and ((for_all(q_:
           integer, ((q_ >= indexrange__first) and (q_ <= p_ - 1)) -> (element(
           flag, [q_]) = red))) and (for_all(r_: integer, ((
           r_ >= p_) and (r_ <= indexrange__last)) -> (element(
           flag, [r_]) = white))))) .
```

Fig. 5. Polish Flag: Post loop VC

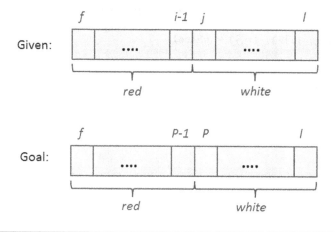

Fig. 6. Polish Flag: Post loop VC picture

verification of the loop invariant with respect to the then-branch. The associated VC is given in Fig. 8 while the corresponding pictorial perspective is shown in Fig. 9. Again we argue that the pictures are more effective at communicating that there are problems, i.e. the contradiction with regards to the colour of element i within the given hypothesis. This contradiction arises because the loop invariant is flawed, i.e. the upper bound of the red segment should be $(i - 1)$ but in the revised loop code it is given as $(i + 1)$.

```
...
loop
--# assert Flag'First<=I and
--#          J<=(Flag'Last+1) and
--#          I<=J and
--# (for all Q in Integer range Flag'First..(I+1) => (Flag(Q)=Red)) and
--# (for all R in Integer range J..Flag'Last => (Flag(R)=White));
          exit when I=J;
          if Flag(I)=White then
              J:=J-1;
              T:=Flag(I);
              Flag(I):=Flag(J);
              Flag(J):=T;
          else
           I:=I+1;
          end if;
end loop;
...
```

Fig. 7. Revised Polish Flag code

```
procedure_partition_section_4.
...
H3:     i <= j .
H4:     for_all(q_: integer, ((q_ >= indexrange__first) and (
            q_ <= i + 1)) -> (element(flag, [q_]) = red)) .
H5:     for_all(r_: integer, ((r_ >= j) and (r_ <=
            indexrange__last)) -> (element(flag, [r_]) =
            white)) .
...
H12:    not (i = j) .
...
H17:    element(flag, [i]) = white .
...

        ->

...
C4:     for_all(q_: integer, ((q_ >= indexrange__first) and (
            q_ <= i + 1)) -> (element(update(update(flag, [i], element(
            flag, [j - 1])), [j - 1], element(flag, [i])), [
            q_]) = red)) .
C5:     for_all(r_: integer, ((r_ >= j - 1) and (r_ <=
            indexrange__last)) -> (element(update(update(
            flag, [i], element(flag, [j - 1])), [j - 1], element(
            flag, [i])), [r_]) = white)) .
...
```

Fig. 8. Polish Flag: Loop invariant VC - then branch (revised code)

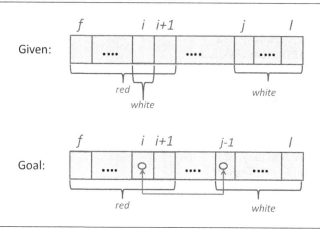

Fig. 9. Polish Flag: Loop invariant VC picture - then branch (revised code)

4   Experimental Implementation and Results

We now describe how the basic approach outlined above has been implemented in an experimental tool called Auto-VCV. As shown in Fig. 10, Auto-VCV involves three phases:

Parser: given a raw VCG file all information relating to arrays is extracted.
Translator: from the extracted information the relative ordering of array elements and segments is determined.
Picture Generator: the relative ordering information is mapped onto the absolute positioning of the array pictures.

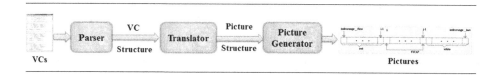

Fig. 10. Auto-VCV architecture

We focus in particular on the core algorithm which extracts information from VCs that is relevant to drawing pictures of arrays. The algorithm takes three input files:

vcg: contains all the VCs related to a specific procedure.
fdl: records type information as well as the variables and constants associated with the procedure. Any user defined proof functions that are used within assertions are also recorded.

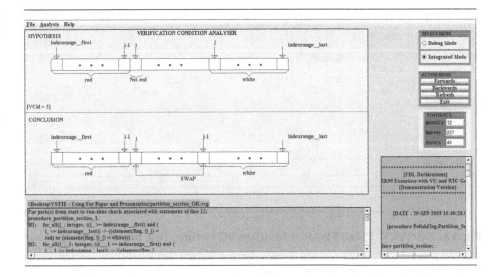

Fig. 11. Auto-VCV screenshot

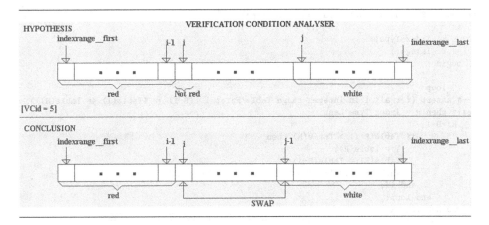

Fig. 12. Auto-VCV: Polish Flag loop invariant VC picture - else branch

rul: contains the definition of proof functions supplied by the user.

Parsing the raw VCs, along with the information in the **fdl**[3] and **rul** files, the algorithm performs the following four tasks for each VC:

1. Identification of the arrays that are explicitly referenced within the given hypotheses and conclusions.

---

[3] FDL stands for Functional Description Language [1].

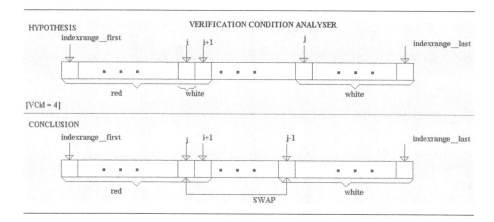

Fig. 13. Auto-VCV: Polish Flag loop invariant VC picture - then branch (revised code)

```
subtype Index_Type is Integer range 1 .. 9;
   type Array_Type is array (Index_Type)
   of Integer;
...
procedure Bubble_Max(Table: in out Array_Type)
   is
      R: Index_Type;
      T: Integer;
   begin
      R:= 1;
      loop
--# assert (for all I in Integer range Table'First .. (R-1) => (Table(I) <= Table(R)));
exit when R = Index_Type'Last;
   R:=R+1;
            if Table(R-1) > Table(R) then
               T:= Table(R);
               Table(R):= Table(R-1);
               Table(R-1):= T;
            end if;
         end loop;
   end Bubble_Max;
```

Fig. 14. Bubble Max code

2. Extraction of properties and relations with respect to elements and segments that are contained within the identified arrays, including constraints on index variables and upper and lower bounds.
3. Ordering the elements and segments that are explicitly identified above, this may involve elementary reasoning with regards to the constraints extracted for index variables.
4. Positioning the elements and segments, i.e. determining if segments (and elements) are (i) adjoining, (ii) non-adjoining, (iii) overlapping. Implicit gaps and overlaps are calculated, i.e. either a fixed number of consecutive elements of a segment.

```
procedure_bubble_max_3.
H1:     for_all(i_: integer, ((i_ >= index_type__first) and (
            i_ <= r - 1)) -> (element(table, [i_]) <= element(
            table, [r]))) .
...
H18:    element(table, [r + 1 - 1]) > element(table, [r + 1]) .
...

        ->
C1:     for_all(i_: integer, ((i_ >= index_type__first) and (
            i_ <= r + 1 - 1)) -> (element(update(update(
            table, [r + 1], element(table, [r + 1 - 1])), [r + 1 - 1], element(
            table, [r + 1])), [i_]) <= element(update(update(
            table, [r + 1], element(table, [r + 1 - 1])), [r + 1 - 1], element(
            table, [r + 1])), [r + 1]))) .
...
```

Fig. 15. Bubble Max: Loop invariant VC - then-branch (true)

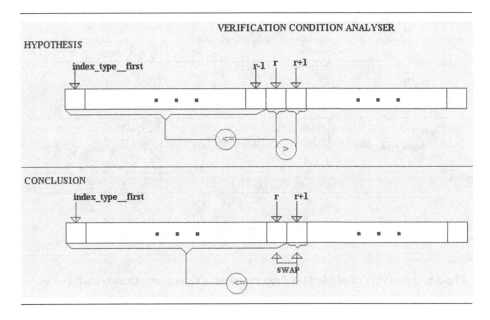

Fig. 16. Auto-VCV: Bubble Max loop invariant VC picture - then-branch (true)

The basic tasks outlined above can be applied in two distinct modes within Auto-VCV. Firstly, in what is called *debug mode* pictures are extracted from individual hypotheses (or conclusions) one at a time for each VC. Secondly, in *integrated mode* all the individual pictures are combined to give a single picture for the given VC. The actual picture drawing aspect of the system maps the abstract information extracted from the VCs onto concrete positions within the Auto-VCV interface panels.

```
procedure_bubble_max_4.
H1:     for_all(i_: integer, ((i_ >= index_type__first) and (
            i_ <= r - 1)) -> (element(table, [i_]) <= element(
            table, [r]))) .
...
H18:    not (element(table, [r + 1 - 1]) > element(table, [r + 1])) .
        ->
C1:     for_all(i_: integer, ((i_ >= index_type__first) and (
            i_ <= r + 1 - 1)) -> (element(table, [i_]) <= element(
            table, [r + 1]))) .
...
```

Fig. 17. Bubble Max: Loop Invariant VC - then-branch (false)

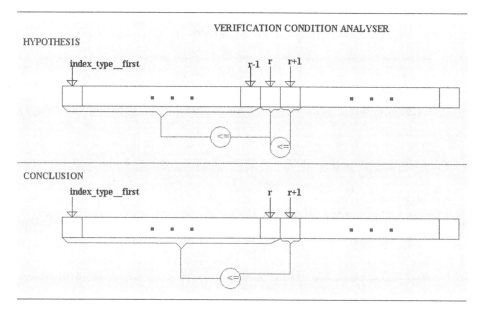

Fig. 18. Auto-VCV: Bubble Max loop invariant VC picture - then-branch (false)

Auto-VCV has an object oriented design and is implemented in Java SDK 1.7 version using AWT and Swing utilities along with the Java 2D graphics library [7]. The GUI for Auto-VCV is shown in Fig. 11, note that as well as displaying pictures of arrays it also allows the user to view the related VC (bottom panel) and FDL file (bottom right panel). Mode selection and other navigation options are shown in the panel on the right.

Returning to our running example, the pictures generated by Auto-VCV for the VC given in Fig. 3 are shown in Fig. 12, while the pictures generated for the VC given in Fig. 8 are shown in Fig. 13. In order to illustrate pictures involving relations, consider the Bubble_Max procedure given in Fig. 14 - a procedure in which the largest value within an array "bubbles" up to the top, i.e. the element with the largest index. The VC associated with the then-branch is given in Fig. 15 while the corresponding Auto-VCV generated picture is shown in Fig. 16. The VC and pictures associated with the path that avoids the then-branch are given in Figs. 17 and 18 respectively. Again we would argue that the validity of these VCs is more immediate when viewed as pictures.

5   Related and Future Work

We are unaware of any other work that directly addresses the visualization of array based VCs. As part of a previous project, which focused on separation logic [11], we built an animation tool [10] which supports the visualization of programs that manipulate the heap. The spatial operators associated with separation logic makes it particularly amenable to extracting pictures from formulas.

Further testing and development of the Auto-VCV tool is required. For instance we need to develop the tool so that it can represent relations between distinct pictures, e.g. when proving sorting algorithms one needs to specify that the output array is a permutation of the input array. Moreover, to deal effectively with more comprehensive functional specifications definitions become important. Handling definitions is currently under development, and accounts for the **rul** (file) input to our algorithm discussed above. Multi-dimensional arrays as well as records are also part of our future work plans. Following the motivations of Reynolds [12] mentioned in the introduction, we are also keen to explore the role of pictures within proof.

In terms of SPARK users, we have received positive feedback on Auto-VCV from software engineers within BAE Systems that use SPARK. We also intend to make use of our work within a MSc programme which covers SPARK and program proof. Another potential direction will be to target Boogie, a generic verification condition generator [5]. Following the Boogie route would allow our approach to be more easily applied to other programming languages.

6   Conclusion

We have presented an approach to visualizing VCs associated with array based code. The core of the approach has been demonstrated via our Auto-VCV prototype tool which extracts pictures from SPARK VCs. While still very much an experimental tool, we believe that it demonstrates the value of visualizing VCs as pictures, both as an aid to proof as well as debugging code and specifications.

Acknowledgements. This research was supported by EPSRC Platform Grant EP/J001058. Our thanks go to Alan Bundy, Gudmund Grov, Paul Jackson, Jacques Fleuriot, Ewen Maclean for their feedback on the work, as well as to John Moore and Ben Gorry (BAE Systems, Warton UK) for their feedback on an early prototype of Auto-VCV. We also thank three anonymous VSTTE 2014 referees for their constructive feedback.

References

1. Barnes, J.: High Integrity Software: The SPARK Approach to Safety and Security. Addison-Wesley, Reading (2003)
2. Bergeretti, J.-F., Carré, B.A.: Information-flow and data-flow analysis of while-programs. ACM Trans. Program. Lang. Syst. (TOPLAS) **7**(1), 37–61 (1985)
3. Cormen, T.H., Leiserson, C.E., Rivest, R.L., Stein, C.: Introduction to Algorithms, 3rd edn. MIT Press, Cambridge (2009)
4. Gordon, M.J.: Programming Language Theory and its Implementation. International Series in Computer Science. Prentice-Hall, Upper Saddle River (1988)
5. Le Goues, C., Leino, K.R.M., Moskal, M.: The boogie verification debugger (Tool Paper). In: Barthe, G., Pardo, A., Schneider, G. (eds.) SEFM 2011. LNCS, vol. 7041, pp. 407–414. Springer, Heidelberg (2011)
6. Gries, D.: The Science of Programming. Springer, New York (1981)
7. Hardy, V.J.: Java 2D API graphics. Sun Microsystems Press Java series. Sun Microsystems Press, Palo Alto (2000)
8. Hoare, C.A.R.: Proof of a program: find. CACM **14**(1), 39–45 (1971)
9. Hoare, C.A.R., Misra, J., Leavens, G.T., Shankar, N.: The verified software initiative: a manifesto. ACM Comput. Surv. **41**(4), 1–8 (2009)
10. Maclean, E., Ireland, A., Grov, G.; The core system: animation and functional correctness of pointer programs. In: Proceedings of the 16th IEEE Conference on Automated Software Engineering (ASE 2011): Tool Demonstration Paper, Lawrence, Kansas. IEEE (2011)
11. O'Hearn, P.W., Reynolds, J.C., Yang, H.: Local reasoning about programs that alter data structures. In: Fribourg, L. (ed.) CSL 2001. LNCS, vol. 2142, pp. 1–19. Springer, Heidelberg (2001)
12. Reynolds, J.C.: The Craft of Programming. Prentice-Hall, Englewood Cliffs (1981)
13. Wirth, N.: Algorithms + Data Structures = Programs. Prentice-Hall, Engelwood Cliffs (1976)

Formal Modeling and Verification of CloudProxy

Wei Yang Tan[1], Rohit Sinha[1]([✉]), John L. Manferdelli[2], and Sanjit A. Seshia[1]

[1] University of California, Berkeley, CA, USA
rsinha@eecs.berkeley.edu
[2] Intel Science and Technology Center for Secure Computing, Berkeley, USA

Abstract. Services running in the cloud face threats from several parties, including malicious clients, administrators, and external attackers. CloudProxy is a recently-proposed framework for secure deployment of cloud applications. In this work, we present the first formal model of CloudProxy, including a formal specification of desired security properties. We model CloudProxy as a transition system in the UCLID modeling language, using term-level abstraction. Our formal specification includes both safety and non-interference properties. We use induction to prove these properties, employing a back-end SMT-based verification engine. Further, we structure our proof as an "assurance case", showing how we decompose the proof into various lemmas, and listing all assumptions and axioms employed. We also perform some limited model validation to gain assurance that the formal model correctly captures behaviors of the implementation.

1 Introduction

With computation shifting to the cloud, security in cloud computing has become a concern. Providers of Infrastructure as a Service (IaaS) lease data center resources (processors, disk storage, etc.) to mutually non-trusting users. While IaaS providers use virtualization to isolate users on a physical machine, even if the virtualization software is assumed to be secure, a malicious user may still exploit misconfigurations or vulnerabilities in management software to gain complete control over data center networks and machines. Moreover, a malicious data center administrator can steal or modify unprotected disk storage. This can be catastrophic because applications may save persistent secrets (e.g. databases, cryptographic key) and virtual machine images (containing trusted program binaries) to disk. These threats are a challenge for deploying security-critical services to the cloud.

CloudProxy [16] is a recently-proposed framework for securely deploying cloud applications on commodity data center hardware. It implements a trusted service that is available to applications to (1) protect confidentiality and integrity of secrets stored on secondary storage, (2) cryptographically prove that they are running unmodified programs, and (3) securely communicate with other applications over untrusted networks.

© Springer International Publishing Switzerland 2014
D. Giannakopoulou and D. Kroening (Eds.): VSTTE 2014, LNCS 8471, pp. 87–104, 2014.
DOI: 10.1007/978-3-319-12154-3_6

We consider the problem of formal specification and verification of Cloud-Proxy. We are concerned with proving that CloudProxy provides a set of security properties to any application that uses its API. To that end, we model the internals of CloudProxy in the presence of arbitrary, non-deterministic applications. Our first challenge is that the security guarantees listed above are informal and fairly high-level; it is non-trivial to formulate these properties for a detailed model of CloudProxy. Therefore, we construct an assurance case [20] that decomposes our proof into several axioms, assumptions about our trusted computing base, and lemmas that must be proved. The assurance case argues that our lemmas are complete — under our documented assumptions, our lemmas imply the high-level security goals outlined by the authors of CloudProxy [16]. In formalizing these lemmas, we use well-known characterizations of non-interference [10] and semantic information flow [13]. Finally, we build a detailed term-level [5] model of CloudProxy, and prove these properties using a Satisfiability Modulo Theories (SMT) based theorem prover [3].

In summary, the primary contributions of this paper include:

- a formal model of CloudProxy (see Sect. 4)
- an assurance case for systematically decomposing our proof into a set of assumptions made by CloudProxy, and properties that must be proved on the model (see Sect. 3: Fig. 2 and Table 1)
- a semi-automatic, machine-checked proof of our properties on the formal model (see Sect. 5).

2   Background

2.1   CloudProxy's Threat Model

We outline CloudProxy's threat model, which is described in greater detail in [16]. The adversary controls everything outside of the protected application's trusted computing base (TCB): hardware and OS/hypervisor that is running CloudProxy. That is, the adversary has physical access to all data center hardware and infrastructure, except the hardware (i.e. CPU, memory, chipset, backplane, disks) on which the protected application is currently running — there is no direct access to the hardware during operation and for a few minutes thereafter (to prevent cold boot attacks [12]). In practice, providers of Infrastructure as a Service (IaaS) may enclose racks of processors in cages to prevent physical access. However, a malicious administrator can remove, examine, modify the disk, and later re-install the modified disk on a CloudProxy machine. The adversary also controls all data center networks. In this threat model, CloudProxy protects the protected application's secrets that (1) reside locally on the machine, and (2) are communicated to other trusted applications over an untrusted network channel.

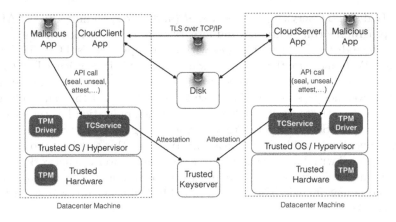

Fig. 1. Overview of CloudProxy architecture

2.2   Overview of CloudProxy Architecture

Figure 1 gives a structural overview of the CloudProxy architecture. CloudProxy assumes that it runs on trusted hardware, which includes a trusted CPU, and a trusted motherboard containing a secure co-processor called the TPM [17]. The TPM serves as a root of trust for secure boot, cryptographic *sealing/unsealing* of secrets, and *attestation* of applications. *Sealing* encrypts the secret, and also binds it to the measurement of the application invoking the API; *unsealing* decrypts the sealed secret if and only if the measurement of the caller matches the bound measurement of the ciphertext. A measurement is a cryptographic hashing on the state of the entity of concern. The TPM protects the sealing keys within its hardware, thereby protecting the keys from software attacks. *Attestation* is a mechanism by which a remote party can verify that the local platform has a desired measurement, and then provision secrets to the local platform. The TPM-enabled boot eventually launches the operating system, which is also trusted by CloudProxy – Sect. 3 describes what guarantees we require from a trusted OS. At the time of writing, CloudProxy uses a hardened Linux kernel. The crux of CloudProxy is the TCService process which exposes an API (see Sect. 2.4) to its mutually trusting applications. The application uses this API to (1) *seal* its secrets before saving them to disk storage, (2) *measure* itself and the underlying OS to prove that it is running unmodified code, and (3) authenticate itself to remote CloudProxy applications via the *attest* API.

We briefly describe how this architecture protects us from an adversary with capabilities as described in the threat model above. First, CloudProxy uses a trusted OS/hypervisor layer for isolating the protected application's execution from other adversarial applications. We argue that apart from vulnerabilities in the application logic (which is beyond our scope), the TCService API is the only remaining means of attack from adversaries. In this paper, we prove that TCService prevents any application's API request from interfering with another application's API response. Secondly, to protect from insider attacks that steal or modify disks, TCService provides a *seal* (and corresponding *unseal*) API to add cryptographic confidentiality and integrity protection before writing secrets to disk. Since disks also store binaries within an application's TCB, TCService uses the TPM to measure the entire software stack (OS, TCService, CloudClient) before executing it. Lastly, to protect from attacks that observe or tamper messages sent over network, TCService provides an *attest* API that an application can use to authenticate itself to a KeyServer. If the application has the expected measurement, TCService will return a certificate (signed by KeyServer) containing the application's public key. The application uses this certificate to establish a secure channel with another CloudProxy application over the network, thereby preventing network attacks. We use an assurance case in Sect. 3 to make a systematic argument for why CloudProxy provides sufficient defense against this threat model.

2.3 Deploying and Initializing CloudProxy

CloudProxy is deployed in two parts: (1) a virtual machine image containing the trusted OS and all CloudProxy applications, and (2) the trusted *KeyServer*. The *KeyServer* is deployed with the desired measurement of TCService, and desired measurements of each application. When the machine boots up and starts TCService, TCService uses the TPM to measure its trusted computing base (the OS and TCService binary), and sends a TPM's attestation to this measurement along with TCService's public key to the *KeyServer*. If the measurement matches the expected value, the *KeyServer* returns a certificate binding TCService to its public key. This establishes trust between the *KeyServer* and TCService for all future communication. Next, TCService starts the application, e.g. CloudClient in Fig. 1. To establish trust with the *KeyServer*, CloudClient uses TCService to measure its trusted computing base (the OS, TCService, and CloudClient binary), and sends the TCService's attestation to this measurement along with the CloudClient's public key to the KeyServer. In response, the *KeyServer* produces a signed certificate binding CloudClient to its public key. From hereon, CloudClient uses this certificate for establishing secure connections with other applications such as the CloudServer. The application also generates a private attestation key, which it *seals* using TCService and saves to disk for future use. Note that the TPM acts as a hardware root of trust in this entire process.

2.4 CloudProxy API

Once the applications have been initialized, they may invoke any of the following CloudProxy API, in any order. We now briefly describe the semantics of each API function (details found in [16]).

1. *GetHostedMeasurement()*: computes the measurement of the calling application.
2. *Attest(data)*: returns a certificate (signed by TCService) binding *data* to the caller by including the caller's measurement in the certificate.

3. *GetAttestCertificate()*: returns a certificate (signed by KeyServer) binding the caller's public key.
4. *Seal(secret)*: encrypts the concatenation of *secret* and the caller's measurement. Then the message authentication code (MAC) of this ciphertext is attached to the ciphertext.
5. *Unseal(sealed_secret)*: performs integrity check on the MAC, and decrypts the input data if the integrity check succeeds. Next, TCService checks if the caller's measurement is equal to the measurement field in the plaintext. If this check succeeds, the plaintext is returned to the caller.
6. *GetEntropy(n)*: returns a cryptographically-strong random number of size n bits.

3   Assurance Case

We prove that CloudProxy protects its client applications from the threats allowed in our threat model. However, the description of the threat model and desired properties in the original CloudProxy paper are quite informal. Our first contribution in this work is to formalize these high-level security properties into a set of axioms, assumptions, and lemmas that are expressible within a model of CloudProxy. Although we formalize our assumptions and lemmas, we rely on an informal assurance case as a meta-level argument for why our lemmas and assumptions fulfill the high-level security properties. In Sect. 4, we build a formal model of CloudProxy, and in Sect. 5, we prove a set of lemmas on this model.

An assurance case is a documented body of evidence that provides a systematic, albeit informal, argument that a system satisfies a set of properties [20]. An assurance case first starts with a goal, and then iteratively decomposes it into constituent goals and assumptions, until all goals are supported by direct evidence. We follow the Goal Structuring Notation (GSN) as described in the GSN Community Standard [2]. A goal or a claim (marked by box labeled G) is a lemma we would like to prove. An assumption (marked by oval labeled A) represents an assumption or an axiom in our proof. A context (labeled Ct) is used to limit scope of our work. An evidence (marked by circle labeled E) refers to a proof and is used to support a goal. We use circles with dashed lines to indicate proofs that are in progress.

As shown in Fig. 1, CloudProxy relies on several components: a trusted hardware, a trusted OS/hypervisor layer, to-be-verified TCService, and a trusted remote key server. In this work, we only verify TCService, and assume that properties about other components hold. This is encoded as assumption **A1** in Fig. 2: the hardware, the hypervisor, and the OS (including the TPM driver) are trusted.

For ease of exposition, we use the term "protected application" to refer to a CloudProxy application whose secrets we seek to protect, and the term "malicious application" to refer to any other CloudProxy application or program running on the same machine. Proving that CloudProxy protects the protected application's secrets (**G1**) is decomposed into 3 goals **G2** - **G4**, one for each

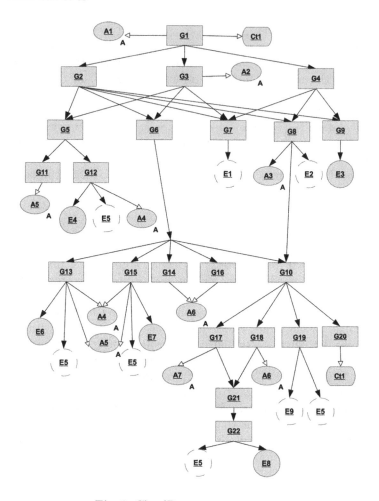

Fig. 2. CloudProxy assurance case.

ability granted to our adversary by the threat model. It must be noted that CloudProxy does not prevent an application from erroneously leaking its secrets to the adversary; it only exports an API that, if used correctly, enables the application to protect its secrets. As a result, verifying application logic is out of scope (**Ct1**). Each goal in **G2 - G4** is defined in terms of one or more goals in **G5 - G9**. **G7** protects the application from attacks that change the application's binary or TCService's binaries on disk before the machine boots up. **G7** is supported by a proof of correctness of the measured launch sequence (**E1**), which uses the TPM to compute a cryptographic hash of the binaries before launching TCService and applications. We need not measure binaries after they launch because (1) we trust the OS/hypervisor to enforce memory protections, and (2) our threat model prevents an insider from physically accessing the memory chip of a machine running CloudProxy (**A2**). Note that all high-level goals

G2 - G4 depend on **G7** because successfully mounting a compromised TCService binary will nullify all security guarantees. In addition to **G7**, we need **G5** and **G6** to guarantee **G2**: a protected application's secrets are not observable in plaintext by malicious programs on that machine. **G5** enforces that a malicious program does not observe a protected application's execution. Our notion of execution only considers application's state updates and side-effects via system calls; we do not consider information leaks via side channels. **G6** enforces that the protected application's secrets have cryptographic confidentiality and integrity protections before being saved to disk. **G8** and **G9** together protect an application's secret that is sent over the network. **G8** relies remote attestation to prove to a third-party that each protected application and TCService are running unmodified binaries. Following remote attestation, **G9** enforces that future communication takes place over a cryptographically secure channel. CloudProxy uses TLS (**E3**) for secure communication – we do not verify the TLS implementation in this work (this problem is explored in [4]).

Consider the assurance case for **G5**. This responsibility is shared between the OS protections (**G11**) and the TCService API guarantees (**G12**). **G11** stipulates that our OS (1) protects an application's address space from reads or writes by other programs, and (2) TCService is in full ownership of the TPM device. Both requirements can be fulfilled by a separation kernel [18]. While separability is a strict and possibly unreasonable requirement for commodity OS, for this discussion we assume we have a separation kernel via **A4**. As a result, TCService interface is the last remaining means by which a malicious application can interfere with the protected application's execution. To that end, **G12** stipulates a non-interference property on TCService: responses to the protected application's API requests is independent of the malicious application's API requests. We prove this property (**E4**) on our UCLID model, and make an initial attempt of validating this model with respect to the implementation (**E5**). Model validation proves that all behaviors in the implementation are captured by the model (see Sect. 6).

Consider the assurance case for **G6**. If secrets are sealed using TCService's *seal* API, then an adversary is unable to observe a secret's plaintext (confidentiality) and is also unable to tamper a secret's ciphertext without being detected (integrity). The proof for **G6** hinges on two sets of lemmas: (1) **G13-G16**: TCService's implementation of *seal* preserves confidentiality and integrity, and (2) **G10**: TCService never reveals its sealing key. For **G13-G16**, we assume (**A6**) that we have a Dolev-Yao [9] adversary — analyzing the strength of cryptographic operations is beyond our scope. In other words, our proof uses axioms of strong encryption, pre-image resistance of hash functions, second pre-image resistance, and strong collision resistance of hash functions. TCService performs *seal* by first encrypting the secret, and then appending the MAC (implemented using hash function) of the ciphertext. Goal **G14** is fulfilled by the confidentiality assumption about ideal encryption scheme. Goal **G16** is fulfilled by the pre-image resistance, second pre-image resistance, and the strong collision resistance axiom about hash function used in MAC. We assume that the cryptographic

Table 1. **Node** refers to the assurance case node in Fig. 2. **Proof Obligations** are either nodes in the assurance case, or property number(s) in Sect. 5.

Node	Description	Proof Obligation
A1	Hardware, hypervisor and OS are trusted	
A2	Adversary cannot physically access computers that are running CloudProxy	
A3	KeyServer is trusted	
A4	Hypervisor and OS layers enforce separability	
A5	Unique *pid* to all CloudProxy apps during TCService's lifetime	
A6	Cryptographic primitives *seal*, *unseal*, SHA are implemented perfectly	
A7	TPM driver does not leak TCService's secrets	
Ct1	Verifying app logic is out of scope	
E1	Verify measured launch mechanism	
E2	Verify remote attestation protocol	
E3	Use verified TLS implementation for network communication	
E4	Prove **G12** on UCLID model.	Ppty (1), (2)
E5	Validate UCLID model	
E6	Prove **G13** on UCLID model	Ppty (6)
E7	Prove **G15** on UCLID model	Ppty (7)
E8	Prove **G22** on UCLID model	Ppty (9)
E9	Prove **G19** on UCLID model	
G1	CloudProxy API secures protected app's secrets	A1, G2-G4
G2	Secure against malicious programs running on same machine	G5-G9
G3	Secure against malicious physical access of disk storage	A2, G5-G7
G4	Secure against network attacks	G7-G9
G5	Executions of any app do not affect other apps	G11-G12
G6	Sealed secrets on disk have confidentiality and integrity protection	G10,G13-G16
G7	Protected app and TCService are launched from unmodified code	E1
G8	Remote attestation via untrusted channels	A3, E2, G10
G9	Use TLS for establishing cryptographically secure channels	E3
G10	Protected app and TCService do not reveal attestation and sealing keys	G17-G20
G11	Isolation of address space belonging to TCService and apps	A5
G12	Non-interference: Applications cannot affect each other through TCService API	A4, E4-E5
G13	TCService *seal* API provides data confidentiality	A4-A5, E5-E6
G14	Cryptographic library's *seal()* provides data confidentiality	A6
G15	TCService *seal* API provides data integrity	A4-A5, E5, E7
G16	Cryptographic library's *seal()* provides data integrity	A6
G17	TCService does not reveal keys during initialization	A7, G21
G18	Protected app does not reveal keys during initialization	A6, G21
G19	TCService does not leak keys within responses to API calls	E5, E9
G20	Protected app does not reveal keys after initialization	
G21	CloudProxy initialization process does not reveal keys	G22
G22	Arguments of system calls do not leak keys	E5, E8

library satisfies these axioms about encryption and hash functions. TCService also appends the application's measurement within the sealed secret. This measurement is used to decide if TCService should return the unsealed secret to the requester — the requester's measurement must match the measurement at the time of sealing. To that end, we also need goals **G13** (fulfilled by **E6**) and **G15** (fulfilled by **E7**) to prove that TCService does not *unseal* the protected application's secret on behalf of a malicious application. While building a formal model, we identified a design flaw (presented here as assumption **A5**) that the OS does not reuse process identifiers throughout the lifetime of TCService— TCService uses the process identifier (*pid*) to identify the application invoking the API call.

Consider the assurance case for **G10**. We must prove that this property holds during (1) TCService's initialization (**G17**), (2) application's initialization (**G18**), and (3) servicing of API request by TCService (**G19**). Although verifying application logic is out of scope, the application's initialization is handled by CloudProxy. **G18** proves that this initialization process does not leak keys. Both TCService and application use the same initialization routine, with the exception that the application uses the TCService's API for cryptographic operations, while TCService uses the TPM's API. This allows us to share **G21** for fulfilling both **G17** and **G18**. **E8** fulfills **G22** by proving that each write (e.g. file write, socket send) out of the application's address space is either sealed or the written value is independent of the keys. Finally, the proof in **E9** fulfills goal **G19**: TCService does not leak its sealing and attestation key in response to an API request. **G19** is necessary even after proving the non-interference property in **G12**. This is because TCService may leak the protected application's secrets by erroneously revealing its own sealing key.

4   Formal Modeling

Our assurance case in Sect. 3 allows us to focus our verification effort on the composition of TCService with the protected and malicious applications. Thus, we do not model the entire TCB consisting of the OS and hardware, since this TCB is not the focus of our verification effort. Instead, we use axioms and assumptions about the TCB in our model.

Figure 3 presents the structural overview of our model[1], for which we use the UCLID [5] modeling language. This model is a synchronous composition of four transition systems: (1) Protected application *App*, (2) Malicious application *Mal_App*, (3) *Scheduler*, and (4) TCService. The model captures the initialization routine (Sect. 2.3) of TCService and applications, as well as the semantics of each CloudProxy API. Recall that CloudProxy does not place any constraints on the application's behavior; secrets will get compromised if the application erroneously leaks the plaintext secrets or the private sealing keys. Therefore, we verify TCService in the presence of an arbitrary *App* and an arbitrary *Mal_App*. When triggered, *App* and *Mal_App* non-deterministically choose an API call and arguments

---

[1] The model is available on http://uclid.eecs.berkeley.edu/cloudproxy.

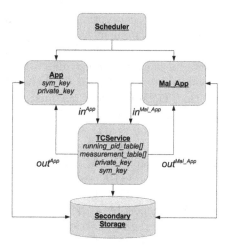

Fig. 3. UCLID model is a synchronous composition of *App*, *Mal_App*, *Scheduler*, and TCService.

to TCService in each step of execution. The *Scheduler* non-deterministically triggers either *App* or *Mal_App* to execute in each step. We choose interleaving semantics because the TCService implementation serializes all API requests onto a FIFO buffer, and handles each request atomically. Since *Mal_App* is completely non-deterministic, our proofs apply to CloudProxy executions containing an unbounded number of malicious applications. TCService maintains the following state variables: (1) a private key (*private_key*) for remote attestation, (2) a symmetric key (*sym_key*) for use in *seal* and *unseal*, (3) *running_pid_table[]* for process identifiers of all running CloudProxy applications, and (4) measurements *measurement_table[]* of all running CloudProxy applications. Each API operation may involve reading and writing to *Secondary_storage*, which is modeled as an unbounded memory in the theory of Arrays.

As we are not analyzing the strength of cryptographic operations, we adopt the Dolev-Yao abstraction [9] in our model. Messages, keys, and state variables are modeled as terms. Cryptographic operations are uninterpreted functions over terms. The cryptographic operations are *perfect* — we apply axioms about strong encryption, pre-image resistance, second pre-image resistance, and strong collision resistance of hash functions.

The following lists the assumptions on the capabilities of *Mal_App* in our model:

1. *Mal_App* is able to execute any cryptographic operations as well as invoke any API of TCService.
2. At initial state, *Mal_App* does not have the knowledge of either *App* secrets or TCService keys in plaintext.
3. *Mal_App* is *not* able to eavesdrop on data returned by *TCService* to *App*. This assumption is sound since we assume that the OS is trusted, and the OS controls the response/request channel.

4. The malicious application has unlimited storage for data learned from invoking TCService APIs and cryptographic functions at every transition step. In other words, *Mal_App* may learn and generate new data from any combination of arbitrary function call.

During our modeling, we found a bug in the implementation. When a process terminates, the entry for that process *pid* is not removed from the *running_pid_table[]* and *measurement_table[]*. If the OS spawns a new application with the same *pid*, then the new application can start unsealing secrets belonging to the terminated CloudProxy application. Having identified this bug, we introduce an assumption (**A5** in assurance case) that the *pid* will not be reused throughout the lifetime of TCService.

5   Verification

In this section, we formalize and verify properties on the UCLID model for each evidence in our assurance case. As mentioned previously, the evidences marked with a dashed line represent proofs that are currently in progress or left for future work. Each proof was performed using UCLID's internal decision procedures [5, 15].

5.1   Non-interference between Applications

G12 in Fig. 2 stipulates that the responses to an application's API requests is independent of the malicious application's API requests. This means that *Mal_App*'s inputs to TCService can be removed without affecting TCService outputs to *App*, and vice versa. In the context of CloudProxy, this property requires two proofs:

1. **non-interference (secrecy)**: *App*'s secrets are not leaked to *Mal_App* when *Mal_App* invokes an API request
2. **non-interference (integrity)**: results of *App*'s API calls are unaffected by *Mal_App*'s API requests

We adopt Goguen and Meseguer's formalization of non-interference for both checks [10]. A trace is a sequence of states. Let T be the set of infinite traces allowed by the composition of $TCService \parallel App \parallel Mal\_App$. Also, let $in^{App}(t)$ and $in^{Mal\_App}(t)$ be the sequence of API requests invoked by App and Mal_App, respectively, in a trace t. Similarly, let $out^{App}(t)$ and $out^{Mal\_App}(t)$ be the sequence of API responses by TCService to App and Mal_App, respectively, in a trace t. The following property checks **non-interference (secrecy)** to Mal_App:

$$\forall t_1, t_2 \in T : (in^{App}(t_2) = \varepsilon \wedge in^{Mal\_App}(t_1) = in^{Mal\_App}(t_2)) \Rightarrow$$
$$(out^{Mal\_App}(t_1) = out^{Mal\_App}(t_2)) \tag{1}$$

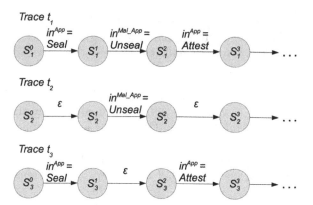

Fig. 4. The figure shows three traces t_1, t_2 and t_3, where trace t_2 replaces *App* API requests in t_1 with ε, and t_3 replaces *Mal_App* API requests in t_1 with ε.

and the following property checks **non-interference (integrity)** from *Mal_App*'s API requests:

$$\forall t_1, t_3 \in T : (in^{Mal\_App}(t_3) = \varepsilon \wedge in^{App}(t_1) = in^{App}(t_3)) \Rightarrow$$
$$(out^{App}(t_1) = out^{App}(t_3)) \tag{2}$$

where ε denotes no API invocation (modeled as stuttering steps). Note that this definition only applies if two conditions are met: (1) TCService must be deterministic (*App* and *Mal_App* need not be deterministic), and (2) TCService's transition function must be total with respect to inputs (Fig. 4).

A hyperproperty is a set of sets of possibly infinite execution traces [7]. As Properties (1) and (2) reason over a pair of traces, they are both are hyperproperties. We can rewrite them as 2-safety properties [7] and prove them using induction. As Fig. 5(a) illustrates, we first construct a 2-fold parallel self-composition of the system, resulting in two instances Sys_1 and Sys_2 of TCService that run synchronously and use the same transition relation R. Let s_1 and s_2 be the state of TCService in Sys_1 and Sys_2 respectively. Let in_1 and in_2 be the input to TCService in Sys_1 and Sys_2 respectively. We also let in_n^{App} and $in_n^{Mal\_App}$ be to *App*'s input and *Mal_App*'s input to TCService in Sys_n respectively. Similarly, let $out^{App}(s)$ and $out^{Mal\_App}(s)$ refer to TCService's output in state s to *App* and *Mal_App* respectively. For **non-interference (secrecy)**, we prove the following inductive property:

$$\forall s_1, s_2. Init(s_1) \wedge Init(s_2) \Rightarrow \Phi_{Mal\_App}(s_1, s_2) \tag{3}$$

$\forall s_1, s_1', s_2, s_2', in_1, in_2.$
$$(\Phi_{Mal\_App}(s_1, s_2) \wedge R(s_1, in_1, s_1') \wedge R(s_2, in_2, s_2') \wedge in_2^{App} = \varepsilon \wedge in_1^{Mal\_App} = in_2^{Mal\_App})$$
$$\Rightarrow \Phi_{Mal\_App}(s_1', s_2') \tag{4}$$

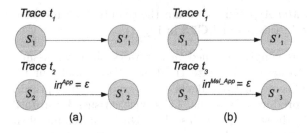

Fig. 5. S denotes the state of TCService in our UCLID model. We prove non-interference (secrecy) in (a) by proving that Mal_App cannot distinguish s_1' from s_2'. We prove non-interference (integrity) in (b) by proving that App cannot distinguish s_1' from s_3'.

where

$$\Phi_{Mal\_App}(s_a, s_b) \doteq \forall s_a', s_b', in.$$
$$R(s_a, in, s_a') \wedge R(s_b, in, s_b') \Rightarrow (out^{Mal\_App}(s_a') = out^{Mal\_App}(s_b')) \tag{5}$$

For any pair of states s_a and s_b, predicate $\Phi_{Mal\_App}(s_a, s_b)$ is *true* if and only if those states are indistinguishable to Mal_App — for the same API call, TCService produces identical output in both s_a and s_b. We also use a transition predicate $R(s, i, s')$ which is *true* iff the system can transition from state s to s' under input i. Property 3 checks the base case that Φ_{Mal_App} holds on any pair of initial states. The inductive step (Property 4) proves that from any pair of states s_1 and s_2 that is indistinguishable to Mal_App, TCService must transition to a pair of states s_1' and s_2' (respectively) that are also indistinguishable to Mal_App. We also need an auxiliary invariant to discharge the induction proof: if the App's *pid* entries of the measurement table in TCService in s_1 and s_2 are the same, then these entries have the same values in s_1' and s_2'.

Proving **non-interference (integrity)** between App and Mal_App requires a similar inductive proof – the preceding discussion applies verbatim if App is substituted for Mal_App and vice versa. UCLID took about 5 s to prove each property.[2]

5.2 Data Confidentiality

Here, we describe our proof of **G7**: Mal_App cannot acquire the plaintext of a sealed secret belonging to App. Recall from Fig. 2 that we split this goal into two lemmas:

– **Lemma 1**: Mal_App cannot obtain the plaintext by breaking the underlying cryptography (goal **G14** in Fig. 2).

---

[2] UCLID was running on VirtualBox and the machine was a 2.6 GHz quad-core with 2 GB of memory space allocated to this VirtualBox environment.

– **Lemma 2**: *Mal_App* cannot obtain the plaintext by invoking a sequence of CloudProxy API calls (goal **G13** in Fig. 2).

Lemma 1 is simply assumed in our work since we assume a Dolev-Yao adversary [9]. In accordance with the Dolev-Yao model, our model represents data as terms of some abstract algebra, and cryptographic primitives operate on those terms to produce new terms. TCService satisfies **Lemma 2** by appending measurement to the secret prior to sealing. During unsealing, if the secret's measurement does not match the measurement of API requester, then the request fails. In what follows, we prove that TCService implements this logic correctly.

Let m be a measurement, m_{App} be the *App*'s measurement, and $\mathbb{D}$ be the set of terms from an abstract algebra. Also, let ENC_MAC be the authenticated encryption function that first encrypts the plaintext, and then appends an integrity-protecting MAC of the ciphertext. Let $in_{API}^{Mal\_App}$ be the API call from the *Mal_App* to TCService, and let $in_{arg}^{Mal\_App}$ be the arguments of the API call from the *Mal_App* to TCService. $out_{success}^{Mal\_App}(s)$ denotes whether TCService successfully performed the API request invoked by Mal_App. $out_{result}^{Mal\_App}(s)$ is the return output of TCService to the *Mal_App*. sK_{TCS} denotes the symmetric key used by TCService to *seal* or *unseal*. We define **Lemma 2** as follows.

$\phi(s) \doteq \forall secret \in \mathbb{D}, s', m_{App}, in.$

$\quad (in_{API}^{Mal\_App} = unseal \wedge in_{arg}^{Mal\_App} = ENC\_MAC(sK_{TCS}, secret, m_{App})) \wedge$

$\quad R(s, in^{Mal\_App}, s') \Rightarrow \neg out_{success}^{App}(s') \hfill (6)$

where $ENC\_MAC(sK_{TCS}, secret, m_{App})$ is a term encoding any arbitrary sealed secret that can belong to *App*, as *secret* is an unconstrained symbolic constant. This allows us to only consider API calls whose argument has this form. This property guarantees that TCService never returns the plaintext secret as a result of calling *unseal* API. **Lemma 1** guarantees that the adversary cannot obtain the plaintext from a sealed secret by breaking the underlying cryptography.

We prove **Lemma 2** via 1-step induction. UCLID took about 30 s to prove this property. Moreover, we discovered the following necessary assumption to prevent spurious counter-examples to the inductive proof: *Mal_App* has a different measurement than *App*, i.e. $m_{Mal\_App} \neq m_{App}$. This is reasonable because they run different binaries, and hash functions are assumed to be collision free.

5.3 Data Integrity

Similar to confidentiality, we prove that TCService enforces integrity protection: the adversary cannot tamper a sealed secret and still have TCService successfully *unseal* it on behalf of *App*. Again, we assume perfect integrity protection of $ENC\_MAC(key, ., .)$, and hence any modification to $ENC\_MAC(key, ., .)$ should *not* be able to *unseal* successfully. Only data that was previously sealed by TCService can be successfully unsealed by TCService– any other data would fail the MAC check since the MAC check uses TCService's symmetric key sK_{TCS}.

This leaves the adversary with only one attack: replace *App*'s sealed data with *Mal_App*'s sealed data. Therefore, the following property checks that TCService does not *unseal* another application's sealed data on behalf of *App*.

Let $\mathbb{M}$ be the set of measurements, and $\mathbb{D}$ be the set of data. We prove that an *unseal* request satisfies the property:

$$\phi(s) \doteq \forall secret \in \mathbb{D}, \forall m \in \mathbb{M}, s', in.$$
$$in_{API}^{App} = unseal \wedge in_{arg}^{App} = ENC\_MAC(sK_{TCS}, secret, m)$$
$$\wedge\, m \neq m_{App} \wedge R(s, in^{App}, s') \Rightarrow \neg out_{success}^{App}(s') \tag{7}$$

where $ENC\_MAC(sK_{TCS}, secret, m)$ is a term encoding any sealed secret that can belong to an application other than *App*, as *secret* and m are unconstrained symbolic constants.

UCLID took less than 5 s to prove this property. A caveat to note here is that CloudProxy does not currently have a mechanism to check for the *freshness* of data. The adversary may perform a replay attack by replacing the *App*'s sealed secret on disk with an older secret sealed by the *App*.

5.4   Protecting Keys

During initialization, TCService generates a symmetric sealing key sK_{TCS}, and a private attestation key pK_{TCS}. Similarly, a CloudProxy application uses TCService to generate a symmetric key sK_{App} and private attestation key pK_{App}. In this section, we prove that keys sK_{App} and pK_{App} are never leaked in writes outsides the *App*'s address space (goal **G18**). We only focus our attention on *App*'s keys in this section; the property and proof for TCService is identical. We defer proof for TCService as it uses the same initialization routine as the application. We express this property in the semantic information flow framework introduced by [13]. For any pair of traces, where the traces start from symbolic states differing in values of sK_{App} and pK_{App} (but all other state variables are identical), the unencrypted outputs along the two traces must be identical – the keys will affect the values of encrypted data. In other words, values written to disk are not a function of the keys. Once again, this is a 2-safety property of $TCService \parallel App \parallel Mal\_App$. We use a 1-step induction to prove this property.

First, we define a specification state variable $\mathcal{S}$ that gets updated each time *App* invokes TCService *seal* API on some data or during initialization.

$$\mathsf{next}(\mathcal{S}(x)) = \begin{cases} true & in_{API}^{App} = seal \wedge x = ENC\_MAC(sK_{TCS}, in_{arg}^{App}, m_{App}) \\ true & init^{App} = true \wedge x = ENC\_MAC(sK_{App}, pK_{App}, m_{App}) \\ \mathcal{S}(x) & \text{otherwise} \end{cases}$$
$$\tag{8}$$

where $init^{App}$ is a boolean value that indicates whether *App* is at the initialization phase. In addition, $\forall x.\mathcal{S}_0(x) = false$ where $\mathcal{S}_0$ is the initial state of $\mathcal{S}$.

Let s_1 and s_2 be a pair of states, where $pK_{App,1}$ and $pK_{App,2}$ are *App*'s private keys in s_1 and s_2 respectively. $sK_{App,1}$ and $sK_{App,2}$ are *App*'s symmetric keys in s_1 and s_2 respectively. $s_1 \setminus \{pK_{App,1}, sK_{App,1}\}$ denotes the set of all state variables in s_1 excluding the two keys. Finally, $out^{disk}(s_1)$ denotes the output to disk in state s_1, and $out^{disk}(s_2)$ denotes the output to disk in state s_2. We formulate this property as follows:

$$\forall s_1, s_2, s_1', s_2', in.$$
$$(s_1 \setminus \{pK_{App,1}, sK_{App,1}\}) = (s_2 \setminus \{pK_{App,2}, sK_{App,2}\})$$
$$\wedge\, R(s_1, in^{App}, s_1') \wedge R(s_2, in^{App}, s_2')$$
$$\wedge\, (\neg \mathcal{S}(out^{disk,1}(s_1')) \vee \neg \mathcal{S}(out^{disk,2}(s_2'))) \Rightarrow$$
$$(out^{disk}(s_1') = out^{disk}(s_2')) \tag{9}$$

UCLID took about two seconds to prove this property. An important caveat is that we only prove this property for writes that the CloudProxy initialization code of *App* makes via the system call interface (e.g. file write to disk). The soundness of this proof relies on the model validation proof that we have captured all possible writes to disk in our model.

6   Model Validation

Although we have proved the security properties of CloudProxy on the formal UCLID model, we are left with an important question: is the model a sound abstraction of the original system? A valid model must encode all behaviors that are allowed in the original system. We make first steps in using KLEE [6] to validate our UCLID model against the C++ implementation, using techniques proposed by Sturton et al. [21].

Since we do not precisely model all computation within TCService (e.g. messages are abstracted away as terms), we need to show that the unmodeled code does not affect the subset of TCService state that we have modeled. Let $\mathcal{V}$ denote the state variables that are present in our UCLID model. We manually identify code paths that will be *pruned* away from our modeling. Then, we prove that the *pruned* code does not affect any state variable within $\mathcal{V}$. This proof uses the *Data-Centric Model Validation* (DMV) technique from [21]. Once we have validated our pruning, we must further prove that the model correctly abstracts the pruned program. This is termed as *Operation-Centric Model Validation* (OMV) in [21]. Both validation steps are a work in progress.

The entire TCService has about 58k lines of code (LoC), of which about 8k LoC is used to build our model. The cryptographic keys, measurement table, and the *pid* table in TCService are our $\mathcal{V}$ set, and only approximately 1k LoC modifies $\mathcal{V}$. After the DMV step, we model in UCLID the remaining 1K LoC. We encountered several challenges in performing OMV, and delay that to future work.

7   Related Work

There has been some use of formal methods for building trustworthy cloud infrastructure. CertiKOS [11] is a verified hypervisor architecture that ensures correct information flow between different guest users. They use a compositional proof technique to decompose their proof into individual lemmas that can be proved using different proof engines. Klein et al. [14] provide a machine-checked verification of the seL4 microkernel in Isabelle. These efforts are especially relevant since CloudProxy needs a trusted OS/hypervisor layer. While both efforts use interactive theorem proving for building machine checked proofs, we use a more automated methodology based on model checking. Another alternative approach is to directly prove the implementation code by inserting annotations and assertions, and then run a verifier on the code. VCC has been developed to verify the Hyper-V implementation using this approach [8]. More importantly, a carefully constructed model can raise the level of abstraction enough to prove such properties efficiently.

We structure our proof of correctness as an assurance case. Assurance cases have been applied in practice to present the support for claims about properties or behaviors of a system. ASCAD [1] presents safety cases (a slight variant of assurance case) for safety critical systems such as military systems. Shankar et al. [19] use Evidential Tool Bus to construct claims, and to integrate different formal tools to provide evidence for each claim.

8 Conclusion

We present the first formal model of CloudProxy, and an assurance case to systematically construct a proof that CloudProxy protects an application's secrets in our threat model. The assurance case lists practical assumptions we make about the trusted computing base of CloudProxy applications. During our modeling and verification of CloudProxy, we have uncovered a flaw and few unintended assumptions in the design (e.g. no reuse of *pid* during TCService's lifetime). Security properties and lemmas derived from the assurance case (e.g. non-interference) are formalized and proved in our model. In ongoing work, we are exploring a model validation technique to prove that our model encodes all the behaviors allowed by CloudProxy's implementation.

Acknowledgments. We sincerely thank David Wagner and Petros Maniatis for their valuable feedback. This work was funded in part by the Intel Science and Technology Center for Secure Computing, and SRC contract 2460.001.

References

1. Adelard: ASCAD The Adelard Safety Case Development (ASCAD) Manual (1998)
2. GSN Community Standard Version 1, November 2011
3. Barrett, C., Sebastiani, R., Seshia, S., Tinelli, C.: Satisfiability modulo theories. In: Biere, A., Heule, M.J.H., van Maaren, H., Walsh, T. (eds.) Handbook of Satisfiability, Chap. 26. Frontiers in Artificial Intelligence and Applications, vol. 185, pp. 825–885. IOS Press, Amsterdam (2009)

4. Bhargavan, K., Fournet, C., Corin, R., Zălinescu, E.: Verified cryptographic implementations for TLS. ACM Trans. Inf. Syst. Secur. **15**(1), 3:1–3:32 (2012)
5. Bryant, R.E., Lahiri, S.K., Seshia, S.A.: Modeling and verifying systems using a logic of counter arithmetic with lambda expressions and uninterpreted functions. In: Brinksma, E., Larsen, K.G. (eds.) CAV 2002. LNCS, vol. 2404, pp. 78–92. Springer, Heidelberg (2002)
6. Cadar, C., Dunbar, D., Engler, D.: Klee: unassisted and automatic generation of high-coverage tests for complex systems programs. In: OSDI'08, pp. 209–224, Berkeley, CA, USA (2008)
7. Clarkson, M., Schneider, F.: Hyperproperties. In: IEEE 21st Computer Security Foundations Symposium, CSF '08, pp. 51–65 (2008)
8. Cohen, E., Dahlweid, M., Hillebrand, M., Leinenbach, D., Moskal, M., Santen, T., Schulte, W., Tobies, S.: VCC: a practical system for verifying concurrent C. In: Berghofer, S., Nipkow, T., Urban, C., Wenzel, M. (eds.) TPHOLs 2009. LNCS, vol. 5674, pp. 23–42. Springer, Heidelberg (2009)
9. Dolev, D., Yao, A.C.: On the security of public key protocols. IEEE Trans. Inf. Theory **29**(2), 198–208 (1983)
10. Goguen, J.A., Meseguer, J.: Security policies and security models. In: IEEE Symposium on Security and Privacy, pp. 11–20 (1982)
11. Gu, L., Vaynberg, A., Ford, B., Shao, Z., Costanzo, D.: Certikos: a certified kernel for secure cloud computing. In: Proceedings of the Second Asia-Pacific Workshop on Systems, APSys '11, pp. 3:1–3:5. ACM, New York (2011)
12. Halderman, J.A., Schoen, S.D., Heninger, N., Clarkson, W., Paul, W., Calandrino, J.A., Feldman, A.J., Appelbaum, J., Felten, E.W.: Lest we remember: cold-boot attacks on encryption keys. Commun. ACM **52**(5), 91–98 (2009)
13. Joshi, R., Leino, K.M.: A semantic approach to secure information flow. Sci. Comput. Program. **37**(1–3), 113–138 (2000)
14. Klein, G., Elphinstone, K., Heiser, G., Andronick, J., Cock, D., Derrin, P., Elkaduwe, D., Engelhardt, K., Kolanski, R., Norrish, M., Sewell, T., Tuch, H., Winwood, S.: sel4: formal verification of an os kernel. In: Symposium On Operating Systems Principles, pp. 207–220. ACM (2009)
15. Lahiri, S.K., Seshia, S.A.: The UCLID decision procedure. In: Alur, R., Peled, D.A. (eds.) CAV 2004. LNCS, vol. 3114, pp. 475–478. Springer, Heidelberg (2004)
16. Manferdelli, J., Roeder, T., Schneider, F.: The cloudproxy tao for trusted computing. Technical report UCB/EECS-2013-135, University of California, Berkeley, July 2013
17. Parno, B.: Bootstrapping trust in a "trusted" platform. In: Proceedings of the 3rd Conference on Hot Topics in Security, HOTSEC'08, pp. 9:1–9:6, Berkeley, CA, USA (2008)
18. Rushby, J.: Proof of separability–a verification technique for a class of security kernels. In: Dezani-Ciancaglini, M., Montanari, U. (eds.) International Symposium on Programming. LNCS, vol. 137, pp. 352–367. Springer, Heidelberg (1982)
19. Shankar, N.: Building assurance cases with the evidential tool bus, March 2014. http://chess.eecs.berkeley.edu/pubs/1061.html
20. Stephen Blanchette, J.: Assurance cases for design analysis of complex system of systems software. Technical report, Software Engineering Institute, Carnegie Mellon University, April 2009
21. Sturton, C., Sinha, R., Dang, T.H., Jain, S., McCoyd, M., Tan, W.-Y., Maniatis, P., Seshia, S.A., Wagner, D.: Symbolic software model validation. In: Proceedings of the 10th ACM/IEEE International Conference on Formal Methods and Models for Codesign, October 2013

Using Promela in a Fully Verified Executable LTL Model Checker

René Neumann[(✉)]

Technische Universität München, Munich, Germany
rene.neumann@in.tum.de

Abstract. In [4] we presented an LTL model checker whose code has been completely verified using the Isabelle theorem prover. The intended use of the checker is to provide a trusted reference implementation against which more advanced checkers can be tested. However, in [4] the checker still used an ad-hoc, primitive input language.

In this paper we report on CAVA, a new version of the checker accepting inputs written in Promela. We report on our formalization of the Promela semantics within Isabelle, which is used both to define the semantics and to automatically generate code for the computation of the state space. We report on experiments on standard Promela benchmarks comparing our tool to SPIN.

1 Introduction

Nearly every hand-written software in the ecosystem suffers from bugs. This is almost inevitable when the software is geared towards high performance and therefore uses highly complicated algorithms and data structures which are not easily provable.

On the other hand, it is in general not feasible to thoroughly prove correctness of the code itself, though exceptions exist [10]. But other measures, like model checkers, allow to nevertheless increase trust in the software. As such, the tool is in the role of a trust-multiplier. Hence, their verdict must not be wrong. Now the recursion begins – or as [17] puts it: *"Quis custodiet ipsos custodes?"* – "Who will watch the watchmen?"

Different approaches to tackle this problem exist (an overview is given in [6]). We proposed a pragmatic solution in a previous paper [4]: a verified *reference implementation* of an LTL model checker for finite-state systems à la SPIN [9], *CAVA*. This model checker follows the well-known automata-theoretic approach [19]: Given a finite-state program P and a formula ϕ, two Büchi automata are constructed that recognize the executions of P, and all potential executions of P that violate ϕ, respectively. Then the product of the two automata is computed and tested on-the-fly for emptiness.

To prove full functional correctness of executable code, we define the program in the logic HOL (roughly: combination of functional programming language with logic) of the interactive theorem prover Isabelle [12]. After proving the

Research supported by DFG grant CAVA, *Computer Aided Verification of Automata*.

D. Giannakopoulou and D. Kroening (Eds.): VSTTE 2014, LNCS 8471, pp. 105–114, 2014.
DOI: 10.1007/978-3-319-12154-3_7

program correct in Isabelle/HOL, ML (or OCaml, Haskell or Scala) code can be generated *automatically* from those definitions [8]. Using refinement, abstract but proof-friendly definitions can be rewritten as efficient, more complex variants, while still preserving correctness (cf. [4,11]).

In our implementation *CAVA*, the four parts (system construction, LTL-to-Büchi conversion, product construction, emptiness check) are not fixed. Instead, an interface in form of proof obligations and types is defined. Anything fulfilling those obligations and exposing functions of the specified type can therefore be used for the corresponding part. LTL-to-Büchi conversion and product construction currently offer no alternative, using the algorithm of Gerth et al. [7] and the standard on-the-fly construction, respectively. Emptiness checking is currently implemented by different flavors of nested depth-first search algorithms [3,16]. For system construction, we offer the modeling languages *Boolean programs* [4] and Promela [2]. The first is an ad-hoc approach and fairly limited in its expressiveness, while Promela is a powerful, widely used language.

This paper will focus on the novel support for Promela models. By sharing the modeling language with SPIN, we strengthen our position as a reference implementation. Further, we enhance the comparability of timing results by removing the problem of different state space sizes, which complicates comparisons [4]. What is more, our work also serves as a formalization of Promela semantics. This allows implementation of optimizations proven to preserve semantics, but also serves as a source of documentation.

We will give a short overview about our Promela support in Sect. 2 with more formalization details following in Sect. 3. In Sect. 4 we will outline the trustworthiness of the resulting program. We will then conduct experiments and elaborate on the results in Sect. 5. In the final Sect. 6 we talk about (possible) future work.

The tool and all supporting material, including the ML code, can be found online at http://cava.in.tum.de/VSTTE14.

2   Promela

Promela [2] is a modeling language, mainly used in the model checker SPIN [9]. It offers a C-like syntax and allows to define processes to be run concurrently. Those processes can communicate via shared global variables or by message-passing via channels. Inside a process, constructs exist for non-deterministic choice, starting other processes and enforcing atomicity. It furthermore allows different means for specifying properties: LTL formulae, assertions in the code, never claims (i.e. an automata that explicitly specifies unwanted behavior) and others.

Some constructs found in Promela models, like `#include` and `#define`, are not part of the language Promela itself, but belong to the language of the C preprocessor. SPIN does not process those, but calls the C compiler internally to process them. In CAVA we do the same.

Though there are approaches for giving a formal semantics of Promela [5,18,20], none of them shows that its definition matches reality. Moreover, some refer to outdated versions of the language.

Therefore, observing the output of SPIN and examining the generated graphs often is the only way of determining the semantics of a certain construct. This is complicated further by SPIN unconditionally applying optimizations. For the current formalization we chose to copy the semantics of SPIN, including the aforementioned optimizations. For some constructs, we had to restrict the semantics, i.e. some models are accepted by SPIN, but not by CAVA. Those deviations are:

- run is a statement instead of an expression. SPIN here has a complicated set of restrictions unto where run can occur inside an expression. The sole use of it is to be able to get the ID of a spawned process. We omitted this feature from CAVA to guarantee expressions to be free of side-effects.
- Variable declarations which got jumped over are seen as not existing. In SPIN, such constructs show surprising behavior:
int i; goto L; i = 5; L: printf("%d", i) yields 0, while
goto L; int i = 5; L: printf("%d", i) yields 5.
The latter is forbidden in CAVA (it will get rejected with "unknown variable i"), while the first behaves as in SPIN.
- Violating an assert does not abort, but instead sets the variable __assert__ to true. This needs to be checked explicitly in the LTL formula. We plan on adding this check in an automatic manner.
- Types are bounded. Except for well-defined types like booleans, overflow is not allowed and will result in an error. The same holds for assigning a value that is outside the bounds. SPIN does not specify any explicit semantics here, but solely refers to the underlying C-compiler and its semantics. This might result in two models behaving differently on different systems when run with SPIN, while CAVA, due to the explicit bounds in the semantics, is not affected.

Additionally, some constructs are currently not supported, and the compilation will abort if they are encountered: d_step[1], typedef, remote references, bit-operations, unsigned, and property specifications except ltl and assert. Other constructs are accepted but ignored, because they do not change the behavior of a model: advanced variable scoping, xr, xs, print*, priorities, and visibility of variables.

Nonetheless, for models not using those unsupported constructs, we generate the very same number of states as SPIN does. An exception applies for large goto chains and when simultaneous termination of multiple processes is involved, as SPIN's semantics is too vague here.

3   Formalization and Implementation

Any formalization of a program needs to specify three things: How to encode the program structure (i.e. the operations and the control flow), how to encode the program state, and how to compute the set of successor program states (i.e. execute a program).

---

[1] This can be safely replaced by atomic, though larger models will be produced then.

```
record pState =                          record gState =
   pid        -- "Process identifier"       vars      -- "Global variables"
   vars       -- "Local variables"          channels  -- "Channels are always global"
   pc         -- "Program counter"          timeout   -- "No process can make transition"
   channels   -- "Reference local channels" procs     -- "List of all running processes"
   s_idx      -- "Reference program"

                    record edge =
                       cond    -- "Necessary condition"
                       effect  -- "Effect on states"
                       target  -- "Next state"
                       prio    -- "Priority"
                       atomic  -- "Atomicity information"
```

Fig. 1. Structure definitions

A Promela program does not consist of a single thread of action, but instead consists of multiple processes which run independent of one another except for when they interact. This is reflected in our formalization.

The program structure of Promela is represented by a set of transition systems: For each process p_i, we define $T_i = (S_i, I_i \in S_i, \delta_i \subseteq S_i \times E)$, where $S_i \subseteq \mathbb{N}$ (the set of program points) and E is the set of all records of type edge, as defined in Fig. 1, i.e. δ_i is the transition relation (the target is encoded in edge). I_i then is the initial program point for this process.

The program state is encoded in two different types of environments, also given in Fig. 1: gState for the global state and pState for the state of each process. Naturally, the global state contains the set of all current pStates (field procs).

The program is constructed from an abstract syntax tree (AST), enriched with semantic information (e.g. variables annotated by their type), which gets translated into the aforementioned set of transition systems, and an initial gState structure.

Calculating the next steps of execution is formalized by the *successor* function (SPIN calls it *semantic engine*), as required by CAVA to serve as a system implementation. For a given configuration and program, it specifies the set of all possible transitions and resulting states. For each process, the set of all edges from the current state is taken into account. The effect of each edge whose cond evaluates to true under the current environment is then applied to yield a new environment. In case of an atomic block, successors are computed until either no further transition is possible (atomicity is lost), or the block is left. Only the last environment is then presented in the result set. As this part is based on SPIN, more information can be found in [9, Chap. 7].

As noted, the translation into a set of transition systems requires an enriched AST. This is achieved in two steps: A hand-written SML parser translates the Promela source into an abstract syntax tree. This data structure is then enriched in Isabelle with the semantic information and some constructs (e.g. for-loops) get replaced by semantically equal parts (de-sugaring). This step allows to keep the *semantic engine* more concise and explicit, also straightening proofs.

stmntToState (*StmntAssign v e*) (*lbls, pri, pos, nxt, _*) =
  ([[(|*cond* = *ECTrue, effect* = *EEAssign v e, target* = *nxt, prio* = *pri, atomic* = *NonAtomic*|)]],
  Index pos, lbls)

stmntToState (*StmntCond e*) (*lbls, pri, pos, nxt, _*) =
  ([[(|*cond* = *ECExpr e, effect* = *EEId, target* = *nxt, prio* = *pri, atomic* = *NonAtomic*|)]],
  Index pos, lbls)"

stepToState (*StepStmnt s* (*Some u*)) (*lbls, pri, pos, nxt, onxt, _*) = (
  let
  (∗ *the 'unless' part* ∗)
  (*ues,_,lbls'*) = *stmntToState u* (*lbls, pri, pos, nxt, onxt, True*);
  (∗ *'u' is the guard for the whole unless; 'ues' the rest* ∗)
  u = *last ues; ues* = *butlast ues;*
  pos' = *pos* + *length ues;*
  (∗ *find minimal current priority* ∗)
  pri' = *min_prio u pri;*
  (∗ *the main part –*
    priority is decreased, because there is now a new unless part with higher prio ∗)
  (*ses,spos,lbls''*) = *stmntToState s* (*lbls', pri* − *1, pos', nxt, onxt, False*);
  (∗ *add an edge to the unless part for each generated state* ∗)
  ses = *map* (*List.append u*) *ses*
  in (*ues@ses,spos,lbls''*))

Fig. 2. Construction of transition system (excerpt)

In Fig. 2 we show the construction of the edges for three exemplary nodes in the enriched AST: The first two, **StmntAssign** and **StmntCond**, are representative examples for most of the AST-nodes: A specific condition and effect are set, and control passes to the next statement. It is to note, that **cond** for the first node and **effect** for the second one each resemble a no-op, as expected. The third example is an {**s**} **unless** {**u**} construct, which is one of the more complicated control structures in Promela: from each step in the sequence **s**, control can go the **unless**-part **u** as soon as the first expression in **u** becomes true. In general, all constructs influencing the control flow (e.g. **do** or **if**) are complex. To a great degree, this is due to SPIN's semantic trying to minimize the use of intermediate states, something commonly happening with nested loops – even more when (nested) **unless** is involved. Another complication for constructing the control flow originates from atomicity, which can be passed between processes (by handshakes), lost (on blocks), or chained (by **goto**).

In Fig. 3 we display snippets from the evaluation function for the condition on the edges. Again, this is in most cases rather straightforward. Those examples amount to: expressions must evaluate to something non-zero; spawning a new process requires the number of currently running processes to be below some upper bound[2]; and for sending something over a channel, the capacity of this channel must not be exhausted.

The structure for evaluating the effects is similar, as shown in Fig. 4: a variable is set to the correct value; a new process is started; the __assert__ variable is set, if the expression is true. For sending and receiving (not shown) more effort is necessary, stemming mostly from the different variants and from the fact, that

---

[2] A necessary condition for a finite state-space.

$evalCond\ (ECExpr\ e)\ g\ l \leftrightarrow exprArith\ g\ l\ e \neq 0$
$evalCond\ (ECRun\ \_)\ g\ l \leftrightarrow length\ (procs\ g) < 255$
$evalCond\ (ECSend\ v)\ g\ l \leftrightarrow withChannel\ v\ (\lambda\_\ c.$ **case** c **of**
$Channel\ cap\ \_\ q \Rightarrow length\ q < cap$
$|\ HSChannel\ \_ \Rightarrow True)\ g\ l$

Fig. 3. Evaluation of conditions (excerpt)

$evalEffect\ (EEAssign\ v\ e)\ \_\ g\ l = setVar\ v\ (exprArith\ g\ l\ e)\ g\ l$
$evalEffect\ (EERun\ name\ args)\ prog\ g\ l =$ **let** $(g,\_) = runProc\ name\ args\ prog\ g\ l$ **in** (g,l)
$evalEffect\ (EEAssert\ e)\ \_\ g\ l =$ **if** $exprArith\ g\ l\ e = 0$
then $setVar\ assert\ 1\ g\ l$
else (g,l)

Fig. 4. Evaluation of effects (excerpt)

receiving can compare values, evaluate variables, and set variables at the same time.

The formalization presented is, as explained, currently quite SPIN-centric and therefore in parts too specific and concrete, especially concerning optimizations. But the current work now allows to abstract into a more concise formalization. Thereafter, the current implementation can be shown to adhere to the same semantics. As was done in the other parts of CAVA, further optimizations can then be applied. Using the refinement approach [11], this does not affect the abstract formalization.

To give some insight about the size of development: The Isabelle theories regarding Promela span about 2100 lines, with the generated code being about 3100 lines of ML. Additional 2400 lines are added by the parser.

4   Trustworthiness

When speaking about something being *verified*, one needs to state explicitly which properties the result is guaranteed to have. Also, except when noted otherwise, some parts are assumed to be correct, like compiler, hardware, and operating system.

For CAVA, the property to hold is the correctness theorem about the model checker: A lasso is found iff the property does not hold for the system (cf. [4]), and, if existing, the lasso is a counter-example. As some parts of CAVA are programmed directly in SML (especially the user-interface and the parsers), no correctness assumption can be made about them. For example, CAVA may return a correct lasso, but the output might still be erroneous, due to a mistake in the printing function. But as those parts are (a) easily checkable by hand and (b) no useful correctness properties can be shown for them (how would one express, that the result of a parser is correct without adding another unproven layer on top?), we still claim the result to be verified.

It remains to show, that the properties hold on the generated code. By design of Isabelle/HOL as an LCF-style theorem prover, every proof-construction is done by primitives of a small trusted kernel [12]. Therefore the proofs in it are correct deductions in the logic and the properties hold. The task of the code-generator [8] then is to translate the definitions from HOL syntax to the target syntax; one can see it as a pretty-printer. Because of this translation on a syntactic level, the properties also hold on the exported code.

What is not covered here is the actual formalization of the properties itself, i.e. whether the HOL term represents the informal claim one is expecting. As [15] lays down in detail, this problem is inherently unsolvable in an automatic fashion and can only be checked by the interested human itself.

5   Evaluation

With the support for Promela, it is now possible to test the very same models in both SPIN and CAVA. For this, we used models from [1,13], with some minor modifications to match modern Promela syntax. The tests were performed on a Core i7 with 2.7 GHz, memory being hard-limited to 6.5 GB. Also, a timeout of 800 s was set for each run.

CAVA was compiled with MLton 20130715. SPIN (version 6.2.5) was used without optimizations, especially partial-order reduction: `spin` was run with `-o1 -o2 -o3` and the code compiled with `-DNOREDUCE`. During the benchmark, SPIN's search depth was set to $6 * 10^7$ (`-m60000000`).

Further, `-Dd_step=atomic` was passed to both SPIN and CAVA, replacing `d_step` blocks by `atomic` blocks, as the former is not supported by CAVA. Since `d_step` is an optimized and restricted form of the latter (collapsing the sequence into one state), this is semantically sound, but influences the size of the state space.

The benchmark consists of 306 single tests, 4 of which got removed, as they contained failing asserts which CAVA ignores by default (cf. Sect. 2). Further, 50 tests included features not supported in CAVA, 77 led to failures in SPIN (most often out-of-memory and exhausted search depth), 94 timed out on CAVA (a test may occur in multiple of those categories). In total 157 tests performed successfully on both tools. To ensure a complete search of the state space the property used together with those tests is G true. Each test was run 5 times, the worst and best time removed and the remaining three averaged. Two timed out runs mark the whole test as timed out.

This benchmark shows, that overall CAVA is about 20 times slower than SPIN. Figure 5a plots the results of the benchmark: the line represents $t_{SPIN} = 20t_{CAVA}$, so anything above represents a test where CAVA was less than 20 times slower than SPIN (dots below analogously). Tests on which it timed out, had a mean run time of 89.18 s in SPIN, lying far above $\frac{timeout}{20}$. This is a good result for a verified and generated software, especially as SPIN builds a tailored checker for each model, whereas CAVA's is general.

Further, we tested multiple properties on scaling versions of the leader election protocol and the "Dining Philosophers". Here, the LTL-to-Büchi translation is important. As of this time, the implementation in CAVA is tailored to verification, not efficiency. This leads to larger-than-necessary state spaces, in particular

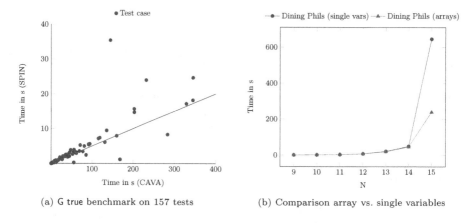

(a) G true benchmark on 157 tests   (b) Comparison array vs. single variables

Fig. 5. Benchmark results

for formulas containing U. Therefore the slowdown is a factor between 9 and 70. For negative properties, SPIN found 75 of 77 counter-examples in less than 10 s, CAVA 70 of 77.

The main reason for the difference in performance is the lack of destructive updates in a purely functional program. In particular we must use trees as our main data structure, yielding a logarithmic overhead. Arrays can only be used when updates are seldom, as they cannot be updated in-place but need to be copied in full. Moreover we cannot utilize pointers for keeping a reference to a changing structure, but have to look up information each time. The consequences are shown in Fig. 5b. We ran "Dining Philosophers" modeled in two different ways: using three arrays of length N, and using $3N$ different variables. The amount of variables has a very notable impact on performance, even though this does not influence the state-space.

6   Future Work

In the previous sections we outlined the current state of the Promela implementation for our model checker CAVA. As already indicated throughout the paper, there still are additional targets which are to be addressed.

In Sect. 2 we mentioned different parts of Promela which are not implemented yet. For those where it is possible, we strive to add support. This also includes overflowing for integer types, as there may be valid use cases.

Furthermore, the current formalization should see further separation between abstraction and implementation, as was done in the other parts of CAVA. This also allows for an even better presentation of the semantics of Promela for one, and, due to possible refinement, additionally clears the way for implementing optimizations without changing semantics.

As already hinted in the previous section, there are several opportunities for performance enhancements. For faster lookups, we already employ hashing. Here, a theory of consistent hashes is planned, to introduce a technique eliminating the rehashing of unchanged structures.

Further future work includes the introduction of new algorithms for emptiness detection, yielding an even better performance.

An important topic to work on are the additional non-trivial optimizations of SPIN, this includes partial-order reduction [14]. This technique is an important optimization used in SPIN to drastically reduce the size of the state-space. This technique needs to be formalized in Isabelle/HOL and then be integrated into CAVA.

Acknowledgements. We are very grateful for the help and input of Javier Esparza, Dennis Kraft, Peter Lammich, Andreas Lochbihler, Philipp Meyer, and Tobias Nipkow.

References

1. Promela database. http://www.albertolluch.com/research/promelamodels. Accessed: 15 January 2013
2. Promela manual pages. http://spinroot.com/spin/Man/promela.html. Accessed: 07 February 2013
3. Courcoubetis, C., Vardi, M., Wolper, P., Yannakakis, M.: Memory-efficient algorithms for the verification of temporal properties. Formal Methods Syst. Des. 1(2/3), 275–288 (1992)
4. Esparza, J., Lammich, P., Neumann, R., Nipkow, T., Schimpf, A., Smaus, J.-G.: A fully verified executable LTL model checker. In: Sharygina, N., Veith, H. (eds.) CAV 2013. LNCS, vol. 8044, pp. 463–478. Springer, Heidelberg (2013)
5. Gallardo, M.D.M., Merino, P., Pimentel, E.: A generalized semantics of PROMELA for abstract model checking. Formal Aspects Comput. 16(3), 166–193 (2004)
6. Gava, F., Fortin, J., Guedj, M.: Deductive verification of state-space algorithms. In: Johnsen, E.B., Petre, L. (eds.) IFM 2013. LNCS, vol. 7940, pp. 124–138. Springer, Heidelberg (2013)
7. Gerth, R., Peled, D., Vardi, M.Y., Wolper, P.: Simple on-the-fly automatic verification of linear temporal logic. In: Dembinski, P., Sredniawa, M. (eds.) Proceedings of the International Symposium Protocol Specification, Testing, and Verification. IFIP Conference Proceedings, vol. 38, pp. 3–18. Chapman & Hall (1996)
8. Haftmann, F., Nipkow, T.: Code generation via higher-order rewrite systems. In: Blume, M., Kobayashi, N., Vidal, G. (eds.) FLOPS 2010. LNCS, vol. 6009, pp. 103–117. Springer, Heidelberg (2010)
9. Holzmann, G.J.: The Spin Model Checker - Primer and Reference Manual. Addison-Wesley, Boston (2003)
10. Klein, G., Elphinstone, K., Heiser, G., Andronick, J., Cock, D., Derrin, P., Elkaduwe, D., Engelhardt, K., Kolanski, R., Norrish, M., Sewell, T., Tuch, H., Winwood, S.: seL4: formal verification of an OS kernel. In: Matthews, J.N., Anderson, T.E. (eds.) Proceedings of the ACM Symposium Operating Systems Principles, pp. 207–220. ACM (2009)
11. Lammich, P., Tuerk, T.: Applying data refinement for monadic programs to Hopcroft's algorithm. In: Beringer, L., Felty, A. (eds.) ITP 2012. LNCS, vol. 7406, pp. 166–182. Springer, Heidelberg (2012)

12. Nipkow, T., Paulson, L.C., Wenzel, M. (eds.): Isabelle/HOL – A Proof Assistant for Higher-Order Logic. LNCS, vol. 2283. Springer, Heidelberg (2002)

13. Pelánek, R.: BEEM: benchmarks for explicit model checkers. In: Bošnački, D., Edelkamp, S. (eds.) SPIN 2007. LNCS, vol. 4595, pp. 263–267. Springer, Heidelberg (2007)

14. Peled, D.: Combining partial order reductions with on-the-fly model-checking. In: Dill, D.L. (ed.) CAV 1994. LNCS, vol. 818, pp. 377–390. Springer, Heidelberg (1994)

15. Pollack, R.: How to believe a machine-checked proof. In: Sambin, G., Smith, J. (eds.) Twenty Five Years of Constructive Type Theory. Oxford University Press, Oxford (1998)

16. Schwoon, S., Esparza, J.: A note on on-the-fly verification algorithms. In: Halbwachs, N., Zuck, L.D. (eds.) TACAS 2005. LNCS, vol. 3440, pp. 174–190. Springer, Heidelberg (2005)

17. Shankar, N.: Trust and automation in verification tools. In: Cha, S.S., Choi, J.-Y., Kim, M., Lee, I., Viswanathan, M. (eds.) ATVA 2008. LNCS, vol. 5311, pp. 4–17. Springer, Heidelberg (2008)

18. Sharma, A.: A refinement calculus for Promela. In: ICECCS, pp. 75–84. IEEE (2013)

19. Vardi, M.Y., Wolper, P.: An automata-theoretic approach to automatic program verification. In: LICS, pp. 332–344. IEEE Computer Society (1986)

20. Weise, C.: An incremental formal semantics for PROMELA. In: Proceedings of the 3rd International SPIN Workshop (1997)

Hypervisors and Dynamic
Data Structures

Store Buffer Reduction with MMUs

Geng Chen[1,2], Ernie Cohen[3], and Mikhail Kovalev[1($\boxtimes$)]

[1] Saarland University, Saarbrücken, Germany
{gengchen,kovalev}@wjpserver.cs.uni-saarland.de
[2] University of Electronic Science and Technology of China, Chengdu, China
[3] University of Pennsylvania, Philadelphia, USA
ernie.cohen@acm.org

Abstract. A fundamental problem in concurrent system design is to identify flexible programming disciplines under which weak memory models provide sequential consistency. For x86-TSO, a suitable reduction theorem for threads that communicate only through shared memory was given by Cohen and Schirmer [6]. However, this theorem cannot handle programs that edit their own page tables (e.g., memory managers, hypervisors, and some device drivers). The problem lies in the interaction between a program thread and the hardware MMU that provides its address translation: the MMU cannot be treated as a separate thread (since it implicitly communicates with the program thread), nor as part of the program thread itself (since MMU reads do not snoop the store buffer of the program thread). We generalize the Cohen-Schirmer reduction theorem to handle programs that edit their page tables. The added conditions prevent the MMU of a thread from walking page table entries owned by other threads.

Keywords: Store buffer reduction · MMU · TLB · Sequential consistency · Verification

1 Introduction

When reasoning about concurrent software, programmers typically assume sequential consistency (SC) [10], a model in which all threads see all memory accesses in a linear order. However, as providing SC in hardware is relatively expensive, modern multicore processors typically implement weaker memory models, in which writes can appear in different orders to different threads. To use SC when reasoning about low-level programs written to execute directly on such hardware, we need practical program criteria that guarantee that any execution is simulated by an SC one.

In this paper, we consider one of the more prevalent non-SC memory models, x86-TSO [12], the native memory model provided by x86/x64 family processors. In x86-TSO, when a processor retires an instruction, its stores are queued in a FIFO *store buffer* (SB); only when such a store emerges from the SB is it applied to the global, shared memory, and made visible to other processors.

© Springer International Publishing Switzerland 2014
D. Giannakopoulou and D. Kroening (Eds.): VSTTE 2014, LNCS 8471, pp. 117–132, 2014.
DOI: 10.1007/978-3-319-12154-3_8

To make SBs transparent to single-threaded programs, when a processor issues a load for an address, it first checks whether there is a store to that address in its SB. If there is such a buffered store, the most recent one is used to satisfy the load; otherwise, it loads the value from memory. Thus, a store from a processor becomes visible to (later) loads from that processor as soon as it enters the SB, and so becomes visible to the thread issuing the store before it becomes visible to threads running on other processors. Thus, stores can appear in different order for different threads, violating SC. For example:

```
T1: a1:=1                    T2: a2:=1
    if(a2==0)                    if(a1==0)
        critical section             critical section
```

In an SC execution, it is impossible for both threads to enter the critical section. But under x86-TSO, both tests might succeed before stores a1 and a2 emerge from their respective SBs, allowing both threads to enter the critical section.

One way to reason about programs running on x86-TSO is to materialize the SBs explicitly in the programming model. This approach is hopelessly impractical; for example, the postcondition of a function call would have to explicitly talk about the stores left in the SB, exposing the internal details of the function implementation to its callers and destroying modular program reasoning.

A discipline guaranteeing SC, like the one presented in this paper, disallows programs such as the one above; typically, it requires a thread to flush its SB at some point between a volatile store[1] (like the assignment to a1 above) and a subsequent volatile load (like the read of a2). An SB reduction theorem, giving such a discipline for x86-TSO, was given by Cohen and Schirmer in [6]. The main challenge in making such a discipline practical is avoiding introducing flushing obligations related to accesses that do not race with other threads; the reduction theorem from [6] achieves this by means of an ownership discipline, where conformance to the ownership discipline is itself verified assuming SC.

A complication arises in trying to extend the SB reduction theorem to a hardware model that includes virtual address translation. (Such translation is invisible to most user-space programs, but is visible to programs that edit their own page tables, such as memory managers and hypervisors.) Since the MMU (which can speculatively read PTEs and cache address translations) is naturally modelled as a separate thread, it is tempting to try to apply the SB reduction theorem directly. The problem is that the SB reduction theorem assumes the processors communicate only through shared memory, whereas a processor and its MMU implicitly share address translations cached in the Translation Lookaside Buffer (TLB). The TLB cannot simply be treated as volatile shared memory,

---

[1] We rely on a C-idiom, where shared portions of memory are identified by a `volatile` tag. The `volatile` tag prevents a compiler from applying certain optimizations to shared accesses which could cause undesired behavior, e.g., store intermediate values in registers instead of writing them to the memory. Shared memory accesses are also called volatile.

since an SC discipline would require the processor to flush its SBs between each of its volatile writes and the implicit TLB read needed to fetch the next address translation; this amounts to a flush after each volatile write, rendering the discipline impractical. The purpose of this paper is to extend the reduction theorem to accommodate SBs, without introducing such flushes.

The rest of the paper is structured as follows. In Sect. 2, we briefly describe our model of the x86/x64 MMU. In Sect. 3, we describe our programming discipline. In Sect. 4, we formalize the models and the discipline. In Sect. 5, we state the reduction theorem and give a proof strategy. We conclude in Sect. 6.

2   MMUs

In the presence of address translation, there is a private MMU and SB component for each thread (Fig. 1). We model the TLB as part of the MMU state. The MMU component can speculatively walk the page tables, one level at a time, setting accessed and dirty bits as it goes, and caching complete or incomplete translations in the TLB. When a thread runs in translated mode, memory access requires a suitable address translation for the virtual address of the access to be cached in the TLB. Page tables are ordinary memory pages, and so can be either thread-local or shared between different MMUs.

A thread can read and write page tables (even tables being used by other threads), changing the set of possible address translations. Such writes are typically accompanied by flushes of the TLB to eliminate stale translations before accessing memory through the new page table entries (PTEs).

Some possible violations of sequential consistency in the presence of an MMU (even in a single threaded environment) are illustrated in the following example:

> T1: pte2.p:=0   MMU1: pte1.a:=1
>   t0:=pte1.a   t1:= pte2

Suppose `pte1` and `pte2` are page table entries, `pte1` points to `pte2`, the present bit in both entries is set[2], and the access bit `pte1.a` is clear. `t0` and `t1` are read

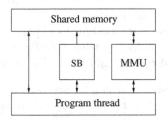

Fig. 1. Abstract view of x86-TSO with the address translation

---

[2] Non-present PTEs cannot be used to produce an address translation. Instead, they are used to signal a page fault.

temporaries in T1 and MMU1 respectively. Consider a TSO execution where the steps of the thread are executed before the steps of the MMU, and the write to pte2 is put to the SB. After this execution, t0 is 0 and the MMU reads pte2 with the present bit set. As a result, the MMU gets an address translation that goes through pte1 and pte2. But such a translation cannot be obtained in an SC execution that ends with t0 = 0: in such an execution, the MMU would have to read pte2 after the assignment to t0, at which point pte2 has been marked nonpresent and so cannot be used for translation.

3   Programming Discipline

The programming discipline introduced here is an extension of the programming discipline from [6] and is based on ownership sets, which have to be maintained explicitly with ghost code. A memory access is classified as either shared (volatile) or local and must be *safe*, i.e., obey the programming discipline. Semantically, there is no difference between the two types of access, but the different types are subject to different rules. Interlocked accesses, i.e., those accesses which flush the SB as a side effect, follow the same rules as volatile accesses.

In [6], each location is classified as shared or unshared, unowned or owned (by a unique thread), read-only or read-write. We extend this classification by adding a specialized type of "owned page table" addresses and allow shared, unowned read-write locations to contain shared page tables:

- Shared, unowned read-write locations are used to implement locks [8], lock-free algorithms or shared page tables. Every thread can perform volatile reads and writes to these addresses, and any MMU is allowed to read and write this memory.
- Shared, unowned read-only addresses are used for static data. Every thread can perform volatile and non-volatile reads from these addresses.
- Shared, owned read-write addresses are used for single-writer-multiple-reader data structures. Every thread can perform volatile reads, but only the owner is allowed to do volatile writes to these addresses.
- Unshared, owned read-write addresses are used for thread-local data or for data protected by a lock. The owner is allowed to write and read the data with volatile and non-volatile accesses.
- Owned page table addresses are used for local page tables. The owning thread can read or write these addresses with volatile accesses. The MMU of the owning thread is allowed to read and write this memory.

Note that the set of addresses that can be accessed by the MMU of a thread is defined by the set of incomplete translations cached in the TLB and the set of PTEs reachable from the page table origin (PTO), which is stored in a register. Hence, our discipline requires every reachable PTE address to be either in the set of local page table addresses or to be in the set of shared, unowned read-write addresses. The latter is useful in situations when several concurrent threads are sharing the same set of page tables for address translation. Moreover, a local page table can point to a page table shared by MMUs of several threads, which allows splitting the address space of a thread into local and shared parts.

Ownership can be transfered either by a non-blocking ghost update or as part of an (atomic) volatile or interlocked write operation. The latter is helpful, e.g., when one acquires a lock and wants to get the ownership of the memory protected by the lock. A thread can take ownership of unowned addresses and release the ownership of addresses it owns. When a thread acquires ownership of an address, it can make it unshared, shared, or an owned page table address. When releasing an owned address a thread can make it shared read-write or shared read-only. It can also make an address that it owns unshared.

The SB flushing rule of our programming discipline is unchanged from [6]: an SB has to be flushed between every volatile write and a subsequent volatile read. This is the only flushing required. Equivalently, we maintain for each thread a *dirty flag* that is set on a (nonflushing) volatile write and cleared when the SB is flushed, and require the flag to be clear when performing a (nonflushing) volatile read. This guarantees that updates from a thread to shared state are made visible to other threads before it reads similar updates from other threads. Local page tables are, in this regard, treated as state shared between a thread and its MMU. The programming discipline can be checked assuming SC, making it suitable for integration into a verifier for concurrent software such as VCC [4].

We reconsider the example with a thread and an MMU from Sect. 1.

```
T1: assert(ownedpt(pte2))          MMU1: pte1.a:=1
    vol pte2.p:=0 {D:=1}                 t1:= pte2
    FENCE {D:=0}
    assert(ownedpt(pte1) && D==0)
    vol t0:= pte1.a
```

(Ghost updates, like the operations on D above, are written in braces, and volatile operations are prefixed by vol.) Before accesses to pte1 and pte2, we assert that both PTEs are present in the local page table set of the thread. (Alternatively, we could consider shared unowned page table entries). The write to pte2 has to be volatile, which means that the dirty flag D of the thread is set. A read of pte1 also has to be volatile. As a precondition of volatile reads we requires the dirty flag to be clear. Hence, between the write and the read we insert a fence, the only effect of which is to flush the SB, which clears the thread's dirty flag. A TSO execution that previously caused a problem is ruled out now: at the time when the thread reads pte1, the store to pte2 is already committed to the memory. Hence, if the thread execution ends with $t0 = 0$, we can be sure that the MMU will not get an address translation going through pte1 and pte2.

However, adding these annotations to the code of the program is not enough. We also have to make sure that the MMU can only perform safe accesses, i.e., accesses to the local and shared page tables. To check this in VCC we explicitly model the MMU in the ghost state of the program and introduce a ghost T1' thread, which nondeterministically executes all possible MMU steps [2]:

```
T1: assert(ownedpt(pte2))              T1': ...
    vol pte2.p:=0 {D:=1}                   assert(ownedpt(pte1))
    FENCE {D:=0}                           {pte1.a:=1}
    assert(ownedpt(pte1) && D==0)          assert(ownedpt(pte2))
    vol t0:= pte1.a                        {t1:= pte2}
                                           ...
```

Note that the programming discipline refers to translated physical addresses, rather than untranslated virtual addresses. Showing that the translated physical addresses of memory accesses are safe can be done if one keeps track of the set of all possible address translations for a given thread. This set can be maintained as part of the MMU state in the ghost state of the program [2].

4 Formalization

Let $\mathbb{N}$ denote the set of natural numbers, $\mathbb{B}$ the Booleans, $\mathbb{A}$ the set of memory addresses, $\mathbb{V}$ the set of memory values, and $\mathbb{T}$ the set of names of temporaries. Memory is modeled as a map from $\mathbb{A}$ to $\mathbb{V}$; $m(a \mapsto v)$ denotes the memory that maps a to v and other addresses as m. We also use nested record updates, e.g., $c[c_1.X := v]$. The n-th element of list l can be selected with $l[n]$ or $l_{[n]}$.

4.1 MMU Abstraction

The MMU model considered here is very abstract. We don't model the MMU in detail here because we present only a *reduction theorem*, i.e., it only allows us to ignore the SBs. The only important property we rely on in our proof is the monotonicity of the MMU, which we state as an assumption here. To reason about a program with the MMU or to verify properties of the translations provided by the MMU (e.g., compliance to our programming discipline), one can instantiate the model presented here by a detailed, architecture-specific MMU model in the style of [2].

The set of MMU configurations is denoted by $\mathbb{U}$. The MMU state subsumes the TLB state and the value of the PTO register (*CR3* register in x86). The set of all possible access rights is denoted by $\mathbb{R}$. A single page table entry (PTE) occupies a single cell in the memory and has the same type $\mathbb{V}$ as all other memory values. Our MMU model relies on the following (uninterpreted) functions:

- $atran(mmu, va, mode, r) \in 2^{\mathbb{A}}$. Given an MMU state $mmu \in \mathbb{U}$, a virtual address $va \in \mathbb{A}$, translation mode $mode \in \mathbb{B}$ (1 - translated mode, 0 - untranslated mode) and the set of access rights $r \in \mathbb{R}$, the function returns the set of translated physical addresses for the specified access. In case there are no available translations the returned set is empty. For the untranslated mode function $atran$ should return $\{va\}$.
- $can\text{-}access(mmu, pa) \in \mathbb{B}$. For a physical address $pa \in \mathbb{A}$ the predicate denotes that the MMU can perform an access to a PTE located at address pa. This is the case when the MMU has an incomplete translation leading to the PTE located at address pa.

- $\delta_{mmur}(mmu, pa, pte) \in 2^{\mathbb{U}}$. For page table entry $pte \in \mathbb{V}$ located at address pa the function returns the set of possible MMU states after the MMU has processed pte. After this step the MMU can have complete or incomplete translations through pte buffered in its TLB. We use this function to obtain the new state of the MMU after the MMU read step.
- $\delta_{mmuw}(mmu, pa, pte) \in 2^{\mathbb{V}}$. This function returns the set of possible PTE values which can be written by the MMU at address pa, given that pte is the current value of the PTE located at address pa. This step models setting of access and dirty bits in a page table entry.
- $can\text{-}page\text{-}fault(mmu, va, r, pa, pte) \in \mathbb{B}$. The predicate denotes that the page fault for the virtual address va and access rights r can be signalled by the MMU. The condition for the page fault must be present in the page table entry pte located at address pa and the MMU must already have an incomplete address translation leading to pte.
- $\delta_{flush}(mmu, F) \in \mathbb{U}$. For the set of (virtual) addresses $F \in 2^{\mathbb{A}}$ the function performs a TLB flush, removing translations for addresses in F from the TLB, and returns the new MMU state after the flush is performed.
- $\delta_{wpto}(mmu, v) \in \mathbb{U}$. The function performs a complete TLB flush and sets the new value $v \in \mathbb{V}$ for the PTO.

We assume *monotonicity* of the MMU, i.e., after the MMU performs a read of a PTE its set of buffered address translations can only grow:

$$\forall mmu' \in \delta_{mmur}(mmu, pa, pte):$$
$$atran(mmu, va, mode, r) \subseteq atran(mmu', va, mode, r).$$

Such an assumption might seem too strong, since the real hardware TLBs are limited in size and typically only contain one (complete) translation for a given virtual address. However, modern architectures use multiple TLBs per processor (e.g., based on page size, instruction/data), so multiple translations for a virtual address can coexist. Moreover, as there is no way to force a walk other than flushing, no real program leverages nonmonotonicity (just as no software leverages the limited length of SBs or limited number of cache lines).

4.2 Instructions

The set of memory instructions $\mathbb{I}$ is defined as a datatype

$$\mathbb{I} = \textbf{Read } vol\ va\ t\ r\ |\ \textbf{Write } vol\ va\ (D, f)\ r\ annot\ |\ \textbf{Ghost } annot$$
$$|\ \textbf{RMW } va\ t\ (D, f)\ r\ cond\ annot\ |\ \textbf{Fence }|\ \textbf{Switch } mode$$
$$|\ \textbf{INVLPG } F\ |\ \textbf{WritePTO } v$$

The parameter vol denotes whether the memory access is volatile. $annot$ is a tuple consisting of the ownership annotations, va is a virtual address, t is a read temporary, r denotes the set of access permissions used for the translation of va, function f takes as a parameter the map from temporaries to values and returns a value to be stored in the memory, D specifies the set of temporaries on which function f operates, predicate *cond* tests on whether a write has to be performed by an RMW instruction, F is a set of addresses to be flushed from the TLB and v is the new value for the PTO.

The ownership annotations $annot = (A, L, R, W, A_{pt}, R_{pt})$ contain the following sets of addresses: acquired addresses A, the local portion of acquired addresses L, released addresses R, the writable portion of released addresses W, acquired page table addresses A_{pt} and released page table addresses R_{pt}.

To distinguish between different kinds of instructions, we introduce predicates $R(I)$, $W(I)$, $G(I)$ (for read, write and ghost), $RMW(I)$, $FENCE(I)$, $SWITCH(I)$, $INVLPG(I)$ and $WPTO(I)$. Volatile and non-volatile operations are distinguished by prefixes v and nv respectively (e.g., $vR(I)$ and $nvR(I)$). We denote the individual fields X of instruction I as $I.X$.

4.3   Virtual Machine

The virtual machine is an abstract machine with sequentially consistent memory and address translation, but without SBs. The virtual machine maintains additional ghost information that allows enforcement of the ownership-based programming discipline both for instructions and for MMU memory accesses.

The configuration c of a virtual machine is given by the tuple

$$c = (m, shared, ro, ts),$$

where $ts_{[i]}$ is the thread-local configuration of thread i, $m \in \mathbb{A} \to \mathbb{V}$ is the shared memory of the machine, $shared \in 2^{\mathbb{A}}$ is the (ghost) set of shared addresses, and ro is the (ghost) set of read-only addresses.

The thread-local configuration $c.ts_{[i]}$ of thread i is defined as

$$c.ts_{[i]} = (p, is, \vartheta, mmu, \mathcal{D}, \mathcal{O}, pt, mode),$$

where $p \in \mathbb{P}$ is the (uninterpreted) program state of the thread, $is \in \mathbb{I}^*$ is the instruction list, $\vartheta \in \mathbb{T} \to \mathbb{V}$ is the set of read temporaries (a read buffer), $mmu \in \mathbb{U}$ is the MMU state, $\mathcal{D} \in \mathbb{B}$ is the (ghost) dirty flag, $\mathcal{O} \in 2^{\mathbb{A}}$ is the (ghost) thread-local ownership set, $pt \in 2^{\mathbb{A}}$ is the (ghost) set of local page table addresses, and $mode \in \mathbb{B}$ is the translation mode. For components X of thread local configuration $c.ts_{[i]}$ we abbreviate $c.X_{[i]}$. By $c.ghst_{[i]} = (c.\mathcal{O}_{[i]}, c.pt_{[i]}, c.shared, c.ro)$ we abbreviate the ghost information of thread i (except the dirty flag) and the shared ghost information.

Let $ghst = (\mathcal{O}, pt, shared, ro)$ be the ghost information of thread i. Then the ownership transfer $otran(ghst, i, I) = (\mathcal{O}', pt', shared', ro')$, performed by a ghost, volatile write or RMW instruction I in thread i is defined as:

$$ro' = ro \cup (I.R \setminus I.W) \setminus (I.A \cup I.A_{pt}) \qquad \mathcal{O}' = \mathcal{O} \cup I.A \setminus I.R$$
$$shared' = shared \cup I.R \cup I.R_{pt} \setminus (I.L \cup I.A_{pt}) \quad pt' = pt \cup I.A_{pt} \setminus I.R_{pt}$$

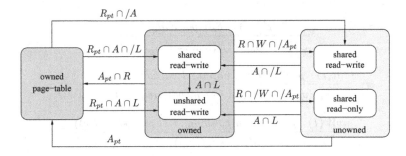

Fig. 2. Ownership transfer.

The possible status changes of an address due to the ownership transfer are shown in Fig. 2.

The computation of the virtual machine is defined by a non-deterministic transition relation $c \Rightarrow c'$, where every step is either a program step, a memory step, an MMU step or a page fault step of thread i. A program step of thread i applies (uninterpreted) function δ_p to the program state and the set of temporaries of the thread to obtain a new program state and newly generated instructions, which are then appended to the old instruction list (Fig. 3).

A memory step of thread i is defined by a case split on the type of instruction $I = hd(c.is_{[i]})$ to be executed (Fig. 3). In case of a read, write or RMW instruction we first translate the virtual address $I.va$ using access rights $I.r$ and choose a physical address pa from the set of available address translations provided by the function $atran$. A read instruction updates temporary $I.t$ with the read value $c.m(pa)$. For a write instruction, we obtain the store value by applying the function $I.f$ to the current set of temporaries and store this value at pa. A volatile write also performs the ownership transfer and sets the dirty flag. An RMW instruction first performs a read of memory cell $c.m(pa)$ into temporary $I.t$, then checks condition $I.cond$ on the updated set of temporaries. If the test succeeds, we obtain the store value by applying $I.f$ to the updated set of temporaries, store this value at address pa, and perform the ownership transfer. Regardless of the test result, we reset the dirty flag. Fence and ghost instructions do not update the non-ghost part of the state (except for the length of the instruction list). A ghost instruction just performs the ownership transfer; a fence instruction clears the dirty flag. Mode switch, INVLPG, and write to PTO instructions also clear the dirty flag. On a mode switch, we change the translation mode to $I.mode$. An INVLPG instruction removes the invalidated translation from the MMU using function δ_{flush}, and a write to PTO instruction applies function δ_{wpto} to the current MMU state.

The MMU of thread i (Fig. 4) can either perform a read from the page tables or a write setting control bits. In case of a read the new MMU state is chosen from the set of MMU states provided by function δ_{mmur} and in case of a write we chose the value to be written from the set of values provided by function δ_{mmuw}. A page fault step is triggered in translated mode when instruction in

$$\frac{(p', is') = \delta_p(c.p_{[i]}, c.\vartheta_{[i]})}{c \xrightarrow{\text{p}}_i c[p_{[i]} := p', is_{[i]} := c.is_{[i]} \circ is']}$$

$$\frac{R(I) \quad pa \in (atran(c.mmu_{[i]}, I.va, c.mode_{[i]}, I.r))}{c \xrightarrow{\text{m}}_i c[\vartheta_{[i]} := c.\vartheta_{[i]}(I.t \mapsto c.m(pa)), is_{[i]} := tl(c.is_{[i]})]}$$

$$\frac{nvW(I) \quad pa \in (atran(c.mmu_{[i]}, I.va, c.mode_{[i]}, I.r))}{c \xrightarrow{\text{m}}_i c[m := c.m(pa \mapsto I.f(\vartheta_{[i]})), is_{[i]} := tl(c.is_{[i]})]}$$

$$\frac{vW(I) \quad pa \in (atran(c.mmu_{[i]}, I.va, c.mode_{[i]}, I.r)) \quad ghst' = otran(c.ghst_{[i]}, i, I)}{c \xrightarrow{\text{m}}_i c[m := c.m(pa \mapsto I.f(\vartheta_{[i]})), ghst_{[i]} := ghst', \mathcal{D}_{[i]} := 1, is_{[i]} := tl(c.is_{[i]})]}$$

$$\frac{RMW(I) \quad pa \in (atran(c.mmu_{[i]}, I.va, c.mode_{[i]}, I.r)) \quad \vartheta' = c.\vartheta_{[i]}(I.t \mapsto c.m(pa))}{(m', ghst') = (I.cond(\vartheta') ? (c.m(pa \mapsto I.f(\vartheta')), otran(c.ghst_{[i]}, i, I)) : (c.m, c.ghst_{[i]}))}{c \xrightarrow{\text{m}}_i c[m := m', \vartheta_{[i]} := \vartheta', ghst_{[i]} := ghst', \mathcal{D}_{[i]} := 0, is_{[i]} := tl(c.is_{[i]})]}$$

$$\frac{G(I) \quad ghst' = otran(c.ghst_{[i]}, i, I)}{c \xrightarrow{\text{m}}_i c[ghst_{[i]} := ghst', is_{[i]} := tl(c.is_{[i]})]} \qquad \frac{FENCE(I)}{c \xrightarrow{\text{m}}_i c[\mathcal{D}_{[i]} := 0, is_{[i]} := tl(c.is_{[i]})]}$$

$$\frac{SWITCH(I)}{c \xrightarrow{\text{m}}_i c[mode_{[i]} := I.mode, \mathcal{D}_{[i]} := 0, is_{[i]} := tl(c.is_{[i]})]}$$

$$\frac{WPTO(I) \vee INVLPG(I)}{mmu' = (WPTO(I) ? \delta_{wpto}(c.mmu_{[i]}, I.v) : \delta_{flush}(c.mmu_{[i]}, I.F))}{c \xrightarrow{\text{m}}_i c[mmu_{[i]} := mmu', \mathcal{D}_{[i]} := 0, is_{[i]} := tl(c.is_{[i]})]}$$

Fig. 3. Program and memory steps of thread i of the virtual machine. In the memory step we execute instruction I, where $I = hd(c.is_{[i]})$.

$$\frac{mode_{[i]} \quad can\text{-}access(c.mmu_{[i]}, pa) \quad mmu' \in (\delta_{mmur}(c.mmu_{[i]}, pa, c.m(pa)))}{c \xrightarrow{\text{mu}}_i c[mmu_{[i]} := mmu']}$$

$$\frac{mode_{[i]} \quad can\text{-}access(c.mmu_{[i]}, pa) \quad v' \in (\delta_{mmuw}(c.mmu_{[i]}, pa, c.m(pa)))}{c \xrightarrow{\text{mu}}_i c[m := c.m(pa \mapsto v')]}$$

$$\frac{mode_{[i]} \quad can\text{-}access(c.mmu_{[i]}, pa) \quad I = hd(c.is_{[i]}) \quad (R(I) \vee W(I) \vee RMW(I))}{can\text{-}page\text{-}fault(c.mmu_{[i]}, I.va, I.r, pa, c.m(pa)) \quad p' = \delta_{pf}(c.p_{[i]}, I.va, I.r, c.m(pa))}{c \xrightarrow{\text{pf}}_i c[is_{[i]} := [], p_{[i]} := p', mmu_{[i]} := \delta_{flush}(c.mmu_{[i]}, \{I.va\}), \mathcal{D}_{[i]} := 0]}$$

Fig. 4. MMU steps and page fault step of thread i of the virtual machine.

the head of the instruction list requires address translation and the page fault for the address of the instruction can be signalled. As an effect of the page fault we (i) update the program state using (uninterpreted) function δ_{pf} which loads the information about the faulty translation to the program state, (ii) flush all translations for the faulty virtual address from the MMU and (iii) clear the instruction list. Additionally, we reset the dirty flag.

Note that reading a faulty entry and signalling a page fault is done in a single atomic transition, i.e., the MMU is not allowed to pre-fetch a faulty PTE first and then use it for signalling a page fault some time later. This allows modeling silent rights granting in page tables (i.e., when the user grants more rights in a PTE without a consequent TLB flush) and setting of the present bit in a PTE without TLB flushing. In a real x86 TLB, the same behaviour is achieved by performing a fresh re-walk of page tables in case of a page fault [1].

Safety for instruction I in thread i (Fig. 5) restricts the sets of translated physical addresses that can be accessed by read, write, and RMW instructions and sets the rules for the ownership transfer. Safety of a volatile read requires the dirty flag to be cleared (this is due to our flushing rule). An MMU access to physical address pa is safe if pa belongs a local page table or to the shared portion of the memory that is not owned by anyone and that does not belong to the read only memory. Configuration c of the virtual machine is safe if first instructions in the instruction lists of all threads are safe and all MMU steps that can be performed from c are safe.

Note that the ownership is essential to the discipline here (and in [6]) because flushing obligations both for SBs and for TLBs can arise through the giving up

$$safe\text{-}instr(c, i, I) \equiv (\forall pa \in atran(c.mmu_{[i]}, I.va, c.mode_{[i]}, I.r).$$
$$(vR(I) \rightarrow pa \in c.\mathcal{O}_{[i]} \cup c.shared \cup c.pt_{[i]} \wedge \neg c.\mathcal{D}_{[i]}) \wedge$$
$$(nvR(I) \rightarrow pa \in c.\mathcal{O}_{[i]} \cup c.ro) \wedge$$
$$(vW(I) \rightarrow \forall j \neq i.\ pa \notin c.\mathcal{O}_{[j]} \cup c.pt_{[j]} \wedge pa \notin c.ro) \wedge$$
$$(nvW(I) \rightarrow pa \in c.\mathcal{O}_{[i]} \wedge pa \notin c.shared) \wedge$$
$$(RMW(I) \wedge \neg I.cond(\vartheta') \rightarrow pa \in c.\mathcal{O}_{[i]} \cup c.shared \cup c.pt_{[i]}) \wedge$$
$$(RMW(I) \wedge I.cond(\vartheta') \rightarrow \forall j \neq i.\ pa \notin c.\mathcal{O}_{[j]} \cup c.pt_{[j]} \wedge pa \notin c.ro)) \wedge$$
$$(vW(I) \vee G(I) \vee (RMW(I) \wedge I.cond(\vartheta'))) \rightarrow \forall j \neq i.\ I.L \subseteq I.A \wedge$$
$$(I.A \cup I.A_{pt}) \cap (c.\mathcal{O}_{[j]} \cup c.pt_{[j]}) = \emptyset \wedge I.R \subseteq c.\mathcal{O}_{[i]} \wedge I.R_{pt} \subseteq c.pt_{[i]} \wedge$$
$$I.A \subseteq c.\mathcal{O}_{[i]} \cup c.shared \cup I.R_{pt} \wedge I.A_{pt} \subseteq c.pt_{[i]} \cup c.shared \cup I.R \wedge$$
$$I.A \cap I.R = \emptyset \wedge I.A_{pt} \cap I.R_{pt} = \emptyset \wedge I.A_{pt} \cap I.A = \emptyset)$$
$$safe\text{-}mmu\text{-}acc(c, pa, i) \equiv pa \in c.pt_{[i]} \cup c.shared \wedge pa \notin c.ro \wedge \forall j.\ pa \notin c.\mathcal{O}_{[j]}$$
$$safe\text{-}state(c) \equiv \forall i.\ safe\text{-}instr(c, i, hd(c.is_{[i]})) \wedge$$
$$\forall i, pa.\ can\text{-}access(c.mmu_{[i]}, pa) \rightarrow safe\text{-}mmu\text{-}acc(c, pa, i).$$

Fig. 5. Safety of instruction I in thread i, where $\vartheta' = c.\vartheta_{[i]}(I.t \mapsto c.m(pa))$.

of ownership. If a thread with a dirty flag set, for instance, releases an owned unshared address (thus, making it shared and safe to access for other threads) and then performs a volatile read from that address, it has to flush an SB beforehand. If a thread acquires (i.e., makes it owned, unshared) a local page-table address that is accessible by its MMU (e.g., after detaching a page table), it has first to perform an INVLPG because, otherwise, the address would still remain accessible after the ownership transfer and the MMU safety would be violated. If a thread acquires a shared, unowned read-write address that was accessible by MMUs of other threads (e.g., after detaching a shared page table), it has to force an INVLPG on those threads as well. Thus, TLB flushing is governed by the programming discipline just as SB flushing is. The only difference is that we argue about the MMU/TLB state in an SC environment explicitly, while the SBs are abstracted by the dirty flags.

4.4   Store Buffer Machine

The SB machine is obtained by adding SBs to the virtual machine. The ghost fields carried from the virtual machine configuration are used to simplify the simulation proof. Store buffers are used not only to buffer memory stores but also to collect history information about the steps of the execution. This information is used to couple the current state of the SB machine with the corresponding state of the virtual machine. The ghost fields carried from the virtual machine do not influence the execution of the SB machine in any way, and the history information recorded in the SB does not influence the non-ghost components (except for the length of the SB when the history information retires). Hence, proving simulation between an SB machine without the ghost and history components and with them is a trivial task and we omit it here.

Configuration of the SB machine c_{sbh} has the same components as configurations of the virtual machine. Thread-local configuration $c_{sbh}.ts_{[i]}$ has all components from the local configuration of the virtual machine plus an SB component $c_{sbh}.ts_{[i]}.sb \in \mathbb{I}_{sb}^*$, which is a list of *SB instructions*:

$$\mathbb{I}_{sb} = \mathbf{Write_{sb}} \text{ vol va } (D, f) \text{ r annot pa v} \mid \mathbf{Read_{sb}} \text{ vol va t r pa v}$$
$$\mid \mathbf{Ghost_{sb}} \text{ annot} \mid \mathbf{Prog_{sb}} \text{ p p' is}.$$

The only SB instruction with a non-ghost effect is $\mathbf{Write_{sb}}$, which stores value v to memory address pa (the other fields of the instruction contain the history information). For reads, ghost instructions and program steps we only record the history. For program steps we record the program state p before the step and the program state p' after the step, along with the newly generated instruction sequence is. For a given read, write, or ghost instruction $I \in \mathbb{I}$, we use the function $sbins(I, pa, v) \in \mathbb{I}_{sb}$ to convert instruction I to a corresponding SB instruction. We overload the predicates $R(I)$, $W(I)$, etc. to work also on SB instructions, and introduce predicate $P(I)$ for the recorded program step.

The behavior of the SB machine is given by a non-deterministic transition relation $c_{sbh} \Rightarrow c'_{sbh}$, where every step is either a program step, a memory step,

$$\frac{(p', is') = \delta_p(p_{[i]}, \vartheta_{[i]}) \quad I' = \mathbf{Prog_{sb}} \; p \; p' \; is'}{c_{sbh} \overset{p}{\Longrightarrow}_i c_{sbh}[p_{[i]} := p', sb_{[i]} := sb_{[i]} \circ I', is_{[i]} := is_{[i]} \circ is']}$$

$$\frac{R(I) \quad pa \in (atran(mmu_{[i]}, I.va, mode_{[i]}, I.r)) \quad v = fwd(sb_{[i]}, c_{sbh}.m, pa)}{c_{sbh} \overset{m}{\Longrightarrow}_i c_{sbh}[\vartheta_{[i]} := \vartheta_{[i]}(I.t \mapsto v), sb_{[i]} := sb_{[i]} \circ [sbins(I, pa, v)], is_{[i]} := tl(is_{[i]})]}$$

$$\frac{W(I) \quad pa \in (atran(mmu_{[i]}, I.va, mode_{[i]}, I.r)) \quad \mathcal{D}' = vW(I) \vee \mathcal{D}_{[i]}}{c_{sbh} \overset{m}{\Longrightarrow}_i c_{sbh}[sb_{[i]} := sb_{[i]} \circ [sbins(I, pa, I.f(\vartheta_{[i]}))], is_{[i]} := tl(is_{[i]}), \mathcal{D}_{[i]} := \mathcal{D}']}$$

$$\frac{G(I)}{c_{sbh} \overset{m}{\Longrightarrow}_i c_{sbh}[sb_{[i]} := sb_{[i]} \circ [sbins(I, pa, v)], is_{[i]} := tl(is_{[i]})]}$$

$$\frac{W(I) \quad ghst' = (nvW(I) \; ? \; ghst_{[i]} : otran(ghst_{[i]}, i, I))}{c_{sbh} \overset{sb}{\Longrightarrow}_i c_{sbh}[m := c_{sbh}.m(I.pa \mapsto I.v), ghst_{[i]} := ghst', sb_{[i]} := tl(sb_{[i]})]}$$

$$\frac{R(I) \vee P(I)}{c_{sbh} \overset{sb}{\Longrightarrow}_i c_{sbh}[sb_{[i]} := tl(sb_{[i]})]} \qquad \frac{G(I) \quad ghst' = otran(ghst_{[i]}, i, I)}{c_{sbh} \overset{sb}{\Longrightarrow}_i c_{sbh}[ghst_{[i]} := ghst', sb_{[i]} := tl(sb_{[i]})]}$$

Fig. 6. Program, memory and SB steps of thread i of the SB machine. For component X of thread configuration $c_{sbh}.ts_{[i]}$, we simply write $X_{[i]}$. For the memory step we only consider execution of read, write or ghost instruction I, where $I = hd(is_{[i]})$. For the SB step we take $I = hd(sb_{[i]})$. As in the case of the virtual machine, we abbreviate by $ghst_{[i]}$ the ghost state of thread i and the shared ghost information.

an SB step, an MMU step, or a page fault step of thread i. A program step of the SB machine has the same effect as in the virtual machine and is recorded as history information in the SB (Fig. 6). A read instruction performs the read and is recorded to the SB as history information; the read value is obtained with the function $fwd(sb_{[i]}, c_{sbh}.m, pa)$, which returns the most recent store to pa present in the SB, or if there are no such stores, the memory value $c_{sbh}.m(pa)$. A write instruction is not executed immediately, but is buffered in the SB together with the ghost history information. A ghost instruction is likewise recorded into the SB without an immediate effect on the configuration. All other memory instructions, as well as page fault steps, can be executed only when the SB is empty, and have the same semantics as defined for the virtual machine, so we omit them here. We also leave out the MMU read and write steps, which have exactly the same semantics as in the virtual machine. When a write instruction leaves SB, it delivers the corresponding buffered store to the memory and performs the ownership transfer if the write is volatile. A ghost SB instruction only performs the ownership transfer. Read and program SB instructions that exit the SB do nothing.

5   Simulation

Our main result is stated in the following simulation theorem.

Theorem 1 (Reduction)

$$c_{sbh} \Rightarrow^* c'_{sbh} \wedge c_{sbh} \sim c \wedge initial(c) \wedge sbempty(c_{sbh}) \wedge safe\text{-}reach(c) \rightarrow$$
$$\exists c'. \; c \Rightarrow^* c' \wedge c'_{sbh} \sim c'$$

We consider only executions that start with empty SBs. Predicate $safe\text{-}reach(c)$ denotes that any configuration reachable from configuration c is safe. The initial configuration of the SB machine can be obtained from the initial configuration of the virtual machine by simply copying all components. Predicate $initial(c)$ assumes the ghost state of the virtual machine to be correctly initialized, i.e., that the ownership sets are disjoint and the read-only set is a subset of shared addresses. The coupling relation $c_{sbh} \sim c$ guarantees equality of the local thread configurations (excluding the SB component) when the SBs are empty.

The proof of Theorem 1 is done by forward simulation: for every step of the SB machine, we find a (possibly empty) corresponding sequence of steps of the virtual machine that preserves the coupling relation. Here the scheduling of the virtual machine becomes crucial. In particular, we have to make sure that the reads (including the MMU reads) performed in both machines get the same value. Two obvious ways to try to do the scheduling are: (i) executing an instruction on the virtual machine when this instruction is executed on the SB machine and (ii) executing an instruction on the virtual machine when this instruction leaves the SB (i.e., delaying the virtual machine until this point). The history information recorded in the SB in this case helps to reconstruct the instructions which yet have to be executed in the virtual machine. However, neither of these approaches work. Executing instructions simultaneously on both machines would cause inconsistency of the shared memory (because of the volatile writes committed to the SB on the SB machine and directly to the memory on the virtual machine). Since any thread is allowed to read the shared portion of the memory, this might lead to inconsistent read results between SB and virtual machines. Delaying all instructions in the virtual machine also does not work, because while a volatile read is delayed in the virtual machine, its read value might get invalidated by a volatile write from another thread.

The scheduling policy which does provide consistent read results executes instructions of thread i simultaneously on both machines until a volatile write enters the SB. At that point, thread i of the virtual machine is delayed until this volatile write leaves the SB. When it does, the virtual machine executes this volatile write together with the instructions (and program steps) recorded in the SB of thread i after that write but before the next volatile write. Clearly, such a strategy keeps the shared portion of the memory consistent between the machines. In a safe execution when a volatile read is executed in the virtual machine the dirty bit must be cleared. A cleared dirty bit of a thread means that the SB of this thread does not contain any volatile writes (we maintain this property as an invariant). Hence, the volatile reads are never delayed and are executed simultaneously in both machines.

Additionally, we want the content of local page tables to be always consistent between the machines. The reason for that is that local PTEs may point to shared page tables and delaying the MMU writes to local PTEs would force us to delay the MMU writes to the shared memory as well. As a result, we have to execute all MMU steps simultaneously in both machines. Together with the possible delay in instruction execution, this leads to reordering of MMU steps with respect to executed instructions in a given thread, but this reordering is always done to the left of the instruction sequence. This behaviour is fine, because the monotonicity property of our MMU model guarantees that once added the address translations are never removed from the MMU (until explicitly flushed). In the virtual machine, some address translations will be added to the MMU earlier than in the SB machine (if one counts time by the number of executed instructions), but they will still remain there when the instructions that might rely on these address translations are executed.

For the formal definition of the coupling relation and for the detailed proofs of Theorem 1 refer to our technical report [3].

6   Conclusion

We presented a programming discipline for concurrent programs running in translated mode and racing with MMUs. Our reduction theorem guarantees, that if such a program satisfies the safety conditions in an SC environment, then execution of this program under TSO also preserves sequential consistency. As a result, one can derive properties for TSO executions by verifying programs in a sequentially consistent model of executions. The safety criteria from Fig. 5 might seem very much suited towards verification experts and not towards programmers. However, the core verification discipline, and the methodology for how to manage ownership and add suitable ghost code, is essentially based on VCC. This discipline is there not just to avoid data races; its there to allow modular, thread-local reasoning about fine-grained concurrent software. Because one has to track ownership anyway, the additional burdens arising from the use of MMUs and SBs are themselves fairly minimal. VCC has been used to verify more than 100KLOC of real-world concurrent software, so the annotation is indeed practical; typical annotation overheads are on the order of 2/1 (i.e., twice as much annotation as source code).

Our main motivation for extending the SB reduction theorem with MMUs was driven by the results obtained during the Verisoft XT project [13], which aimed at the formal verification of the Microsoft Hyper-V hypervisor in VCC. When the project ended in 2010 many crucial portions of the hypervisor code were verified. Yet, the overall theory of the multi-core hypervisor verification was far from being completed, even on paper. Since then, many pieces of the theory have been worked out [5]. This paper is intended to close another open gap in that theory and to allow verification of software that manages page tables.

Related work. The programming discipline presented here is an extension of [6] and can be used to verify both data race free (DRF) andnon-DRF programs. There are simpler, ownership-free criteria to guarantee SC for non-DRF programs in the presence of SBs (such as the absence of triangular races [11] or quadrangular races [7]), but they guarantee a condition stronger than SC, and thereby allow non-racing accesses to induce flushing obligations. Neither of these disciplines considers address translation. Kolanski [9] develops a programming logic based on separation logic that specifically materializes page tables and address translation. However, it considers neither concurrency, caches (such as TLBs), nor store buffering.

References

1. Advanced Micro Devices: AMD64 Architecture Programmer's Manual Volume 2: System Programming, 3.19 edn., Sep 2011
2. Alkassar, E., Cohen, E., Kovalev, M., Paul, W.J.: Verification of TLB virtualization implemented in C. In: Joshi, R., Müller, P., Podelski, A. (eds.) VSTTE 2012. LNCS, vol. 7152, pp. 209–224. SPRINGER, Heidelberg (2012)
3. Chen, G., Cohen, E., Kovalev, M.: Store buffer reduction with MMUs: complete paper-and-pencil proof. Technical report, Saarland University, Saarbrücken (2013). http://www-wjp.cs.uni-saarland.de/publikationen/CCK13.pdf
4. Cohen, E., Dahlweid, M., Hillebrand, M., Leinenbach, D., Moskal, M., Santen, T., Schulte, W., Tobies, S.: VCC: a practical system for verifying concurrent C. In: Berghofer, S., Nipkow, T., Urban, C., Wenzel, M. (eds.) TPHOLs 2009. LNCS, vol. 5674, pp. 23–42. Springer, Heidelberg (2009)
5. Cohen, E., Paul, W., Schmaltz, S.: Theory of multi core hypervisor verification. In: van Emde Boas, P., Groen, F.C.A., Italiano, G.F., Nawrocki, J., Sack, H. (eds.) SOFSEM 2013. LNCS, vol. 7741, pp. 1–27. Springer, Heidelberg (2013)
6. Cohen, E., Schirmer, B.: From total store order to sequential consistency: a practical reduction theorem. In: Kaufmann, M., Paulson, L.C. (eds.) ITP 2010. LNCS, vol. 6172, pp. 403–418. Springer, Heidelberg (2010)
7. Gotsman, A., Musuvathi, M., Yang, H.: Show no weakness: sequentially consistent specifications of tso libraries. In: Aguilera, M.K. (ed.) DISC 2012. LNCS, vol. 7611, pp. 31–45. Springer, Heidelberg (2012)
8. Hillebrand, M., Leinenbach, D.: Formal verification of a reader-writer lock implementation in C. In: 4th International Workshop on Systems Software Verification (SSV09). Electronic Notes in Theoretical Computer Science, vol. 254, pp. 123–141. Elsevier Science B. V. (2009)
9. Kolanski, R.: Verification of programs in virtual memory using separation logic. Ph.D. thesis, School of Computer Science and Engineering, University of NSW, Sydney 2052, Australia, July 2011
10. Lamport, L.: How to make a multiprocessor computer that correctly executes multiprocess programs. IEEE Trans. Comput. **28**(9), 690–691 (1979)
11. Owens, S.: Reasoning about the implementation of concurrency abstractions on x86-TSO. In: D'Hondt, T. (ed.) ECOOP 2010. LNCS, vol. 6183, pp. 478–503. Springer, Heidelberg (2010)
12. Sewell, P., Sarkar, S., Owens, S., Nardelli, F.Z., Myreen, M.O.: x86-TSO: a rigorous and usable programmer's model for x86 multiprocessors. Commun. ACM **53**(7), 89–97 (2010)
13. Verisoft XT Consortium: The Verisoft XT Project (2007–2010). http://www.verisoftxt.de

Separation Kernel Verification: The Xtratum Case Study

David Sanán[1], Andrew Butterfield[1($\boxtimes$)], and Mike Hinchey[2]

[1] Trinity College Dublin, Dublin, Ireland
{andrew.butterfield,david.sanan}@scss.tcd.ie
[2] University of Limerick, Limerick, Ireland
mike.hinchey@lero.ie

Abstract. The separation kernel concept was developed as an architecture to simplify formal kernel security verification, and is the basis for many implementations of integrated modular avionics in the aerospace domain. This paper reports on a feasibility study conducted for the European Space Agency, to explore the resources required to formally verify the correctness of such a kernel, given a reference specification and a implementation of same. The study was part of an activity called Methods and Tools for On-Board Software Engineering (MTOBSE) which produced a natural language Reference Specification for a Time-Space Partitioning (TSP) kernel, describing partition functional properties such as health monitoring, inter-partition communication, partition control, resource access, and separation security properties, such as the security policy and authorisation control. An abstract security model, and the reference specification were both formalised using Isabelle/HOL. The C sources of the open-source XtratuM kernel were obtained, and an Isabelle/HOL model of the code was semi-automatically produced. Refinement relations were written manually and some proofs were explored. We describe some of the details of what has been modelled and report on the current state of this work. We also make a comparison between our verification explorations, and the circumstances of NICTA's successful verification of the sel4 kernel.

1 Introduction

The separation kernel concept was introduced by Rushby [1] to aid in achieving high assurance in critical systems. A separation kernel creates a secure environment providing temporal and spatial partitioning of applications. In this environment each application can only access the set of resources that the kernel assigns, by being isolated into partitions where there is no flow of data beyond explicitly authorized channels.

In the last decade the use of separation kernels has increased, with architectures such as the Multiple Independent Levels of Security and Safety architecture

Funded by ESTEC CONTRACT No. 4000106016, and supported, in part, by Science Foundation Ireland grant 10/CE/I1855

D. Giannakopoulou and D. Kroening (Eds.): VSTTE 2014, LNCS 8471, pp. 133–149, 2014.
DOI: 10.1007/978-3-319-12154-3_9

(MILS) [2], appearing, as well as standards such as Common Criteria (CC) [3] and the associated Separation Kernel Protection Profile (SKPP) [4] for security requirements, or ARINC-653 [5] for functional requirements. In particular, in the space environment, the IMA for Space (IMA-SP) platform proposed by the European Space Research and Technology Centre (ESTEC) uses a separation kernel, which helps with fault containment.

Based on those standards and architectures, different implementations of the separation kernel have emerged, such as PikeOS [6], seL4 [7], XtratuM [8], or Air2 [9] among others. The SKPP assurance requirements only require, from the formal methods point of view, that a certified kernel design is semiformally verified and to provide a formal security policy model. However, for simple and small designs it is technically possible to go beyond those levels and perform a full verification of the implementation to ensure the absence of errors.

A separation kernel implementation is too complex for a direct approach to the verification of the implementation's code. Aiming to reduce the verification complexity, projects like L4.Verified [7], VerisoftXT [6], and the verification of the software for the so called Embedded Device (ED) [10] have successfully applied techniques such as refinement verification, where the properties are verified over an abstract model, which is less detailed and therefore easier to verify. Then, by means of so-called forward simulation, the implementation model is verified. L4.Verified and VerisoftXT respectively aim to verify the general purpose kernels seL4 and PikeOS, each composed of around 10 K lines of code. On the other hand, the verification in [10] targets a software-based embedded device of around 3k lines of code. L4.Verified fully verified security and functional properties of the seL4 kernel down to the C implementation and machine code. VerisoftXT fully verifies functional correctness of PikeOS, including memory separation correctness as well. Finally the work in [10] is focused on Common Criteria certification and verification is restricted to security properties. The significance of secure micro-kernel verification is still increasing and new on-going projects continue to arise, like [11] where non-interference has been proved on Prosper, a simple separation micro-kernel targeting the ARM architecture, and [12] where the information flow policy for the SAFE security kernel was verified.

Within the project *Methods and Tools for On-Board Software Engineering (MTOBSE)*[1] we developed an abstract model which captures requirements of a reference specification, for a partition-separation kernel, which was also developed under this project, guided by the SKPP and the IMA-SP specification [13]. We also formalised an abstract model of a security policy, and we provide a formal refinement relation between this and the reference model. We selected the open source XtratuM kernel [8] as the code verification target. Using existing model extraction tools, we have partially modeled the XtratuM microkernel and we have formalised the refinement relation between the abstract model and the XtratuM implementation model.

Unlike L4.Verified, VerisoftXT, and the verification of the ED kernel, we are not either starting from a particular specification and deriving verifiable

---

[1] Funded by ESTEC CONTRACT No. 4000106016

code (L4.Verified), or taking existing code and abstracting out a specification (VerisoftXT and ED kernel). In our case we have written a general reference specification and have constructed an abstract model of that specification. We are exploring the feasibility of verifying third-party kernel implementations, such as XtratuM, against our reference abstract model, which we expect to be more difficult as a result of the independent development of the model and implementation.

As work in progress, we describe the methodologies and toolchain we are using to formally verify the XtratuM kernel w.r.t. the abstract model, and we also detail the process used to obtain the implementation model from the source code, as well as the issues that arise regarding feasibility.

2   About the Partitioned-Separation Kernel: A Reference Specification

Before John Rushby introduced the concept of a separation kernel [1], security models for high assurance kernels were too complex for feasible sound verification. The separation kernel approach uses simpler notions of partition and separation to result in a security kernel for which proof is much easier, but the necessary characteristics are still covered. To achieve process isolation, a secure kernel considers the spatial separation of resources and temporal separation of execution. Spatial separation restricts the set of resources each process can access to a designated set, while temporal separation ensures the execution of each process occurs at well defined times, without being changed or delayed by activities elsewhere in the system. These two concepts ensure that processes have the perception of being executed in independent environments. However, it is necessary to allow flows of information among processes. Since those information flows break the spatial separation principle, the separation kernel protection profile (SKPP) [4] establishes a Partition Information Flow Policy (PIFP) that relaxes the separation, but only for appropriate information flows.

The natural language reference specification [14], developed in the MTOBSE project, consists of software requirements, interface requirements, and the architectural design. Both the software requirements and the interface requirements are based on the requirements baseline for the IMA-SP platform [13] and ESA's own suggestions. Based on the specified requirements, the architectural design describes the data structures, component internal interfaces, and component functionalities.

The main sources from which the software requirements are drawn are the Arinc-653 standard specification [5] for functional requirements (partitioning aspects) and the Separation Kernel Protection Profile (SKPP) [4] for security requirements (separation aspects). To achieve temporal partitioning as defined in the ARINC-653 standard, IMA-SP requires the use of a static cyclic scheduler, where partitions are assigned to execution windows called Partition Time Windows (PTW), which are strictly dispatched according to their assigned execution quotas and period. IMA-SP allows the static configuration of a set of schedulers, and during execution system partitions can invoke system calls to change the active scheduler to one of that set. Additionally, spatial partitioning is achieved by memory protection hardware, and forbidding any partition communication not explicitly allowed by an inter-partition communication channel, enforced by the separation kernel's PIFP.

Although the developed reference specification is guided by these standards, it does not intend to be fully compliant with them. For example, a non-standard view is taken of requirements for processes, intra-partition communication, and the health monitor. The ESA view is that management of those aspects are handled by a partition guest OS for processes and intra-partition communication, or a system partition for the health monitor. Also, as far as possible drivers are not part of the kernel in order to keep it as simple as it is possible. Only clock drivers are part of the kernel since they are necessary for the partition scheduler. A system partition is responsible for allocating drivers for other devices. User partitions cannot have direct access to devices, and any communication between a device and a user partition is through an explicit inter-partition communication channel between the user partition and the driver system partition.

In the case of security and separation requirements this reference specification follows the SKPP recommendations, and it includes requirements tailored to the space environment for audit, user data protection, identification and authentication, security management, protection of the security functions, and resource utilisation.

Figure 1 shows the diagram for the architectural design. It includes the components required by the reference specification, including cores to manage partitions, communication, global and local time, exceptions not concerned with the kernel security functionality, interrupts and devices, and finally the Kernel

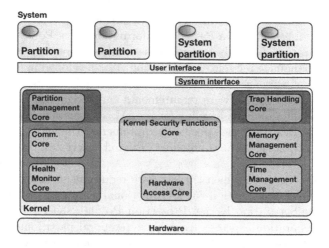

Fig. 1. Separation kernel design

Security Functions (KSF) core. User and System partitions can access the functionality the kernel provides through the interface that these modules implement.

3 Verification Methodology and Toolchain

The complexity of verifying a separation kernel makes it necessary to use verification based on layer abstractions such as refinement.

Our approach to refinement verification is fairly standard, as we take a *forward simulation* approach. We determine a refinement relation $\mathcal{R}_{AI}$ between the states S_A of an abstract model $\mathcal{M}_A$ and the states S_I of an implementation model $\mathcal{M}_I$. Given $op_I : s_I \mapsto s'_I$ and $op_A : s_A \mapsto s'_A$, showing that op_I data-refines op_A is a matter of showing, given any s_I and s_A, that the diagram in Fig. 2 commutes: Generally, the relation between $\mathcal{R}_{AI}$ is not trivial, mapping one abstract state to a set of corresponding implementation states. Additionally, in particular when aiming the full kernel verification, data and behavioral simplification of the abstract model bring new invariants in the implementation model that must be verified. So, to simplify the refinement task and the verification, it is typically necessary to introduce intermediate models $\mathcal{M}_{IM_0} \cdots \mathcal{M}_{IM_n}$ with higher levels of abstraction such that $\mathcal{M}_A \sqsubseteq \mathcal{M}_{IM_0} \cdots \mathcal{M}_{IM_n} \sqsubseteq \mathcal{M}_I$.

Although it is well known that refinement preserves safety but not liveness properties [15], in [16] it is shown that it is possible to formulate liveness properties in such a way that they are preserve by refinement.

Our property verification effort will be concentrating on proving system-call correctness and verifying security properties. Proofs for system calls will use classical Hoare triples based on pre- and post-conditions, ensuring that system calls satisfy their functional requirements. With regard to security properties, they will be verified using invariant preservation over data structures related to a security property.

The whole verification process is being carried out using the Isabelle/HOL theorem prover [17]. Isabelle/HOL Higher-Order Language (HOL) allows us to model the kernel abstraction, and to describe the properties representing the security and functional requisites and the refinement relation between models. In order to apply refinement verification we need to obtain an implementation model, which can be obtained using a semantic model of the implementation language over the source code. To that aim, we are using the C-Parser tool [18] developed by NICTA (Australia's Information and Communications Technology

$$\text{Model } \mathcal{M}_A : \qquad s_A \xrightarrow{\quad op_A \quad} s'_A$$

$$\mathcal{R}_{AI} \Big\downarrow \qquad \mathcal{R}_{AI} \Big\downarrow$$

$$\text{Model } \mathcal{M}_I : \qquad s_I \xrightarrow{\quad op_I \quad} s'_I$$

Fig. 2. Refinement (forward simulation)

(ICT) Research Centre of Excellence), that takes as input code a subset of C-99[2], and automatically provides a set of Isabelle/HOL theories defining an imperative model of that code. C-Parser introduces proof automation, discharging translation correctness, so the tool ensures that the model is correct with regard the provided semantic model, and additionally it automatically proves properties about memory access correctness.

4   Modelling the Separation Partitioning Kernel

Refinement verification requires the construction of an abstract model of the requirements, simple enough to make the verification feasible. However, it is important to have simplicity in mind as a compromise between verification of requirements and refinement verification, to obtain a transition relation which eases the refinement verification.

The partitioning-separation formal model is composed of more than thirty Isabelle/HOL theories where the kernel architecture and behaviour are defined according to the reference specification. These theories cover the spectrum from low-level machine data-types up to high-level kernel security behaviour. This range of abstract levels is required both to ease the construction of refinement relations, and cover aspects of security that themselves have low-level hardware-related aspects.

Therefore, the abstract model includes elements present in implementations like XtratuM: e.g., partial support for function pointer structures, and features such partitions with two virtual timers (global and local).

4.1   Kernel Data Structures

The kernel global state is modelled as an Isabelle/HOL record containing the current state of the partition-separation kernel components described in Sect. 2, and an additional field representing the current machine state, which is necessary to ensure that setup of hardware (e.g. MMU configuration) enforces data separation.

```
record state=
    partition_manager ::partition_manager_type
    communication_state ::communication_type
    health_monitor :: health_monitor_type
    ksf :: ksf_state
    trap_management :: trap_management_type
```

Collections of objects uniquely identified, like partitions, or communications channels, are specified using partial functions from the field identifying the object (e.g. the partition identifier) to the object itself. Since Isabelle functions are

---

[2] C-99 refers to the revised standard of ANSI C, or C-89, released in 1999

total, partial functions are specified using datatype *option*, which returns *None* for those identifiers not mapped to any object and *Some obj* for those mapped to object *obj*.

The State and Function Pointers. Operating systems implement trap and interrupt functions using a table mapping traps and interrupts to the function handling them. So, on incoming interrupts or traps, the OS goes to the lookup table and executes the management functions. To model this behaviour on Isabelle/HOL it should be enough to define a function mapping traps and interrupts to higher order functions managing the interrupts. Since traps and interrupt management functions usually modify global variables, it is necessary to model them as functions modifying the state, which can be done using monads.

However, Isabelle/HOL requires that datatype constructors involving the type constructor $\rightarrow$ for the full function space, do not use the newly defined datatype in the $\rightarrow$ lefthandside, i.e. all occurrence must be strictly positive [19]. This is because having a constructor which recursively uses a new type τ on the left side of $\rightarrow$ means that the cardinality of τ would be at least that of the powerset of τ, which by Cantor's theorem would be strictly greater than the cardinality of τ. Therefore, due to this restriction it is not possible to include state modifier functions in the global state, nor in the state of any kernel component.

One work around, is to define the *state* without considering function pointers, and create a new record extending the original state with the set of possible functions being pointed to by these pointers. But that is not enough to allow state components using function pointers, like the machine state, to directly reference those function pointers, since they belong to the *extended_state* definition, which is not visible to them. To solve this, the field extending the *state* containing the functions pointed to by function pointers, is mapped from naturals to higher order functions modifying the state, and function pointer variables keep the natural number associated with the relevant function pointer in the mapping function. Invoking the function pointer means getting the function mapped to that natural. The relevant excerpt from the model is immediately below, noting that we have two different kinds of function pointer: interrupts and trap-handlers. Both take the interrupt or trap being handled and return a monad over a partial state.

```
record extended_state = state + funct_pointers :: funct_pointer_map
type_synonym interrupt_handler = "pointer ⇒ hw_irq ⇒ unit ps_monad"
type_synonym trap_handler = "hw_fault ⇒ unit ps_monad"
datatype funct_pointer = FunctionPointer_1 "trap_handler"
                       |FunctionPointer_2 "interrupt_handler"
type_synonym funct_pointer_map = "funct_pointer_ind ⇀ funct_pointer"
```

However, this work around also has limitations. The most important one is that functions pointed to by function pointers cannot invoke other function pointers. This is because the actual function is a monad to *partial_state*, which does not include the function pointer mapping. Nonetheless, none of the function pointers modelled are affected by this limitation.

Using *record* related Isabelle/HOL functions is possible to define maps from *state* to *partial_state* and vice versa:

definition *s_2_ps::"state ⇒ partial_state"*
where *"s_2_ps s ≡ partial_state.truncate s"*
definition *ps_2_s::" funct_pointer_map ⇒ partial_state ⇒ state"*
where *"ps_2_s fp ps ≡ partial_state.extend ps (state.fields fp)"*

Health Monitor. In the presence of hardware faults, the trap manager sends the trapped fault to the health monitor. The health monitor is modelled as a record containing a fault management table, modelled as a total function from faults to monitoring actions, and a fault record. The fault management table specifies one of the following actions: system restart (cold or warm), shutdown, halt, or ignore. This last action keeps a fault log accessible by the health monitor system partition, as specified by the IMA-SP.

Partition Virtual Machines. As mentioned in Sect. 2 the separation kernel provides a virtual machine to partitions in such a way that they have (apparently) unique access to the hardware. To that aim, in addition to user context registers and the program counters, the partition manager keeps the partition cache status, for both data and code caches, interrupt state, and virtual timers.

Partition cache virtualization keeps the state of cache-enabled and frozen bits for data and cache in the MMU configuration, restoring them on each partition switch from the cache virtualization data of the incoming partition. In addition, on each partition switch the contents of the cache for the outgoing partition is flushed for cache sanitation.

In partition virtualization, interrupt management plays a big role. Fields in charge of interrupt management determine whether virtual interrupts are enabled for the partition and the priority level. Two total functions provide a mapping from hardware and system traps to addresses in the partition trap handler table, with the possibility of masking traps and keeping track of unattended traps. Partitions' trap routines are user code and their execution are beyond the scope of the kernel model. The Isabelel/HOL structure for partition interrupt virtualization is:

```
record trap_info = hw_mask :: trap_mask
   hw_pending :: trap_pending
   ext_mask :: trap_mask
   ext_pending :: trap_pending
   t_enabled :: trap_enabled
   t_PIL :: pil        t_line :: trap_line
   hw_vector :: "hw_irq ⇒ vector_index"
   sys_vector :: "ext_irq + ext_fault⇒ vector_index"
   sw_trap :: "sw_trap option"
```

Machine State. Although the kernel model does not aim at hardware verification, we need a hardware model of those parts which require a correct setup to ensure spatial separation. The machine model depends heavily on the target hardware platform, which in the case of the current project, is the Sparc V8 architecture [20].

In particular, we have modeled the following:

1. *Processor registers* to control supervisor mode and incoming traps and interrupts
2. *User general purpose registers* to check register sanitation on context switches
3. *Input/output devices' address space* to verify correct setup of devices
4. *Memory Management Unit (MMU)* to ensure the directory entries for virtual memory are correctly configured.

(i) and (ii) are modelled by `CPU_context` and `user_context`, defined as total functions from a register datatype, specified as a datatype providing a constructor for each register, to a machine word, specified as a 32-bit word. (iii) is modelled by `io_memory` as a partial function, from the set of devices memory addresses to machine words. Finally `MMU_state` models (iv) and contains the MMU registers, modeled also as total functions from MMU register name to machine words, the data and code cache, and the memory.

4.2   Kernel Behaviour

The separation kernel is an event-oriented model. Indeed, partitions are run owning the microprocessor until some event raises a trap, to wake up the kernel, which will handle the event. Conforming to this, the top Isabelle/HOL theory in the modelled kernel is an entry point waiting for incoming events, i.e. traps and partition calls to kernel services. In addition, as we are concerned with spatial separation verification, memory access events are also considered. With a correct MMU set-up, a partition accessing virtual memory addresses not assigned to that partition shall cause a memory access error.

The kernel states are shown in Fig. 3. The entry point only handles traps, system calls and access to memory when the kernel is in NORMAL or MAINTENANCE states, these being software events ignored in any other state. The BOOT state is partially modelled by a booting function returning an initial kernel state for the given initial configuration.

Traps, Interrupts, and Health Monitor. The model captures hardware traps and device interrupts with a partial function from traps and interrupts to the function handling them. By default, the health monitor handles kernel traps, but partition traps are delivered to a system partition, which carries out health monitor functions. Whether an incoming trap is delivered to the system partition is decided by a configuration table with the actions to take on traps. Interrupts and traps are considered non-preemptive.

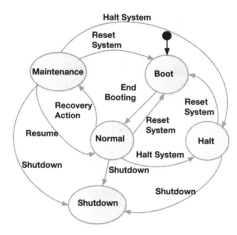

Fig. 3. Kernel state transition graph

Similarly to traps, device interrupts are also handled by a system partition. When a device interrupts the kernel it sets the bit corresponding to that interrupt in the partition virtual machine for the system partition handling interrupts. The kernel only provides handlers for the hardware timers. In particular it provides two handlers: one is for the system time, incrementing the system clock and the running partition system clock; the other is for system timers, which control the partition scheduler and virtual timers for partitions.

The Security Model. The SKPP [4] functional security requirements include: security audit, user data protection, identification and authentication, security management, self-protection, and resource utilization. The most important parts from the temporal and spatial isolation perspective are those defining the flow control functions, and temporal quotas.

The flow control function is modelled in the Kernel Security Function (KSF) module as a function mapping partitions and resources to the allowed operations of partitions over the resources, following a flow control policy based on the Least Privilege abstraction [21] (LP). The LP function defines, for each pair (*partition* × *resource*), acceptance or denial of a given operation (*write/read* allowed or not). In the case the operation is not specified, and the value for that pair is *unspecified*, then the flow control is based on a function mapping operations between partitions, following in that case a partition-pair abstraction. Here the partition pair function PP defines, for each pair (*partition* × *partition*), the acceptance or denial of a given operation, and in the case that the value is *unspecified* any operation involving those partitions is forbidden.

The IMA-SP specification [13] forbids shared memory, and the only flow between partitions is using inter-partition communication channels, which communicate via ports uniquely assigned to partitions. Communication channels fix the direction of the communication so each channel has to be composed of a source port, which writes to the corresponding destination port, ensuring a one way communication flow. Considering inter partition communication, the flow control function model shall allow an operation op between partitions $P1$, $P2$ using a inter partition channel $ch = \langle sp \times dp \rangle$, with sp a source port in $P1$, dp a destination port in $P2$, if $LP\ P1\ dp = Write\_Allowed \vee (LP\ P1\ dp = Undefined \wedge PP\ P1\ P2 = Write\_Allowed) \wedge LP\ P2\ sp = Read\_Allowed \vee (LP\ P2\ sp = Undefined \wedge PP\ P2\ P1 = Read\_Allowed)$.

In the case of multi-cast channels with one source port sp and multiple destination ports $dp_1, \ldots, dp_n$, the operation will be allowed if for all pairs $(sp \times dp_1) \ldots (sp \times dp_n)$ the relation above holds.

For the KSF to enforce temporal quotas, it manages the global clock and the set of Major Time Frames (MTF) defining the scheduler. It is in charge of switching partitions, detecting if some partition has exceed its temporal quota and ensuring that residual information is removed. The reason that a partition can exceed its temporal quota is because a partition can invoke a system service just before the current PTW finishes and, since the kernel is not preemptive, the timer interrupt would not be handled until that call finishes. This could be solved by allowing preemption, but making the kernel more complex, or establishing a time in the MTF after which system calls are not allowed.

With regard to security, the KSF models authorization access to kernel privileged operations. The KSF records, for each partition, a set of authorized operations. For the sake of kernel simplicity, system partitions own authorization to all privileged operations, whereas non-system partitions own no rights.

Kernel Services. Kernel services typically change the kernel state into another one modifying some kernel variables, so they are modelled using state monads. The kernel offers two types of services: privileged services like changing the state of a partition or halting the kernel, and non-privileged services such as sending a message to a communication port, or modifying some partition virtual machine property like enabling the data cache. Before invoking any kernel service, the kernel checks out the current partition privileges to detect if the current partition is authorized to perform the operation (check phase). Also, the service arguments are examined to check they are correct (decode phase). Only if the partition has the necessary privileges and the arguments passed to the service are correct the service is invoked (invocation phase), otherwise the kernel will return the corresponding error code.

4.3 The Abstract Security Model

We represent the separation kernel concept with an abstract security model (ASM, Fig. 4) whose configuration is composed of the tuple $< P, \alpha, \beta, \sigma >$, where P is a set of partition-ids, α is an action policy representing a set of allowed actions for each partition-id, β is a set of applications as a function from partitions to sequence of actions, and σ is a schedule, modelled as a sequence of partition-ids, each occurrence denoting the corresponding partition performing one (the next) action from its corresponding sequence.

$$run \ : \ Sys \rightarrow RunHist$$
$$run(\alpha, \sigma, \beta) = execute_\alpha(\sigma, \beta)$$
$$execute \ : \ ActPol \rightarrow (Sched \times Apps) \rightarrow RunHist$$
$$execute_\alpha(\langle\rangle, \_) = \langle\rangle$$
$$execute_\alpha(p : \sigma, \beta) = perform^{\beta,p}_{\alpha,\sigma}\beta(p)$$

$$perform \ : \ (ActPol \times Sched) \rightarrow (Apps \times PId) \rightarrow Run \rightarrow RunHist$$
$$perform^{\beta,p}_{\alpha,\sigma}\langle\rangle = execute_\alpha(\sigma, \beta)$$
$$perform^{\beta,p}_{\alpha,\sigma}(a : r) = \begin{cases} (p, a) : execute_\alpha(\sigma, \beta \dagger \{p \mapsto r\}) \ , a \in \alpha(p) \\ \langle\rangle \qquad\qquad\qquad\qquad\qquad\quad\ , a \notin \alpha(p) \end{cases}$$

Fig. 4. Abstract security model

We say that a run-history run, defined as a sequence of pairs $(Pid \times actions)^*$, is consistent with an action policy α, $hpConsistent_\alpha \ run$, if for every partition/action pair $(p, a) \in run$, α allows p to perform a.

The key property in ASM is that the execution of actions for each scheduled partition, given by $run(\alpha, \sigma, \beta)$, is consistent with the policy:
$hpConsistent_\alpha \ run(\alpha, \sigma, \beta)$.

Run takes as input the action policy (α), the scheduler (σ), and the sequence of actions that partitions execute (β), and it returns the run-history. If the sequence of partitions defined by the scheduler is empty, run finishes; otherwise if it is equal to $p : \sigma$ (: is the list constructor) it adds the pair (p, a) to the run history, where a is the next action in the sequence of actions for partition p, $\beta(p)$, and a is taken out from the list of actions for $\beta(p)$ († is the map override operator). If there is no next action a for p, $\beta(p) = \langle\rangle$, the next partition in σ is scheduled and the run history is not modified. If action a is not allowed for partition p, expressed as $a \notin \alpha(p)$, then we simply stop, and return an empty history.

4.4 Refinement Relation between ASM and the Reference Model

For refinement verification (Fig. 5) we define the relation $\mathcal{R}^{ASM}$ between states belonging to ASM and the abstract model of the reference specification (rm). This relates the sequence of actions for partitions β, the scheduler σ, and the action policy α, with the set of partitions defined in the partition manager, the scheduler, and the security policy, respectively.

Function f used in $\mathcal{R}^P$ and $\mathcal{R}^{SP}$ defines a function from partition-ids in the very abstract model to partition-ids in the abstract model. Function h associates the partition sequence of actions in ASM with segment codes in the abstract model. Similarly, g associates in $\mathcal{R}^P$ the partition's set of allowed action with the set of allowed operations in the partition security model. For $\mathcal{R}^S$, a prefix p^* of σ must be equal to the partition window ($PTWid$) in the abstract model's

$$\mathcal{R}^{ASM} \ (\beta, \sigma, \alpha) \ rm \equiv \ \mathcal{R}^P \ \beta \ rm.partition\_manager \land \mathcal{R}^S \ \sigma \ rm.scheduler \ \land$$
$$\mathcal{R}^{SP} \ \alpha \ rm.security\_model$$
$$\mathcal{R}^P \beta \ pm \equiv \exists f, h.Dom \ \beta = f`(Dom \ pm.partitions) \ \land$$
$$\forall i \in Dom \ \beta.\beta \ i = h(pm.partitions(f \ i))$$
$$\mathcal{R}^S \ \sigma \ sch \equiv \ \sigma = p^* : \sigma_1 \land partition \ sch[sch.current][sch.PTWid] = p \ \land$$
$$\exists pv.\sigma_1 = pv \ sch$$
$$\mathcal{R}^{SP} \ \alpha \ sp \equiv \exists f, g. \ Dom \ \alpha = f`(Dom \ sp) \land$$
$$\forall i \in Dom \ \alpha.\alpha \ i = g(pm.partitions(f \ i))$$

Fig. 5. Abstract security model refinement relation

current scheduler *sch.current*. ' represents set image function, and : the concatenation operator. Variable *pv* is a prophecy variable [15] introduced to simulate non-deterministic changes of the current scheduler when a partition invokes the corresponding system call as defined by IMA-SP.

5   Towards Separation Kernel Verification: The Xtratum Case

The XtratuM kernel [8] is a general partitioning microkernel, which provides basic hardware access to allocated partitions and is in compliance with the IMA-SP reference specification [13]. XtratuM provides temporal and spatial separation, using specific hardware to access memory and a deterministic cyclic scheduler to provide partitions with spatial and temporal isolation, inter-partition communication, and health monitoring for partition fault management.

5.1   Getting an Implementation Model

To get the implementation model, we used Xtratum 3, release 33, dated June 2012 and we modified it to make it compliant with Nicta's C-Parser 1.13, dated May 2013. Xtratum, version 3-33, is composed of more than 10 K. Lines of C code and 440 functions. Therefore, although it is really small in comparison with general purpose kernels (e.g., Linux v3 kernel has more than 19,000 K LoC) it is still big enough to necessitate that the implementation model is obtained automatically.

However, the C-Parser tool imposes some restrictions due to verification decisions and parsing considerations. The most significant ones are: function calls and assignments are not considered statements, but expressions, so side-effect expressions are not allowed such as assignments in control flow conditions; to simplify the memory model, pointers referencing local variables are not allowed; union and bitfields are considered unsafe since they violate the abstraction of the C semantic model and hence are forbidden.

XtratuM makes use of a subset of C not covered by C-Parser, so it has been necessary to edit XtratuM's source code to make it compliant with the parsing tool. With that aim, side-effect expressions where split using temporary variables to store the side-effect modification, and referenced local variables were moved out of the local context to the global kernel context. Unions and bitfields have been manually transformed into arrays of bytes of the size of the largest union field. C operators accessing union fields are substituted with functions that access the field in the resulting array of bytes. Note that currently those modifications are implemented to make the use of C-Parser possible, but this means we need to verify of the correctness of our modifications. Nicta uses a specific tool to automate this transformation and provide a translation proof, but as of this time it is not publicly available.

In addition, it is necessary to modify the XtratuM source code to find workarounds to bugs or undocumented C statements not handled by the parser, such as C comments at the end of a line using "//", or the `volatile` type quali-fier. The above issues are resolved by their removal from the source code because they do not affect the functional behaviour of the implementation. Other prob-lems are resolved by replacement with equivalent but compliant code. While deriving the partial implementation model, we found 14 different incompatibili-ties between the XtratuM code and the parsing tool.

So far, we have partially extracted an implementation model for XtratuM, having extracted the kernel data definitions and the scheduler functions, and those functions the on which scheduler depends. To obtain a complete model using `C-Parser`, it is necessary to restructure the source code and to provide a model of the kernel's assembly code, which the parser ignores. First, as is usual in a Kernel's code organization, XtratuM is organized in different mod-ules which are independently compiled, and later linked into the final executable file. In this scheme, inter-module dependencies are resolved by exporting func-tion prototypes that other modules use. It is common to find cyclic depen-dencies between modules which are resolved during the linking stage. On the other hand, `C-Parser`'s input is a unique C file, where such cyclic dependen-cies are not allowed. Hence, it was necessary to carefully re-structure the source code to be compatible with `C-Parser`. In future we may also explore the use of the CIL tool (http://sourceforge.net/projects/cil/) to merge all the C files into one without such cycles. Indeed, we are getting a modified kernel where for-mal verification ensures its correctness and that its behaves as expected by the specification. Second, kernels use assembly code in their lower layers to access the hardware, especially for functionality concerning interrupt management and hardware configuration. Although at this stage it is not intended to perform machine code verification, it is at least necessary to provide a minimum model to ensure hardware configuration correctness, especially of critical elements for supporting isolation such as the MMU.

5.2   Refinement Model

The construction of the abstract model was developed considering both the ref-erence specification [14] and the XtratuM implementation foreseeing the refine-ment relation with the implementation model. Nevertheless, and although both models have a similar architecture, some of the data structures in the implementation differ dramatically from the abstract model, therefore the refinement relation is not straightforward. This may have a negative impact on the cost of the refinement proof. In particular, most of the data structures in the abstract model are represented as partial functions, while the implementation uses static arrays or linked lists, and often the implementation splits the data structures into multiple arrays or lists, aiming for efficiency, but requiring us to check that the partial functions in the abstraction truly correspond with the implementation.

It is worth noting, that although the refinement relation must connect the whole model with the implementation model, there are some components like the KSF's security policy that are not currently refined since the implementation does not provide an explicit model of it, although there is a functional implementation of it implicit in inter-partition communication.

6   Future Work

Verifying a kernel is a major task, with complete verification requiring several years of effort, even in the case of a small separation kernel consisting of only a few thousands of lines of code. After finishing the abstract model that spans functional and security requirements, there are still two big steps to carry out: Requirement verification over the abstract models and proof of refinement between the abstract model and the implementation model.

Although verification of requirements can be considered a conceptually straightforward task, albeit with a lot of attention to a lot of detail, mostly focused on invariants and Hoare-triplet verification, it is still necessary to bring forth a proof of separation to support a guarantee of partition isolation in this architecture.

The proof of refinement will require collaboration with the XtratuM team which will help to produce a modified C-Parser compliant kernel. Additionally it may be necessary to modify the model extractor to be a better fit to XtratuM, or other alternative implementations, with particular features (e.g., total parser support for function pointers). Moreover, the refinement verification could require an intermediate layer to cover the gap between the abstract model and the implementation model.

What is very clear, is that an approach that requires verifying a refinement relation between independently developed specifications and implementations, is more complex than one where one end of the refinement relation was developed with the other end already known and understood. The MTOBSE project was looking at the situation where a customer issues the specification, and then seeks suppliers to tender their implementations, in open competition — a situation very common were customers are tax-payer/government funded entities such as ESA.

References

1. Rushby, J.M.: Design and verification of secure systems. SIGOPS Oper. Syst. Rev. **15**, 12–21 (1981)
2. Alves-Foss, J., Oman, P.W., Taylor, C., Harrison, S.: The MILS architecture for high-assurance embedded systems. IJES **2**(3/4), 239–247 (2006)
3. Criteria, C.: Common criteria for information technology security evaluation, version 2.3. Technical report ISO/IEC 15408:2005, Common Criteria (2005)
4. Directorate, I.A.: Protection profile for separation kernels in environments requiring high robustness. Technical report, U.S. Government, June 2007
5. ARINC, Arinc specification 653–2: Avionics application software standard interface part 1 - required services. Technical report, Aeronautical Radio INC (2005)
6. Baumann, C., Beckert, B., Blasum, H., Bormer, T.: Better avionics software reliability by code verification a glance at code verification methodology in the verisoft xt project. In: Embedded World 2009 Conference (2009)
7. Klein, G., et al.: seL4: formal verification of an OS kernel. CACM **53**, 107–115 (2010)
8. Crespo, A., Ripoll, I., Masmano, M.: Partitioned embedded architecture based on hypervisor: The xtratum approach. In: Eighth European Dependable Computing Conference, EDCC-8 2010, Valencia, Spain, 28–30 April, pp. 67–72. IEEE Computer Society (2010)
9. Consortium, A.-I.: AIR II (2013). http://air.di.fc.ul.pt/air-ii/. Accessed 5 Nov 2013
10. Heitmeyer, C., Archer, M., Leonard, E., McLean, J.: Applying formal methods to a certifiably secure software system. IEEE Trans. Softw. Eng. **34**, 82–98 (2008)
11. Dam, M., Guanciale, R., Khakpour, N., Nemati, H., Schwarz, O.: Formal verification of information flow security for a simple arm-based separation kernel. In: Proceedings of the 2013 ACM SIGSAC Conference on Computer & #38; Communications Security, CCS '13, pp. 223–234 (2013)
12. de Amorim, A.A., Collins, N., DeHon, A., Demange, D., Hritcu, C., Pichardie, D., Pierce, B.C., Pollack, R., Tolmach, A.: A verified information-flow architecture. In: 41st ACM SIGPLAN-SIGACT Symposium on Principles of Programming Languages (POPL) (2014)
13. de Ferluc, R.: Report D10 – TSP Services Specification. IMA-SP/D10 Issue 2.1, ESTEC. Contract ESTEC 4000100764, March 2012
14. Butterfield, A., Sanan, D.: Reference specification for a partitioning kernel and a separation kernel. Technical Report Version 4.1, Lero. ESTEC Contract No. 4000106016, 3 parts: MTOBSE_D03i4-SRS,-ICD,-ADD (2013)
15. Abadi, M., Lamport, L.: The existence of refinement mappings. Theor. Comput. Sci. **82**, 253–284 (1991)
16. Alves-Foss, J., Rinker, B., Benke, M., Marshall, J., O'Connel, P., Taylor, C.: The idaho partitioning machine. Technical report (2002)
17. Paulson, L.C. (ed.): Isabelle: A Generic Theorem Prover. LNCS, vol. 828. Springer, Heidelberg (1994)
18. Winwood, S., Klein, G., Sewell, T., Andronick, J., Cock, D., Norrish, M.: Mind the gap: a verification framework for low-level C. In: Berghofer, S., Nipkow, T., Urban, C., Wenzel, M. (eds.) TPHOLs 2009. LNCS, vol. 5674, pp. 500–515. Springer, Heidelberg (2009)
19. Berghofer, S., Wenzel, M.: Inductive datatypes in HOL - lessons learned in formal-logic engineering. In: Bertot, Y., Dowek, G., Hirschowitz, A., Paulin, C., Théry, L. (eds.) TPHOLs 1999. LNCS, vol. 1690, p. 19. Springer, Heidelberg (1999)

20. C. SPARC International Inc., The SPARC architecture manual: version 8. Upper Saddle River, NJ, USA: Prentice-Hall Inc. (1992)
21. Saltzer, J.H., Schroeder, M.D.: The protection of information in computer systems. Proc. IEEE **63**, 1278–1308 (1975)

Separation Algebras for C Verification in Coq

Robbert Krebbers[(✉)]

ICIS, Radboud University Nijmegen, Nijmegen, The Netherlands
mail@robbertkrebbers.nl

Abstract. Separation algebras are a well-known abstraction to capture common structure of both permissions and memories in programming languages, and form the basis of models of separation logic. As part of the development of a formal version of an operational and axiomatic semantics of the C11 standard, we present a variant of separation algebras that is well suited for C verification.

Our variant of separation algebras has been fully formalized using the Coq proof assistant, together with a library of concrete implementations. These instances are used to build a complex permission model, and a memory model that captures the strict aliasing restrictions of C.

1 Introduction

Separation logic [19] is widely used to reason about imperative programs that use mutable data structures and pointers. Its key feature is the *separating conjunction* $P * Q$ that allows to split the memory into two disjoint parts; a part described by P, and another part described by Q. The separating conjunction is used for example in the *frame rule*.

$$\frac{\{P\}\, s\, \{Q\}}{\{P * R\}\, s\, \{Q * R\}}$$

This rule enables local reasoning about parts of a program. Given a Hoare triple $\{P\}\, s\, \{Q\}$, this rule makes it possible to derive that the triple also holds when the memory is extended with a disjoint part described by R.

In previous work, we have extended separation logic to deal with intricate features of the C programming language. In [15] we have extended separation logic to support non-local control flow in the presence of block scope variables (with pointers to those), and in [13] we have extended that separation logic to deal with non-determinism and sequence points in C.

A shortcoming of this first version of our separation logic for C is its rather basic memory model that merely supports integers and pointers, but no array, struct, and union types. In order to support these data-types together with the *strict-aliasing restrictions* of C11 [10, 6.5p6-7], which allow compilers to perform type-based alias analysis, one needs a rich memory model. For that reason, we have developed a memory model based on forests structured according to the shape of data types in C to accurately describe these restrictions [12].

In this paper, we will show how separation algebras are used for the integration of our separation logic and our memory model.

© Springer International Publishing Switzerland 2014
D. Giannakopoulou and D. Kroening (Eds.): VSTTE 2014, LNCS 8471, pp. 150–166, 2014.
DOI: 10.1007/978-3-319-12154-3_10

Separation logic for C. The key observation of our separation logic in [13] is the correspondence between non-determinism in expressions and a form of concurrency. Inspired by the rule for the parallel composition [18], we have the following kinds of rules for each operator ⊚.

$$\frac{\{P_1\}\, e_1\, \{Q_1\} \qquad \{P_2\}\, e_2\, \{Q_2\}}{\{P_1 * P_2\}\, e_1 \circledcirc e_2\, \{Q_1 * Q_2\}}$$

The intuitive idea of the above rule is that if the memory can be split up into two parts, in which the subexpressions e_1 respectively e_2 can be executed safely, then the full expression $e_1 \circledcirc e_2$ can be executed safely in the whole memory. Since the separating conjunction ensures that both parts of the memory do not have overlapping parts that will be written to, it is guaranteed that no interference of the side-effects of e_1 and e_2 occurs. It thus effectively rules out expressions as (*p = 3) + (*p = 4) that have undefined behavior [10, 6.5p2].

Our separation logic uses permissions [4], and therefore the singleton assertion has the shape $e_1 \overset{x}{\mapsto} e_2$ where x is the permission of the object e_2 at address e_1. Fractional permissions [5] are used to make sharing of read only memory of multiple subexpressions possible. This is needed in *p + *p for example.

Permissions are also used to keep track of whether an object has been locked due to a previous assignment. This is needed to ensure that no undefined behavior because of a sequent point violation occurs (modifying an object in memory more than once between two sequence points). Furthermore, since C only allows pointer arithmetic on addresses that exist (*i.e.* have not been deallocated), we need *existence permissions*. Bornat *et al.* [4] left existence permissions for future work, but our permission model incorporates these.

Since permissions are used to account for various constraints, they become very complex, especially when used in a memory model for a real-world language like C. We will use separation algebras to factor out common structure and to build the permission and memory model in a more compositional way.

Approach. Separation algebras, as originally defined by Calcagno *et al.* [6], are used as models of separation logic. Given a *separation algebra*, which is a partial cancellative commutative monoid $(A, \emptyset, \cup)$, a shallow embedding of separation logic with assertions $P, Q : A \to$ Prop can be defined as:

$$\mathsf{emp} := \lambda x \,.\, x = \emptyset$$
$$P * Q := \lambda x \,.\, \exists x_1\, x_2 \,.\, x = x_1 \cup x_2 \wedge P\, x_1 \wedge Q\, x_2$$

The prototypical instance of a separation algebra is a heap, where $\emptyset$ is the empty heap, and $\cup$ the disjoint union. Other useful instances include the booleans (bool, false, $\vee$) and fractional permissions $([0,1]_\mathbb{Q}, 0, +)$ [4,5] where 0 denotes no access, 1 exclusive access, and $0 < \_ < 1$ read-only access. Separation algebras are closed under various many (products, finite functions, *etc.*), and hence complex instances can be built compositionally.

When formalizing separation algebras in the Coq proof assistant, we quickly ran into some problems:

1. Dealing with partial operations is cumbersome.
2. Dealing with subsets types (modeled as Σ-types) is inconvenient.
3. Operations like the difference operation $\setminus$ cannot be defined constructively from just the laws of a separation algebra.

To deal with problem 1 of partiality, we turn $\cup$ into a total binary operation, and axiomatize a binary relation $x \perp y$ that describes that x and y are *disjoint*. Only if $x \perp y$ holds, $x \cup y$ is required to satisfy the algebraic laws.

Problem 2 already appears in the simple case of fractional permissions $[0, 1]_\mathbb{Q}$, where the $\cup$-operation (here $+$) can 'overflow'. We remedy this problem by having all operations operate on pre-terms (here $\mathbb{Q}$) and axiomatize a predicate valid that describes that a pre-term is valid (here $0 \leq \_ \leq 1$).

Although problems 1 and 2 seem relatively minor for trivial separation algebras like Booleans and fractional permissions, these problems become more evident for more complex (recursive) separation algebras like those that appear in our memory model. Our approach makes using plain ML/Haskell-style types possible. In order to deal with problem 3, we axiomatize the relation $\subseteq$ and the operation $\setminus$. Using a choice operator, the $\setminus$-operation can be defined in terms of $\cup$, but in Coq (without axioms) that is impossible.

Since the aforementioned problems merely concern ease of formalization, our solution so far is just a different form of presentation and does not fundamentally change the notion of a separation algebra. Although our solution results in more laws, these are generally trivial to prove. Moreover, we describe some machinery to deal with the additional conditions.

A more fundamental problem is that the standard definition of a separation algebra allows for very strange instances that do not correspond to a reasonable separation logic. To that end, Dockins *et al.* [8] have described various restrictions of separation algebras: splittability, positivity, disjointness, *etc.* Of course, we rather avoid the need to formalize a complex algebraic hierarchy in Coq. Hence, we define *one* variant that fits our whole development.

Our variant also includes additional features to abstractly describe exclusive ownership, which is needed for our permission and memory model.

Related work. Separation algebras were originally defined by Calcagno *et al.* [6], but their work dealt with a rather idealized language, and was not aimed at formalization in proof assistants. However, many researchers have used separation algebras and separation logic for realistic languages in proof assistants.

Dockins *et al.* [8] have formalized separation algebras together with various restrictions in Coq. They have dealt with the issue of partiality by treating $\cup$ as a relation instead of a function. However, this is unnatural, because equational reasoning becomes impossible and one has to name all auxiliary results.

Bengtson *et al.* [2] formalized separation algebras in Coq to reason about object-oriented programs. They have defined $\cup$ as a partial function, and did not define any complex permission models. Yet another formalization of separation algebras is by Klein *et al.* [11] using the Isabelle proof assistant. Their approach to partial operations is similar to ours. Section 2 contains a comparison.

In our previous paper on a separation logic for non-determinism and sequence points in C [13] we used an extension of *permission algebras* to describe permissions abstractly. Separation algebras are more general: the previous abstraction contained notions specific to permissions, and therefore the memory model itself was not an instance. Moreover, separation algebras include an ∅-element, which is necessary to split the trees of our memory model. The permission model that we present in this paper is based on our previous one [13], but it is built more compositionally, and it supports existence permissions.

There has been a significant amount of previous work on formalized memory models for the C programming language, most notably by Leroy *et al.* [17] and Beringer *et al.* [3] in the context of the CompCert compiler [16]. However, no previous memory models apart from our own [12] have taken the strict aliasing restrictions of C11 into account. Thus, in particular no previous work has dealt with separation logic for such a memory model.

Contribution. Our contribution is fivefold:

- We define a variant of separation algebras that works well in Coq (Sect. 2).
- We present a complex permission model for an operational and axiomatic semantics of the C programming language (Sects. 3 and 4).
- We present a generalization of the memory model that we described in [12] and show that it forms a separation algebra (Sect. 5).
- We present an algebraic method to reason about disjointness (Sect. 6).
- All proofs have been formalized using the Coq proof assistant (Sect. 7).

Because this paper is part of a large formalization effort, we often omit details and proofs. The interested reader can find all details online as part of the Coq development at http://robbertkrebbers.nl/research/ch2o.

2   Simple Separation Algebras

We first describe our version of separation algebras that is equivalent to traditional non-trivial, positive, and cancellative separation algebras.

Definition 2.1. *A simple separation algebra consists of a set A, with:*

- *An element $\emptyset : A$*
- *A predicate* valid $: A \to$ Prop
- *Binary relations* $\perp, \subseteq\; : A \to A \to$ Prop
- *Binary operations* $\cup, \setminus\; : A \to A \to A$

Satisfying the following laws:

1. *If $x \perp y$, then $y \perp x$ and $x \cup y = y \cup x$*
2. *If* valid x, *then $\emptyset \perp x$ and $\emptyset \cup x = x$*
3. *If $x \perp y$ and $x \cup y \perp z$, then*
   (a) *$y \perp z$, $x \perp y \cup z$ and*
   (b) *$x \cup (y \cup z) = (x \cup y) \cup z$*

4. If $z \perp x$, $z \perp y$ and $z \cup x = z \cup y$, then $x = y$
5. If $x \perp y$, then valid x and valid $(x \cup y)$
6. There exists an $x \neq \emptyset$ with valid x
7. If $x \perp y$ and $x \cup y = \emptyset$, then $x = \emptyset$
8. If $x \perp y$, then $x \subseteq x \cup y$
9. If $x \subseteq y$, then $x \perp y \setminus x$ and $x \cup y \setminus x = y$

To deal with partiality, we turned $\cup$ into a total operation. Only if x and y are *disjoint*, notation $x \perp y$, we require $x \cup y$ to satisfy the algebraic laws.

Laws 2–4 describe the traditional laws of a separation algebra: identity, commutativity, associativity, and cancellativity. Law 5 ensures that valid is closed under $\cup$. Law 6 ensures that the separation algebra is non-trivial, together with law 5 this yields valid $\emptyset$. Law 7 describes positivity, and laws 8 and 9 fully axiomatize the $\subseteq$-relation and $\setminus$-operation. Using positivity and cancellativity, we obtain that $\subseteq$ is a partial order and that $\cup$ is order preserving and respecting.

Definition 2.2. *The* simple Boolean separation algebra bool *is defined as:*

$$\text{valid } x := \text{True} \qquad\qquad \emptyset := \text{false}$$
$$x \perp y := \neg x \vee \neg y \qquad\qquad x \cup y := x \vee y$$
$$x \subseteq y := x \rightarrow y \qquad\qquad x \setminus y := x \wedge \neg y$$

Boyland's fractional permissions $[0, 1]_\mathbb{Q}$ [5] where 0 denotes no access, 1 exclusive access, and $0 < \_ < 1$ read-only access, form a simple separation algebra.

Definition 2.3. *The* simple fractional separation algebra $\mathbb{Q}$ *is defined as:*

$$\text{valid } x := 0 \leq x \leq 1 \qquad\qquad \emptyset := 0$$
$$x \perp y := 0 \leq x, y \wedge x + y \leq 1 \qquad\qquad x \cup y := x + y$$
$$x \subseteq y := 0 \leq x \leq y \leq 1 \qquad\qquad x \setminus y := x - y$$

The version of separation algebras by Klein *et al.* [11] in Isabelle also treats $\cup$ as a total operation and uses a relation $\perp$. There are some differences:

1. We include a predicate valid to prevent having to deal with subset types.
2. They have weaker premises for associativity (law 3b), namely $x \perp y$, $y \perp z$ and $x \perp z$ instead of $x \perp y$ and $x \cup y \perp z$. Ours are more natural, *e.g.* for fractional permissions one has $0.5 \perp 0.5$ but not $0.5 + 0.5 \perp 0.5$, and it thus makes no sense to require $0.5 \cup (0.5 \cup 0.5) = (0.5 \cup 0.5) \cup 0.5$ to hold.
3. We axiomatize $\setminus$ because Coq does not have a choice operator.

3   Permissions and Separation Logic for C

Our semantics for the C programming language needs a complex permission system to account for whether certain operations are allowed or not. We classify the C permissions using the following *permission kinds*.

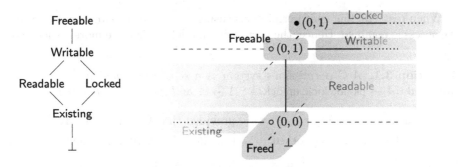

Fig. 1. Left: the lattice of permission kinds. Right: the actual permissions.

- Freeable. All operations (reading, writing, deallocation) are allowed.
- Writable. Just reading and writing is allowed.
- Readable. Solely reading is allowed.
- Existing. Objects with permissions of this kind are allowed to have pointers to them, which can be used for pointer arithmetic but cannot be dereferenced. Permissions of this kind are called *existence permissions* in [4].
- Locked. Permissions of this kind are used temporarily for objects that have been locked due to a write. The original permission of these objects will be restored at a subsequent sequence point [13].
  For example, in (x = 3) + (*p = 4); the assignment x = 3 will lock the object x. The purpose of this lock is to describe the *sequence point restriction* of C that disallows to assign to the same object multiple times during the execution of the same expression. Hence, if p points to x, the expression will have undefined behavior. At the sequence point ;, the object x will be unlocked, and its original permission will thereby be restored.
- ⊥. No operations are allowed at all, and pointers to objects with permission of this kind are indeterminate. For example, free(p); return (p-p); has undefined behavior. After the call to free, the pointer p refers to an object with a permission of kind ⊥. Therefore, p becomes indeterminate [10, 6.2.4p2], and cannot be used for pointer arithmetic anymore.

As displayed in Fig. 1, permission kinds form a lattice (pkind, ⊆) where $k_1 \subseteq k_2$ expresses that k_1 allows fewer operations than k_2. We use permission kinds as an abstract view of the permission model to allow the operational semantics to determine if certain operations are allowed. However, for our separation logic we have to deal with sharing. This is needed to:

- Split a Writable or Readable permission into Readable ones. This is needed in x + x where both parts require read ownership of x.
- Split a Freeable permission into an Existing and Writable one. This is needed in *(p + 1) = *p = 1 where one part requires write ownership of *p, and another performs pointer arithmetic on p (which is only allowed if *p exists).

When reassembling split permissions (using $\cup$), we need to know when exclusive access is regained. Hence, the permission model needs to be more structured.

Definition 3.1. *A* C permissions system *is a separation algebra* A *with functions* kind $: A \to$ pkind, lock, unlock, $\frac{1}{2} : A \to A$ *and* token $: A$ *satisfying:*

$$\text{unlock (lock } x) = x \qquad \text{provided that Writable} \subseteq \text{kind } x \qquad (1)$$

$$\text{kind (lock } x) = \text{Locked} \qquad \text{provided that Writable} \subseteq \text{kind } x \qquad (2)$$

$$\text{kind}\left(\tfrac{1}{2}x\right) = \begin{cases} \text{Readable} & \text{if Writable} \subseteq \text{kind } x \\ \text{kind } x & \text{otherwise} \end{cases} \qquad (3)$$

$$\text{kind token} = \text{Existing} \qquad (4)$$

$$\text{kind } (x \setminus \text{token}) = \begin{cases} \text{Writable} & \text{if kind } x = \text{Freeable} \\ \text{kind } x & \text{if Existing} \subset \text{kind } x \end{cases} \qquad (5)$$

The $\frac{1}{2}$-operation is used to split a Writable or Readable permission x into two Readable permissions $\frac{1}{2}x$. Permissions of kind Locked cannot be split using $\frac{1}{2}$ because such permissions require exclusive write ownership. The $\setminus$-operation is used to take an *existence permission* token of some permission. In particular, it is used to split a Freeable permission x into an Existing permission token and Writable permission $x \setminus$ token. The existence permission token has kind Existing and thus allows solely pointer arithmetic.

A possible permission model satisfying these laws is (a subset of) the following three dimensional space:

$$\{\text{Freed}\} + \{\circ, \bullet\} \times \mathbb{Q} \times [0, 1]_{\mathbb{Q}}.$$

Figure 1 displays how the elements of this model project onto their kinds. This permission model combines fractional permissions to account for read/write ownership with counting permissions to account for the number of existence permissions (*i.e.* tokens) that have been handed out. The annotations $\{\circ, \bullet\}$ describe whether a permission is locked $\bullet$ or not $\circ$. Although counting permissions are traditionally modeled by natural numbers [4], our model uses rational numbers to allow the counting part to be splittable as well.

Our organization of permissions is inspired by CompCert [17], but has the additional Locked node. Since CompCert only deals with an operational semantics for C, it does not need to make a distinction between permissions and permission kinds. Therefore, a coarse permission model suffices.

4   Extended Separation Algebras

In this section we extend simple separation algebras with some features that will be used for our memory model. Moreover, we present various instances of separation algebras that will be used to contruct a C permission system.

Definition 4.1. *A* separation algebra *extends a* simple separation algebra *with:*

- *Predicates* splittable, unmapped, unshared $: A \rightarrow$ Prop
- *A unary operation* $\frac{1}{2} : A \rightarrow A$

Satisfying the following laws:

10. *If* $x \perp x$, *then* splittable $(x \cup x)$
11. *If* splittable x, *then* $\frac{1}{2}x \perp \frac{1}{2}x$ *and* $\frac{1}{2}x \cup \frac{1}{2}x = x$
12. *If* splittable y *and* $x \subseteq y$, *then* splittable x
13. *If* $x \perp y$ *and* splittable $(x \cup y)$, *then* $\frac{1}{2}(x \cup y) = \frac{1}{2}x \cup \frac{1}{2}y$
14. unmapped $\emptyset$, *and if* unmapped x, *then* valid x
15. *If* unmapped y *and* $x \subseteq y$, *then* unmapped x
16. *If* $x \perp y$, unmapped x *and* unmapped y, *then* unmapped $(x \cup y)$
17. unshared x *iff* valid x *and for all* y *with* $x \perp y$ *we have* unmapped y

The predicate unmapped describes whether storage with given permission is allowed to contain content or should be empty. Dually, unshared x describes whether a permission x has exclusive ownership of its storage. This means that all permissions disjoint to x do not allow their storage to contain content. The following table describes how the C permissions are classified using the predicates unmapped and unshared.

unshared	unmapped	Examples
		Readable permissions
	✓	The $\emptyset$ permission and Existing permissions
✓		Freeable, Writable and Locked permissions
✓	✓	The Freed permission

For separation algebras where unmapped and unshared make no sense (for example, the memory model in Sect. 5), we let unmapped $x := x = \emptyset$ and unshared $x :=$ False. These definitions trivially satisfy laws 14–17.

The $\frac{1}{2}$-operation is partial because permissions without read ownership (for example those of kind Locked) cannot be split. Similar to the treatment of $\cup$, we turn $\frac{1}{2}$ into a total function and let splittable describe if a permission can be split (laws 10 and 11). Law 12 makes sure that splittable permissions are infinitely splittable, and law 13 ensures that $\frac{1}{2}$ distributes over $\cup$.

Definition 4.2. *The* Boolean separation algebra bool *is extended with:*

$$\text{splittable } x := \neg x \qquad\qquad \frac{1}{2}x := x$$
$$\text{unmapped } x := \neg x \qquad\qquad \text{unshared } x := x$$

Definition 4.3. *The* fractional separation algebra $\mathbb{Q}$ *is extended with:*

$$\text{splittable } x := 0 \leq x \leq 1 \qquad\qquad \tfrac{1}{2}x := 0.5 \cdot x$$
$$\text{unmapped } x := x = 0 \qquad\qquad \text{unshared } x := x = 1$$

A crucial part of the C permissions is the ability to lock permissions after an assignment to describe the sequence point restriction [13]. The *lockable separation algebra* adds annotations $\{\circ, \bullet\}$ to account for whether a permission is locked $\bullet$ or not $\circ$. Permissions that are locked have exclusive write ownership, and are thus only disjoint from those that do not allow content.

Definition 4.4. *Given a separation algebra A, the* lockable separation algebra $\mathcal{L}(A) := \{\circ, \bullet\} \times A$ *over A is defined as:*

$$\text{valid } (\circ\, x) := \text{valid } x \qquad\qquad \text{valid } (\bullet\, x) := \text{unshared } x$$
$$\emptyset := \circ\, \emptyset$$
$$\circ x \perp \circ y := x \perp y \qquad\qquad \circ x \perp \bullet y := x \perp y \wedge \text{unmapped } x \wedge \text{unshared } y$$
$$\bullet x \perp \bullet y := \text{False} \qquad\qquad \bullet x \perp \circ y := x \perp y \wedge \text{unshared } x \wedge \text{unmapped } y$$
$$\circ x \cup \circ y := \circ\,(x \cup y) \qquad\qquad \circ x \cup \bullet y := \bullet\,(x \cup y)$$
$$\bullet x \cup \bullet y := \bullet\,(x \cup y) \qquad\qquad \bullet x \cup \circ y := \bullet\,(x \cup y)$$

We omitted the definition of some relations and operations in the previous and coming definitions due to space restrictions.

The C permission model needs existence permissions that allow pointer arithmetic but do not supply read or write ownership. The *counting separation algebra* over A has elements (x, y) with $x \in \mathbb{Q}$ and $y \in A$. Here, x counts the number of existence permissions that have been handed out. Existence permissions are elements $(x, \emptyset)$ with $x < 0$. To ensure that the counting separation algebra is closed under $\cup$ and preserves splittability, the counter x is rational.

Definition 4.5. *We let z_1 and z_2 denote the first and second projection of z.*

Definition 4.6. *Given a separation algebra A, the* counting separation algebra $\mathcal{C}(A) := \mathbb{Q} \times A$ *over A is defined as:*

$$\text{valid } x := \text{valid } x_2 \wedge (\text{unmapped } x_2 \to x_1 \leq 0) \wedge (\text{unshared } x_2 \to 0 \leq x_1)$$
$$\emptyset := (0, \emptyset)$$
$$x \perp y := x_2 \perp y_2 \wedge (\text{unmapped } x_2 \to x_1 \leq 0) \wedge (\text{unmapped } y_2 \to y_1 \leq 0)$$
$$\wedge (\text{unshared } (x_2 \cup y_2) \to 0 \leq x_1 + y_1)$$
$$x \cup y := (x_1 + y_1, x_2 \cup y_2)$$

Finally, we need to extend permissions with a permission Freed to keep track of whether storage has been deallocated. Deallocated storage is not allowed to contain any content, and pointers to deallocated storage are indeterminate and thereby cannot be used for pointer arithmetic.

Definition 4.7. *Given a separation algebra A, the* freeable separation algebra $\mathcal{F}(A) := \{\text{Freed}\} + A$ *over A is defined by extending the separation algebra with:*

$$\text{valid Freed} := \text{True} \qquad\qquad x \perp \text{Freed} := x = \emptyset$$

$$\text{Freed} \perp \text{Freed} := \text{False} \qquad\qquad \text{Freed} \perp y := y = \emptyset$$

$$x \cup \text{Freed} := \text{Freed}$$

$$\text{Freed} \cup \text{Freed} := \text{Freed} \qquad\qquad \text{Freed} \cup y := \text{Freed}$$

$$\text{unmapped Freed} := \text{True} \qquad\qquad \text{unshared Freed} := \text{True}$$

Combining the previous separation algebras, we now define the C permission model. It is easy to verify that it satisfies the laws of Definition 3.1.

Definition 4.8. C permissions *are defined as*

$$\text{perm} := \mathcal{F}(\mathcal{L}(\mathcal{C}(\mathbb{Q})))$$

with:

$$\text{kind } z := \begin{cases} \text{Freeable} & \text{if } z = \circ\,(0,\,1) \\ \text{Writable} & \text{if } z = \circ\,(x,\,1) \text{ with } x \neq 0 \\ \text{Readable} & \text{if } z = \circ\,(x,\,y) \text{ with } 0 < y < 1 \\ \text{Existing} & \text{if } z = \circ\,(x,\,0) \text{ with } x \neq 0 \\ \text{Locked} & \text{if } z = \bullet\,(x,\,y) \\ \perp & \text{otherwise} \end{cases}$$

$$\text{lock } z := \begin{cases} \bullet\,(x,\,y) & \text{if } z = \circ\,(x,\,y) \\ z & \text{otherwise} \end{cases}$$

$$\text{unlock } z := \begin{cases} \circ\,(x,\,y) & \text{if } z = \bullet\,(x,\,y) \\ z & \text{otherwise} \end{cases}$$

$$\text{token} := \circ\,(-1,\,0)$$

5 The C Memory Model and Strict Aliasing

In *type-based alias analysis*, type information is used to determine whether pointers are aliased or not. Consider:

```
float f(int *p, float *q) { float x = *q; *p = 10; return x; }
```

Here, a compiler should be able to assume that p and q are not aliased because their types differ. However, the (static) type system of C is too weak to enforce this restriction since a union type can be used to call f with aliased pointers.

```
union INT_FLT { int x; float y; } u = { .y = 3.14 };
f(&u.x, &u.y);
```

A union is the C version of the sum type, but contrary to traditional sum types, unions are *untagged* instead of *tagged*. This means that the variant of a union cannot be obtained. Unions destroy the property that each memory area has a unique type that is statically known. The *effective type* [10, 6.5p6-7] of a memory area hence depends on the *run-time behavior* of the program.

The *strict-aliasing restrictions* of C11 [10, 6.5p6-7] ensure that a pointer to a variant of a union type (not to the whole union itself) can only be used for an access (a read or store) if the union has that particular variant. Calling g with aliased pointers (as in the example where u has the y variant, and is accessed through a pointer p to the x variant) results in undefined behavior.

Under certain circumstances it is nonetheless allowed to access a union using a pointer to another variant than its current one, this is called *type-punning* [10, 6.5.2.3]. For example, the function g has defined behavior (on architectures with size_of(int) ≤ size_of(float) and where ints do not have trap values):

```
int g() { union INT_FLT u; u.y = 3.0; return u.x; }
```

Type-punning may only be performed directly via an l-value of union type. The function h below thus exhibits undefined behavior because type-punning is performed indirectly via a pointer p to a variant of the union.

```
int h() { union INT_FLT u; int *p = &u.x; u.y = 3.0; return *p; }
```

Significant existing formal versions of C (*e.g.* those by Leroy *et al.* [17] and Ellison and Rosu [9]) model the memory as a finite partial function to objects, where each object consists of an array of bytes. Since these existing formal versions of C do not keep track of the variants of unions, they cannot capture the strict-aliasing restrictions of C11.

Instead of using an array of bytes to represent the contents of each object, our memory model [12] uses structured trees that have arrays of bits that represent base values (integers and pointers) on the leafs. This modification captures the strict-aliasing restrictions: effective types are modeled by the state of these trees.

A generalization of our memory model [12], where the leafs of the trees are elements of a separation algebra instead of just bits, forms a separation algebra. The original version of the memory model can be re-obtained by instantiating the generalized version with (permission annotated) bits.

Definition 5.1. C-trees *over a separation algebra A are defined as:*

$$w \in \text{ctree } A ::= \text{base}_{\tau_b} \vec{x} \mid \text{array}_\tau \vec{w} \mid \text{struct}_s \overrightarrow{w \vec{x}} \mid \text{union}_u (i, w, \vec{x}) \mid \overline{\text{union}_u \vec{x}}$$

where $x \in A$. C-maps (m $\in$ cmap A) are finite partial functions of a countable set of memory indexes (o $\in$ index) to pairs of booleans and C-trees.

In the above definition, $s, u \in$ tag range over struct and union names (called *tags*), $\tau_b \in$ basetype ranges over *base types* (signed char, unsigned int, $\tau*$, ...), and $\tau \in$ type ranges over *types* (τ_b, $\tau[n]$, struct s, union s).

C-trees have two kinds of union nodes: $\mathrm{union}_u\,(i, w, \vec{x})$ represents a union in a particular variant i with padding $\vec{x}$, and $\overline{\mathrm{union}_u}\,\vec{x}$ represents a union whose variant is unknown. Unions of the latter kind can be obtained by byte-wise copying and appear in uninitialized memory. When accessing (reading or writing) a union $\overline{\mathrm{union}_u}\,\vec{x}$ using a pointer to variant i, the bits $\vec{x}$ will be interpreted as a C-tree w of variant i, and the node is changed into $\mathrm{union}_u\,(i, w, \vec{x}')$ where $\vec{x}'$ corresponds to the remaining padding. It is important to note that the variant of a union is internal to the memory model, and should not be exposed through the operational semantics because an actual machine does not store it.

Padding between struct fields is stored in the current version of our memory model, whereas it was absent in the original version [12]. For the actual instantiation, we have defined a predicate in the Coq formalization to ensure that padding always consists of indeterminate bits so as to be C11 compliant[1].

The nodes (w, β) of C-maps are annotated with a boolean β to account for whether storage has been allocated dynamically using `malloc` (if $\beta = \mathsf{true}$) or statically as a block scope variable (if $\beta = \mathsf{false}$).

The original version of the memory model used specific nodes for objects that have been deallocated. In the current version we make it more uniform and represent such objects by a tree with Freed permissions at all leafs.

Definition 5.2. Bits *are defined as:*

$$b \in \mathsf{bit} ::= 1 \mid 0 \mid (\mathsf{ptr}\ p)_i \mid\ ?$$

where $p \in \mathsf{ptr}$ ranges over pointers represented as paths through C-trees (see [12] for the formal definition).

A bit is either a concrete bit 0 or 1, the ith fragment bit $(\mathsf{ptr}\ p)_i$ of a pointer p, or the indeterminate bit ?. As shown in Fig. 2, integers are represented by concrete sequences of bits, and pointers by sequences of fragments. This way of representing pointers is similar to Leroy *et al.* [17], but is on the level of bits instead of bytes. The actual bit representation flatten w of a C-tree w is obtained by flattening it. For the C-tree w_s in Fig. 2 we have:

$$\mathsf{flatten}\ w_s = 10000100\ 01000100\ ????????\ ????????\ (\mathsf{ptr}\ p)_0\ (\mathsf{ptr}\ p)_1 \ldots (\mathsf{ptr}\ p)_{31}$$

In order to re-obtain the actual memory model, we instantiate C-maps with permission annotated bits. For that, we use the *tagged separation algebra* that extends each element of an existing separation algebra with a tag.

---

[1] In particular: "When a value is stored in an object of structure or union type, including in a member object, the bytes of the object representation that correspond to any padding bytes take unspecified values" [10, 6.2.6.1p6].

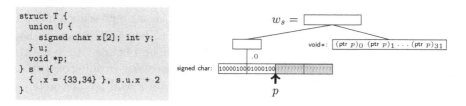

```
struct T {
  union U {
    signed char x[2]; int y;
  } u;
  void *p;
} s = {
  { .x = {33,34} }, s.u.x + 2
}
```

Fig. 2. The C-tree w_s corresponding to the object **s** declared in the C code on the left (on the x86 architecture). Permissions are omitted for simplicity.

Definition 5.3. *Given a separation algebra A and a set of tags T with default tag $t \in T$, the tagged separation algebra $\mathcal{T}_{t:T}(A) := A \times T$ over A is defined as:*

$$\text{valid } x := \text{valid } x_1 \wedge (\text{unmapped } x_1 \rightarrow x_2 = t)$$

$$\emptyset := (\emptyset, t)$$

$$x \perp y := x_1 \perp y_1 \wedge (\text{unmapped } x_1 \vee x_2 = y_2 \vee \text{unmapped } y_1)$$
$$\wedge (\text{unmapped } x_1 \rightarrow x_2 = t) \wedge (\text{unmapped } y_1 \rightarrow y_2 = t)$$

$$x \cup y := \begin{cases} (x_1 \cup y_1, y_2) & \text{if } x_2 = t \\ (x_1 \cup y_1, x_2) & \text{otherwise} \end{cases}$$

The tagged separation algebra $\mathcal{T}_{t:T}(A)$ ensures that each element $x \in A$ with unmapped x element has the default tag t. For the case of permission annotated bits $\mathcal{T}_{?:\text{bit}}(\text{perm})$, we use the symbolic bit ? that represents indeterminate storage as the default tag to ensure that unmapped permissions have no content.

Definition 5.4. The C memory *is defined as:*

$$\text{mem} := \text{cmap}\,(\mathcal{T}_{?:\text{bit}}(\mathcal{F}(\mathcal{L}(\mathcal{C}(\mathbb{Q}))))).$$

C-trees do not form a separation algebra because they do not have a single $\emptyset$ element (they have one for each type). However, apart from $\emptyset$ all other relations and operations can be defined by lifting those of the underlying separation algebra from the leafs to the trees. Defining the separation algebra structure on C-maps is then straightforward, the operations on the trees are lifted to finite functions, and the $\emptyset$ element is defined as the empty partial function.

The $\cup$-operation on (disjoint) C-trees is defined as follows:

$$\text{base}_{\tau_b} \vec{x}_1 \cup \text{base}_{\tau_b} \vec{x}_2 := \text{base}_{\tau_b} (\vec{x}_1 \cup \vec{x}_2)$$

$$\text{array}_\tau \vec{w}_1 \cup \text{array}_\tau \vec{w}_2 := \text{array}_\tau (\vec{w}_1 \cup \vec{w}_2)$$

$$\text{struct}_s \overrightarrow{w_1 \vec{x}_1} \cup \text{struct}_s \overrightarrow{w_2 \vec{x}_2} := \text{struct}_s (\overrightarrow{w_1 \vec{x}_1} \cup \overrightarrow{w_2 \vec{x}_2})$$

$$\text{union}_u (i, w_1, \vec{x}_1) \cup \text{union}_u (i, w_2, \vec{x}_2) := \text{union}_u (i, w_1 \cup w_2, \vec{x}_1 \cup \vec{x}_2)$$

$$\text{union}_u (i, w_1, \vec{x}_1) \cup \overline{\text{union}_u \vec{x}_2} := \text{merge}_\cup (\text{union}_u (i, w_1, \vec{x}_1)) \vec{x}_2$$

$$\overline{\text{union}_u \vec{x}_1} \cup \text{union}_u (i, w_2, \vec{x}_2) := \text{merge}_\cup (\text{union}_u (i, w_2, \vec{x}_2)) \vec{x}_1$$

Here, $\mathsf{merge}_f\ w\ \vec{x}$ yields a modified version of w in which the elements on the leaves are combined with $\vec{x}$ using the function f.

The above definition makes it possible to split storage of compound datatypes into smaller parts. However, splitting a union into a part with write ownership and a part with mere existence permissions is quite subtle because the variant of a union can change at run-time:

$$\mathsf{union}_u\,(i, w_1, \vec{x_1}) = \mathsf{union}_u\,(i, w_1', \vec{x_1'}) \cup \boxed{\text{part with existence permissions}}$$

$$\Downarrow \quad \text{switching from variant } i \text{ to } j$$

$$\mathsf{union}_u\,(j, w_2, \vec{x_2}) = \mathsf{union}_u\,(j, w_2', \vec{x_2'}) \cup \boxed{\text{part with existence permissions}}$$

Hence, for the part of a union that has mere existence permissions we always use the node $\overline{\mathsf{union}_u\ \vec{x}}$ with unknown variant. This restriction is enforced in the rules for disjointness and validity. Some representative rules are listed below:

$$\frac{\mathsf{valid}\ \vec{x}}{\mathsf{valid}\ (\overline{\mathsf{union}_u\ \vec{x}})} \qquad \frac{\mathsf{valid}\ w \quad \mathsf{valid}\ \vec{x} \quad \neg(\mathsf{unmapped}\ w \wedge \mathsf{unmapped}\ \vec{x})}{\mathsf{valid}\ (\mathsf{union}_u\,(i, w, \vec{x}))}$$

$$\frac{\mathsf{flatten}\ w_1 \mathbin{+\!\!+} \vec{x_1} \perp \vec{x_2} \quad \mathsf{valid}\ w_1 \quad \neg(\mathsf{unmapped}\ w_1 \wedge \mathsf{unmapped}\ \vec{x_1}) \quad \mathsf{unmapped}\ \vec{x_2}}{\mathsf{union}_u\,(i, w_1, \vec{x_1}) \perp \overline{\mathsf{union}_u\ \vec{x_2}}}$$

Since operations that change the variant (type-punning and byte-wise copying) are only allowed if the entire union has exclusive write ownership, the constraint $\mathsf{unmapped}\ \vec{x}_2$ ensures that disjointness is preserved under such operations.

6   Reasoning About Disjointness

For the soundness proof of the axiomatic semantics in [13] we often had to reason about preservation of disjointness under memory operations. To ease that kind of reasoning, we have defined some machinery. In this section we will show that the machinery of [13] extends to any separation algebra.

Definition 6.1. *Disjointness of a sequence $\vec{x}$, notation $\perp \vec{x}$, is defined as:*

1. $\perp[\,]$
2. If $x \perp \bigcup \vec{x}$ and $\perp \vec{x}$, then $\perp (x :: \vec{x})$

Notice that $\perp \vec{x}$ is stronger than merely having $x_i \perp x_j$ for each $i \neq j$. For example, using fractional permissions, we do not have $\perp[0.5, 0.5, 0.5]$ whereas we clearly do have $0.5 \perp 0.5$. Using disjointness of sequences we can for example state the associativity law (law 3 of Definition 2.1) in a more symmetric way:

$$\text{if } \perp[x, y, z] \quad \text{then} \quad x \cup (y \cup z) = (x \cup y) \cup z.$$

Next, we define a relation $\vec{x}_1 \equiv_\perp \vec{x}_2$ that captures that sequences $\vec{x}_1$ and $\vec{x}_2$ behave equivalently with respect to disjointness.

Definition 6.2. Equivalence of $\vec{x_1}$ and $\vec{x_2}$ with respect to disjointness, *notation* $\vec{x_1} \equiv_\perp \vec{x_2}$, *is defined as:*

$$\vec{x_1} \leq_\perp \vec{x_2} := \forall x \,.\, \perp (x :: \vec{x_1}) \to \perp (x :: \vec{x_2})$$
$$\vec{x_1} \equiv_\perp \vec{x_2} := \vec{x_1} \leq_\perp \vec{x_2} \wedge \vec{x_2} \leq_\perp \vec{x_1}$$

It is straightforward to show that $\leq_\perp$ is reflexive and transitive, is respected by concatenation of sequences, and is preserved by list containment. Hence, $\equiv_\perp$ is an equivalence relation, a congruence with respect to concatenation of sequences, and is preserved by permutations. The following results allow us to reason algebraically about disjointness.

Lemma 6.3. *If* $\vec{x_1} \leq_\perp \vec{x_2}$, *then* $\perp \vec{x_1}$ *implies* $\perp \vec{x_2}$.

Lemma 6.4. *If* $\vec{x_1} \equiv_\perp \vec{x_2}$, *then* $\perp \vec{x_1}$ *if and only if* $\perp \vec{x_2}$.

Theorem 6.5. *We have the following algebraic properties:*

$$\emptyset :: \vec{x} \equiv_\perp \vec{x} \tag{6}$$

$$(x_1 \cup x_2) :: \vec{x} \equiv_\perp x_1 :: x_2 :: \vec{x} \qquad \text{provided that } x_1 \perp x_2 \tag{7}$$

$$\bigcup \vec{x_1} :: \vec{x_2} \equiv_\perp \vec{x_1} \mathbin{+\!\!+} \vec{x_2} \qquad \text{provided that } \perp \vec{x_1} \tag{8}$$

$$x_2 :: \vec{x} \equiv_\perp x_1 :: (x_2 \setminus x_1) :: \vec{x} \quad \text{provided that } x_1 \subseteq x_2 \tag{9}$$

7   Formalization in Coq

All proofs in this paper have been fully formalized using Coq [7]. We used Coq's notation mechanism combined with unicode symbols and type classes to let the code correspond as well as possible to the definitions in this paper. The Coq development contains many parts that are not described in this paper, including the features of the original memory model [12].

In the Coq development, we used Coq's setoid machinery [20] to conveniently rewrite using the relations $\leq_\perp$ and $\equiv_\perp$ (see Definition 6.2). Using this, we have implemented a tactic that automatically solves entailments of the form:

$$H_0 : \perp \vec{x_0}, \ \dots, \ H_n : \perp \vec{x_n} \quad \vdash \quad \perp \vec{x}$$

where $\vec{x}$ and $\vec{x_i}$ (for $i \leq n$) are arbitrary Coq expressions built from $\emptyset$, $\cup$ and $\bigcup$. This tactic works roughly as follows:

1. Simplify hypotheses using result 6–8 of Theorem 6.5.
2. Solve side-conditions by simplification using the same results and a solver for list containment (implemented by reflection).
3. Repeat these steps until no further simplification is possible.
4. Finally, solve the goal by simplification and list containment.

The Coq definitions corresponding to our memory model involve a lot of list surgery to translate between bit sequences and trees. To ease proofs about list surgery, we have developed a large library of general purpose theory. This library not only includes theory about lists, but also about finite sets, finite functions, and other data structures that are used heavily in the formalization.

8   Conclusions and Further Research

The eventual goal of this research is to develop an operational and axiomatic semantics (based on separation logic) for a large part of the C11 programming language [14]. This paper is an important step towards combining our separation logic [13,15] with our memory model [12]. However, a separation logic that can deal with the full (non-concurrent) C memory model remains future work.

For the operational semantics, one only needs a memory model that uses a coarse permission system, like the one used in CompCert [17]. In order to obtain a more concise operational semantics, one may therefore like to separate the memory model used in the operational semantics (with coarse permissions) from the one used in the axiomatic semantics (with rich permissions). The approach of *juicy memories* by Stewart and Appel [1, Chapter 42] might be useful.

It may be interesting to investigate what other permission models satisfy our requirements (see Definition 3.1). The permission model of Dockins *et al.* [8] may be a candidate.

Acknowledgments. I thank Freek Wiedijk and the anonymous referees for their helpful comments. This work is financed by NWO.

References

1. Appel, A.W. (ed.): Program Logics for Certified Compilers. Cambridge University Press, Cambridge (2014)
2. Bengtson, J., Jensen, J.B., Sieczkowski, F., Birkedal, L.: Verifying object-oriented programs with higher-order separation logic in Coq. In: van Eekelen, M., Geuvers, H., Schmaltz, J., Wiedijk, F. (eds.) ITP 2011. LNCS, vol. 6898, pp. 22–38. Springer, Heidelberg (2011)
3. Beringer, L., Stewart, G., Dockins, R., Appel, A.W.: Verified compilation for shared-memory C. In: Shao, Z. (ed.) ESOP 2014 (ETAPS). LNCS, vol. 8410, pp. 107–127. Springer, Heidelberg (2014)
4. Bornat, R., Calcagno, C., O'Hearn, P. W., Parkinson, M. J.: Permission accounting in separation logic. In: POPL, pp. 259–270 (2005)
5. Boyland, J.: Checking interference with fractional permissions. In: Cousot, R. (ed.) SAS 2003. LNCS, vol. 2694, pp. 55–72. Springer, Heidelberg (2003)
6. Calcagno, C., O'Hearn, P. W., Yangm, H.: Local action and abstract separation logic. In: LICS, pp. 366–378 (2007)
7. Coq Development Team. The Coq Proof Assistant Reference Manual (2012)
8. Dockins, R., Hobor, A., Appel, A.W.: A fresh look at separation algebras and share accounting. In: Hu, Z. (ed.) APLAS 2009. LNCS, vol. 5904, pp. 161–177. Springer, Heidelberg (2009)
9. Ellison, C., Rosu, G.: An executable formal semantics of C with applications. In: POPL, pp. 533–544 (2012)
10. International Organization for Standardization. ISO/IEC 9899-2011: Programming languages - C. ISO Working Group 14 (2012)
11. Klein, G., Kolanski, R., Boyton, A.: Mechanised separation algebra. In: Beringer, L., Felty, A. (eds.) ITP 2012. LNCS, vol. 7406, pp. 332–337. Springer, Heidelberg (2012)

12. Krebbers, R.: Aliasing restrictions of C11 formalized in Coq. In: Gonthier, G., Norrish, M. (eds.) CPP 2013. LNCS, vol. 8307, pp. 50–65. Springer, Heidelberg (2013)
13. Krebbers, R.: An operational and axiomatic semantics for non-determinism and sequence points in C. In: POPL, pp. 101–112 (2014)
14. Krebbers, R., Wiedijk, F.: A Formalization of the C99 Standard in HOL, Isabelle and Coq. In: Davenport, J.H., Farmer, W.M., Urban, J., Rabe, F. (eds.) MKM 2011 and Calculemus 2011. LNCS, vol. 6824, pp. 301–303. Springer, Heidelberg (2011)
15. Krebbers, R., Wiedijk, F.: Separation logic for non-local control flow and block scope variables. In: Pfenning, F. (ed.) FOSSACS 2013 (ETAPS 2013). LNCS, vol. 7794, pp. 257–272. Springer, Heidelberg (2013)
16. Leroy, X.: Formal verification of a realistic compiler. CACM **52**(7), 107–115 (2009)
17. Leroy, X., Appel, A.W., Blazy, S., Stewart, G.: The CompCert memory model, Version 2. Research report RR-7987, INRIA (2012)
18. O'Hearn, P.W.: Resources, concurrency and local reasoning. In: Gardner, P., Yoshida, N. (eds.) CONCUR 2004. LNCS, vol. 3170, pp. 49–67. Springer, Heidelberg (2004)
19. O'Hearn, P.W., Reynolds, J.C., Yang, H.: Local reasoning about programs that alter data structures. In: Fribourg, L. (ed.) CSL 2001 and EACSL 2001. LNCS, vol. 2142, pp. 1–19. Springer, Heidelberg (2001)
20. Sozeau, M.: A new look at generalized rewriting in type theory. J. Formal Reasoning **2**(1), 41–62 (2010)

Automatically Verified Implementation of Data Structures Based on AVL Trees

Martin Clochard[1,2]([✉])

[1] Ecole Normale Supérieure, 75005 Paris, France
[2] Univ. Paris-Sud and INRIA Saclay and LRI-CNRS, 91405 Orsay, France
martin.clochard@lri.fr

Abstract. We propose verified implementations of several data structures, including random-access lists and ordered maps. They are derived from a common parametric implementation of self-balancing binary trees in the style of Adelson-Velskii and Landis trees. The development of the specifications, implementations and proofs is carried out using the Why3 environment. The originality of this approach is the genericity of the specifications and code combined with a high level of proof automation.

1 Introduction

Formal specification and verification of the functional behavior of complex data structures like collections of elements is known to be challenging [1,2]. In particular, tree data structures were considered in many formal developments using various verification environments. In this paper, we consider self-balancing binary trees, in the style of the so-called AVL trees invented by Adelson-Velskii and Landis [3]. We design a generic implementation of these self-balancing trees from which we derive and verify three instances: random access lists, ordered maps and mergeable priority queues. To reach the appropriate level of genericity in the common part of this development we use an abstract binary search mechanism, based in particular on a notion of monoidal measure on stored data. This notion is shared with an approach proposed by Hinze and Paterson [4] for the development of another general-purpose tree data structure they called *finger trees*. This abstraction allows us to clearly separate the concepts of balanced trees on one hand and search trees on the other hand.

Our development is conducted using the Why3 program verifier, and automated theorem provers to discharge proof obligations. The genericity of the development is obtained by using a *module cloning* mechanism of Why3, which we present briefly in Sect. 2. Section 3 develops the structure of self-balancing trees, independently of any notion of search. Then Sect. 4 presents an abstract notion of search trees based on generic *selectors*. Finally we present and verify the three proposed instances in Sect. 5. Related work in discussed in Sect. 6.

The Why3 formalization is available at http://www.lri.fr/~clochard/AVL/avl-why3.tgz.

© Springer International Publishing Switzerland 2014
D. Giannakopoulou and D. Kroening (Eds.): VSTTE 2014, LNCS 8471, pp. 167–180, 2014.
DOI: 10.1007/978-3-319-12154-3_11

2   Preliminary: Cloning Modules in Why3

In Why3, generic development of components is done via the notion of *cloning* [5]. Cloning a module amounts to copy its contents while substituting some abstract symbols (types, predicates, functions, procedures) and eliminating some axioms by creating proof obligations for them. In case of procedure substitution, proof obligations are generated as well to check for specification inclusion. This cloning mechanism is used both as an instantiation mechanism for generic development as well as a way to declare standard parameters. For example, suppose that we want to write a development generic with respect to a structure of monoid. Then fresh parameters can be created by cloning a standard abstract module for monoid:

```
module Monoid
  type t
  constant zero : t
  function op t t : t
  axiom neutral : forall x. op x zero = x = op zero x
  axiom associative : forall x y z. op (op x y) z = op x (op y z)
end
module Generic
  clone export Monoid
  (* Generic definitions here *)
end
```

And the generic module can later be specialized to a concrete monoid, say integers, by instantiating the monoid abstract symbols.

```
clone Generic with type t = int,constant zero = Int.zero,
  function op = (+), lemma neutral, lemma associative
```

3   Balanced Binary Trees in AVL Style

We first present a certified implementation of the rebalancing operations for AVL trees. Moreover, this implementation is used to directly derive a logarithmic-time implementation of catenable dequeues.

3.1   Representation and Logic Model

The very first step of a verified data structure implementation is to decide not only what is its internal representation but as importantly what it should represent, i.e. its logical meaning. Having a simple logical reflection of the structure usually makes reasoning much easier. The internal representation of an AVL tree is a binary tree storing the height at every node for efficiency reasons.

```
type t 'a = Empty | Node (t 'a) (D.t 'a) (t 'a) int
```

The namespace D corresponds to the abstract data stored in the tree.

The chosen model is the list of data stored in the tree in infix order, since it is the part expected to be invariant by rebalancing. However, in order to specify rebalancing, the tree structure cannot be completely abstracted away because of the height requirements, so we also add the height to this model. Here is the Why3 formalization (++ denotes list concatenation):

```
type m 'a = { lis : list (D.t 'a); hgt : int } (* type of the model *)
function list_model (t:t 'a) : m 'a = match t with Empty → Nil
  | Node l d r _ → list_model l ++ Cons d (list_model r) end
function height (t:t 'a) : int = match t with Empty → 0
  | Node l d r _ → let hl = height l in let hr = height r in
    1 + if hl < hr then hr else hl
  end
function m (t:t 'a) : m 'a = { lis = list_model t; hgt = height t }
```

3.2   Representation Invariant

The balancing criterion for AVL is that the difference between the heights of two sibling trees does not exceed a given positive bound. The structural invariants are readily transformed into the following Why3 predicate:

```
predicate c (t:t 'a) = match t with Empty → true
  | Node l d r h → -balancing ≤ height r - height l ≤ balancing ∧
    c l ∧ c r ∧ h = height t
  end
```

Note that the constant **balancing** is left abstract as a positive integer. Most implementations use a concrete value, which is a trade-off between the potential tree depth and the cost of re-balancing the tree. Since the only impact of keeping it abstract showed to be writing a name instead of a constant, that decision was left to client code.

3.3   Code and Verification

Balancing is performed via smart constructors for tree nodes and catenation operators, specified in terms of the model to build the expected lists. The parts about the height are a bit more complex, as the information about the resulting height has to be precise enough for proof purposes. For example, here is the specification for the core balancing routine, which simulates the construction of a tree node when the two child sub-trees are slightly off balance:

```
val balance (l:t 'a) (d:D.t 'a) (r:t 'a) : t 'a
  requires { c l ∧ c r }
  requires { -balancing-1 ≤ (m l).hgt - (m r).hgt ≤ balancing+1 }
  ensures { let hl = (m l).hgt in let hr = (m r).hgt in
    let he = 1 + (if hl < hr then hr else hl) in
    let hres = (m result).hgt in 0 ≤ he - hres ≤ 1 ∧
    (-balancing ≤ hl - hr ≤ balancing → he = hres) }
  ensures { c result ∧ (m result).lis = (m l).lis ++ Cons d (m r).lis }
```

More complex balancing is done via another smart constructor making no hypothesis on the relative height of the two trees, and two catenation operators similar to the node constructors.

As for the verification part, it did not require any human help once the right specifications were written. All proof obligations were completely discharged by automated theorem provers.

Finally, the catenable dequeue implementation is immediate from the balancing code: catenation is provided, and all other operations (push and pop at both ends) are internal sub-routines of rebalancing. It is logarithmic-time, and also features a constant-time nearly-fair scission operation directly derived from pattern-matching over the tree.

4   Selection of Elements in Balanced Trees

AVL trees were first introduced as binary search trees, so most operations over them involve a binary search by comparison. However, Hinze and Paterson [4] have shown that using a generalization of binary search based on monoidal annotations, one could implement a variety of data structures. In this section, we present and verify a generalized implementation of usual AVL routines (insertion, deletion, etc.) using a similar approach.

4.1   Monoidal Summary

The usual search mechanism in binary search trees is search by comparison using a total order. However, by keeping summaries of the contents in each subtrees, one can provide a variety of other mechanisms. For example, keeping the number of elements in each subtree gives positional information, which can be used to perform efficient random access. Hinze and Paterson [4] proposed monoids as a general mechanism to keep track of those summaries: the content of each subtree is summarized by the sum of the measures of its elements in some given monoid.

We use those annotations as well to provide different search mechanisms. They are integrated in the development with minimal changes as the height bookkeeping is done the same way. We also add parameters corresponding to an abstract monoid and measure.

4.2   Abstracting the Binary Search Mechanism

In their paper about finger trees, Hinze and Paterson suggest to implement most data structure operations using a splitting mechanism, which finds an element where a predicate over the monoidal abstraction of the prefix flips. We could have used this technique, but it has some flaws when considering AVL trees. First and foremost, it completely ignores the fact that the internal tree nodes contain elements that could – and would – be used to guide the search. This is not the case for finger trees as elements are stored in the leaves. Second, the usual insertion/deletion/lookup routines coming with AVL trees would be replaced by much slower (though still logarithmic-time) implementations based on complete splitting of the tree followed by catenation of the parts back together.

This last part, however, is perfectly fit for specification since what binary search does is exactly selecting a split of the list model.

Splits are formalized by the following definitions:

```
type split 'a = { left : list 'a; middle : option 'a; right : list 'a }
function rebuild (s:split 'a) : list 'a =
  s.left ++ option_to_list s.middle ++ s.right
```

The structure of splits corresponds exactly to the two possible outcomes of a binary search in the tree: either finding an element in a node or ending on an empty leaf. In order to describe the particular splits we wish to find, we use an abstract *selector* parameter:

```
type selector
predicate selected (s:selector) (sp:split (D.t 'a))
predicate selection_possible (s:selector) (l:list (D.t 'a))
```

Informally, the `selector` describes the class of splits we want to find, represented by the `selected` predicate. The `selection_possible` describes the lists in which splits corresponding to the `selector` can be found using binary search. This compatibility mean that one can reduce the problem of finding a split in its class by bisection over the node structure, potentially using the summary of the branches to guide the search. We achieve this decription by adding an abstract routine parameter performing this reduction:

```
type part = Here | Left selector | Right selector
val selected_part (ghost llis rlis:list (D.t 'a))
  (s:selector) (l:M.t) (d:D.t 'a) (r:M.t) : part
  requires { selection_possible s (llis ++ Cons d rlis) }
  requires { l = M.sum D.measure llis ∧ r = M.sum D.measure rlis }
  returns { Here →
      selected s { left = llis; middle = Some d; right = rlis }
    | Left sl → selection_possible sl llis ∧
      forall sp. selected sl sp ∧ rebuild sp = llis →
        selected s { sp with right = sp.right ++ Cons d rlis }
    | Right sr → selection_possible sr rlis ∧
      forall sp. selected sr sp ∧ rebuild sp = rlis →
        selected s { sp with left = llis ++ Cons d sp.left } }
```

Note that the routine is expected to compute new selectors as the reduced problem may be different. Also, we need to ensures that whenever the search ends on a leaf, the only possible split is the selected one. This is expressed by an axiom:

```
axiom selection_empty : forall s:selector. selection_possible s Nil →
  selected s { left = Nil; middle = None; right = Nil }
```

4.3   Certified Routines Based on Binary Search

Using the abstract binary search mechanism, we certified the implementation of a generalization of the usual routines over AVL trees: lookup, insertion, deletion, as well as splitting. The code is skipped here as it is standard, it is just a matter of replacing the decisions usually done by comparison by a case analysis on the result of `selected_part`, interested readers may find the code for those routines in Appendix A.3. We then focus on the specifications of those routines. For example, let us see how we could specify insertion. Earlier, we mentioned that those procedures could be build on top of splitting: one could perform insertion by splitting the tree, replacing the potential middle element, and rebuilding it afterwards. It turns out to be the right specification for insertion:

```
val insert (ghost r:ref (split (D.t 'a))) (s:selector)
    (d:D.t 'a) (t:t 'a) : t 'a
  requires { selection_possible s (m t).lis ∧ c t }
  ensures { c result ∧ (m result).lis = !r.left ++ Cons d !r.right }
  ensures { selected s !r ∧ rebuild !r = (m t).lis }
  writes { r }
```

Note that we use a ghost reference instead of an existential quantifier for the split. While using an existential is possible, there are two reasons for using such a reference instead. First, existentially quantified goals tend to be hard for automated provers. In this case, we can very easily give them an explicit witness via the reference. Second, in case the client code is really hard to prove, one can help the automated provers by providing logical cuts. Such cuts will be much easier to write if the existentially quantified value is known.

The three remaining routines have pretty similar specification:

– Deletion is the converse of insertion: any potential middle element is removed of the split before rebuilding.
– Lookup amounts to return the middle of the split.
– Splitting returns a split with lists represented by AVL trees.

5   Verified Instances

5.1   Random-Access Sequences

The first instance use positional selection, which naturally gives random-access sequences. This is obtained by instantiating the monoid by integers and measuring all elements by 1, which gives fast access to the length of the sub-lists. Using that information, binary search is done by finding in which of the three pieces of the list lies the n-th element. Note that reducing the problem to a sub-list requires the index to change. Also, as random-access lists are completely polymorphic, data elements are instantiated with fully polymorphic values (`D.t 'a = 'a`).

The formal specification of this kind of selection is straightforward:

```
type selector = { index : int; hole : bool }
predicate selected (s:selector) (sp:split 'a) =
  s.index = length sp.left ∧ (s.hole ↔ sp.middle = None)
predicate selection_possible (s:selector) (l:list 'a) =
  if s.hole then 0 ≤ s.index ≤ length l else 0 ≤ s.index < length l
```

The extra boolean field is intended to specify whether we want the list to be cut in two pieces or split around the n-th element. Having both allows to derive most positional operations over random-access lists directly from the abstract selection routines:

- Assignment is derived from abstract insertion
- Positional insertion is also derived from abstract insertion
- Positional lookup is implemented by abstract lookup
- Positional deletion is derived from abstract deletion
- Both kind of positional splits are derived from abstract splitting.

However, the specifications had to be rewritten as the obtained ones did not match the desired ones for random-access lists. This was done by writing specification wrappers around those operations. The automatic verification of this wrapper did not required human help beyond making explicit a trivial induction correlating the length of the list to its monoidal summary.

As an example of the resulting specifications, here is the one for the assignment procedure:

```
val set (n:int) (d:'a) (l:t 'a) : t 'a
  requires { c l ∧ 0 ≤ n < length (m l) }
  ensures { c result ∧ length (m result) = length (m l) }
  ensures { forall i:int. i ≠ n → nth i (m result) = nth i (m l) }
  ensures { nth n (m result) = Some d }
```

5.2   Maps and Sets

Another instance correspond to the abstract data structures usually implemented with AVL trees: ordered sets and associative arrays. Those naturally correspond to the case of comparison-based binary search in sorted sequences.

Several new parameters are added to reflect the ordering structure.

- An abstract key datatype
- A function extracting keys from data
- A computable ordering relation over keys

From those parameters, binary search trees lookup, insertion, and deletion are obtained by using straightforward instances for the selection parameters:

- Selection is done by keys, so the selector type is instantiated by keys.
- Selection can be done only in sorted sequences.

  ```
  predicate selection_possible (_:'b) (l:list (D.t 'a)) = increasing l
  ```

- A split is selected by a key if it corresponds to elements with keys lower, equal and greater than the selector respectively.

```
predicate selected (k:Key.t) (sp:split (D.t 'a)) =
  upper_bound k sp.left ∧ lower_bound k sp.right ∧
  match sp.middle with None → true | Some d → eq k (key d) end
```

– Binary search is done by mirroring comparison

As we do not need the extra summaries here, the monoid is instantiated by the unit monoid. Although this instantiation yields a perfectly valid implementation for ordered associative arrays, it is unsatisfactory from the specification point of view as the data structure is still modeled by a list. This is not a suitable model for associative arrays, which are intended to represent finite key-values mappings. In order to get specifications based on such modeling, we wrote specification wrappers over the implementation. The new model was obtained by interpreting the previous list model as an association list:

```
type m 'a = { func : Key.t → option (D.t 'a); card : int }
function association (l:list (D.t 'a)) : Key.t → option (D.t 'a) =
  match l with
  | Nil → \k. None
  | Cons d q → \k. if eq k (key d) then Some d else association q k
  end
function m (t:t 'a) : m 'a = {
  func = association (AVL.m t);
  card = length (AVL.m t);
}
predicate c (t:t 'a) = AVL.c t ∧ increasing (AVL.m t)
```

Note that this instantiation does not break the abstraction barrier: the specification wrappers and selectors are based on the model of the AVL trees only.

The obtained specifications indeed corresponds to the expected behavior of an associative array. For example, here is the specification for insertion (others look alike):

```
val insert (d:D.t 'a) (t:t 'a) : t 'a
  requires { c t }
  ensures { c result }
  ensures { c result ∧ (if (m t).func (key d) = None
      then (m result).card = (m t).card + 1
      else (m result).card = (m t).card) ∧
    forall k:Key.t. if eq k (key d) then (m result).func k = Some d
    else (m result).func k = (m t).func k }
```

The verification of those specification wrappers was not completely immediate, as it required a number of facts over sorted association lists that could be proved only by induction. Mostly, it required a bridge lemma between the notion of selected split of the list and a similar notion stated in terms of key-value mappings. This required a small amount of manual work to state the corresponding lemmas and to make explicit the inductive structure of the proofs.

Finally, certified implementations of ordered maps and sets were derived from this implementation by writing immediate specification wrappers over instances of this implementation.

- Sets were obtained from an instance identifying keys and elements. For specifications, the model was reduced to the predicate of presence.
- Maps were obtained by instantiating the elements with couple formed of a key and a polymorphic value. As keys were irrelevant as outputs of the model mapping, that part was removed from specifications.

5.3   Mergeable Priority Queues

The last instance presented in this paper is selection of the element with the smallest key, which is an immediate implementation of mergeable priority queues. The corresponding monoid is the minimum monoid over keys extended with the positive infinity, which gives fast access to the smallest key of sub-lists. Then, binary search can be done by taking a path leading to a minimum element. For the ordering and keys, we reuse the same setting as for associative arrays.

The specification of minimum selection is quite direct as well: it amounts to say that the split has a middle element and that it is minimal.

```
type selector = unit
predicate selected (_:unit) (sp:split (D.t 'a)) =
  match sp.middle with
  | None → false
  | Some d → lower_bound (key d) sp.left ∧ lower_bound (key d) sp.right
  end
predicate selection_possible (_:unit) (l:list (D.t 'a)) = l ≠ Nil
```

Binary search can obviously be done by taking the path to the minimum element.

From this instantiation, one can map the priority queue operations to the abstract AVL ones:

- finding the minimum is exactly lookup.
- removing the minimum is deletion.
- adding an element can be implemented by prepending the new element.
- merging two priority queues can be done by catenation.

Again, those operations were wrapped under new specifications with a better-suited model. Since the order of the elements inside the structure is irrelevant, the priority queue is represented by a finite bag:

```
type m 'a = { bag : D.t 'a → int; card : int }
function as_bag (l:list 'a) : 'a → int = match l with
  | Nil → \x. 0
  | Cons x q → \y. if x = y then as_bag q y + 1 else as_bag q y
  end
```

Here is an example of the final specifications, namely the one for the remove_min operation:

```
val remove_min (ghost r:ref (D.t 'a)) (t:t 'a) : t 'a
  requires { c t ∧ (m t).card ≥ 1 }
  writes  { r }
  ensures { c result ∧ (m t).card = (m result).card + 1 ∧
    (m t).bag !r = (m result).bag !r + 1 ∧
    (forall d. d ≠ !r → (m t).bag d = (m result).bag d) ∧
    (forall d. (m t).bag d > 0 → le (key !r) (key d)) }
```

6   Related Work

Verified balanced binary search trees. Numerous verified implementation of balanced binary search trees have been proposed. For example, implementations of AVL trees have been verified in Coq [6], Isabelle [7] and ACL2 [8], and similar verifications of red-black trees have been carried out [9–11] http://vacid.codeplex.com. A number of them used some kind of proof automation, though developments in proofs assistants are mostly manual. However, those implementations are not as generic as they are restricted to the usual binary search trees.

Finger trees. Finger trees were introduced by Hinze and Paterson [4] as a structure general enough to derive several common data structure from it, which is exactly the same level of genericity intended by our certified implementation. However, rather few certified implementation of finger trees were carried out. Mathieu Sozeau verified the implementation of Hinze and Paterson using the Program extension of Coq [12], and another verification was carried out using Isabelle [13]. In both cases, proofs are mostly manual while our implementation is verified correct with nearly no human interaction. Also, excepted for Sozeau's implementation of random-access sequences, there was no attempt to check that the specification was indeed strong enough to verify the common instances.

7   Conclusions and Perspectives

This work presents a generic certified implementation of AVL trees and the verification of three common data structures derived from that generic core. The verification overhead is rather light, as it corresponds to less than 1400 non-empty lines of Why3 for the whole presented development, which amounts to about 550 lines of implementation. Moreover, most of this verification cost corresponds to code specification, as proofs are mostly discharged by automated provers without needing to provide hints. Details about the development size can be found in appendix.

In conclusion, we would like to assess that a high level of abstraction in programs like the one used in this development mingles very well with proof automation. This is first caused by the separation between unrelated concepts like balancing and binary search. Mixing such concepts in a single routine widen greatly the search space of automated provers, as they cannot identify that only one of those is related to a particular goal. Also, another benefit of genericity is that some routines are written and proven once, while proving directly the instances would require a lot of duplication.

We expect that such generic approaches would help to the development of certified libraries, which are a first step towards developing verified programs of consequent sizes.

A   Size of the Development

A.1   Lines of Code

	Lines of implementation	Lines of specification/proof hints
Balancing	174	196
Selection	91	59
Associative Array	58	237
Maps	40	180
Sets	31	139
Random-access sequences	63	143
Priority queue	78	219
Association list properties	–	119
Sorted list theory	–	33
Preorder theory	–	22
Monoid theory	–	30
Total	535	1377

Overall, the proof hints corresponds to about 40 lemmas.

A.2   Verification Setting

The verification was carried out using the development version of Why3, which features abstract program substitution during cloning. Though not released yet at the time this paper is written, this corresponds to the version 0.84. Each goal was discharged using one of the four SMT solvers Alt-Ergo, CVC3, CVC4 or Z3. The time limit was set to 5 seconds for the vast majority of them.

Prover	Discharged goals	Average time	Maximum time
Alt-Ergo	471	0.29 s	6.76 s
CVC3	283	0.29 s	3.01 s
CVC4	66	0.68 s	7.39 s
Z3	11	1.37 s	4.84 s

A.3   Code for Insertion, Lookup and Deletion

Note: the expensive list-manipulating code is ghost, and as such is not executed.

```
let rec insert (ghost r:ref (split (D.t 'a))) (s:selector)
  (d:D.t 'a) (t:t 'a) : t 'a
  requires { selection_possible s (m t).lis ∧ c t }
  ensures { c result ∧ (m result).lis = !r.left ++ Cons d !r.right }
  ensures { selected s !r ∧ rebuild !r = (m t).lis }
  writes { r }
  (* extra postcondition needed to prove the recursion. *)
  ensures { 1 ≥ (m result).hgt - (m t).hgt ≥ 0 }
  variant { (m t).hgt }
= match view t with
  | AEmpty → r := { left = Nil; middle = None; right = Nil };
    singleton d
  | ANode tl td tr _ _ → match selected_part (m tl).lis (m tr).lis
      s (total tl) td (total tr) with
    | Left sl → let nl = insert r sl d tl in
      { e with right = (!r).right ++ Cons td (m tr).lis }; balance nl td tr
    | Right sr → let nr = insert r sr d tr in
      r := { !nr with left = (m tl).lis ++ Cons td (!r).left }; balance tl td nr
    | Here → r := { left = (m tl).lis;
        middle = Some td;
        right = (m tr).lis };
      node tl d tr
    end
  end


let rec remove (ghost r:ref (split (D.t 'a))) (s:selector)
  (t:t 'a) : t 'a
  requires { selection_possible s (m t).lis ∧ c t }
  ensures { c result ∧ (m result).lis = !r.left ++ !r.right }
  ensures { selected s !r ∧ rebuild !r = (m t).lis }
  writes { r }
  (* needed to prove the recursion *)
  ensures { 1 ≥ (m t).hgt - (m result).hgt ≥ 0 }
  variant { (m t).hgt }
= match view t with
  | AEmpty → r := { left = Nil; middle = None; right = Nil}; t
  | ANode tl td tr _ _ → match selected_part (m tl).lis (m tr).lis
      s (total tl) td (total tr) with
    | Left sl → let nl = remove r sl tl in
      r := { !r with right = (!r).right ++ Cons td (m tr).lis; balance nl td tr
    | Right sr → let nr = remove r sr tr in
      r := { !r with left = (m tl).lis ++ Cons td (!r).left; balance tl td nr
    | Here → r := { left = (m tl).lis;
        middle = Some td;
        right = (m tr).lis };
      fuse tl tr
    end
  end


let rec get (ghost r:ref (split (D.t 'a))) (s:selector)
  (t:t 'a) : option (D.t 'a)
```

```
  requires { c t ∧ selection_possible s (m t).lis }
  ensures { selected s !r ∧ rebuild !r = t.m.lis }
  ensures { result = (!r).middle }
  writes { r }
  variant { (m t).hgt }
= match view t with
  | AEmpty → r := { left = Nil; middle = None; right = Nil }; None
  | ANode tl td tr _ _ → match selected_part (m tl).lis (m tr).lis
      s (total tl) td (total tr) with
    | Left sl → let res = get r sl tl in
      r := { !r with right = (!r).right ++ Cons td (m tr).lis }; res
    | Right sr → let res = get r sr tr in
      r := { !r with left = (m tl).lis ++ Cons td (!r).left }; res
    | Here → r := { left = (m tl).lis;
        middle = Some td;
        right = (m tr).lis };
      Some td
    end
  end
```

References

1. Leavens, G.T., Leino, K.R.M., Müller, P.: Specification and verification challenges for sequential object-oriented programs. Formal Aspects Comput. **19**(2), 159–189 (2007)
2. Leino, K.R.M., Moskal, M.: VACID-0: Verification of ample correctness of invariants of data-structures. In: Proceedings of Tools and Experiments Workshop at VSTTE (2010)
3. Adel'son-Vel'skiĭ, G.M., Landis, E.M.: An algorithm for the organization of information. Sov. Mathematics-Doklady **3**(5), 1259–1263 (1962)
4. Hinze, R., Paterson, R.: Finger trees: a simple general-purpose data structure. J. Funct. Program. **16**(2), 197–217 (2006)
5. Bobot, F., Filliâtre, J.C., Marché, C., Paskevich, A.: Why3: Shepherd your herd of provers. In: Boogie 2011: First International Workshop on Intermediate Verification Languages, Wrocław, Poland, pp. 53–64, August 2011
6. Filliâtre, J.-C., Letouzey, P.: Functors for proofs and programs. In: Schmidt, D. (ed.) ESOP 2004. LNCS, vol. 2986, pp. 370–384. Springer, Heidelberg (2004)
7. Nipkow, T., Pusch, C.: AVL Trees. Archive of Formal Proofs. Formal proof development, March 2004. http://afp.sf.net/entries/AVL-Trees.shtml
8. Ralston, R.: ACL2-certified AVL Trees. In: Proceedings of the Eighth International Workshop on the ACL2 Theorem Prover and Its Applications, ACL2 '09, pp. 71–74. ACM (2009)
9. Appel, A.: Efficient Verified Red-Black Trees (2011). http://www.cs.princeton.edu/appel/papers/redblack.pdf
10. Charguéraud, A.: Program verification through characteristic formulae. In: Proceedings of the 15th ACM SIGPLAN International Conference on Functional Programming, ICFP '10, pp. 321–332. ACM (2010)
11. Lammich, P., Lochbihler, A.: The Isabelle collections framework. In: Kaufmann, M., Paulson, L.C. (eds.) ITP 2010. LNCS, vol. 6172, pp. 339–354. Springer, Heidelberg (2010)

12. Sozeau, M.: Program-ing finger trees in Coq. In: Hinze, R., Ramsey, N. (eds.) 12th ACM SIGPLAN International Conference on Functional Programming, ICFP 2007, Freiburg, Germany, pp. 13–24. ACM Press (2007)
13. Nordhoff, B., Körner, S., Lammich, P.: Finger Trees. Archive of Formal Proofs, October 2010. http://afp.sf.net/entries/Finger-Trees.shtml. Formal proof development

Certification

A Model for Capturing
and Replaying Proof Strategies

Leo Freitas, Cliff B. Jones[✉], Andrius Velykis, and Iain Whiteside

School of Computing Science, Newcastle University,
Newcastle upon Tyne NE1 7RU, UK
{leo.freitas,cliff.jones,andrius.velykis,
iain.whiteside}@newcastle.ac.uk

Abstract. Modern theorem provers can discharge a significant proportion of Proof Obligation (POs) that arise in the use of Formal Method (FMs). Unfortunately, the residual POs require tedious manual guidance. On the positive side, these "difficult" POs tend to fall into families each of which requires only a few key ideas to unlock. This paper outlines a system that can lessen the burden of FM proofs by identifying and characterising ways of discharging POs of a family by tracking an interactive proof of one member of the family. This opens the possibility of capturing ideas — represented as proof *strategies* — from an expert and/or maximising reuse of ideas after changes to definitions. The proposed system has to store a wealth of meta-information about conjectures, which can be matched against previously learned strategies, or can be used to construct new strategies based on expert guidance.

1 Introduction

Formal methods based on one or another chosen specification language are now used to document different levels of abstraction for many systems. In those methods that adopt a "posit and prove" style of development, engineering decisions are recorded in concrete models and Proof Obligation (POs) are generated whose discharge establishes that the reified model has a behaviour compatible with a more abstract model. (There are also POs that establish internal consistency of one level of model — e.g. respecting invariants.)

Both clever engineering and AI techniques have led to Automated Theorem Prover (ATPs) that can discharge an impressively large proportion of POs but the manual discharge of the remaining POs is an impediment to the wider use of formal methods. The research hypothesis of the AI4FM project is that a system can be built that learns, from interactive proof, ideas that will facilitate automatic discharge of other recalcitrant POs *in the same family*. The emphasised qualification in the previous sentence indicates that the system is not intended to discover general heuristics; the aim is to extract intuition about functions and data structures used in the specific family of POs.

© Springer International Publishing Switzerland 2014
D. Giannakopoulou and D. Kroening (Eds.): VSTTE 2014, LNCS 8471, pp. 183–199, 2014.
DOI: 10.1007/978-3-319-12154-3_12

The design of the AI4FM system is itself being conducted formally. Moreover, exploration of the design space is being undertaken by recording and modifying formal models of the proposed system. This paper reviews such a model, emphasising the meta-information and strategies that contribute to establishing the research hypothesis of the AI4FM project. A similar process was used to considerable effect in the creation of the *mural* theorem proving assistant [JJLM91].

To underpin the explanation of the AI4FM system, Sect. 2 introduces a formal specification of a heap memory manager; POs and proof strategies arising from this example are used to illustrate AI4FM system features. Sections 3 and 4 minimally present the specification of the core of the proposed system, particularly the representation of proof strategies and the important high-level information about POs needed to reuse the strategies. A summary of the specification is given in Appendix A, whereas a complete description can be found in [FJVW13, Chapter 3]. The model of how proof strategies are (re)played and captured is described in Sects. 4 and 5. Proof strategies illustrating the model have been informally—but in more depth—presented in [FW14]. Section 6 reviews some related work and Sect. 7 summarises the conclusions.

2 Background

This section introduces a heap memory model that is used below to illustrate AI4FM. The example is adapted from [JS90, Ch.7], where it was specified using the VDM notation. The *Heap* specification has been formally mechanised (i.e. all the POs have been proved) using both Isabelle [Pau94] and Z/EVES [Saa97] theorem provers. The mechanisation of the proofs is recorded in [FJVW13]. This work has also generated an account of practical proof patterns [FW14], whose descriptions underpin the proof-process modelling presented in this paper.

The heap memory manager is modelled using two operations at two levels of abstraction (here specified using VDM notation):

Loc: the type of a single memory location, represented as $\mathbb{N}$.
Free: the type of the heap as a collection of all free locations. At *level 0*, it is represented as a set of locations $Free0 = Loc\text{-}\mathbf{set}$. At *level 1*, it is represented as a map from start locations to sizes that is constrained by a datatype invariant to be *disj*oint and *sep*arate:

$$Free1 = Loc \xrightarrow{m} \mathbb{N}_1$$

$$\mathbf{inv}\ (f) \triangleq disj(f) \land sep(f)$$
$$disj(f) \quad \triangleq \quad \forall l, l' \in \mathbf{dom}\,f \cdot l \neq l' \Rightarrow locs\text{-}of(l, f(l)) \cap locs\text{-}of(l', f(l')) = \{\}$$
$$sep(f) \quad \triangleq \quad \forall l \in \mathbf{dom}\,f \cdot (l + f(l)) \notin \mathbf{dom}\,f$$

The invariant conditions ensure that the range of locations identified by any two map elements (defined as $\{l \ldots l + f(l)\text{-}1\}$ by *locs-of*) do not intersect (*disj*) and that contiguous memory regions are as large as possible (*sep*).
NEW: takes a size as input and, if available, returns a starting location for a contiguous chunk of memory of the appropriate size after updating the state.

DISPOSE: returns a contiguous chunk of memory to the heap. This operation takes a start location and size as parameters and updates the state.

At level 0, these operations are defined using set operations, whereas at level 1 they are refined to use mapping from locations to their corresponding sizes. The main PO discussed in this paper is feasibility of the *NEW* operation and the associated lemmas needed for the proof At level 1, the *NEW* operation is:

$NEW1 \ (s \colon \mathbb{N}_1) \ r \colon Loc$
ext wr $f_1 \ \colon \ Free1$
pre $\exists l \in \mathbf{dom} \ f_1 \cdot f_1(l) \geq s$
post $r \in \mathbf{dom} \ \overleftarrow{f_1} \wedge (\overleftarrow{f_1}(r) = s \wedge f_1 = \{r\} \triangleleft \overleftarrow{f_1}) \vee$
$\qquad (\overleftarrow{f_1}(r) > s \wedge f_1 = (\{r\} \triangleleft \overleftarrow{f_1}) \cup_m \{r + s \mapsto \overleftarrow{f_1}(r) - s\})$

NEW1 has two behaviours depending on whether a location of exactly the required or strictly larger size has been located. If the size matches, then that element is removed from the map; if the map element refers to a larger region, then the remaining locations in the region must be added back to the heap (hence the map union). The precondition embraces both cases by using $\geq$.

The feasibility PO for *NEW* requires that, for every starting state ($\overleftarrow{f_1}$) and input (s) that satisfy the precondition and invariant, there exists an updated state (f_1) and result (r) that satisfy the postcondition and invariant.

$$\forall s \in \mathbb{N}_1, \overleftarrow{f_1} \in Free1 \cdot \exists l \in \mathbf{dom} \ \overleftarrow{f_1} \cdot \overleftarrow{f_1}(l) \geq s \wedge sep(\overleftarrow{f_1}) \wedge disj(\overleftarrow{f_1})$$
$$\Rightarrow$$
$$\exists f_1 \in Free1, r \in Loc \cdot [r \in \mathbf{dom} \ \overleftarrow{f_1} \wedge (\overleftarrow{f_1}(r) = s \wedge f_1 = \{r\} \triangleleft \overleftarrow{f_1}) \vee$$
$$(\overleftarrow{f_1}(r) > s \wedge f_1 = (\{r\} \triangleleft \overleftarrow{f_1}) \cup_m \{r + s \mapsto \overleftarrow{f_1}(r) - s\})] \wedge sep(f_1) \wedge disj(f_1)$$

The first step of the proof is to expose the postcondition by application of introduction rules, then supply an appropriate witness for the result (l, from the precondition), resulting in a conjecture of the form:

$$\frac{\overleftarrow{f_1} \in Free1, \ s \in \mathbb{N}_1, \ l \in \mathbf{dom} \ \overleftarrow{f_1}, \ l \geq s, \ sep(\overleftarrow{f_1}), \ disj(\overleftarrow{f_1})}{\begin{array}{c} \exists f_1 \in Free1 \cdot [l \in \mathbf{dom} \ \overleftarrow{f_1} \wedge (\overleftarrow{f_1}(l) = s \wedge f_1 = \{l\} \triangleleft \overleftarrow{f_1}) \vee \\ (\overleftarrow{f_1}(l) > s \wedge f_1 = (\{l\} \triangleleft \overleftarrow{f_1}) \cup_m \{l + s \mapsto \overleftarrow{f_1}(l) - s\})] \wedge sep(f_1) \wedge disj(f_1) \end{array}}$$

To progress this proof, a witness for the updated state must be provided; however, a *hidden* case analysis on the $\geq$ in the hypothesis is required because of the alternative behaviours of *NEW*. The two cases, $l > s$ and $l = s$, can then be solved independently. In both cases, the witness for f_1 is explicit in the postcondition. The invariant is challenging. For the $l > s$ case, the goal is:

$$\frac{\overleftarrow{f_1} \in Free1, \ s \in \mathbb{N}_1, \ l \in \mathbf{dom} \ \overleftarrow{f_1}, \ l \geq s, \ sep(\overleftarrow{f_1}), \ disj(\overleftarrow{f_1}}{\begin{array}{c} sep((\{l\} \triangleleft \overleftarrow{f_1}) \cup_m \{l + s \mapsto \overleftarrow{f_1}(l) - s\}) \wedge \\ disj((\{l\} \triangleleft \overleftarrow{f_1}) \cup_m \{l + s \mapsto \overleftarrow{f_1}(l) - s\}) \end{array}}$$

which can be solved by lemmas that distribute the invariant over map operators.

Even in this relatively small case study, the notion of PO families plays an important role. The two main ideas in this proof are: discovering a *hidden* case analysis (i.e. a missing hypothesis) and using lemmas that distribute the map operators over the invariant — and these are exactly what is needed to solve the (more complicated) *DISPOSE* feasibility proof obligation.

3   The AI4FM System

This section describes the abstract model of the AI4FM system that realises the functionality described in the introduction. Specifically, we describe the meta-information content of *conjectures* that enable strategies to be learned and matched against proof situations, as described in Sects. 4 and 5.

The accumulated information in an AI4FM instantiation can be thought of as a collection of bodies (in the sense of "body of knowledge" as meta-information associated to user theories). Each *body* contains proof tasks (conjectures and their justifications), user-defined functions and types, and strategies. This paper focuses on conjectures, justifications and strategies and the reader is referred to [FJVW13, Chapter 3] for a full description of the model.

3.1   Conjectures

A proof task is a *Judgment*, which contains hypotheses and a conclusion, and a *role*. A *role* describes the purpose of this task. In addition there can be any number of (attempts at) justifications. Thus:

$$
\begin{array}{lll}
Conjecture :: & what & : \ Judgement \\
& role & : \ \{\textsc{Axiom}, \textsc{Trusted}, \textsc{Lemma}, \textsc{Subgoal}, \cdots\} \\
& justifs & : \ JusId \xrightarrow{m} Justification \\
& specialises & : \ [ConjId] \\
& \cdots &
\end{array}
$$

An example of a low level conjecture would be a natural deduction proof rule for "or elimination" which might be marked as an axiom (Axiom). Within a body for a VDM specification like the heap, a proof obligation generator will create a *Conjecture* for each PO about the consistency of that single specification. Thus, another conjecture may be the Lemma representing the *NEW* feasibility PO of Sect. 2.

3.2   Justifications

Turning to *Justification*, it is explicitly envisaged that there can be multiple attempts to justify a proof task. When a conjecture is first generated, it will have no justifications. A user might start one proof justification, leave it aside and try another, then come back and complete the first proof. But notice that the notion of whether a proof is complete (in the sense of (transitively) relying only on axioms) is a complex recursive predicate. Overall,

$$Justification :: by \quad : (ConjId \mid ToolOP)$$
$$with : ConjId^*$$

A justification which uses an established inference rule will point to its *ConjId*. The *with* field points to any sub-problems that need to be discharged to complete the proof. Notice that such a justification corresponds to one step in a proof: collecting a whole proof requires tracing the attempts at the sub-conjectures. In practice, TP tools such as Isabelle and Z/EVES are powerful enough that a user will hardly ever interact at the level of the (natural deduction) laws of the logic itself. So, in fact, the most prevalent examples of *Justification* ought come from an attached Theorem Prover. Use of an ATP will be recorded as an instance of *ToolOP* — such output will be specific enough to the ATP that it is not further specified here (e.g. a concrete proof script instance).

3.3 Meta-Information

Finally, conjectures include meta-information (or *features*):

$$Conjecture :: \cdots$$
$$provenance : (Origin \mid Why)^*$$
$$emphTps \quad : TyId \xrightarrow{m} \mathbb{N}$$
$$emphFns \quad : FnId \xrightarrow{m} \mathbb{N}$$
$$other \quad : \cdots$$

The additional features of each *Conjecture*, i.e. *provenance*, *emph*asised types or functions, are the key information collected to enable analysis and creation or execution of proof strategies. The *provenance* feature details a sequence describing the history of how a particular conjecture has arisen. For example, for top-level PO conjectures, it would record the type of PO; for sub-goal conjectures, it would record the strategies that lead to that particular goal, e.g. the *provenance* for the *NEW*1 feasibility *Conjecture* nearing its complete justification could be:

[*EXPOSE-POST, HCA, EXIST-PRE-WITNESS, SINGLE-PT-WITNESS, WITNESSED, SPLIT-INV-POST, INV-BRKDOWN*].

In general, the set of tokens indicating provenance is open ended, yet fairly stable per domain. Registering this information allows simplifying proof strategy search for similar proofs. The AI4FM system could match the provenance with a strategy in an earlier proof and suggest adapting it: e.g. "On a previous similar proof, the next step was this particular strategy" (see Sect. 5.2 for an example).

Moreover, it would be useful if definitions within bodies of knowledge contained information about their use within the proof obligations/conjectures of the body. For example, this could include properties of operators, such as them being distributive and associative but not commutative — they could influence strategy matching.

4 Playing Proof Strategies

The most common mode of operation for AI4FM is the intelligent suggestion and application of "intentful" strategies and lemmas to break down and solve POs.

In general the ethos described fully in [FW14] is to use strategies to deconstruct a high-level PO to the point where so-called *weakening* lemmas (e.g. goal simplification rules) can be suggested to break down the conjectures until automation can kick in to discharge the remaining goals. AI4FM strategies are *intentful* because they advertise their applicability to conjectures by *MTerms* (the 'M' is for *Matching*) and are optionally annotated with an explicit *intent* as a natural language record of a strategy's purpose and is identifiable by machine. The suitability of any strategy for progressing the proof of a given conjecture is given by evaluating the propositional *MTerm* over a *conjecture*'s features (as described in Sect. 3). Such functionality is modelled via two operations: *FIND-STRATEGY* to suggest a list of appropriate strategies for a given conjecture; and, *APPLY* to execute the strategy found.

The following section describes the structure of a strategy in detail and Sect. 4.2 instantiates some example strategies. Then, Sects. 4.3 and 4.4 describe the *FIND-STRATEGY* and *APPLY* operations, respectively.

4.1   Anatomy of a Strategy

The first component of an AI4FM *strategy* is an *intent*, given as a *Why* token:

$$Strategy :: intent : [Why]$$
$$\cdots$$

The *intent* serves a dual purpose:

1. It serves to explain what the strategy does;
2. It is added to the provenance of the (sub)conjectures generated.

The latter enables subsequent strategies to be suggested *because* this strategy has been applied (see Sect. 4.2.3, for example). The purpose of a strategy is to progress proofs and the crucial component that instructs AI4FM how that strategy should be applied is the *by* field:

$$Strategy :: \cdots by : (conjId \mid ToolIP) \cdots$$

The *by* field shows that a strategy can be justified by either a call to an internal conjecture (given by a *conjId*) or an external tool (given by a *ToolIP*). Appeals to inference rules, axioms or previously proved (or even still open) conjectures are given by internal references. Tools can either be part of the theorem prover or can be separately developed "apps" within AI4FM — e.g. [GKL13]. The *script* component of a *ToolIP* indicates that the input to different tools can vary.

$$Strategy :: \cdots weightings : MTerm \xrightarrow{m} Weight$$
$$mvars : mvar^* \cdots$$

The *weightings* map, describes *when* a strategy should be applied and contains the key feature-matching objects: *MTerms*. Each *MTerm* is associated with a natural number that describes the utility of the current strategy for progressing the proof, if that *MTerm* be satisfied. A basic *MTerm* is a proposition built from negation ($\neg$), conjunction ($\wedge$) and an unbounded set of *atomic* (paramaterised) predicates. For example, the atomic *prov-test*(*VDM-FEAS*, *conjId*) checks if the *VDM-FEAS* token is part of the provenance of the conjecture *conjId*.

Rather than permit choice explicitly in *MTerms*, the weightings *map* means that a strategy can have multiple *MTerms* with different associated *weights*. This approach enables multiple (disjunctive) scenarios in which a strategy is applicable and a notion of partial match to be modelled. The weightings are used by the *FIND-STRATEGY* operation to rank strategies by value; matching in a single strategy must therefore return the highest ranking *MTerm* in the *weightings*. Machine learning techniques like PageRank adaptations [KU14] can be used to learn ways to improve the strategies matching rate. For more sophisticated matching, a simple binding mechanism called *matching variables* (*mvars*) for *MTerms* is provided, and is written with the following syntax:

$$\textbf{match} \ ?x \ ?y \ \textbf{with} \ atomic_1(?x, ?y, conjId) \wedge \cdots \wedge atomic_n(?x, ?y, conjId)$$

to mean that evaluation of an *MTerm* must instantiate $?x$ and $?y$ as terms from the *judgement* to satisfy the basic *MTerm* part. Any *mvars* in *MTerms* must be declared in the strategy itself. This means that they can also appear in the tool input *script* to customise the behaviour of a strategy. *MTerms*, *mvars*, and *ToolIP* are exemplified in the next section, but further discussion is postponed until Sect. 4.3, where they are used in the *FIND-STRATEGY* operation. Finally, strategies can be organised into a "taxonomy". The idea is perhaps best illustrated by an example:

NPEANOINDUCT specialises INDUCTIONPROOF
NCOMPLETEINDUCT specialises INDUCTIONPROOF

So the final field becomes:

$Strategy \ :: \ \cdots$
$\qquad specialises \ : \ [StrId]$

Specialisation is a simple example of strategy *capture*, described in Sect. 5.

4.2 *MWhy* Strategies Example

To ground the previous section, with a strong focus on *MTerms*, three example strategies, implementing the proof patterns from [FW14], are given.

4.2.1 VDM Structural Breakdown

The first illustration of an AI4FM strategy is for *structural breakdown*, which simply decomposes a top-level proof obligation (e.g. VDM's feasibility, narrow-postcondition or widen-precondition POs) — by performing safe introduction rules. For example, a feasibility proof obligation of the form:

$$\forall \overleftarrow{\sigma}, \overleftarrow{i} \cdot pre\text{-}OP(\overleftarrow{\sigma}, \overleftarrow{i}) \ \Rightarrow \ \exists \sigma, \bar{o} \cdot post\text{-}OP(\overleftarrow{\sigma}, \overleftarrow{i}, \sigma, \bar{o})$$

(where $\overleftarrow{\sigma}$ and $\overleftarrow{i}$ are the initial state and inputs and σ and $\bar{o}$ represent the updated state and outputs for a particular operation) would be transformed to:

$$\exists \sigma, \bar{o} \cdot post\text{-}OP_1 \wedge \ldots \wedge post\text{-}OP_n \wedge post\text{-}OP\text{-}\sigma\text{-}inv_1 \wedge \ldots \wedge post\text{-}OP\text{-}\sigma\text{-}inv_n$$

That is, quantifiers and assumptions are stripped (and added to the context) and the conclusion is unfolded to a conjunction of postconditions and state invariants.

The result of structural breakdown on the feasibility PO for *NEW* from Sect. 2 would be the following:

$$\frac{\overleftarrow{f_1} \in \textit{Free}1, \; s \in \mathbb{N}_1, \; l \in \textbf{dom} \, \overleftarrow{f_1}, \; l \geq s, \; \textit{sep}(\overleftarrow{f_1}), \; \textit{disj}(\overleftarrow{f_1})}{\begin{array}{c} \exists r \in \mathbb{N}_1, f_1 \in \textit{Free}1 \cdot [r \in \textbf{dom} \, \overleftarrow{f_1} \wedge (\overleftarrow{f_1}(r) = s \wedge f_1 = \{r\} \triangleleft \overleftarrow{f_1}) \vee \\ (\overleftarrow{f_1}(r) > s \wedge f_1 = (\{r\} \triangleleft \overleftarrow{f_1}) \cup_m \{r + s \mapsto \overleftarrow{f_1}(r) - s\})] \wedge \textit{sep}(f_1) \wedge \textit{disj}(f_1) \end{array}}$$

The *intent* for this strategy is given as *EXPOSE-POST* to describe that it is really just exposing the main postcondition. The *weightings* map consists of three individual *MTerms* that check whether the conjecture is one of the required top-level VDM POs. For feasibility, the *MTerm* is:

$$\textit{prov-test}(\textit{FEAS-PO}, \textit{conjId}) \wedge \neg \, \textit{prov-test}(\textit{EXPOSE-POST}, \textit{conjId})$$

Since the *MTerms* for this strategy are straightforward, there are no *mvars* to be recorded and it does not specialise any other strategies.

4.2.2 Hidden Case Analysis

A common technique for progressing a tricky proof is to introduce new hypotheses to help solve the goal. The price to pay is that these hypotheses need to be discharged at some point. Fortunately, some inference rules allow one to make use of new hypotheses, as in disjunction elimination, where the burden is to prove the same goal under different (disjunctive) hypotheses. This use of disjunction elimination is itself a specialisation of a fundamental concept in theorem proving, the "cut rule":

$$\boxed{\text{cut-disj-elim}} \quad \frac{H \vdash C_1 \vee C_2 \quad C_1 \vdash G \quad C_2 \vdash G}{H \vdash G}$$

When there is no explicit disjunction in the goal, yet there is a missing hypothesis to finish the proof, it is called Hidden Case Analysis (HCA). A specific instance of HCA is where the "cut" hypothesis is $\geq$ — its *MTerm* provides a first use of matching variables:

$$\textbf{match } ?\textit{hyp} \textbf{ with } \textit{hyp-test}(?\textit{hyp}, \textit{conjId}) \wedge \textit{top-symb}(?\textit{hyp}, \geq)$$

where a hypothesis with a $\geq$ is matched against the conjecture. This strategy is used in the *NEW* feasibility PO to split $l \geq s$ into $l = s \vee l > s$.

4.2.3 Existential Witnessing

The final example strategy, existential witnessing, is a general strategy for progressing with POs with an existential quantifier, by instantiating it with a witness provided by the user. The *MTerm* is:

$$\textit{prov-test}(\textit{EXPOSE-POST}, \textit{conjId}) \wedge \textit{top-symb}(\exists, \textit{conjId.what.conc})$$

and the intent of this strategy is simply *WITNESS*. Existential witnessing is an example of a strategy that has specialisations: two important examples of such a specialised existential witnessing strategy are *single-point* and *fully witnessed*.

Single-point existential witnessing. A common situation that arises with POs is the need to witness updated state variables — the PO may be of the form $\exists \sigma \cdot \sigma = t \wedge \ldots$. A strategy provided for this situation, with an *MTerm*:

> **match** *?tm ?x ?y* **with**
> *prov-test*(*EXPOSE-POST*, *conjId*)$\wedge$*subtree*(*?tm*, *conjId.what.conc*)
> $\wedge$ *exvar-test*(*?x*, *conjId.what.conc*) $\wedge$
> *top-symb*(=, *?tm*) $\wedge$ *left-child*(*?x*, *?tm*) $\wedge$ *right-child*(*?y*, *?tm*)

which picks out a subterm of the conclusion that has the shape *?x* =*?y* where*?x* is an existentially bound variable. The *by* for this strategy could be a call to an Isabelle tactic with the following script: *apply*(*rule-tac x* =*?y in exI*), which is the Isabelle command for performing existential introduction with explicit witnesses. The matching of *?x* and *?y* as f_1 and $(\{l\} \lhd \overleftarrow{f_1})$ respectively is the appropriate single-point witness for the $l = s$ case of *NEW* feasibility PO.

Fully witnessed. This specialisation of witnessing has a niche purpose: match conjectures that have been witnessed already, and had all the existentials stripped from them. It does nothing to the goal, but adds *WITNESSED* to the provenance of the *Conjecture* enabling further proof strategies to attack the witnessed postconditions and invariant. The *MTerm* for this strategy is:

> *prov-test*(*WITNESS*, *conjId*)$\wedge \neg$ *top-symb*(*conjId.what.conc*, $\exists \cdot$)$\wedge \neg$
> *prov-test*(*WITNESSED*, *conjId*)

Specialisations of strategies must have a higher *weight* than their general versions, to ensure that if it matches, the specialised version will be triggered.

4.3   Finding a Strategy

If a conjecture cannot be solved by proof automation,[1] the *FIND-STRATEGY* operation can be used to search through the set of available strategies and check their applicability to the current conjecture (ranked by *Weight* in order of their applicability). As described above, this requires evaluating the *MTerms* of a strategy. The function for evaluating an *MTerm* has type:

> *match* : *MTerm* $\times$ *ConjId* $\rightarrow$ *Binding*-**set**
>
> *match*(*mt*, *c*) $\triangleq$ ...

where a *Binding* is a map between *mvars* and *terms* (in the theorem prover):

> *Binding* = *mvar* $\xrightarrow{m}$ *term*

A set of bindings is returned because there can be many and each may be interesting to an engineer. Consider, for example, an *MTerm* as follows:

> *hyp-test*(*?hyp*, *conjId*) $\wedge$ *top-symb*(*?hyp*, $\leq$)

---

[1] It is assumed that ATP is always used before strategic intervention is required.

which matches any hypothesis of the conjecture that has a $\leq$ as its top symbol. The strategy associated with this $MTerm$ could, for example, apply case analysis on $\leq$ (introducing the $=$ and $<$ cases). In a goal $x \leq y, x \leq z \vdash \ldots$, there would be two possible matches. A failure to match the $MTerm$ against the conjecture is represented by the empty set. This is different from the case where an $MTerm$ is successfully matched, but has no matching variables, which returns a singleton set containing the empty map. Thus, since each strategy has multiple $MTerms$, it must return the highest weight from all those $MTerms$ that match, which is:

$$Max(ran(\{mt \mid mt \in \mathbf{dom}\ weightings \wedge match(c, mt) \neq \{\}\} \lhd weightings))$$

and if that $MTerm$ contains multiple matches, then each binding must also be returned. This weighted filtering of available strategies is a crucial part of matching evaluated $MTerms$, so that the most suitable strategies with actual instantiations from the current conjecture are found. This means that the operation is:

> $FIND\text{-}STRATEGY\ (f\colon BdId, n\colon ConjId)\ r\colon (StratId \times Weight \times Binding)^*$
> **pre** $n \in \mathbf{dom}\ guts(f)$
> **post** $\ldots \wedge (st, w, bd) \in r$
> $\qquad \Rightarrow \mathbf{dom}\ bd \subseteq st.mvars \wedge \exists mt \in \mathbf{dom}\ weightings \cdot bd \in match(mt, n)$
> $\qquad \wedge \ldots$

We use a sequence since we want to order strategies as most applicable, but leave the $Weight$ to show the distribution of applicability. We give the precondition and the part of the postcondition that ensures that any returned strategies and bindings are indeed a match. We elide the rest of the postcondition for brevity.

4.4 Applying a Strategy

Once an engineer has chosen the strategy to use, based on those found to be applicable, the $APPLY$ operation can be used. $APPLY$ takes the conjecture and a strategy with associated binding and applies it, updating the state by:

1. Adding new conjectures generated by the strategy, including the Why of the applied strategy as part of the $provenance$ of the new conjectures.
2. Adding a justification to the conjecture that the strategy was applied to, including any tool output, $ToolOp$.

If the strategy uses an external tool, then the $Binding$ must be used to instantiate any potential $mvars$ in the $script$ of the tool input, $ToolIP$. If the strategy fails, then the operation will return $false$ and not update the state.

The signature of $APPLY$ and part of the postconditions relevant to the provenance of generated conjectures:

> $APPLY\ (f\colon BdId, n\colon ConjId, s\colon StratId, b\colon Binding)\ r\colon bool \times conjId\text{-}\mathbf{set}$
> **ext wr** Σ
> **pre** $\ldots$
> **post** $(r = (true, cs)$
> $\qquad \Rightarrow \ldots \wedge \forall c \in cs \cdot c \in \mathbf{dom}\ \Sigma.guts \wedge s.intent \in c.provenance \wedge \ldots)$
> $\qquad \wedge (r = (false, cs) \Rightarrow \ldots)$

The postcondition ensures that all of the generated conjectures (the set cs) have been added to the *guts* of the *body*, and that the provenance has been updated to include the *intent* of the applied strategy.

5   Capturing Proof Strategies

When an expert has to intervene to progress a proof, this is identified within AI4FM as an opportunity to learn both new proof techniques and new *why*s of a proof technique. The key aim of AI4FM is to *learn* from expert intervention in a single proof to improve automation in subsequent proof attempts that are similar in some way. We have devised several ways in which AI4FM can learn new strategies and this section describes another example of the most commonly used techniques: strategy capture by *specialisation*.

After showing strategy specialisation for existential variable witnessing, we motivate this technique with another example of HCA. Section 5.1 describes how this can be performed; finally, Sect. 5.2, briefly summarises other ways in which AI4FM can learn from an expert.

5.1   Strategy Specialisation Example: Hidden Case Analysis

As described in Sect. 4.2.2, exposing a HCA is an important technique for progressing proofs. The key step is the act of introducing case analysis by a specialised version of the "cut rule": it introduces the two cases and a lemma that requires showing that the disjunction holds in the current context. For example, applying *cut-disj-elim* with $C_1 = x > y$ and $C_2 = x = y$ is the correct case analysis for the *NEW*1 feasibility proof obligation described in Sect. 4.2.2. The goal $x \geq y \vdash x > y \lor x = y$ can then be proved as a lemma. This example strategy was first created for the *NEW*1 feasibility proof, which requires the hidden case split on the $\geq$ present in its precondition.

To learn a new strategy from the basic inference rule strategy *cut-disj-elim*, we need to provide an *MTerm* and reference the lemma generated as proved. This done, the system can automatically suggest the specialised $\geq$ HCA strategy in similar situations: namely, whenever $\geq$ appears in the hypothesis and the user is stuck (i.e. no known strategy is applicable and the user explicitly asks help to AI4FM), alternative HCA or indeed instantiation of known ones could be suggested. This is detailed below.

5.2   Using Provenance to Specialise Strategies

The process of capturing new strategies works in two ways: a priori, where the expert user interacts and informs AI4FM about novel ideas from previous known successful ones; and post-facto, where searching/clustering procedures can try and learn new strategies from successfully applied ones. So far, we have investigated the former and plan to work on the latter in the future.

Thus, at the point where the (expert-)user suggests the HCA for $\geq$ as a new strategy, the AI4FM system could request the user for alternative hypothesis generating instances of the "cut rule" that would make sense in the context. For example, spotting that $\geq$ is a reflexive pre-order maximises the chance of a strategy generalising this to $\leq, \subseteq, \cdots$. Moreover, assuming the *provenance* information from the *DISPOSE*1 feasibility proof suggests *cut-disj-elim*, but without the knowledge what to plug in for the disjuncts, the user could be asked to suggest something.

*Hidden case analysis in DISPOSE*1. The feasibility proof for *DISPOSE*1 (see details in [FJVW13, App. E.8, F]), needs a specialised version of HCA, where the new hypotheses are about whether the adjoining sets of memory below and above the memory being disposed are empty or not. This is important because it will determine, because of the *sep* invariant, the largest contiguous memory as the correct state update. So, if neither below nor above is empty, the returned value is their unions, whereas if either is empty, the formula in *DISPOSE*1 postcondition is greatly simplified. All of these cases rely on the fact of the application of the HCA strategy, where the hidden disjunction is about emptiness of both sets (leading to 4 cases). A detailed technical explanation for this is in [FJVW13, Appendix E.8, F] and [FJVW13, Section 3.2.3]. It discusses how the HCA strategy applied in *NEW*1 (at the right time) is specialised for *DISPOSE*1, providing the (expert) user informs the system about the hidden disjunct on the empty sets. The capturing was played independently in two proof modes (i.e. tactical and Isar) in Isabelle to the same result.

The interesting observation here is that, despite significant differences of detail, the overall proof strategy for *NEW*1 is quite similar to *DISPOSE*1, as was predicted (in the AI4FM hypothesis). This indicates that with enough strategies available, the level of successful applications to different problems will be higher.

6   Related Work and Status

As discussed above, the system described in this paper should be seen in the wider context of the AI4FM project, where the project partners and collaborators have been working on tools that can be used by the system described here. Three of these related tools are:

Proof Strategy Graph [GKL13] is a tool for encoding proof strategies. PSGraphs can be composed statically based on a notion of *types* on incoming and outgoing goals. The goal types simultaneously allow for additional control of a strategy's behaviour and understanding of its purpose and result. The goal types on PSGraphs correspond closely to our *MTerms*, enabling the learning of new AI4FM strategies from instances of PSGraphs.

Lemology [HKJM13] suggests lemmas by analogy with a similar theorem; furthermore, it can be used to suggest analogous conditions to speculate new lemmas. The AI4FM should capture enough details of proof and conjecture features to detect analogy and suggest applicable lemmas.

IsaCoSy [JDB11] can generate conjectures based on functions and types of interest, run them through a counterexample checker to eliminate obvious false conjectures, then use an automated theorem prover to attempt to prove the remainder. The *emphFns* and *emphTps* from unproven conjectures can be fed into IsaCoSy to help generate lemmas that can progress a proof automatically.

Other related work includes [HK13] where machine learning is used to identify clusters of lemma usefulness. They apply the technique to simple inductive theorems in both the Coq and ACL2 provers. The idea is to try and identify lemmas with high "quality", in the sense of helping solve more goals. A key difference to our approach is that we anticipate the use of meta-information for learning, instead of the actual raw proof data, given it is not easy to gather enough of it (i.e. one would not provide 100 samples of the same proof).

In [KU14], authors describe a way to mine proof tracing information in order to detect lemma relevance, duplication, and ranks them in order of importance. The idea uses machine learning (clustering and PageRank) techniques by sifting through the large amount of data found in the proof object (inference graph). It takes into account intermediate lemmas (or sub-goals), as well as user defined lemmas. Their approach observe the problem at this lowest-level of proof object, as well as at the theorem prover's tactic-application level, where the difference helps determine what is a useful lemma (in terms of its applicability during proof), as opposed to what makes the theorem prover "happy" (in terms of the interaction between the lemma shape and the way it relates to the various proof tactics applied). We are trying to understand their experimental setup data in order to make use of similar techniques in AI4FM. Their work, however, has no notion of user-supplied input, where proof intent (e.g. meta-proof information) is provided in order to search for similar proof strategies on different goals.

Status.   Proof engineering is essential for scalability: it takes a good amount of unrelated proof effort to enable one to tackle the actual proof obligations of interest. Lemmas are useful whenever one needs to either: decompose a complex problem; fine-tune the theorem prover's rewriting abilities to given goals; generalise a solution of some related (usually more abstract) problem; and to provide alternative solutions of the same data structure being modelled; *etc.*

In our experiment we have tested our hypothesis by having the same proof task performed independently by three different people with three different backgrounds (formal methods proof expert, Isabelle proof expert, MSc student), in two different provers (Isabelle/HOL and Z/EVES), and encoded in two different methods (VDM and Z) on medium size refinement problem (i.e. the Heap). We analysed the proof traces and scripts of the Isabelle development (using Perl) looking for commonalities and differences. On the expert proof engineer development, our new lemmas on VDM maps in Isabelle were the ones with highest reuse rate (at 22 %), with other available Isabelle library lemmas reuse being quite high too (at 38 %). On the Isabelle expert, the ratio was slightly different at 16 % and 65 % respectively. The effort on PO-specific weakening lemmas and type bridges was comparable at 23 % and 17 % for each expert. This indicates that a considerable amount of effort (around 20 % for both experts) was related to setting up VDM map operators and lemmas in Isabelle, whereas around the same effort was needed on the actual POs. Arguably, the VDM lemmas are reusable across problems, hence the patterns described for the Heap problem do transfer across problems (in VDM at least). The encoding in Z/EVES was relatively straightforward, as there were no issues with undefinedness and the Z mathematical toolkit is quite similar to VDM's. This part of the experiment was useful, however, in early detection of possible proof-difficulty in the model, which only appeared much latter in the Isabelle development.

Prototype Implementation. For a comprehensive capture of proof strategies, a prototype AI4FM system is being developed. It allows us to track proof histories and provides a convenient user interface and scalable data persistence to record the necessary meta-information about the expert's proof process and strategies [Vel12,FJV14]. The current system implementation[2] supports integration with and proof capture from both Isabelle and Z/EVES proof assistants. While it currently employs an older version of *MWhy* (meta-)information model and requires significant engineering effort to keep up with developments of underlying provers, having tool support for proof capture, strategy extraction and replay expands the AI4FM approach beyond pencil-and-paper exercises.

7   Conclusions

From our experiments, the use of *MWhy* (meta-)information about the proof process has helped reduce the burden of proof within three separate proof exercises (see http://www.ai4fm.org). This confirms our hypothesis that it is possible to learn (or capture) (re-)playable proof strategies across the same FM problem, such that from a few POs and key ideas, remaining (recalcitrant and tedious) POs can be discharged.

This paper describes a summary of our meta-information capturing, playing, and replaying AI4FM system, where *MWhy* represents the state, and several operations over this state represent finding suitable proof strategies (play), applying them to a different goal (replay), as well as suggesting specialisations of available strategies as a means to improve strategy application (capture).

This abstract description of the AI4FM system can be implemented in different ways. The prototype *ProofProcess* framework mentioned above acts as an add-on to different theorem provers by capturing and storing the meta-information externally. Alternatively, the AI4FM system could be closely integrated with a theorem prover, allowing –for example– an expert to specify the meta-information within the formal specification, etc.

Further Work. When discovering different strategies, we need to create specific *MTerms*. So far, we have created *MTerms* common to a category of FM POs. We are working to expand that by performing proof exercises over a variety of examples, as well as tapping into previous proofs by authors from the Grand Challenge experiments [BFW09,FW08,FW09].

---

[2] *ProofProcess* framework, http://github.com/andriusvelykis/proofprocess.

Acknowledgements. Other AI4FM members helped us understand important problems in automated reasoning. We are grateful for discussions with Moa Johansson on lemma generation. EPSRC grants EP/H024204/1 and EP/J008133/1 support our research.

Several interesting questions were raised after the presentation at VSTTE in Vienna. Shankar emphasised the virtue of recording information about proof strategies that fail — this was recognised early in AI4FM [JFV13] but the reminder is timely and a way of handling this will be made more explicit in the model. Christoph Gladisch questioned the extent to which "machine learning" could help improve an AI4FM system: currently mechanised learning is focussed on setting of the *Weight* field — we agreed to pursue a dialogue on the topic. Mike Whalen urged others to make source material available to the AI4FM project — we would obviously welcome this but emphasise that we need (instrumented) proof processes rather than just finished proofs — our proof material is available via http://www.ai4fm.org

A   Model

Σ :: bdm: $BdId \xrightarrow{m} Body$
$bdrels$: $(BdId \times Relationship \times BdId)$-**set**

$Body$ :: $domain$: $Domain$
$functions$: $FnId \xrightarrow{m} FnDefn$
$types$: $TyId \xrightarrow{m} TyDefn$
$guts$: $ConjId \xrightarrow{m} Conjecture$
$strats$: $StratId \xrightarrow{m} Strategy$

$FnDefn$ :: $type$: $Signature$
$tags$: $FnTag$-**set**
$defn$: $[Definition]$

$Conjecture$ :: $what$: $Judgement$
$role$: $\{$Axiom, Trusted, Lemma, Subgoal, $\cdots\}$
$justifs$: $JusId \xrightarrow{m} Justification$
$specialises$: $[ConjId]$
$provenance$: $(Origin \mid Why)^*$
$emphTps$: $TyId \xrightarrow{m} \mathbb{N}$
$emphFns$: $FnId \xrightarrow{m} \mathbb{N}$
$other$: $\cdots$

$Judgement = Typing \mid Equation \mid Ordering \mid \cdots \mid Sequent$

$Sequent$ :: $hyps$: $Judgement^*$
$goal$: $Judgement$

$Justification$ :: by: $(ConjId \mid ToolOP)$
$with$: $ConjId^*$

$ToolOP = \cdots$

$Origin = Token$

$Why = Token$

$FnTag = \{$Inv, Pre, Post, $\ldots\}$

$Strategy$ :: $intent$: $[Why]$
$\quad\quad\quad by$: $(ConjId \mid ToolIP)$
$\quad\quad\quad weightings$: $MTerm \xrightarrow{m} \mathbb{N}$
$\quad\quad\quad mvars$: $mvar^*$
$\quad\quad\quad specialises$: $[StratId]$

$ToolIP$ :: $name$: $\{$ SLEDGEHAMMER, SMT, SIMPLIFY, PSGRAPH, $\cdots \}$
$\quad\quad\quad script$: $Token$

$Atomic = prov\text{-}test \mid tag\text{-}test \mid hyp\text{-}test \mid \cdots$

$MTerm$ :: $mvars$: $mvar^*$
$\quad\quad\quad mterm$: propositional terms over $Atomic$

$Relationship =$ USES $\mid Specialisation \mid Morphism \mid Isomorphism \mid$
$\quad\quad\quad\quad\quad\quad\quad\quad Inherits \mid Sub \mid$ SIMILARITY $\mid \cdots$

References

[BFW09] Butterfield, A., Freitas, L., Woodcock, J.: Mechanising a formal model of flash memory. Sci. Comp. Prog. **74**(4), 219–237 (2009)

[FJV14] Freitas, L., Jones, C.B., Velykis, A.: Can a system learn from interactive proofs?. In: Voronkov, A., Korovina, M. (eds.) HOWARD-60. A Festschrift on the Occasion of Howard Barringer's 60th Birthday, pp. 124–139. EasyChair (2014)

[FJVW13] Freitas, L., Jones, C.B., Velykis, A., Whiteside, I.: How to say why. Technical report CS-TR-1398, Newcastle University, November 2013. www.ai4fm. org/tr

[FW08] Freitas, L., Woodcock, J.: Mechanising mondex with Z/Eves. Formal Aspects Comput. **20**(1), 117–139 (2008)

[FW09] Freitas, L., Woodcock, J.: A chain datatype in Z. Int. J. Softw. Inform. **3**(2–3), 357–374 (2009)

[FW14] Freitas, L., Whiteside, I.: Proof Patterns for Formal Methods. In: Jones, C., Pihlajasaari, P., Sun, J. (eds.) FM 2014. LNCS, vol. 8442, pp. 279–295. Springer, Heidelberg (2014)

[GKL13] Grov, G., Kissinger, A., Lin, Y.: A graphical language for proof strategies. In: McMillan et al. [MMV13], pp. 324–339

[HK13] Heras, J., Komendantskaya, E.: ML4PG in computer algebra verification. In: Carette, J., Aspinall, D., Lange, C., Sojka, P., Windsteiger, W. (eds.) CICM 2013. LNCS, vol. 7961, pp. 354–358. Springer, Heidelberg (2013)

[HKJM13] Heras, J., Komendantskaya, E., Johansson, M., Maclean, E.: Proof-pattern recognition and lemma discovery in acl2. In: McMillan et al. [MMV13], pp. 389–406

[JDB11] Johansson, M., Dixon, L., Bundy, A.: Conjecture synthesis for inductive theories. J. Autom. Reason. **47**(3), 251–289 (2011)

[JFV13] Jones, C.B., Freitas, L., Velykis, A.: Ours *Is* to reason why. In: Liu, Z., Woodcock, J., Zhu, H. (eds.) Theories of Programming and Formal Methods. LNCS, vol. 8051, pp. 227–243. Springer, Heidelberg (2013)

[JJLM91] Jones, C.B., Jones, K.D., Lindsay, P.A., Moore, R.: mural: A Formal Development Support System. Springer, London (1991)

[JS90] Jones, C.B., Shaw, R.C.F. (eds.): Case Studies in Systematic Software Development. Prentice Hall International, Englewood (1990)

[KU14]   Kaliszyk, C., Urban, J.: Learning-assisted theorem proving with millions of
         lemmas. CoRR, abs/1402.3578 (2014)
[MMV13] McMillan, K., Middeldorp, A., Voronkov, A. (eds.): LPAR-19 2013. LNCS,
         vol. 8312. Springer, Heidelberg (2013)
[Pau94] Paulson, L.C. (ed.): Isabelle: A Generic Theorem Prover. LNCS, vol. 828.
         Springer, Heidelberg (1994)
[Saa97] Saaltink, M.: The Z/EVES system. In: Till, D., Bowen, J.P., Hinchey, M.G.
         (eds.) ZUM 1997. LNCS, vol. 1212, pp. 72–85. Springer, Heidelberg (1997)
[Vel12] Velykis, A.: Inferring the proof process. In: Choppy, C., et al. (eds.) FM2012
         Doctoral Symposium, Paris, France, August 2012

A Certifying Frontend for (Sub)polyhedral Abstract Domains

Alexis Fouilhe$^{(\boxtimes)}$ and Sylvain Boulmé

Univ. Grenoble-Alpes, VERIMAG, 38000 Grenoble, France
{alexis.fouilhe,sylvain.boulme}@imag.fr

Abstract. Convex polyhedra provide a relational abstraction of numerical properties for static analysis of programs by abstract interpretation. We describe a lightweight certification of polyhedral abstract domains using the COQ proof assistant. Our approach consists in delegating most computations to an untrusted backend and in checking its outputs with a certified frontend. The backend is free to implement relaxations of domain operators (i.e. a *subpolyhedral* abstract domain) in order to trade some precision for more efficiency, but must produce hints about the soundness of its results. Previously published experimental results show that the certification overhead with a full-precision backend is small and that the resulting certified abstract domain has comparable performance to non-certifying state-of-the-art implementations.

Keywords: Abstract interpretation · Abstract domain of polyhedra · Program verification in COQ

1 Introduction

ASTRÉE [1] is a major success of semantics-based static analysis of programs: it is capable proving the absence of runtime undefined behaviours in large scale real world C programs from avionics. Abstract interpretation [2], on which ASTRÉE is based, formalizes the state analysis of programs and guarantees that the analyzer soundly over-approximates the behaviours of the program under analysis. However, ASTRÉE is itself a complex piece of software. Despite the care put in its development, it may contain bugs. One possible solution consists in proving that the analyzer implementation is sound and having this proof mechanically checked by a proof assistant. Trusting the result of the analyzer is thereby reduced to trusting the proof checker and answering the question: Is what has been proved what we want to prove?

This question is especially relevant in the context of automated C program manipulation, where the semantics of the C programming language are part of the specification. The COMPCERT C compiler [3] is a successful project built with the COQ proof assistant. The VERASCO project aims at building an abstract

---

This work was partially supported by ANR project VERASCO (INS 2011).

D. Giannakopoulou and D. Kroening (Eds.): VSTTE 2014, LNCS 8471, pp. 200–215, 2014.
DOI: 10.1007/978-3-319-12154-3_13

interpreter in a similar manner, reusing the CompCert infrastructure: mainly the formalized semantics of the C programming language and the frontend. Once the semantics of the program under analysis are defined, the correctness proof is composed of two components: the abstract domain must be shown to soundly over-approximate manipulations of sets of reachable states, and the link between the program semantics and the abstract domain must be proved correct.

Our work addresses the problem of proving correct in Coq an implementation of the abstract domain of polyhedra [4], which capture linear relationships between program variables. The abstract domain we built is similar both in features and performance to the core of the polyhedra library in the PPL [5] and Apron [6]. We adopted the same two tier architecture as Besson et al. [7]: an untrusted Ocaml backend performs most of the computations and outputs proof hints for the results it produces, which are used by a frontend developed in Coq to build trustworthy results.

The efficient generation of proof hints, which we call *certificates*, is described elsewhere [8], along with an experimental evaluation of the overall abstract domain. The main contribution of the work described here is the design of the link between the Coq frontend and the untrusted backend. It avoids the conversion and transfer of polyhedra. This makes the coupling between the frontend and the backend very loose. As a result, building other certificate-producing backends is easy and has no impact on the Coq frontend code. Complete freedom is given on the choice of data structures: a backend could use constraint or double representation for polyhedra. Furthermore, since the backend does not give formal precision guarantees, a backend could implement relaxations of domain operators [9,10], trading precision for efficiency.

We also present a lightweight method to ensure the soundness of Ocaml code extracted from the Coq frontend, even when the backend has an internal state, or when the functional purity of the backend is not trusted. Last, we describe the architecture of the frontend as a collection of functors which extends a bare metal abstract domain interface. This approach makes the proof modular: it is simpler and more robust to change.

2   A Certified Interface of Polyhedral Abstract Domains

Let us introduce an small imperative programming language, named *PL*. The syntax of *PL* programs is described on Fig. 1. Letter t stands for an affine term and c is a condition over numerical variables with the following syntax:

s	$x := t$	$s_1; s_2$	$\mathbf{if}(c)\{s_1\}\mathbf{else}\{s_2\}$	$\mathbf{while}(c)\{s : p_i\}$
$\langle p \rangle s$	$p[x := t]$	$\langle \langle p \rangle s_1 \rangle s_2$	$\langle p \sqcap c \rangle s_1$ $\sqcup \langle p \sqcap \neg c \rangle s_2$	$\begin{cases} p_i \sqcap \neg c & \text{if } p \sqsubseteq p_i \wedge \langle p_i \sqcap c \rangle s \sqsubseteq p_i \\ \top \sqcap \neg c & \text{otherwise} \end{cases}$

Fig. 1. Syntax and postcondition computation of *PL*

$$c ::= t_1 \bowtie t_2 \mid \neg c \mid c_1 \wedge c_2 \mid c_1 \vee c_2$$

with $\bowtie \in \{=, \neq, \leq, \geq, <, >\}$. All numbers are rationals.

Let us now sketch how to build a "*sound-by-construction*" static analyzer performing a value analysis for this toy language. This will also introduce our logical interface of abstract domains. For simplicity, we assume here that PL programs are annotated, by an *untrusted* analyzer, with candidate invariants p_i where they are hard to infer: at the loop headers. Hence, we only have to prove the soundness of a postcondition computation, described on Fig. 1, which checks whether the candidate invariants are inductive. Given a precondition p, the postcondition $\langle p \rangle s$ of a statement s is computed using recursion on the syntax of s. If a candidate invariant cannot be shown to be inductive, it is replaced by $\top$, which is always safe. This happens when the candidate invariant does not include the postcondition of the loop body and may have two causes. Either the candidate invariant *is not* inductive, or the abstract domain used for checking inductiveness is not precise enough.

The postcondition computation relies on the operators of the abstract domain. Let us introduce them on the example of the abstract domain of polyhedra. Their COQ formal specifications are presented on Fig. 2. A polyhedron p encodes a formula $\bigwedge_i \boldsymbol{a_i}.\boldsymbol{x} \leq b_i$, where $\boldsymbol{a_i}$ is a row vector of rational constants, b_i is a rational constant and $\boldsymbol{x}$ is a column vector of numerical variables of the program. Its semantics, or concretization, is the *predicate* $[\![p]\!]$ defined as $\lambda m. \bigwedge_i \sum_j a_{ij}.m(x_j) \leq b_i$, where m is a total map from variables to rationals representing a memory state. We omit the definitions of the semantics $[\![t]\!]$ of t and $[\![c]\!]$ of c, as they are standard.

– Polyhedron $\top$ corresponds to the predicate `True`.
– Polyhedron $\bot$ corresponds to the predicate `False`.
– Polyhedron $p \sqcap c$ over-approximates the conjunction of $[\![p]\!]$ and $[\![c]\!]$ (hence, the forward predicate transformer for *guard*).
– Polyhedron $p_1 \sqcup p_2$ over-approximates the disjunction of $[\![p_1]\!]$ and $[\![p_2]\!]$ (hence, the forward predicate transformer for *join*).
– Given a term t and a variable x, polyhedron $p[x := t]$ over-approximates the result of applying the forward predicate transformer for $x := t$ on $[\![p]\!]$.
– Boolean $p_1 \sqsubseteq p_2$ over-approximates the inclusion of predicates: if it is true, then $[\![p_2]\!]$ is a logical consequence of $[\![p_1]\!]$.

Although we have omitted them here, the COQ code of the invariant checker needs to formalize the semantics of PL and prove that the reachable states of a PL program are soundly captured by the postcondition computation defined on Fig. 1. This relies on the abstract domain operations satisfying the specifications on Fig. 2.

These specifications are weak: they only enforce that the operators of the abstract domain perform safe over-approximations. They give no information on the precision of the results. Building an abstract domain satisfying these specifications is our focus in this paper.

$$[\![\top]\!]m \qquad \neg [\![\bot]\!]m \qquad [\![p]\!]m \wedge [\![c]\!]m \Rightarrow [\![p \sqcap c]\!]m \qquad [\![p_1]\!]m \vee [\![p_2]\!]m \Rightarrow [\![p_1 \sqcup p_2]\!]m$$

$$[\![p]\!]m \Rightarrow [\![p[x := t]]\!](m[x := [\![t]\!]m]) \qquad p_1 \sqsubseteq p_2 \wedge [\![p_1]\!]m \Rightarrow [\![p_2]\!]m$$

Fig. 2. Correctness specifications of our main polyhedral operations

3 Result Certification of Polyhedral Abstract Domains

While using CoQ enhances the reliability of software, it sets a number of restrictions on the programs which can be reasoned about. First, the CoQ programming language is restricted to pure functions that must be shown to terminate. The algorithms used by the abstract domain of polyhedra are complex to implement and these CoQ requirements would have made their implementation even harder. The most representative example is the simplex algorithm.

Furthermore, CoQ programs cannot use native machine arithmetic for computing. Instead, numbers are represented as lists of bits. The algorithms operating on polyhedra being arithmetic intensive, this suggests carrying out as much computation outside CoQ as possible. Again, the simplex algorithm is the most representative example.

The arguments required to prove the correctness of the operators of the abstract domain of polyhedra make it convenient to offload much computation to an untrusted oracle and keep only a small amount of code to be proved correct in CoQ. We back up this claim with some background on polyhedra.

3.1 Representing Polyhedra for Certification

A polyhedron can be represented in two ways: as a conjunction of constraints (i.e. affine inequalities) or as a set of generators, as illustrated on Fig. 3.

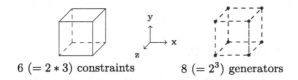

6 ($= 2 * 3$) constraints   8 ($= 2^3$) generators

Fig. 3. Constraint and generator representations of the 3-dimensional hypercube

When working with generator representation, proving correctness of the polyhedral operations specified on Fig. 2 requires proving completeness results. Indeed, forgetting one vertex of the hypercube yields an under-approximation of this hypercube. Correctness of static forward analysis is not preserved through under-approximation, but through over-approximation.

Proving correctness of polyhedral operations in constraint representation is easier, as forgetting one constraint of the result produces a safe over-approximation. The proof can be built incrementally by proving that each produced constraint includes the exact result.

$$[\![p]\!]m \Rightarrow \forall a, [\![p\backslash x]\!](m[x := a]) \qquad\qquad [\![p]\!](m[x_1 := m(x_2)]) \Rightarrow [\![p[x_1 \leftarrow x_2]]\!]m$$

Fig. 4. Correctness specifications of the projection and renaming operators

3.2   Expressing Correctness as Inclusions of Polyhedra

The correctness of each operation reduces to inclusions of polyhedra. However, this reduction requires to first break the complex operations given in Fig. 2 into simpler ones, which compose a *low level interface* of polyhedral abstract domains.

This low level interface has the same inclusion test and join operators as before. The guard is restricted to one affine constraint. There is no forward predicate transformer for assignment, but projection and renaming operators are provided, from which it can be built (see Sect. 6.3). The specifications for projection and renaming are given in Fig. 4. Polyhedron $p\backslash x$ results from the projection of p on the space of variables where dimension x has been removed. Renaming $p[x_1 \leftarrow x_2]$ over-approximates the renaming of x_1 as x_2 in p. Variable x_2 is required to be fresh, but this precondition is not formalized in the CoQ specification as it is not needed for our correctness proofs. A violation of this precondition may result in a precision bug, see Sect. 4.1.

Correctness of the operators of the low level interface can now be reduced to inclusions of polyhedra, with the exception of renaming. However, under the freshness precondition, renaming is a purely syntactic transformation. Three operations remain: the guard of a polyhedron p with an affine constraint c, the projection of a variable x from a polyhedron p and the join of two polyhedra p_1 and p_2. Each constraint c' of their result must be shown to satisfy the inclusion properties specified below.

guard. $\bigwedge_i c_i \wedge c \sqsubseteq c'$, with $p \triangleq \bigwedge_i c_i$
projection. $p \sqsubseteq c'$ (and x should have a nil coefficient in c')
join. $p_1 \sqsubseteq c'$ and $p_2 \sqsubseteq c'$

3.3   Checking Inclusion of Polyhedra

The correctness of the complex low level operations reduces to inclusions of polyhedra. Farkas's lemma further reduces polyhedra inclusion to a linear programming problem on constraint representation of polyhedra. Below, we say that "constraint $a_1.x \leq b_1$ *syntactically entails* $a_2.x \leq b_2$" if and only if $a_1 = a_2$ and $b_1 \leq b_2$.

Farkas's lemma. A polyhedron $p \triangleq \bigwedge c_i$ is included in a one-constraint polyhedron c' if and only if there exists $\lambda_i \geq 0$, such that $\sum_i \lambda_i.c_i$ syntactically entails c'.

Given λ, a vector of λ_i, checking that p is included in c' is straightforward: build the linear combination $c \triangleq \lambda.p$ and check that c syntactically entails c'. This generalizes to a polyhedron $p' \triangleq \bigwedge c'_j$ by supplying a vector of coefficients λ_j

```
type poly

val freshId : poly -> positive
val top : poly
val isEmpty : poly -> (cert option)
val isIncl : poly * poly -> (cert option)
val guard : poly * affineConstraint -> (poly option) * cert
val join : poly * poly -> poly * cert
val project : poly * var -> poly * cert
val rename : var * var * poly -> poly
```

Fig. 5. OCAML interface of the backend

for each constraint c'_j of p'. The vectors λ_j form a matrix Λ such that $p_s \triangleq \Lambda.p$ and the constraints of p_s entail those of p' syntactically. The matrix Λ can be used by a checker to validate the result of an operator: we call Λ an *inclusion certificate*. Nothing is proved when the check fails, however.

3.4   Core Architecture of the Abstract Domain

Farkas's lemma makes result verification cheap. Moreover, it guarantees that producing a certificate to justify an inclusion property is always possible. This motivates the two tier architecture we have chosen for our polyhedral abstract domain.

The abstract domain is split in an untrusted OCAML backend and a frontend which is developed in COQ. The backend performs most complex computations of the low level interface. Its interface is given on Fig. 5. The backend provides certificates of type `cert` that allow the frontend to produce certified results. Type `poly` is the internal representation of polyhedra used by the backend: it remains opaque for the frontend. The functions `isEmpty` and `isIncl` produce a certificate only when inclusion in $\bot$ or in another polyhedron holds. Other operations produce both polyhedra and certificates, except for renaming where a certificate is not needed.

The communication protocol between the backend and the frontend is detailed in next section. Section 5 describes the formalization in COQ of the backend functions. Last, Sect. 6 describes how complex polyhedra operations are built from the low level interface.

4   Using Certificates as Build Instructions

Three polyhedra operators use a certificate from the backend and produce a polyhedron: the guard, join and projection operators. What we have presented leads naturally to a pattern of algorithms for the frontend, which we illustrate for the projection operator. First, polyhedron $p_s \triangleq \Lambda.p$ is built, using the certificate Λ provided by the backend. Syntactic entailment is then checked with the result

```
Definition project (pF, pB) x :=
   let (pB', ce) := Backend.project pB x in
   let pF' := projectUsing ce pF x in
   (pF', pB')
```

Fig. 6. The implementation of the projection in the frontend

$p \backslash x$ actually provided by the backend. An extra check is specific to the projection: verifying that x is free in p.

Checking syntactic entailment is actually unnecessary: p' can be used as a result of the projection operator. It satisfies the inclusion property, by construction. On top of sparing the entailment check, this approach removes the need for the backend to communicate its result to the frontend. The certificate is sufficient. This remark applies to the projection operator, as well as to the guard and join operators.

As a result, the operators follow a simpler pattern, illustrated for the projection operator on Fig. 6. The backend and the frontend both have their own representation of a polyhedron, which we call pB and pF, respectively.

That pB and pF represent the same polyhedron is an invariant property. An operator of the abstract domain consists in invoking the corresponding operator of the backend, thereby obtaining the backend representation pB' for the resulting polyhedron. The backend also produces a certificate ce, from which the frontend computes its representation pF' of the result of the operator, along with a proof that it is correct. This restores the synchronisation between the frontend and backend: pF' and pB' represent the same polyhedron.

4.1 The Impact of Bugs

Previous discussion makes the assumption that all goes well: the certificate is well-formed and yields a representation of the result computed by the backend. However, bugs might lurk in the backend, leading to incorrect results or erroneous certificates. Two possible effects can be observed by the user of the abstract domain.

– If the certificate is well-formed but yields a result different from that of the backend, synchronization is lost and the results built by the abstract domain are likely to be wildly over-approximated, yet correct.
– If an ill-formed certificate (e.g. refers to nonexistent constraints) is output by the backend, the frontend will report a failure. Two failure modes are supported: abort or return a correct $\top$ result.

Unless the backend aborts, the frontend returns correct results in all cases: soundness bugs in the backend induce precision bugs of the abstract domain. These bugs are uncovered using standard software engineering methods.

```
Inductive cert :=
| Implies : list (positive * consCert) → cert
| Empty : linComb → cert
| Bind : positive → consCert → cert → cert.
```

Fig. 7. Coq definition of polyhedron build instructions

```
Inductive consCert :=
| Direct : linComb → consCert
| SplitEq : linComb → linComb → consCert
| JoinCons : linComb → linComb → consCert.
```

Fig. 8. Coq definition of constraint build instructions

4.2   The Certificate Language

The frontend builds correct by construction results using certificates provided by the backend. The type `cert` of the certificates is given in Fig. 7. We will describe the design of the certificates from the ground up on the example of a projection $p \backslash x$ for which the backend has produced a certificate `Implies l`.

From a high level of abstraction, `Implies l` is the sparse representation of a matrix Λ which defines the result $p' \triangleq \Lambda.p$ of the projection. In order to make the certificate compact, the constraints of p are identified by positive numbers and the descriptions of linear combinations, the type `linComb`, refer to constraints by their identifier. Identifier generation is handled by the backend: the frontend requests `freshId pB` when it needs a constraint identifier that does not appear in polyhedron `pB`. The frontend does not check the freshness of identifiers: as described in Sect. 4.1, invalid identifiers may result in precision bugs.

Type `consCert` describes the various ways to build one constraint of p'_1. Its definition appears in Fig. 8. The `Direct` construct is the standard application of Farkas's lemma. For efficiency reasons, a backend may handle equality constraints specially, instead of representing them as pairs of inequalities. Two applications of Farkas's lemma are necessary to build an equality $a.x = b$ from $p \triangleq \bigwedge_i c_i$. One builds $a.x \leq b$ and the other builds $a.x \geq b$. The equality follows from their conjunction and we introduced the `SplitEq` construct to handle this case.

The join operator requires a special construct, `JoinCons`. For each constraint c of the result of $p_1 \sqcup p_2$, it must be shown that $p_1 \sqsubseteq c$ and $p_2 \sqsubseteq c$. To this end, a `JoinCons` certificate contains one linear combination to build $c_1 \triangleq a_1.x \leq b_1$ such that $p_1 \sqsubseteq c_1$ and another for $c_2 \triangleq a_2.x \leq b_2$ such that $p_2 \sqsubseteq c_2$. The frontend checks that $a_1 = a_2$ and then chooses c_1 as the resulting constraint if $b_1 \geq b_2$, or c_2 otherwise. If $a_1 \neq a_2$, the certificate is considered ill-formed.

Type `cert` also provides a construct to build $\bot$, as the result of a guard for example. An `Empty l` certificate is used for this purpose, where the linear combination `l` yields a trivially contradictory constraint, like $0 \leq -1$.

Let us motivate the last construct of type `cert` through a glimpse of the redundancy elimination behind a backend implementation of the guard $p \sqcap c$, with $p \triangleq \bigwedge_i c_i$. Constraint c is rewritten using the equality constraints in p, so as to lower the number of variables involved. The result c' could then be involved in proving that the system of inequalities $\bigwedge_i c_i \wedge c'$ hides an implicit equality e. The new equality e could then used for further rewriting. Building a certificate in that setting is hard. The construct `Bind j cc ce` helps by introducing a new constraint resulting from the linear combination `cc` and giving it identifier `j`. The remainder of the inclusion certificate, `ce`, may then use it.

5 Formalizing the Backend in CoQ

Our abstract domain is split in two components: the frontend, which is developed in CoQ, and the backend, which is written in OCAML. In order to execute the code, the CoQ frontend must be extracted to OCAML code through CoQ extraction mechanism. Extraction roughly consists in removing all the proof-related information from a CoQ development, as OCAML type system is not powerful enough to represent it.

Once extracted, the frontend calls to the backend appear as function calls in the operators code. For the extraction to generate these calls, the backend functions must be declared to CoQ as axioms. Let $\underline{f}$ be an external function of OCAML type $\underline{A} \to \underline{B}$. It is declared to CoQ as a function f, of CoQ type $A \to B$ and the extractor is instructed to replace calls to f with calls to $\underline{f}$. Types $\underline{A}$ and $\underline{B}$ must be the extracted versions of A and B. The OCAML compiler will report an error otherwise.

These declarations prevent the execution of the CoQ development in CoQ virtual machine: the body of the backend functions is not available to CoQ. Furthermore, this process of linking certified CoQ code to untrusted OCAML code may lead to a number of serious pitfalls.

Inconsistency. An axiom like `failwith` : $\forall B,$ `string` $\to B$ introduces inconsistency as it builds a proof of any B from a `string`. In particular, `failwith False ""` gives a proof of `False`. This pitfall is avoided by providing a model of axioms in CoQ: a proof that their CoQ type is inhabited.

Implicit axioms. Inductive type B (e.g. $\{x : \mathbb{Z} \mid x < 5\}$) may be extracted into a strictly larger extracted type $\underline{B}$ (e.g. $\mathbb{Z}$). This introduces an implicit requirement on $\underline{f}$ (i.e. its results are lower than 5) that OCAML typechecker cannot ensure. For our frontend, we have thus carefully checked that CoQ inductive types involved in backend functions are identical to their OCAML extraction.

Memory corruption. Our backend uses the GMP [11] C library. A bug in GMP or its OCAML frontend, ZARITH [12], may corrupt arbitrary memory locations. However, it seems unlikely that such a bug breaks soundness silently.

Implicit purity axiom. Semantics of $\rightarrow$ are different in COQ and in OCAML. In COQ, f is implicitly a pure function: hence $\forall x, f\ x = f\ x$ is provable. On the contrary, $\underline{f}$ in OCAML may use an implicit state such that, for a given x two distinct calls $\underline{f}\ x$ give different results. In other word, axiomatizing $\underline{f}$ as $A \rightarrow B$ in COQ introduces an implicit functional requirement: $\underline{f}$ is observationally pure. Having an implicit state is allowed only if the effect of this implicit state remains hidden (e.g. for memoization). See [13] for details.

However, it may be difficult to ensure that a backend has no observable side effects. In ours, a bug in GMP or ZARITH may break this requirement. Furthermore, our proofs do not rely on the purity of backend functions. The following describes the theory of impure computations we have formalized in COQ in order to declare the backend functions as potentially impure. This theory is inspired by *simulable monads* [14], but from which we drop the notion of prophecy, because we are not interested in generating the backend from COQ.

5.1   *May-Return* Monads: A Simple Theory of Impure Computations

Impure computations are COQ computations that may use external computations in OCAML. For any COQ type A, we assume a type $?A$ to denote impure computations returning values of type A. Type transformer "$?$." is equipped with a monad:

– Operator $\mathbf{bind}_{A,B} : ?A \rightarrow (A \rightarrow ?B) \rightarrow ?B$ encodes OCAML "$\mathbf{let}\ x = k_1\ \mathbf{in}\ k_2$" as "$\mathbf{bind}\ k_1\ \lambda x.k_2$".
– Operator $\mathbf{unit}_A : A \rightarrow ?A$ lifts a pure computation as an impure one.
– Relation $\equiv_A : ?A \rightarrow ?A \rightarrow \mathrm{Prop}$ is a congruence (w.r.t. $\mathbf{bind}$) which represents equivalence of semantics between OCAML computations. Moreover, operator $\mathbf{bind}$ is associative and admits $\mathbf{unit}$ as neutral element.

Last, we assume a relation $\leadsto_A : ?A \rightarrow A \rightarrow \mathrm{Prop}$ and write "$k \leadsto a$" to denote the property that "computation k may return a". This relation is assumed to be compatible with $\equiv_A$ and to satisfy the following axioms:

$$\mathbf{unit}\ a_1 \leadsto a_2 \Rightarrow a_1 = a_2 \qquad \mathbf{bind}\ k_1\ k_2 \leadsto b \Rightarrow \exists a, k_1 \leadsto a \wedge k_2\ a \leadsto b$$

The theory of may-return monads is a very abstract axiomatization of impurity: it does not provide any information about *effects* of impure computations. However, as our frontend only cares about *results* of backend functions, this theory suffices to our needs. Hence, backend functions $\underline{f}$ of type $\underline{A} \rightarrow \underline{B}$ are simply axiomatized in COQ as $f : A \rightarrow ?B$.

Our frontend is parameterized by an implementation of may-return monads: it does not depend on a particular model. Simple transformers over a global state have a denotation in the state monad defined in Fig. 9, using S as type of states. Even if building a model where any OCAML computation is denoted is complex [15] and beyond the scope of this work, this gives us confidence in our frontend being correct when used with a side-effecting backend.

$$?A \triangleq S \to A \times S \qquad k_1 \equiv k_2 \triangleq \forall s, (k_1\ s) = (k_2\ s) \qquad k \rightsquigarrow a \triangleq \exists s, \mathrm{fst}\,(k\ s) = a$$

$$\mathrm{unit}\ a \triangleq \lambda s.(a, s) \qquad \mathrm{bind}\ k_1\ k_2 \triangleq \lambda s_0.\mathbf{let}\ (a, s_1) = (k_1\ s_0)\ \mathbf{in}\ (k_2\ a\ s_1)$$

Fig. 9. The state-transformer model of may-return monads

$$?A \triangleq A \qquad k_1 \equiv k_2 \triangleq k_1 = k_2 \qquad k \rightsquigarrow a \triangleq k = a \qquad \mathrm{unit}\ a \triangleq a \qquad \mathrm{bind}\ k_1\ k_2 \triangleq k_2\ k_1$$

Fig. 10. A trivial implementation of the may-return monad

5.2 Extraction of Impure Computations

The may-return monad is useful to control COQ assumptions that would otherwise be left implicit. However, it is of no other practical interest and is removed at extraction time by providing the trivial implementation given on Fig. 10. The extractor inlines these definitions so that the monad has no runtime overhead.

The trivial implementation of the may-return monad is also used to provide a pure COQ interface to our abstract domain, by exposing that $\rightsquigarrow$ is equality. Although this partly puts the backend in the trusted computing base (TCB), this was actually required to plug our library as an abstract domain of the analyzer developed as part of the VERASCO project [16].

5.3 Backward Reasoning on Impure Computations

Having introduced axioms for impure computations in Sect. 5.1, we sketch below how we automate COQ reasonings about such computations, by using a weakest-precondition calculus programmed as a LTAC tactic.

First, we define in COQ an operator $\mathrm{wlp}_A : ?A \to (A \to \mathrm{Prop}) \to \mathrm{Prop}$ such that $\mathrm{wlp}\ k\ P \triangleq \forall a, k \rightsquigarrow a \Rightarrow (P\ a)$ expresses the weakest precondition ensuring that any result returned by computation k satisfies postcondition P.

For example, let us consider a COQ function g that first calls an external f returning a natural number of $\mathbb{N}$ and second, increments its result. We define $g\,x \triangleq \mathrm{bind}\ (f\,x)\ \lambda n.(\mathrm{unit}\ n+1)$ and express the property that "g returns only strictly positive naturals" as the goal "$\forall x, \mathrm{wlp}\ (g\,x)\ \lambda n.n \neq 0$". Our LTAC tactic simplifies this goal into a trivial consequence of "$\forall n : \mathbb{N}, n+1 \neq 0$".

This tactic proceeds backward on wlp-goals, by applying repeatedly lemmas which are represented below as rules. It first tries to apply backward a *decomposition* rule: one for UNIT or BIND below, or one for pattern-matching over some usual types (booleans, option types, product types, etc.). When no decomposition applies, the tactic applies CUT&UNFOLD. Actually, it tries to discharge the left premise using existing lemmas; if this fails, the definition of wlp is simply unfolded; otherwise, the goal is replaced using the right premise: the unfolding is thus performed with a lemma injection in hypothesis.

$$\text{Decomp-Unit} \ \frac{P\,a}{\text{wlp (unit } a)\, P}$$

$$\text{Decomp-Bind} \ \frac{\text{wlp } k_1 \ \lambda a.(\text{wlp } (k_2\, a)\, P)}{\text{wlp (bind } k_1\, k_2)\, P}$$

$$\text{Cut\&Unfold} \ \frac{\text{wlp } k\, P_1 \qquad \forall a, k \rightsquigarrow a \wedge P_1\, a \Rightarrow P_2\, a}{\text{wlp } k\, P_2}$$

In our CoQ development, this tactic automates most of the bureaucratic reasoning on first-order impure computations. For higher-order impure computations (e.g. invoking a list iterator), equational reasoning is also needed.

6   Modular Construction of the Abstract Domain

We have described in the last two sections a basic interface to the abstract domain of polyhedra. It is a restricted version of the interface described in Sect. 2: the forward predicate transformer for assignment is missing, for example. The gap between the low level interface, closer to what the backend provides, and the fully-fledged interface, that our abstract domain offers to the user, is bridged entirely in the CoQ frontend. The extra functionality is provided through the use of functors. Each functor takes an abstract domain and builds a richer one while lifting the proofs as necessary. This decomposition makes the proofs more manageable and modular.

The overall architecture of the abstract domain is pictured on Fig. 11. The shaded left-hand side is the CoQ frontend. Each of the pictured layers represents a functor. The untrusted backend stands on the right-hand side. While communication between the two is represented by arrows, it reduces to function calls in the extracted frontend code.

6.1   Building the Guard Operator

A first example of our modular construction of some abstract domain features is the guard operator presented in Sect. 3. This operator $p \sqcap c$ accepts an arbitrary propositional formula as constraint c. However, the backend guard operator takes only constraints of the form $t \bowtie 0$, with $\bowtie \in \{=, \leq, <\}$ and t an affine term.

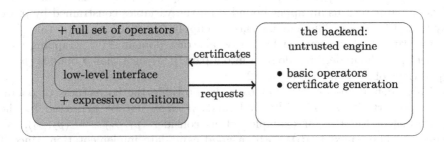

Fig. 11. Overview of the domain architecture

The transformation from the more expressive guards to the basic guards is performed by the frontend by the following steps:

1. Negations are eliminated using De Morgan's laws on binary operators to push negation inwards, eliminating double negations, and taking the dual comparison on atomic formula.
2. Comparison $\neq$ is rewritten as a disjunction of strict inequalities.
3. On $\mathbb{Z}$, $t_1 < t_2$ is rewritten as $t_1 - t_2 + 1 \leq 0$. This increases precision of our polyhedra computations where all variables are in $\mathbb{Q}$.
4. Disjunctions are over-approximated by joins.

For a guard $p \sqcap c$, our algorithm performs a number of polyhedra operations that is linear in the number of operations in c. The functor which provides this extended guard operator to an abstract domain featuring only a basic one also contains the proof that the algorithm described above is sound.

6.2   Framing Potentially Constrained Variables

Generating fresh variables has many applications for program verification: handling local variables, parameter passing during function inlining, implementing the forward predicate transformer for assignment, etc. However, our COQ specifications of abstract domains do not provide any information about the set of variables constrained by a polyhedron. Indeed, these loose specifications allow a modular management of fresh variables: in particular, certification of low-level operations presented at Sect. 3 is not intricated with fresh variables handling.

Hence, this section and the next one introduce generic abstract domains (functors) gluing additional data about constrained variables to the value of an underlying abstract domain. We certify these functors by expressing the invariant of theses additional data through the *concretization function* of the newly introduced domain. We now illustrate the necessity of this trick on a functor that simply frames the variables constrained by an abstract value (e.g. a polyhedron).

Formally, if F is a set of variables, we note $m \equiv_F m'$ if and only if memories m and m' coincide on F. Then, given a polyhedron p, we say that F *frames* p if and only if $\forall m_1 \forall m_2$, $m_1 \equiv_F m_2 \Rightarrow (\llbracket p \rrbracket m_1 \Leftrightarrow \llbracket p \rrbracket m_2)$, and that x *is free in* p if and only if $\{x' \mid x' \neq x\}$ frames p. An operator $\mathrm{bnd}(p)$ can then be defined such that $\{x \mid x \leq \mathrm{bnd}(p)\}$ frames p (variables are represented by positive integers). This operator returns an upper bound β on the variables constrained by p: we say that β *bounds* p. These definitions also apply to conditions and terms.

Operator bnd is provided by a new abstract domain $\mathbb{P}^{\mathrm{bnd}}$ wrapping each element p of the underlying domain into a pair (p, β) such that β bounds (p, β). Operations of $\mathbb{P}^{\mathrm{bnd}}$ are given Fig. 12.

Naive definitions of $\mathbb{P}^{\mathrm{bnd}}$ fail to make provable the correctness of operations: property "$\forall (p, \beta) \in \mathbb{P}^{\mathrm{bnd}}, \beta$ bounds p" may not be preserved by the operations of Fig. 12. For example, let us consider $(p_1, \beta_1) \sqcup^{\mathrm{bnd}} (p_2, \beta_2)$. We expect $(p_1 \sqcup p_2, \max(\beta_1, \beta_2))$ to be a good candidate implementation, since if

$$\mathrm{bnd}((p, \beta)) \triangleq \beta \qquad \top^{\mathrm{bnd}} \triangleq (\top, 1) \qquad \bot^{\mathrm{bnd}} \triangleq (\bot, 1)$$

$$(p_1, \beta_1) \sqcup^{\mathrm{bnd}} (p_2, \beta_2) \triangleq (p_1 \sqcup p_2, \max(\beta_1, \beta_2))$$

$$(p, \beta) \sqcap^{\mathrm{bnd}} c \triangleq (p \sqcap c, \max(\beta, \mathrm{bnd}(c))) \qquad (p_1, \beta_1) \sqsubseteq^{\mathrm{bnd}} (p_2, \beta_2) \triangleq p_1 \sqsubseteq p_2 \wedge \beta_1 \leq \beta_2$$

Fig. 12. Main operators of $\mathbb{P}^{\mathrm{bnd}}$

β_1 bounds p_1 and β_2 bounds p_2, then $\max(\beta_1, \beta_2)$ bounds both p_1 and p_2. However, $\max(\beta_1, \beta_2)$ may not bound $p_1 \sqcup p_2$, as this somewhat contorted, yet correct, implementation of $p_1 \sqcup p_2$ shows when x is chosen above the bound 1:

$$p_1 \sqcup p_2 \triangleq \begin{cases} x \leq 0 & \text{if } p_1 = p_2 = \bot \\ \top & \text{otherwise} \end{cases}$$

Our solution consists in keeping the definitions given in Fig. 12, but changing that of $[\![(p, \beta)]\!]$ so that it implies the property "β bounds (p, β)". Given a concrete memory m, we impose that variables above β are free in $[\![(p, \beta)]\!]m$ by quantifying over any abstract memory $m_\sharp$ that results from the arbitrary update of m on these variables:

$$[\![(p, \beta)]\!]m \triangleq \forall m_\sharp, \; m_\sharp \equiv_{\{x \,|\, x \leq \beta\}} m \; \Rightarrow \; [\![p]\!]m_\sharp$$

6.3 Assignment with Buffered Renaming

The $\mathbb{P}^{\mathrm{bnd}}$ functor can be used to over-approximate the forward predicate transformer of assignment. Indeed, it allows to introduce an auxiliary fresh variable x_0 which names the value of variable x before the assignment:

$$p[x := t] \triangleq (p[x \leftarrow x_0] \sqcap x = t[x \leftarrow x_0]) \setminus x_0 \quad \text{where} \quad x_0 \triangleq \max(\mathrm{bnd}(t), \mathrm{bnd}(p)) + 1$$

However, our abstract domain uses the $\mathbb{P}^{:=}$ functor described below instead, because it performs a lower *amortized number of polyhedra renamings*.

Functor $\mathbb{P}^{:=}$ makes it possible to express relations between memory states in the intermediary computations of the operators. This achieved by duplicating the set of variable names: each variable x can be represented as $x@0$ or $x@1$. Of these two representatives of x, the concretization imposes that exactly one refers to a concrete memory cell. Similarly to what is done in $\mathbb{P}^{\mathrm{bnd}}$, the other representative is arbitrarily updated in abstract memory $m_\sharp$. The concretization involves a function σ that associates its current representative to each variable. It also involves a function π that associates concrete x to both abstract variables $x@0$ and $x@1$, for all x.

$$[\![(p, \sigma)]\!]m \triangleq \forall m_\sharp, \; m_\sharp \equiv_{\{x_\sharp \,|\, x_\sharp = \sigma(\pi(x_\sharp))\}} m \circ \pi \; \Rightarrow \; [\![p]\!]m_\sharp$$

In the $\mathbb{P}^{:=}$ functor, assignment to x switches the representative of x, instead of renaming the variable in the underlying polyhedron as with $\mathbb{P}^{\mathrm{bnd}}$. Renamings from assignments are buffered until joins or inclusions, where they may eventually be performed (only when representatives of identical variables need to be unified). Furthermore, two successive renamings on the same variable in the buffer annihilate (by involution of representative switch).

This functor could be extended so as to buffer projections, which can then be reordered to get smaller intermediate results (in terms of size of representation). The decision to apply projections is delegated to the backend. In this version, the functor introduces a unique representative at each assignment: a kind of SSA form is thus computed on-the-fly in the abstract domain. This extension is not implemented yet.

In conclusion, our modular treatments of assignment depart from [7]: this results in more manageable proofs. In [7], projections are systematically delayed until inclusion tests: we believe that the choice of when to apply projections should be delegated to the backend.

7   Conclusion

We presented one solution to prove the correctness of an implementation of the abstract domain of polyhedra using the CoQ proof assistant. In this setting, correctness reduces to inclusions of polyhedra which, through Farkas's lemma, makes a posteriori verification of results a convenient approach. As a result, our domain is composed of an untrusted backend, to which most of the complex computations are offloaded, and a CoQ frontend which validates the results produced by the backend. This work makes two main contributions.

On one hand, we consider the implicit requirements set when linking certified code to untrusted external code in the CoQ proof assistant. This delicate issue might be carefully considered by certification authorities for e.g. avionics. We partly address it through a lightweight method for declaring the backend functions to CoQ in such a way that the proofs remain trustworthy even when the backend is not functionally pure.

On the other hand, we show how communication between the frontend and the backend can be reduced to certificates, which serve as build instructions for the frontend. The certificate language induces a low coupling between the frontend and the backend: the latter could implement relaxations of some operators [9,10] or use entirely different data structures without requiring changes to the frontend. Although it does not make abstract domain development easier, our approach reduces the impact of bugs.

The complete domain further distinguishes itself from previous work by integrating certificate generation to the backend and by a more modular proof architecture. Experiments shows that it has comparable performance to non-certifying state-of-the-art implementations [8].

The complete code is available on the Web, along with a demonstration application, from http://www-verimag.imag.fr/~boulme/vstte2014.html.

Acknowledgements. We would like to thank Michaël Périn and David Monniaux for their continuous feedback all along this work. We also thank the members of the VERASCO project for their motivating interaction.

References

1. Blanchet, B., Cousot, P., Cousot, R., Feret, J., Mauborgne, L., Miné, A., Monniaux, D., Rival, X.: A static analyzer for large safety-critical software. In: PLDI. ACM (2003)
2. Cousot, P., Cousot, R.: Abstract interpretation: a unified lattice model for static analysis of programs by construction or approximation of fixpoints. In: POPL. ACM (1977)
3. Leroy, X.: Formal verification of a realistic compiler. Commun. ACM **52**(7), 107–115 (2009)
4. Cousot, P., Halbwachs, N.: Automatic discovery of linear restraints among variables of a program. In: POPL. ACM (1978)
5. Bagnara, R., Hill, P.M., Zaffanella, E.: The Parma Polyhedra Library: toward a complete set of numerical abstractions for the analysis and verification of hardware and software systems. Sci. Comput. Program. **72**(1–2), 3–21 (2008)
6. Jeannet, B., Miné, A.: APRON: a library of numerical abstract domains for static analysis. In: Bouajjani, A., Maler, O. (eds.) CAV 2009. LNCS, vol. 5643, pp. 661–667. Springer, Heidelberg (2009)
7. Besson, F., Jensen, T., Pichardie, D., Turpin, T.: Result certification for relational program analysis. Technical report RR-6333, INRIA (2007)
8. Fouilhe, A., Monniaux, D., Périn, M.: Efficient generation of correctness certificates for the abstract domain of polyhedra. In: Logozzo, F., Fähndrich, M. (eds.) Static Analysis. LNCS, vol. 7935, pp. 345–365. Springer, Heidelberg (2013)
9. Laviron, V., Logozzo, F.: SubPolyhedra: a (more) scalable approach to infer linear inequalities. In: Jones, N.D., Müller-Olm, M. (eds.) VMCAI 2009. LNCS, vol. 5403, pp. 229–244. Springer, Heidelberg (2009)
10. Sankaranarayanan, S., Colón, M.A., Sipma, H.B., Manna, Z.: Efficient strongly relational polyhedral analysis. In: Emerson, E.A., Namjoshi, K.S. (eds.) VMCAI 2006. LNCS, vol. 3855, pp. 111–125. Springer, Heidelberg (2006)
11. Free Software Foundation: The GNU Multiple Precision Arithmetic Library, 5.0 edn. (2012)
12. Miné, A., Leroy, X.: ZArith. http://forge.ocamlcore.org/projects/zarith
13. Pottier, F.: Syntactic soundness proof of a type-and-capability system with hidden state. J. Funct. Program. **23**(1), 38–144 (2013)
14. Claret, G., González Huesca, L.D.C., Régis-Gianas, Y., Ziliani, B.: Lightweight proof by reflection using a posteriori simulation of effectful computation. In: Blazy, S., Paulin-Mohring, C., Pichardie, D. (eds.) ITP 2013. LNCS, vol. 7998, pp. 67–83. Springer, Heidelberg (2013)
15. Birkedal, L., Reus, B., Schwinghammer, J., Støvring, K., Thamsborg, J., Yang, H.: Step-indexed Kripke models over recursive worlds. In: POPL. ACM (2011)
16. Blazy, S., Laporte, V., Maroneze, A., Pichardie, D.: Formal verification of a C value analysis based on abstract interpretation. In: Logozzo, F., Fähndrich, M. (eds.) Static Analysis. LNCS, vol. 7935, pp. 324–344. Springer, Heidelberg (2013)

Certification of Nontermination Proofs Using Strategies and Nonlooping Derivations

Julian Nagele, René Thiemann$^{(\boxtimes)}$, and Sarah Winkler

Institute of Computer Science, University of Innsbruck, Innsbruck, Austria
{julian.nagele,rene.thiemann,sarah.winkler}@uibk.ac.at

Abstract. The development of sophisticated termination criteria for term rewrite systems has led to powerful and complex tools that produce (non)termination proofs automatically. While many techniques to establish termination have already been formalized—thereby allowing to certify such proofs—this is not the case for nontermination. In particular, the proof checker CeTA was so far limited to (innermost) loops. In this paper we present an Isabelle/HOL formalization of an extended repertoire of nontermination techniques. First, we formalized techniques for nonlooping nontermination. Second, the available strategies include (an extended version of) forbidden patterns, which cover in particular outermost and context-sensitive rewriting. Finally, a mechanism to support partial nontermination proofs further extends the applicability of our proof checker.

1 Introduction

Program verification aims to establish certain properties of pieces of software, such as termination. But in presence of bugs it is often at least as important to show the negative property by means of a counter-example or, more generally, a disproof, such as a nontermination argument.

In this paper we consider term rewrite systems (TRSs) which constitute a powerful means to express functional programs in a compact way, and are thus a natural input format for program analysis. However, many programming languages employ particular evaluation strategies that are to be considered in program analysis. Thus also TRSs have to be analyzed with respect to specific strategies. In particular, a TRS which is nonterminating when ignoring the strategy may still be terminating when the evaluation respects the strategy.

Sophisticated techniques to analyze termination of TRSs (under strategies) have been developed and implemented in tools for automated termination analysis like AProVE [6] and T$_T$T$_2$ [12]. However, these tools are complex and thus one should not blindly trust them: ever so often some tool delivers an incorrect proof, which remains undetected unless another prover gives the opposite answer on the same TRS. Therefore, it is of major importance to independently certify the

This research was supported by the Austrian Science Fund (FWF): P22767 and I963.

© Springer International Publishing Switzerland 2014
D. Giannakopoulou and D. Kroening (Eds.): VSTTE 2014, LNCS 8471, pp. 216–232, 2014.
DOI: 10.1007/978-3-319-12154-3_14

generated proofs, which can be done using various certifiers [3, 4, 21] that rely on formalizations within some trusted proof assistant. Due to certification, bugs have been revealed in termination tools that have gone unnoticed for years and were easily fixed after they have been detected.

Our certifier for nontermination techniques is developed in the proof assistant Isabelle/HOL [16], and a preliminary version was already described in [23], which however was quite limited: only looping TRSs $\mathcal{R}$ could be treated, i.e., TRSs which admit derivations of the form $t \rightarrow^+_{\mathcal{R}} C[t\mu]$ for some term t, context C, and substitution μ; and the only supported strategy was innermost. There are even more severe restrictions for the other certifiers: [3] only supports loops without strategy, and [4] does not support nontermination proofs at all.

In the meanwhile, we extended our repertoire of formalized nontermination techniques. It now covers techniques for *nonlooping* nonterminating TRSs. Moreover, as strategy specification we now support an extended version of *forbidden patterns* [9], which generalizes many common strategies like (leftmost)-innermost, (leftmost)-outermost, and context-sensitive rewriting [15]. Finally, we also integrated a mechanism to support *partial* nontermination proofs, which further increases the applicability of our certifier and led to the detection of a severe soundness bug of AProVE, which has now been fixed.

We consider our contributions threefold. First and foremost, our extensions significantly increased the number of certifiable nontermination proofs. Second, on the theory level we could drastically simplify one of the algorithms for checking nontermination using forbidden patterns, and relax the preconditions for applying the technique of rewriting dependency pairs (cf. Theorem 14). Finally, we illustrate how termination checkers can benefit from certification: we used Isabelle's code generator [10] to integrate the executable functions from our certifier in T$_{T}$T$_2$, such that this tool is now able to automatically generate nontermination proofs involving general forbidden pattern strategies. This nearly doubled the number of generated nontermination proofs of T$_{T}$T$_2$.

The remainder is structured as follows. In Sect. 2 we give preliminaries. In Sect. 3 we explain our formalization of loop detection involving forbidden patterns. Afterwards, Sect. 4 deals with techniques that allow to disprove termination of nonlooping TRSs, namely the techniques of rewriting and narrowing dependency pairs [7], the switch between innermost termination and termination [8], and a direct technique to disprove termination [5]. Experimental data is provided in Sect. 5 where we also explain how we integrated forbidden patterns in T$_{T}$T$_2$, and why and how we added support for partial nontermination proofs to CeTA. We conclude in Sect. 6.

Our formalization is part of the **Is**abelle **F**ormalization **o**f **R**ewriting (IsaFoR) which also includes our certifier CeTA [21]. Since IsaFoR contains every tiny detail of each proof, in the paper we just highlight some differences between the formalization and the paper proofs. Both IsaFoR and all details on our experiments are available at http://cl-informatik.uibk.ac.at/software/ceta/experiments/ntcert/.

2   Preliminaries

We refer to [2] for the basics of rewriting. We use ℓ, r, s, t, u, w for terms, f, g for function symbols, x, y for variables, σ, μ, τ, δ for substitutions, i, j, k, n, m for natural numbers, o, p, q for positions, C, D for contexts, and $\mathcal{P}$, $\mathcal{R}$ for TRSs. Here, substitutions are mappings from variables to terms, and $t\mu$ is the term t where each variable x in t has been replaced by $\mu(x)$; contexts are terms which contain exactly one hole $\square$, $t[\cdot]_p$ is the context that is obtained by replacing the subterm $t|_p$ of t at position p by the hole $\square$. The term $C[t]$ is the term where the hole in C is replaced by t. We write $s \trianglerighteq t$ if $s = C[t]$ for some context C and $s \triangleright t$ if $s \trianglerighteq t$ and $s \neq t$. A position p is left of q iff $p = o\,i\,p'$, $q = o\,j\,q'$, and $i < j$. The set of positions in a term t is written as $\mathsf{Pos}(t)$ and ε denotes the empty position. The set of variables is $\mathcal{V}$, and $\mathcal{V}(t)$ are the variables within a term t.

A TRS $\mathcal{R}$ is a set of rewrite rules $\ell \to r$. The rewrite relation of $\mathcal{R}$ at position p is defined by $t \to_{\mathcal{R},p} s$ iff $t = C[\ell\sigma]$ and $s = C[r\sigma]$ for some rule $\ell \to r \in \mathcal{R}$, substitution σ, and context C with $C|_p = \square$. In this case, the term $\ell\sigma$ is called a redex at position p. The reduction is outermost iff there is no redex above p, and it is innermost (denoted $\xrightarrow{i}_{\mathcal{R},p}$) iff there are no redexes below p. We often omit p and $\mathcal{R}$ in a reduction $\to_{\mathcal{R},p}$, if $\mathcal{R}$ is obvious from the context, and if p can be chosen freely. A TRS is overlay iff all critical pairs of the TRS are due to root overlaps, i.e., there are no rules $\ell_1 \to r_1$ and $\ell_2 \to r_2$ such that a non-variable proper subterm of ℓ_1 unifies with ℓ_2. A TRS is locally confluent if every critical pair (s, t) is joinable, i.e., there is some u such that $s \to_{\mathcal{R}}^* u$ and $t \to_{\mathcal{R}}^* u$.

We write $t \to^! s$ if both $t \to^* s$ and s is in normal form w.r.t. $\to$, i.e., there is no u such that $s \to u$. Strong normalization of $\to$ is denoted by $SN(\to)$, and $SN_\to(t)$ denotes that t admits no infinite derivation w.r.t. $\to$. We sometimes write $SN_{\mathcal{R}}(t)$ instead of $SN_{\to_{\mathcal{R}}}(t)$. A DP problem is a pair of two TRSs $(\mathcal{P}, \mathcal{R})$ where $\mathcal{P}$ is a set of dependency pairs encoding recursive calls, and $\mathcal{R}$ is used to evaluate the arguments between two recursive calls. A $(\mathcal{P}, \mathcal{R})$ chain is an infinite derivation of the form $s_1\sigma_1 \to_{\mathcal{P},\varepsilon} t_1\sigma_1 \to_{\mathcal{R}}^* s_2\sigma_2 \to_{\mathcal{P},\varepsilon} t_2\sigma_2 \to_{\mathcal{R}}^* \dots$ where each $s_i \to t_i \in \mathcal{P}$. The chain is an innermost chain, iff additionally $t_i\sigma_i \xrightarrow{i}{}^!_{\mathcal{R}} s_{i+1}\sigma_{i+1}$ is satisfied for all i. A TRS $\mathcal{R}$ is (innermost) nonterminating iff $SN(\to_{\mathcal{R}})$ $(SN(\xrightarrow{i}_{\mathcal{R}}))$ does not hold. A DP problem $(\mathcal{P}, \mathcal{R})$ is (innermost) nonterminating iff it admits an (innermost) $(\mathcal{P}, \mathcal{R})$ chain or if $\mathcal{R}$ is (innermost) nonterminating.[1]

Since the paper describes the formalization on an informal level which does not require deep knowledge of Isabelle, we omit an introduction to this proof assistant here. The logic we are using is classical HOL, which is based on simply-typed lambda-calculus, enriched with a simple form of ML-like polymorphism.

3   Forbidden Patterns

This section deals with checking whether a loop is indeed a loop with respect to a particular evaluation strategy: Given a certificate containing a TRS $\mathcal{R}$, a loop

---

[1] In the literature (e.g., in [7]) a nonterminating DP problem is also called *infinite*. This is the reason why in IsaFoR this property is defined as *infinite-dpp*.

and some strategy, our proof checker CeTA can check whether there does indeed exist an infinite $\mathcal{R}$-rewrite sequence which adheres to this strategy.

To support a broad variety of strategies we consider forbidden pattern rewriting, which covers for instance innermost, outermost, and context-sensitive rewriting [9,15]. Hence the formalization of techniques for forbidden pattern strategies has the significant advantage that a wide range of strategies can be treated by the same formalism, so CeTA internally converts all outermost and context-sensitive strategies into forbidden patterns before the certifier for nontermination proofs is invoked, cf. *certify-cert-problem* in `Proof_Checker.thy`. We give a motivating example before recalling some preliminaries on forbidden pattern rewriting.

Example 1. Consider the following applicative TRS which models a buggy implementation of the map function, where ' denotes a binary infix application symbol, and : the cons operator. In the recursive call one forgot to invoke tl on xs and hence the TRS does not terminate.

$$\text{map} \text{ ' } f \text{ ' } xs \rightarrow \text{if ' } (\text{empty ' } xs) \text{ ' nil ' } (: \text{ ' } (f \text{ ' } (\text{hd ' } xs)) \text{ ' } (\text{map ' } f \text{ ' } xs))$$

hd ' $(: ' x ' xs) \rightarrow x$	if ' true ' t ' $e \rightarrow t$	empty ' $(: ' x ' xs) \rightarrow$ false
tl ' $(: ' x ' xs) \rightarrow xs$	if ' false ' t ' $e \rightarrow e$	empty ' nil $\rightarrow$ true

Without strategy there is a loop map ' f ' nil $\rightarrow C[\text{map ' } f \text{ ' nil})]$ for $C = $ if ' (empty ' nil) ' nil ' $(: ' (f ' (\text{hd ' nil})) ' \square)$ which definitely does not show the real problem of map to the user: the loop ignores the common evaluation strategy for if which disallows reductions in the *then* and *else* branches. Note that due to the applicative setting this desired behavior is not expressible by a context-sensitive strategy, but it can be modeled by a forbidden strategy, as shown in Example 3.

3.1   Background

Using forbidden pattern strategies one can specify that the position of any redex may not be below (or above) certain patterns. In this way one can express outermost (or innermost) strategies. We consider the following extended definition of a forbidden pattern which allows for patterns with location R. This admits to also express strategies like leftmost-outermost with special treatment for if.

Definition 2. *A forbidden pattern is a triple (ℓ, o, λ) for a term ℓ, position $o \in \mathcal{P}os(\ell)$, and $\lambda \in \{H, A, B, R\}$. For a set Π of forbidden patterns the relation $\xrightarrow{\Pi}$ is defined by $t \xrightarrow{\Pi}_p s$ iff $t \rightarrow_p s$ and there is no pattern $(\ell, o, \lambda) \in \Pi$ such that there exist a position $o' \in \mathcal{P}os(t)$, a substitution σ with $t|_{o'} = \ell\sigma$, and*

- $p = o'o$ *if $\lambda = $ H (here)*,
- $p > o'o$ *if $\lambda = $ B (below), and*
- $p < o'o$ *if $\lambda = $ A (above)*,
- p *is right of o' if $\lambda = $ R (right of)*.

Example 3. For the TRS in Example 1, the forbidden pattern strategy where Π consists of (if ' b ' t ' e, p, λ) for all $p \in \{12, 2\}$ and $\lambda \in \{H, B\}$ has the intended effect that reductions in the *then* and *else* branches are not allowed.

A TRS $\mathcal{R}$ is forbidden-pattern nonterminating w.r.t. Π iff $\neg SN(\xrightarrow{\Pi})$, which can be proven via *forbidden pattern loops* (Π-loops). To succinctly describe infinite derivations that are induced by loops we use context-substitutions.

Definition 4 [22]. *A* context-substitution *is a pair* (C, μ) *consisting of a context C and a substitution μ. The n-fold application of (C, μ) to a term t, denoted $t(C, \mu)^n$, is inductively defined as $t(C, \mu)^0 = t$ and $t(C, \mu)^{n+1} = C[t(C, \mu)^n \mu]$.*

As an example for context-substitutions, we refer to Fig. 1 which illustrates the term $t(C, \mu)^3$.

Context-substitutions allow to concisely write the infinite derivation induced by a loop $t \to^+ C[t\mu]$ as $t = t(C, \mu)^0 \to^+ t(C, \mu)^1 \to^+ \ldots \to^+ t(C, \mu)^n \to^+ \ldots$.

To facilitate the certification of loops under strategies, one needs to analyze its constituting steps. In the remainder of this section we will consider a loop with starting term t, context C and substitution μ with $C|_p = \square$ of the form

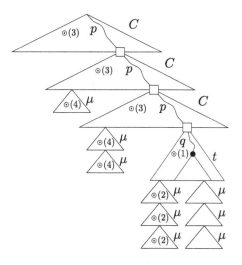

Fig. 1. Redexes left of $p^n q$.

$$t = t(C, \mu)^0 = t_1 \to_{q_1} t_2 \to_{q_2}$$
$$\cdots \to_{q_m} t_{m+1} = t(C, \mu)^1 \qquad (1)$$

A loop of the form (1) is a Π*-loop* iff the step $t_i(C, \mu)^n \to_{p^n q_i} t_{i+1}(C, \mu)^n$ respects the forbidden pattern strategy induced by Π for all $i \leqslant m$ and all $n \in \mathbb{N}$. For instance, assuming that one of the loop's redexes is $t|_q$ as illustrated in Fig. 1, we need to know whether this position remains a redex w.r.t. to the strategy, no matter how many contexts and substitutions are applied around t.

The problem of whether a loop constitutes a Π-loop is decidable. To this end, the following notions from innermost and outermost loops are useful.

Definition 5 [20,22]. *A* matching problem *is a pair* $(u \vartriangleright \ell, \mu)$. *It is* solvable *iff there are n and σ such that $u\mu^n = \ell\sigma$. An* extended matching problem *is a tuple $(D \vartriangleright \ell, C, t, \mathcal{M}, \mu)$ where $\mathcal{M} = \{s_1 \vartriangleright \ell_1, \ldots, s_n \vartriangleright \ell_n\}$. It is* solvable *iff there are m, k, σ, such that $D[t(C, \mu)^m]\mu^k = \ell\sigma$ and $s_i\mu^k = \ell_i\sigma$ for all i. If $\mathcal{M} = \varnothing$, we just omit it.*

A set of (extended) matching problems is solvable iff some element is solvable. Given a loop, in order to decide whether it indeed constitutes a Π-loop one computes a set of (extended) matching problems which has no solution if and only if the loop is indeed a Π-loop.

3.2 From Forbidden Pattern Loops to Matching Problems

A rewrite step is a Π-step iff it adheres to every single pattern $\pi \in \Pi$. In fact a loop (1) is a Π-loop if and only if the following key property holds for all choices of $\pi \in \Pi$, $t = t_i$, $t' = t_{i+1}$ and $q = q_i$ where $1 \leqslant i < m$ [24]:

Property 6. For a forbidden pattern $\pi = (\ell, o, \lambda)$ and $t \to_q t'$ all reductions $t(C, \mu)^n \to_{p^n q} t'(C, \mu)^n$ are allowed with respect to π, i.e., there are no n, o', and σ such that $t(C, \mu)^n|_{o'} = \ell\sigma$ and $p^n q = o'o$ if $\lambda = $ H, $p^n q < o'o$ if $\lambda = $ A, $p^n q > o'o$ if $\lambda = $ B, and $p^n q$ is right of o' if $\lambda = $ R.

This property can be decided by a case analysis on λ, defining suitable sets of (extended) matching problems for each case. In the following paragraphs we give these sets for patterns of type $(\cdot, \cdot, R)$ and $(\cdot, \cdot, B)$. The other cases are similar, details can be found in the formalization.

Forbidden Patterns of Type $(\cdot, \cdot, R)$. For patterns $\pi = (\ell, o, R)$, it has to be checked whether $p^n q$ occurs to the right of o'. There are four possibilities, as illustrated in Fig. 1: (1) o' ends in t, (2) o' ends in a term $t\mu^k$, (3) o' ends in a position of C^k, or otherwise (4) o' ends in a position of $C^k\mu^{k-1}$, for some $k \leqslant n$. Let $W(t) = \bigcup_{k \in \mathbb{N}} V(t\mu^k)$ denote the set of variables introduced by the substitution μ when applied iteratively. Then each case can be covered by a set of matching problems as follows:

Definition 7. *Let $\mathcal{M}_{R,\pi}$ denote the union of the following four sets:*

$$\mathcal{M}_{R,1} = \{(u \rhd \ell, \mu) \mid q' \in \mathcal{P}os(t), q' \text{ is left of } q, \text{ and } u = t|_{q'}\}$$
$$\mathcal{M}_{R,2} = \{(u \rhd \ell, \mu) \mid q' \in \mathcal{P}os(t), q' \text{ is left of } q, x \in W(t|_{q'}), \text{ and } u \trianglelefteq x\mu\}$$
$$\mathcal{M}_{R,3} = \{(u \rhd \ell, \mu) \mid p' \in \mathcal{P}os(C), p' \text{ is left of } p, \text{ and } u = C|_{p'}\}$$
$$\mathcal{M}_{R,4} = \{(u \rhd \ell, \mu) \mid p' \in \mathcal{P}os(C), p' \text{ is left of } p, x \in W(C|_{p'}), \text{ and } u \trianglelefteq x\mu\}$$

For the formalization of patterns $(\cdot, \cdot, R)$, we first had to incorporate support for the *left-of* relation on positions. However, the most effort was spent on the case analysis, i.e., an induction proof showing that any position in a context-substitution $t(C, \mu)^n$ fits into one of the four cases.

Forbidden Patterns of Type $(\cdot, \cdot, B)$. For patterns $\pi = (\ell, o, B)$ the position $o'o$ has to be strictly above the redex, i.e., $p^n q > o'o$. Here two cases can be distinguished: $o'o$ may end in t, so $o'o \geqslant p^n$, or it may end in some occurrence of C, so $o'o < p^n$ (similar to cases (1) and (3) in Fig. 1).

In case of the former, $o'o$ has finitely many possibilities to hit a position in t above q. Thus, this case reduces to finitely many $(\cdot, \cdot, H)$ cases.

In the latter case, $o'o$ is a non-hole position of C^n, i.e., $p^n > o'o$ (and hence $p > \varepsilon$). We consider all possibilities for non-empty subcontexts D, and compute a number n_0 such that it suffices to consider the term $t(C, \mu)^{n_0}$ in order to account for all loop iterations.[2] A detailed analysis of these two cases leads to the following sets of matching problems $\mathcal{M}_B$ and $\mathcal{E}_B$:

Definition 8. *The (extended) matching problems* $\mathcal{M}_{B,\pi} = \mathcal{M}_{B,1} \cup \mathcal{E}_{B,2}$ *are*

$$\mathcal{M}_{B,1} = \bigcup_{\bar{q} < q} \mathcal{M}_{H,(\ell,\bar{q},H)}$$

$$\mathcal{E}_{B,2} = \{(D \rhd \ell, C\mu, t(C,\mu)^{n_0}\mu, \mu) \mid \Box \lhd D \unlhd C, \ D|_{p''} = \Box, \ p''p^{n_0} > o\}$$

where $\mathcal{M}_{H,(\ell,\bar{q},H)}$ *refers to the* H *matching problem for* t, q, *and* (C,μ), *and* n_0 *is, dependent on* p'', *the minimal number satisfying* $|p''| + n_0|p| > |o|$.

Unsolvability of the respective sets of (extended) matching problems is a sufficient and necessary condition for Property 6:

Theorem 9 [24]. *Let* $t \to_q t'$ *and let* (C,μ) *be a context-substitution such that* $C|_p = \Box$. *All reductions* $t(C,\mu)^n \to_{p^n q} t'(C,\mu)^n$ *are allowed with respect to the pattern* $\pi = (\ell, o, \lambda)$ *if and only if* $\mathcal{M}_{\lambda,\pi}$ *is not solvable.*

As to be expected from the technical definitions, the soundness and completeness results for the respective cases required a considerable amount of reasoning about contexts and positions. We preferred contexts over positions whenever possible: position reasoning tends to be tedious because one always needs to ensure that they are valid in the term where they are to be used. For instance, IsaFoR internally represents forbidden patterns as triples $(\ell[\cdot]_o, \ell|_o, \lambda)$ rather than (ℓ, o, λ) to avoid the obvious side condition $o \in \mathcal{P}os(\ell)$. The amount of bureaucracy on valid positions required throughout the formalization was nevertheless substantial. Apart from this, the proofs for all cases could be formalized along the lines of the paper proof. For the case of B patterns the results crucially rely on the new solving procedure for extended matching problems.

3.3   Deciding Solvability of Extended Matching Problems

Solvability of (extended) matching problems is known to be decidable [20,22], and in [23] we already formalized and simplified the decision procedure for non-extended matching problems. In the remainder of this section we present our algorithm to decide solvability of extended matching problems—these problems originate from the outermost loop checking procedure and are also required in the case of forbidden patterns, cf. Definition 8.

As in [23], our proofs deviate from the paper proofs considerably and result in a simplified decision procedure which we also integrated in termination tools. For example, in AProVE we have been able to delete some sub-algorithms (180 lines) and replace them by a single line of code.

---

[2] More precisely, n_0 can be set to 0 if $p = \varepsilon$ and to $\lceil \frac{|o| \dotdiv |q|}{|p|} \rceil$ otherwise.

The decision procedure in [22] works in three phases: first, any extended matching problem is simplified to solved form; second, from the simplified matching problem a set of (extended) identity problems is generated, and finally, solvability of the identity problems is decided. We followed this general structure in the formalization, and only report on the first and the third phase, since the second phase was straightforward.

The algorithm for the first phase consists of a set of strongly normalizing inference rules. It contains rules for decomposition and symbol clash as in a standard matching algorithm[3], but also incorporates rules to apply a (context-) substitution in cases where a standard matching algorithm would fail.

Definition 10 [22, Definition 5]. *Let* $MP = (D \gg \ell_0, C, t, \mathcal{M}, \mu)$ *be an extended matching problem where* $\mathcal{M} = \{s_1 \gg \ell_1, \ldots, s_m \gg \ell_m\}$ *and* $C \neq \square$. *Then* MP *is in* solved form *iff each* ℓ_i *is a variable. Let* $\mathcal{V}_{incr,\mu} = \{x \in \mathcal{V} \mid \exists n : x\mu^n \notin \mathcal{V}\}$ *be the set of increasing variables.*

We define a relation $\Rightarrow$ *which simplifies extended matching problems that are not in solved form, so suppose* $\ell_j = f(\ell'_1, \ldots, \ell'_{m'})$.

(v) $MP \Rightarrow \perp$ *if* $s_j \in \mathcal{V} \backslash \mathcal{V}_{incr,\mu}$
(vi) $MP \Rightarrow (D\mu \gg \ell_0, C\mu, t\mu, \{s_i\mu \gg \ell_i \mid 1 \leqslant i \leqslant m\}, \mu)$ *if* $s_j \in \mathcal{V}_{incr,\mu}$
(vii) $MP \Rightarrow \top$ *if* $j = 0$, $D = \square$, *and* $(\mathcal{M} \cup \{t \gg \ell_0\}, \mu)$ *is solvable*
(viii) $MP \Rightarrow (C \gg \ell_0, C\mu, t\mu, \mathcal{M}, \mu)$ *if* $j = 0$, $D = \square$, *and* $(\mathcal{M} \cup \{t \gg \ell_0\}, \mu)$
    is not solvable

As in [23], where we formalized the inference rules for simplifying non-extended matching problems, we implemented these rules directly as a function *simplify-emp-main* using Isabelle's function package [13]. In this way, we did not have to formalize confluence of $\Rightarrow$.

Note that for this function one faces the problem of getting it terminating and efficient at the same time: if one has to recompute $\mathcal{V}_{incr,\mu}$ in every iteration, the function becomes inefficient; on the other hand, if one passes $\mathcal{V}_{incr,\mu}$ using an additional parameter (e.g., V_i) then the function is not necessarily terminating as it is not guaranteed that V_i is indeed instantiated by $\mathcal{V}_{incr,\mu}$. To see this, suppose the simplification algorithm is invoked on the problem $(D \gg \ell, C, t, \{x \gg \mathsf{c}\}, \mu)$ where μ is the empty substitution but V_i a set containing x. Then an application of Rule (vi) immediately leads to a recursive call with the same arguments.

To solve this problem, in [23] it was proposed to write two functions: The main soundness result is proven for a terminating but inefficient one where $\mathcal{V}_{incr,\mu}$ gets recomputed in every recursive call. A second, possibly nonterminating function has V_i as additional argument and is proven to be equivalent to the first function if invoked with the right arguments, i.e., in this case with $V_i = \mathcal{V}_{incr,\mu}$.

Although this solution leads to an efficient and sound implementation, it imposes quite some overhead. First, one has to write the simplification algorithm twice, and second one has to perform an equivalence proof of the two functions.

Therefore we propose a different solution for *simplify-emp-main*. The simple idea is to pass the pair (μ, V_i) as an argument to *simplify-emp-main*, where this

---

[3] Rules (i)–(iv) in [22, Definition 5], which are omitted here for brevity.

pair is encapsulated in a new type with the invariant that $V_i = \mathcal{V}_{\mathsf{incr},\mu}$. Thus, in the implementation one just has to provide selectors from the new type to both μ and V_i, where it now suffices to write only one implementation of *simplify-emp-main*. Moreover, the whole quotient construction—creation of the new type, writing the selectors, reasoning about this new type—can conveniently be done via the lifting and transfer-package of Isabelle [11]. Note that in the meantime we also rewrote the simplification algorithm for matching problems in [23] using the same idea, again by using lifting and transfer.

For the third phase where (extended) identity problems are to be solved, we could of course reuse the algorithm for non-extended identity problems that has been developed in [23]. However, we did not stick to the complicated algorithm of [22] for extended identity problems, since it requires several auxiliary algorithms and the soundness proofs are difficult or tedious to formalize. (The whole description takes 3.5 pages in [22] where these pages do not even cover all proofs.) Instead, we developed a new, partial algorithm which is easy to implement and easy to formalize. In detail, we show that all extended identity problems that are constructed for forbidden patterns via *simplify-emp-main* belong to a special class of extended identity problems where the context within such a problem is large in comparison to the other terms. This class of problems can easily be translated into non-extended identity problems via the following mini-algorithm: an extended identity problem $(D \approx s, \mu, C, t)$ is solvable iff the identity problem $(D[t] \approx s, \mu)$ is solvable, provided there is some i such that $C \rhd s\mu^i$. For more details on (extended) identity problems and our new proofs we refer to [22] and lemmas *eident-prob-to-ident-prob* and *simplify-emp-main-large-C* within the theory `Outermost_Loops.thy`.

4   Nonlooping Nontermination

While in the previous section we restricted ourselves to loops (though for every forbidden pattern strategy), we now aim at possibly nonlooping nonterminating TRSs, but only consider innermost strategies. More precisely, we consider the variant of innermost rewriting which corresponds to $\xrightarrow{\Pi}$ where $\Pi = \{(\ell, \varepsilon, \mathsf{A}) \mid \ell \in \mathcal{Q}\}$ for some set of terms $\mathcal{Q}$. The corresponding rewrite relation is *qrstep* within IsaFoR, and it generalizes rewriting without strategy ($\mathcal{Q} = \varnothing$) and innermost rewriting ($\mathcal{Q} = \{\ell \mid \ell \to r \in \mathcal{R}\}$). To ease the presentation, in the paper we just consider the special cases $\to_{\mathcal{R}}$ and $\xrightarrow{i}_{\mathcal{R}}$ in the following. In total, we discuss three different techniques which can be used to disprove termination for nonlooping nonterminating TRSs. One disregards the strategy completely (Sect. 4.1), one performs rewrite steps which may violate the strategy (Sect. 4.2), and one directly constructs infinite possibly nonlooping derivations (Sect. 4.3).

4.1   Switching Between Innermost Termination and Termination

Example 11. Let $\mathcal{R}'$ be a confluent overlay TRS which encodes a Turing machine $\mathcal{A}$ via innermost rewriting. We assume that the computation starts in a constant

$\mathsf{tm}_{\mathsf{init}}$ which represents the initial configuration of $\mathcal{A}$. Now consider the TRS $\mathcal{R} = \mathcal{R}' \cup \{\mathsf{run\text{-}again}(x) \to \mathsf{run\text{-}again}(\mathsf{tm}_{\mathsf{init}})\}$ where run-again is some fresh symbol.

Obviously, $\mathcal{R}$ is not innermost terminating: if $\mathcal{A}$ terminates in some final configuration represented by a term t, then $\mathsf{run\text{-}again}(\mathsf{tm}_{\mathsf{init}}) \xrightarrow{i}^*_{\mathcal{R}} \mathsf{run\text{-}again}(t) \xrightarrow{i}_{\mathcal{R}}$ $\mathsf{run\text{-}again}(\mathsf{tm}_{\mathsf{init}})$ is an innermost loop. Otherwise, there is an infinite evaluation of $\mathsf{run\text{-}again}(\mathsf{tm}_{\mathsf{init}})$ when trying to rewrite the argument $\mathsf{tm}_{\mathsf{init}}$ to a normal form.

Observe that in the first case, the derivation may be long and thus hard to find, e.g., $\mathcal{A}$ may compute the Ackermann function; and in the latter case, there might be no looping derivation at all.

However, disproving termination of $\mathcal{R}$ is simple when disregarding the strategy: the loop $\mathsf{run\text{-}again}(\mathsf{tm}_{\mathsf{init}}) \to_{\mathcal{R}} \mathsf{run\text{-}again}(\mathsf{tm}_{\mathsf{init}})$ is easily detected. Hence, for nontermination analysis one tries to get rid of strategy restrictions, and indeed there are known criteria where $SN(\xrightarrow{i}_{\mathcal{R}})$ and $SN(\to_{\mathcal{R}})$ coincide: for example, locally confluent overlay TRSs fall into this class [8]. Thus, the simple loop above constitutes a valid innermost nontermination proof.

We formalized the criterion of [8], though we did not follow the original proof structure, but developed a simpler proof via dependency pairs [1]. To this end, we first integrated a similar theorem for DP problems, as it is utilized in AProVE, cf. *switch-to-innermost-proc* in `Innermost_Switch.thy`.

Theorem 12. *Let $\mathcal{P}$ and $\mathcal{R}$ be TRSs such that $\mathcal{R}$ is locally confluent and such that there is no overlap between $\mathcal{P}$ and $\mathcal{R}$. Then any $(\mathcal{P}, \mathcal{R})$ chain shows the existence of some innermost $(\mathcal{P}, \mathcal{R})$ chain.*

Theorem 12 can not only be used on its own—to switch from innermost termination to termination for DP problems—but it can also be utilized to derive Gramlich's result to switch from innermost termination to termination for TRSs.

Theorem 13 [8]. *Let $\mathcal{R}$ be some finite TRS, let there be infinitely many symbols. If $\mathcal{R}$ is locally confluent and overlay, then $\neg SN(\to_{\mathcal{R}}) \implies \neg SN(\xrightarrow{i}_{\mathcal{R}})$.*

Proof. Let $\mathcal{P}$ be the set of dependency pairs of $\mathcal{R}$. If $\mathcal{R}$ is not terminating, then by soundness of dependency pairs there must be some $(\mathcal{P}, \mathcal{R})$ chain. By Theorem 12 we conclude that there also is some innermost $(\mathcal{P}, \mathcal{R})$ chain: $\mathcal{R}$ is locally confluent by assumption and there is no overlap between $\mathcal{P}$ and $\mathcal{R}$ since $\mathcal{R}$ is an overlay TRS. Finally, by completeness of dependency pairs we conclude from the innermost chain that $\mathcal{R}$ must be innermost nonterminating.   □

The formalization of this proof was straightforward: IsaFoR already contained the required results on critical pairs, confluence, and dependency pairs [18,21], cf. *switch-to-innermost-locally-confluent-overlay-finite* in `Innermost_Switch.thy`.

The formalization also reveals side conditions which one never finds in paper proofs: Finiteness of $\mathcal{R}$ and an unbounded supply of function symbols are taken for granted, but are crucial to construct fresh function symbols (fresh symbols are required in order to build the set of dependency pairs). With more bureaucracy, one would be able to drop the condition that $\mathcal{R}$ is finite—by arguing that in an infinite reduction only countably many symbols can occur, and by implementing Hilbert's hotel one can always construct enough fresh symbols—but since for certification we are only interested in finite TRSs, we did not spend this additional effort.

In order to guarantee local confluence we had to provide new means for checking joinability. Whereas in [18] the main algorithm was a comparison of normal forms of s and t, this is no longer the best solution in our setting, since $\mathcal{R}$ is usually nonterminating. To this end, we now offer a breadth-first-search algorithm to check joinability. The certificate just has to set a limit on the search depth which ensures termination of the algorithm.

In total, we can now easily certify innermost nontermination proofs like the one for Example 11: the certificate just has to contain the looping derivation run-again$(\mathsf{tm}_{\mathsf{init}}) \to_{\mathcal{R}}$ run-again$(\mathsf{tm}_{\mathsf{init}})$ and an indication in how many steps each critical pair of $\mathcal{R}$ can be joined.

4.2   Rewriting and Narrowing Dependency Pairs

In this section we consider two techniques of [7] that allow to ignore the strategy for one step. Given a DP problem $(\mathcal{P}, \mathcal{R})$, they replace one of the pairs $s \to t$ in $\mathcal{P}$ by new ones which result from rewriting or narrowing $s \to t$.

One advantage over the result from the previous subsection is that we only need unique normal forms for the *usable rules* while previously we had to consider the whole TRS. Here, the usable rules of a term t are any subset $\mathcal{U}(t)$ of $\mathcal{R}$ such that whenever $t\sigma \xrightarrow{\mathsf{i}}{}^*_{\mathcal{R}} s$ for some σ which instantiates all variables by normal forms, then in this derivation all applied rules must be from $\mathcal{U}(t)$. There are various estimations of usable rules where the simplest one is provided in [1]. The following theorem already generalizes [7, Theorem 31] which requires nonoverlappingness instead of unique normal forms.

Theorem 14. *Let $(\mathcal{P} \uplus \{s \to t\}, \mathcal{R})$ be a DP problem and suppose $t \to_{\mathcal{R},p} t'$ with rule $\ell \to r \in \mathcal{R}$ and substitution μ. If for $\mathcal{U} = \mathcal{U}(t|_p)$ the rewrite relation $\xrightarrow{\mathsf{i}}_{\mathcal{U}}$ has unique normal forms and there are only trivial critical pairs between $\ell \to r$ and $\mathcal{U}$ then the following holds: if $(\mathcal{P} \uplus \{s \to t'\}, \mathcal{R})$ is innermost nonterminating then $(\mathcal{P} \uplus \{s \to t\}, \mathcal{R})$ is also innermost nonterminating.*

In the formalization we closely followed the original paper proof where we were able to slightly relax the preconditions: it is sufficient to consider the usable rules with respect to all arguments of $t|_p$ instead of $t|_p$ itself. To check that $\mathcal{U}$ has unique normal forms we use the following easy but sufficient criterion: if all critical pairs of $\mathcal{U}$ at the root level are trivial then $\xrightarrow{\mathsf{i}}_{\mathcal{U}}$ is confluent and thus has unique normal forms. The following TRS can be shown innermost nonterminating via Theorem 14, but it requires the more relaxed preconditions.

Example 15. Consider the TRS $\mathcal{R}$ consisting of $\mathcal{R}'$ of Example 11 and the rules:

$$\mathsf{c}(x, y) \to x \qquad \mathsf{c}(x, y) \to y \qquad \mathsf{f}(\mathsf{a}) \to \mathsf{f}(\mathsf{c}(\mathsf{a}, \mathsf{tm}_{\mathsf{init}}))$$

Note that the result from the previous subsection is not applicable, since the system is not locally confluent. However, since $\mathcal{U}(\mathsf{a}) = \varnothing$ and $\mathcal{U}(\mathsf{tm}_{\mathsf{init}}) = \mathcal{R}'$ is confluent, we can rewrite the dependency pair $\mathsf{f}^\sharp(\mathsf{a}) \to \mathsf{f}^\sharp(\mathsf{c}(\mathsf{a}, \mathsf{tm}_{\mathsf{init}}))$ to $\mathsf{f}^\sharp(\mathsf{a}) \to \mathsf{f}^\sharp(\mathsf{a})$ and obtain an obvious loop.

To certify such a nontermination proof, one only has to provide the rewrite step that is performed and a nontermination proof for the modified problem. All preconditions are automatically checked by CeTA.

The second technique considers narrowing of dependency pairs, where a rule $s \to t \in \mathcal{P}$ is first instantiated to $s\sigma \to t\sigma$ and subsequently $t\sigma$ gets rewritten to u, yielding a new rule $s\sigma \to u$. Since instantiation is obviously correct for nontermination analysis, completeness of narrowing is a straightforward consequence of the completeness result for rewriting, cf. `Rewriting.thy`, `Instantiation.thy`, and `Narrowing.thy`.

4.3   Nonterminating Derivations

To finally detect nontermination, one requires a technique which actually finds infinite derivations. As stated before, one can consider loops $t \to^+ C[t\mu]$, however, there are also techniques which are able to detect a larger class of nonterminating derivations [5,17] which are both available in CeTA.

The idea in [5] is to derive *pattern rules* of the form $s\sigma^n\tau \hookrightarrow t\delta^n\mu$ which state that for each n there is a rewrite sequence $s\sigma^n\tau \to^+ t\delta^n\mu$. To this end, there are several inference rules which allow to derive pattern rules, and there is a sufficient criterion when a pattern rule implies nontermination.

Example 16. Consider the following nonterminating TRS.

$$\mathsf{s}(x) > 0 \to \mathsf{true} \qquad\qquad 0 > y \to \mathsf{false}$$
$$\mathsf{s}(x) > \mathsf{s}(y) \to x > y \qquad\qquad \mathsf{f}(\mathsf{true}, x, y) \to \mathsf{f}(x > y, \mathsf{s}(x), \mathsf{s}(y))$$

It is nonlooping, as in the infinite derivation

$$\mathsf{f}(\mathsf{true}, \mathsf{s}^2(0), \mathsf{s}^1(0)) \to \mathsf{f}(\mathsf{s}^2(0) > \mathsf{s}^1(0), \mathsf{s}^3(0), \mathsf{s}^2(0))$$
$$\to^2 \mathsf{f}(\mathsf{true}, \mathsf{s}^3(0), \mathsf{s}^2(0)) \to \mathsf{f}(\mathsf{s}^3(0) > \mathsf{s}^2(0), \mathsf{s}^4(0), \mathsf{s}^3(0))$$
$$\to^3 \mathsf{f}(\mathsf{true}, \mathsf{s}^4(0), \mathsf{s}^3(0)) \to \dots$$

it takes more and more steps to rewrite $\mathsf{s}^{n+1}(0) > \mathsf{s}^n(0)$ to true when n is increased. However, using the inference rules, one can first derive the pattern rule $(\mathsf{s}(x) > \mathsf{s}(y)) \{x/\mathsf{s}(x), y/\mathsf{s}(y)\}^n \{x/\mathsf{s}(x), y/0\} \hookrightarrow \mathsf{true}\,\varnothing^n\,\varnothing$ which states that it is possible to rewrite each term $\mathsf{s}^{n+2}(x) > \mathsf{s}^{n+1}(0)$ to true ($\varnothing$ denotes the empty substitution). And afterwards, it is easy to combine this pattern rule with the rule for f to detect nontermination, again using the methods of [5].

To be able to certify this kind of nontermination proofs, in `Nonloop.thy` we first proved correctness of all inference rules on an abstract level, e.g., where substitutions are modeled as functions from variables to terms. In order to check concrete proofs, in `Nonloop_Impl.thy` we then introduced a datatype to represent proofs, i.e., sequences of inference steps, where also the type of substitutions was changed from the abstract type to a list based representation.

Using this approach, most of the paper proofs have been easily integrated into Isabelle. We here only report on some issues we had to solve during the formalization. To this end, consider the following two inference rules of [5].

$$\frac{s\,\varnothing^n\,\varnothing \hookrightarrow t\,\varnothing^n\,\varnothing}{s\,\sigma^n\,\varnothing \hookrightarrow t[z]_p\,(\sigma \cup \{z/t[z]_p\})^n\,\{z/t|_p\}}\text{if } p \in \mathcal{P}\mathsf{os}(t),\ s = t|_p\sigma,\ z \text{ is fresh} \quad \text{(III)}$$

$$\frac{s\,\sigma_s^n\,\mu_s \hookrightarrow t\,\sigma_t^n\,\mu_t}{s\,(\sigma_s\rho)^n\,\mu_s \hookrightarrow t\,(\sigma_t\rho)^n\,\mu_t}\text{if } \delta\rho = \rho\delta \text{ for each } \delta \in \{\sigma_s, \mu_s, \sigma_t, \mu_t\} \quad \text{(VII)}$$

One of the small problems we encountered is the underspecification in Rule (III): the condition "z is fresh" does not contain the information w.r.t. which other variables z has to be fresh—in the formalization this is clarified, namely $\mathcal{V}(s) \cup \mathcal{V}(t) \cup \bigcup_{x:\sigma(x)\neq x}(\{x\} \cup \mathcal{V}(\sigma(x)))$.

Moreover, there have been several operations on substitutions which first had to be defined, e.g. for domain renamings [5, Definition 3], one defines substitutions like $\{x\rho/s\rho \mid x/s \in \sigma\}$ where ρ has some further properties. Before showing properties of this substitution, in the formalization we first had to prove that this substitution is well-defined, i.e., that the properties of ρ ensure that $x\rho$ is always a variable, and that there are no conflicting assignments.

Further operations on substitutions became necessary for certification. For example, in Rule (VII) one has to check equality of substitutions. Here, it turned out that checking equality of the lists which represent the substitutions was not sufficient, as some correct proofs have been rejected by our certifier, e.g., since $[(x,t),(y,s)] \neq [(y,s),(x,t),(x,t)]$, but both lists represent the same substitution $\{x/t, y/s\}$. Instead, we had to implement a function *subst-eq* which decides whether two substitutions which are represented by lists are identical.

We finally remark on an extension of the original approach that was required in the formalization: while the technique in [5] is presented on the level of TRSs, the implementation in AProVE also applies the method on DP problems, where in the inference rules one has to distinguish between $\mathcal{P}$- and $\mathcal{R}$-steps. Moreover, AProVE also uses the following inference rule, which was not described in [5].

$$\frac{s\,\sigma_s^n\,\mu_s \hookrightarrow t\,\sigma_t^n\,\mu_t}{s\sigma_s^k\,\sigma_s^n\,\mu_s \hookrightarrow t\sigma_t^k\,\sigma_t^n\,\mu_t}X \quad \text{(X)}$$

All these extensions have been integrated in IsaFoR and CeTA.

The technique of [17] is quite similar to [5] in the sense that there are also derivation patterns which can be derived via some inference rules, until some pattern is detected which immediately implies nontermination. In fact, [5] is an extension of [17] as the latter only considers string rewrite systems, i.e., TRSs with only unary function symbols. But since it is currently unknown whether [5] can fully simulate [17], we also formalized the technique of [17] directly, which was a relatively easy task: since everything in [17] works on strings, there was no tedious reasoning on substitutions and renamings of variables required, cf. Nonloop_SRS.thy.

For certification we require the full inference tree that derives the final pattern, where in each inference rule all parameters have to be specified. For example, for (III) we explicitly require σ, p, and z; and for (VII) the substitution ρ has to be provided. Moreover, for pretty-printing and early error detection we require that every derived pattern is explicitly stated within the certificate.

5   Experiments and Partial Nontermination Proofs

We tested our certifier using the TRSs from the termination problem database (TPDB 8.0.7). To be more precise, we considered all 596 first-order TRSs where at least one tool in 2013 has generated a nontermination proof. In our experiments, we tested the following termination tools which all print their proofs in a structured proof format (CPF).

- AProVE'13 and T$_T$T$_2$'13 are the versions of AProVE and T$_T$T$_2$ that participated in the certified category of the termination competition in 2013. Both tools are restricted to nontermination techniques of [23].
- AProVE'14 is the current version of AProVE. It can even apply nontermination techniques that are not supported by CeTA.
- T$_T$T$_2$'14 is the current version of T$_T$T$_2$.

Table 1. Experimental data.

	AProVE'13	AProVE'14	T$_T$T$_2$'13	T$_T$T$_2$'14
# successful nontermination proofs	276	575	221	417
# certified proofs	276	563	221	417
# partially certified proofs	–	12	–	–

Table 1 clearly shows the significance of our formalizations: we doubled the number of certifiable nontermination proofs for AProVE, and can now certify 98 % of the generated proofs.

Since AProVE'13, T$_T$T$_2$'13, and T$_T$T$_2$'14 use only techniques supported by CeTA, it comes as no surprise that all these proofs were certified. In contrast, 12 proofs by AProVE'14 were refused as the applied nontermination techniques are not available in CeTA, e.g., proofs for equational rewrite systems (modulo AC).

To still increase the reliability for these proofs, we added support for partial proofs in CeTA. To be more precise, we added a proof technique called "unknown proof" to CPF which logically states that the certifier may assume the implication $\neg SN(a_1) \wedge \cdots \wedge \neg SN(a_n) \implies \neg SN(a_0)$ where each a_i may be some arbitrary binary relation, including textual descriptions like "equational rewrite relation of ..." which are not formally specified. As a consequence, every technique that is not supported by CeTA can be exported as an unknown proof, and then CeTA can still check all the proofs for the subgoals $\neg SN(a_i)$ with $i > 0$.

Using partial certification, CeTA can check in average 70 % of the proof steps within each of the 12 partial proofs. Interestingly, due to the partial certification capabilities of CeTA, we could even spot and fix one real soundness bug within AProVE. In one example a terminating TRS $\mathcal{R}_1$ was transformed into a nonterminating TRS $\mathcal{R}_2$ although it was claimed that the termination behavior of $\mathcal{R}_1$ and $\mathcal{R}_2$ is equivalent. Since AProVE was not able to finally disprove termination of $\mathcal{R}_2$—and hence there was no complete nontermination proof of $\mathcal{R}_1$—this bug was only discovered due to partial certification, where even for incomplete proofs every single nontermination technique could be checked by CeTA.

To support partial certification in CeTA, major restructuring was required. Previously, there was a hierarchical structure of nontermination proofs where the hierarchy was given by the input: nontermination proofs for DP problems have been a leaf, proofs for TRSs have been the next layer, and proofs for relative termination have been at the top of the hierarchy. However, now for every input there is the "unknown proof" which may contain subproofs for all other inputs. Therefore, the proof types for every input are modeled via one large mutual recursive datatype (it is the datatype definition . . . -*nontermination-proof* at the beginning of Check_Nontermination.thy), which takes considerably more time to process by Isabelle than the hierarchical sequence of non-mutual recursive datatypes that we had before. Similarly, also all functions and proofs for the overall certification procedure had to be defined and proven simultaneously for all inputs. Whereas most of this adaptation was straightforward, we also encountered problems, that some packages in Isabelle do not support mutual recursion. For example, in order to define our parser for CPF, we first had to add support for mutual recursion to the partial functions package of [14]. We refer to [19] for further details on this extension.

In order to obtain input examples for CeTA's forbidden pattern loop check, we integrated support for forbidden pattern loops into $\mathsf{T_TT_2}$. More precisely, we added a forbidden pattern loop check to the already present unfold strategy which searches for loops. To that end, we exported IsaFoR's loop checking procedure to OCaml using Isabelle's code generator. Though interfacing IsaFoR's data structures required some overhead, this proved to be a fast way to integrate a reliable implementation in $\mathsf{T_TT_2}$. Support of forbidden pattern loops allows $\mathsf{T_TT_2}$'14 to show nontermination of all those TRSs in our test set of 596 problems that feature an innermost, outermost, or context-sensitive strategy (197 problems in total), as well as Example 3. In total, by just integrating CeTA's forbidden pattern loop check, we could nearly double the number of nontermination proofs of $\mathsf{T_TT_2}$'13: from 221 to 417, cf. Table 1.

6   Conclusion

In summary, we formalized several new nontermination techniques which cover nonlooping derivations and looping derivations under strategies. In total this formalization increased the size of IsaFoR by around 10k lines. Due to our work, CeTA is now able to certify the vast majority of nontermination proofs that are generated by automated tools for TRSs.

Acknowledgments. The authors are listed in alphabetical order regardless of individual contributions or seniority.

References

1. Arts, T., Giesl, J.: Termination of term rewriting using dependency pairs. Theoret. Comput. Sci. **236**, 133–178 (2000)
2. Baader, F., Nipkow, T.: Term Rewriting and All That. Cambridge University Press, Cambridge (1998)
3. Blanqui, F., Koprowski, A.: CoLoR: a Coq library on well-founded rewrite relations and its application to the automated verification of termination certificates. Math. Struct. Comput. Sci. **4**, 827–859 (2011)
4. Contejean, E., Courtieu, P., Forest, J., Pons, O., Urbain, X.: Automated certified proofs with CiME3. In: Proceedings of the RTA '11. LIPIcs, vol. 10, pp. 21–30 (2011)
5. Emmes, F., Enger, T., Giesl, J.: Proving non-looping non-termination automatically. In: Gramlich, B., Miller, D., Sattler, U. (eds.) IJCAR 2012. LNCS(LNAI), vol. 7364, pp. 225–240. Springer, Heidelberg (2012)
6. Giesl, J., Schneider-Kamp, P., Thiemann, R.: AProVE1.2: automatic termination proofs in the dependency pair framework. In: Furbach, U., Shankar, N. (eds.) IJCAR 2006. LNCS (LNAI), vol. 4130, pp. 281–286. Springer, Heidelberg (2006)
7. Giesl, J., Thiemann, R., Schneider-Kamp, P., Falke, S.: Mechanizing and improving dependency pairs. J. Autom. Reason. **37**(3), 155–203 (2006)
8. Gramlich, B.: Abstract relations between restricted termination and confluence properties of rewrite systems. Fund. Inform. **24**, 3–23 (1995)
9. Gramlich, B., Schernhammer, F.: Extending context-sensitivity in term rewriting. In: Proceedings of the WRS '09. EPTCS, vol. 15, pp. 56–68 (2010)
10. Haftmann, F., Nipkow, T.: Code generation via higher-order rewrite systems. In: Blume, M., Kobayashi, N., Vidal, G. (eds.) FLOPS 2010. LNCS, vol. 6009, pp. 103–117. Springer, Heidelberg (2010)
11. Huffman, B., Kunčar, O.: Lifting and transfer: a modular design for quotients in Isabelle/HOL. In: Gonthier, G., Norrish, M. (eds.) CPP 2013. LNCS, vol. 8307, pp. 131–146. Springer, Heidelberg (2013)
12. Korp, M., Sternagel, C., Zankl, H., Middeldorp, A.: Tyrolean termination tool 2. In: Treinen, R. (ed.) RTA 2009. LNCS, vol. 5595, pp. 295–304. Springer, Heidelberg (2009)
13. Krauss, A.: Partial and nested recursive function definitions in higher-order logic. J. Autom. Reason. **44**(4), 303–336 (2010)
14. Krauss, A.: Recursive definitions of monadic functions. In: Proceedings of the PAR '10. EPTCS, vol. 43, pp. 1–13 (2010)
15. Lucas, S.: Context-sensitive computations in functional and functional logic programs. J. Funct. Logic Program. **1**, 1–61 (1998)
16. Nipkow, T., Paulson, L.C., Wenzel, M. (eds.): Isabelle/HOL. LNCS, vol. 2283. Springer, Heidelberg (2002)

17. Oppelt, M.: Automatische Erkennung von Ableitungsmustern in nichtterminieren-den Wortersetzungssystemen. Diploma thesis, HTWK Leipzik, Germany (2008)
18. Sternagel, C., Thiemann, R.: Formalizing Knuth-Bendix orders and Knuth-Bendix completion. In: Proceedings of the RTA '13. LIPIcs, vol. 21, pp. 287–302 (2013)
19. Thiemann, R.: Mutually recursive partial functions. Arch. Formal Proofs, February 2014. Formal Proof Development. http://afp.sf.net/entries/Partial_Function_MR.shtml
20. Thiemann, R., Giesl, J., Schneider-Kamp, P.: Deciding innermost loops. In: Voronkov, A. (ed.) RTA 2008. LNCS, vol. 5117, pp. 366–380. Springer, Heidelberg (2008)
21. Thiemann, R., Sternagel, C.: Certification of termination proofs using CeTA. In: Berghofer, S., Nipkow, T., Urban, C., Wenzel, M. (eds.) TPHOLs 2009. LNCS, vol. 5674, pp. 452–468. Springer, Heidelberg (2009)
22. Thiemann, R., Sternagel, C.: Loops under strategies. In: Treinen, R. (ed.) RTA 2009. LNCS, vol. 5595, pp. 17–31. Springer, Heidelberg (2009)
23. Sternagel, C., Thiemann, R.: Certification of nontermination proofs. In: Beringer, L., Felty, A. (eds.) ITP 2012. LNCS, vol. 7406, pp. 266–282. Springer, Heidelberg (2012)
24. Thiemann, R., Sternagel, C., Giesl, J., Schneider-Kamp, P.: Loops under strategies ... continued. In: Proceedings of the IWS '10, vol. 44, pp. 51–65 (2010)

Real Time and Security

.

Parameterized Model-Checking of Timed Systems with Conjunctive Guards

Luca Spalazzi and Francesco Spegni[✉]

DII - Università Politecnica Delle Marche, Ancona, Italy
{spalazzi,spegni}@dii.univpm.it

Abstract. In this work we extend the Emerson and Kahlon's cutoff theorems for process skeletons with conjunctive guards to Parameterized Networks of Timed Automata, i.e. systems obtained by an *apriori* unknown number of Timed Automata instantiated from a finite set $U_1, \ldots, U_n$ of Timed Automata templates. In this way we aim at giving a tool to universally verify software systems where an unknown number of software components (i.e. processes) interact with continuous time temporal constraints. It is often the case, indeed, that distributed algorithms show an heterogeneous nature, combining dynamic aspects with real-time aspects. In the paper we will also show how to model check a protocol that uses special variables storing identifiers of the participating processes (i.e. PIDs) in Timed Automata with conjunctive guards. This is non-trivial, since solutions to the parameterized verification problem often relies on the processes to be symmetric, i.e. indistinguishable. On the other side, many popular distributed algorithms make use of PIDs and thus cannot directly apply those solutions.

1 Introduction

Software model-checking emerged as a natural evolution of applying model checking to verify hardware systems. Some factors, among several ones, that still make software model checking challenging are: the inherently dynamic nature of software components, the heterogeneous nature of software systems and the relatively limited amount of modular tools (both theoretical and practical) for verifying generic software systems.

Software systems definable as an arbitrary number of identical copies of some process template, are called parameterized systems, and are an example of infinite state systems [17]. Sometimes the nature of a software system is heterogeneous, meaning that it combines several "characteristics" (e.g. a clock synchronization algorithm is supposed to work with an arbitrary number of processes but also to terminate within a certain time). The scarcity of modular tools is witnessed by the fact that almost everyone trying to model check a software system, has to build his/her own toolchain that applies several intermediate steps (usually translations and abstractions) before building a model that can be actually model checked.

© Springer International Publishing Switzerland 2014
D. Giannakopoulou and D. Kroening (Eds.): VSTTE 2014, LNCS 8471, pp. 235–251, 2014.
DOI: 10.1007/978-3-319-12154-3_15

Despite such obstacles, several industries already apply model checking as part of their software design and/or software testing stages. (e.g., Microsoft [8], NASA [25], Bell Labs [20], IBM [9], UP4ALL[1]). In the aerospace industry, the DO178C international standard [27] even consider software model checking (or more generally, software verification) an alternative to software testing, under suitable assumptions.

The core of our work is an extension of the Emerson and Kahlon's Cutoff Theorem [15] to *parameterized and timed systems*. Assuming a parameterized system based on Timed Automata $U_1, \ldots, U_m$ that synchronize using conjunctive Boolean guards, the cutoff theorem allows to compute a list of positive numbers $(c_1, \ldots, c_m)$ such that, let ϕ be a given specification, then:

$$\forall i \in [1, m].(\forall n_i \in [0, \infty) \ . \ (U_1, \ldots, U_m)^{(n_1, \ldots, n_m)} \models \phi \ \textit{iff}$$
$$\forall n_i \in [0, c_i] \ . \ (U_1, \ldots, U_m)^{(n_1, \ldots, n_m)} \models \phi)$$

Intuitively, the proof shows that the cutoff configuration is *trace equivalent* to each "bigger" system.

The contribution of this work is multifold, w.r.t. the aforementioned factors: it reduces the problem of model checking an *infinite state* real-time software system to model checking a finite number of finite state systems; it shows a concrete example of how to combine verification algorithms from distinct domains, to verify what we call a *heterogeneous* software systems; the cutoff theorem for real-time systems is a theoretical tool that can be applied as a first step when verifying a parameterized and real-time algorithm. A second contribution is methodological: this paper describes how to exploit the cutoff theorem to model variables that store process identifiers (PIDs) of processes participating to the distributed algorithm. This is non trivial, since the former relies on the fact that processes should be symmetrical, thus indistinguishable. In order to show this, we will use a popular benchmark protocol, viz. the Fischer's protocol for mutual exclusion. To the best of our knowledge, this is the first time that the Fischer's protocol has been verified using model checking techniques, for an *apriori* unknown number of processes.

2   Related Work

Infinite State System. Timed Automata and Parameterized Systems are two examples of infinite state systems [17]. In general, the problem of model checking infinite state systems is undecidable [6]. A classic approach to overcome this limitation, is to find suitable subsets of infinite state systems that can be reduced to model checking of finitely many finite state systems, e.g. identifying a precise abstraction (e.g. clock-zones for Timed Automata [10]). Other approaches are based on the idea of finding a finite-state abstraction that is correct but not complete, such that a property verified for the abstract system holds for the

---

[1] http://www.uppaal.com/index.php?sida=203\&rubrik=92 URL visited on April'14.

original system as well [7,14,19,30]. Some other approaches are based on the idea of building an invariant representing the common behaviors exhibited by the system [24]. When a given relation over the invariant is satisfied, then the desired property is satisfied by the original system. Its limitation is that building the abstraction or the invariant is usually not automatic.

Cutoffs for Parameterized Systems. Concerning the use of cutoff for model checking parameterized systems, there exists two main approaches: computing the cutoff number of process replications or the cutoff length of paths. The former consists in finding a finite number of process instances such that if they satisfy a property then the same property is satisfied by an arbitrary number of such processes. Emerson and Kahlon [15] established a cutoff value of about the number of template states, for a clique of interconnected process skeletons. In the case of rings, a constant between 2 and 5 is enough [18]. For shared resources management algorithms [11], the cutoff value is the number of resources plus the quantified processes (in the decidable fragment of processes with equal priority). Other works proved that one process per template is enough, for certain grids [26]. Recently, in [5] it has been showed that certain parameterized systems may admit a cutoff which is not computable, while Hanna *et al.* [22] proposed a procedure to compute a cutoff for Input-Output Automata that is independent of the communication topology. On the other hand, computing the cutoff length of paths of a parameterized system consists in finding an upper bound on the number of nodes in its longest computation path. When a property is satisfied within the bounded path, then the property holds for a system with unbound paths, i.e., with an arbitrary number of process instances. The classic work from German and Sistla [19], Emerson and Namjoshi [16] proved that such a cutoff exists for the verification of parameterized systems composed of a control process and an arbitrary number of user processes against indexed LTL properties. Yang and Li [29] proposed a sound and complete method to compute such a cutoff for parameterized systems with only rendezvous actions. In that work, the property itself is represented as an automaton. Lately it has been also showed that parameterized systems on pairwise rendezvous do not admit, in general, a cutoff [7]. To the best of our knowledge, cutoff theorems have not been stated previously for timed systems. Surprisingly enough, extending Emerson and Kahlon cutoff theorems [15] to timed systems does not increase the cutoff value.

Parameterized Networks of Timed or Hybrid Automata. The realm of real-time systems (timed automata and, more in general, hybrid automata) with a finite but unknown number of instances has been explored. Abdulla and Jonsson [1] proposed in their seminal work to reduce safety properties to reachability properties. They worked with a network composed by an arbitrary set of identical timed automata controlled by a controller (i.e. a finite timed automaton as well). Abdulla et al. show also that checking safety properties in networks of timed automata with multiple clocks is an undecidable problem [2], as well as the problem of determining if a state is visited infinitely often, in the continuous time model (in the discrete time model, instead, it is decidable) [3]. It should be remarked that in their undecidability proof, the network of timed automata must rely on synchronous rendezvous in order to prove the undecidability results. This motivated us to explore timed automata with different synchronization mechanisms in this work. Ghilardi et al. [13], reduced model checking safety properties to reachability problem. Similarly to Abdulla and Jonsson, they applied their approach to networks composed by an arbitrary set of timed automata interacting with a controller. Their original contribution consisted in the usage of Satisfiability Modulo Theories techniques. Göthel and Glesner [21] proposed a semi-automatic verification methodology based on finding network invariants and using both theorem proving and model checking. Along the same line, Johnson and Mitra [23] proposed a semi-automatic verification of safety properties for parameterized networks of hybrid automata with rectangular dynamics. They based their approach on a combination of invariant synthesis and inductive invariant proving. Their main limitation is that specifications are often not inductive properties (e.g. the mutual exclusion property it is not an inductive property). In this case one must show that a set of inductive invariants can imply the desired property. This last step is often not fully automatic.

We consider systems composed of a finite number of templates, each of which can be instantiated an arbitrary number of times. We limit Timed Automata to synchronize using Conjunctive Guards, instead of the classic Pairwise Rendezvous [10], because, as already mentioned, parameterized systems with pairwise rendezvous do not admit, in general, a cutoff [7]. Finally, the verification proposed in this paper is completely automatic.

3   Parameterized Networks of Timed Automata

This work introduces Parameterized Networks of Timed Automata (PNTA), an extensions of Timed Automata that synchronize using conjunctive Boolean guards. We also introduce Indexed-Timed CTL*, a temporal logic that integrates TCTL and MTL [12], for reasoning about timed processes, together with Indexed-CTL*\X [15], for reasoning about parametric networks of processes. In the following definition we will make use of a set of *temporal constraints* $TC(C_l)$, defined as:

$$TC(C) ::= \top \mid \neg\, TC(C) \mid TC(C) \,\vee\, TC(C) \mid$$
$$C \,\sim\, C \mid C \,\sim\, \mathbb{Q}^{\geq 0}$$

where $\sim\, \in\, \{<, \leq, >, \geq, =\}$, C is a set of clock variables and $\mathbb{Q}$ denotes the set of rational numbers.

Definition 1 (Timed Automaton Template). *A Timed Automaton (TA) Template U_l is a tuple $\langle S_l, \hat{s}_l, C_l, \Gamma_l, \tau_l, I_l \rangle$ where:*

- S_l *is a finite set of states, or locations;*
- $\hat{s}_l \in S_l$ *is a distinguished initial state;*
- C_l *is a finite set of clock variables;*

- Γ_l is a finite set of Boolean guards built upon S_l;
- $\tau_l \subseteq S_l \times TC(C_l) \times 2^{C_l} \times \Gamma_l \times S_l$ is a finite set of transitions;
- $I_l : S_l \to TC(C_l)$ maps a state to an invariant, such that $I_l(\hat{s}_l) = \top$;

We will denote with $|U_l| = |S_l|$ the size of the timed automaton. A network of timed automata can be defined as a set of k TA templates, where each TA template (say U_l) is instantiated an arbitrary number (say n_l) of times.

Definition 2 (PNTA). *Let $(U_1, \ldots, U_k)$ be a set of Timed Automaton templates. Let $(n_1, \ldots, n_k)$ be a set of natural numbers. Then*

$$(U_1, \ldots, U_k)^{(n_1, \ldots, n_k)}$$

is a Parameterized Network of Timed Automata denoting the asynchronous parallel composition of timed automata $U_1^1 || \ldots || U_1^{n_1} || \ldots || U_k^1 || \ldots || U_k^{n_k}$, such that for each $l \in [1, k]$ and $i \in [1, n_l]$, then U_l^i is the i-th copy of U_l.

Let us remark that every component of U_l^i is a disjoint copy of the corresponding template component. In the following will be described how every process U_l^i, also called instance, can take a local step after having checked that the neighbors' states satisfy the transition (conjunctive) Boolean guard. In such system a process can check it is "safe" to take a local step, but it cannot induce a move on a different instance. A PNTA based on conjunctive guards is defined as follows.

Definition 3 (PNTA with Conjunctive Guards). *Let $(U_1, \ldots, U_k)^{(n_1, \ldots, n_k)}$ be a PNTA. Then, it is a PNTA with Conjunctive Guards iff every $\gamma \in \Gamma_l^i$ is a Boolean expression with the following form:*

$$\bigwedge_{\substack{m \in [1, n_1] \\ m \neq i}} (\hat{s}_l(m) \vee s_l^1(m) \vee \cdots \vee s_l^p(m)) \wedge \bigwedge_{\substack{h \in [1, k] \\ h \neq l}} (\bigwedge_{j \in [1, n_j]} (\hat{s}_h(j) \vee s_h^1(j) \vee \cdots \vee s_h^q(j)))$$

where, for all $l \in [1, k]$, $i \in [1, n_l]$ and $p > 0$, $\{s_l^1, \ldots, s_l^p\} \subseteq S_l$, $s_l(i) \in S_l^i$ and $\hat{s}_l$ is the initial states of U_l. The initial states $\hat{s}_l(m)$ and $\hat{s}_h(j)$ must be present.

We remark that our definitions of Timed Automaton template, PNTA and PNTA with Conjunctive Guards are variants of the notion of *timed automata* and *networks of timed automata* found in literature (e.g. [10]).

The *operational semantics* of PNTA with conjunctive guards is expressed as a transition system over *PNTA configurations*.

Definition 4 (PNTA Configuration). *Let $(U_1, \ldots, U_k)^{(n_1, \ldots, n_k)}$ be a PNTA. Then a configuration is a tuple:*

$$\mathfrak{c} = (\langle \overline{s}_1, \overline{u}_1 \rangle, \ldots, \langle \overline{s}_k, \overline{u}_k \rangle)$$

where, for each $l \in [1, k]$:

- $\overline{s}_l : [1, n_l] \to S_l$ *maps an instance to its current state, and*
- $\overline{u}_l : [1, n_l] \to (C_l \to \mathbb{R}^{\geq 0})$, *maps an instance to its clock function, s.t.*

$$\forall i \, . \, \overline{u}_l(i) \models I_l^i(\overline{s}_l(i)) \tag{1}$$

$\mathfrak{C}$ *is the set of all the configurations.*

Intuitively, let $(\ldots, \langle \overline{s}_l, \overline{u}_l \rangle, \ldots)$ be a configuration, then $\overline{s}_l(i) \in S_l$ denotes the state where instance U_l^i is in that configuration. $\overline{u}_l(i)$ is the clock assignment function (i.e., $\overline{u}_l(i) : C_l \to \mathbb{R}^{\geq 0}$) of instance U_l^i in that configuration. In other words, for each $c \in C_l$, $\overline{u}_l(i)(c)$ is the current value that the clock variable c assumes for instance U_l^i. Any assignment to such clock variables must satisfy the invariant for the corresponding state (see Eq. (1)). The notion of transition requires some auxiliary notations. Let $l \in [1, k]$, and let $i \in [1, n_l]$, then we call:

- *initial configuration*
  $\hat{\mathfrak{c}} \in \mathfrak{C}$ such that, for each $l \in [1, k]$, for each $i \in [1, n_k]$:
  $\overline{s}_l(i) = \hat{s}_l^i$, and
  $\forall c \in C_l, \overline{u}_l(i)(c) = 0$.
- *projection*
  $\forall \mathfrak{c} = (\langle \overline{s}_1, \overline{u}_1 \rangle, \ldots, \langle \overline{s}_l, \overline{u}_l \rangle, \ldots, \langle \overline{s}_k, \overline{u}_k \rangle) \in \mathfrak{C}$,
  $\mathfrak{c}(l) = \langle \overline{s}_l, \overline{u}_l \rangle$, and
  $\mathfrak{c}(l, i) = \langle \overline{s}_l(i), \overline{u}_l(i) \rangle$.
- *state-component*
  $\forall \mathfrak{c} = (\langle \overline{s}_1, \overline{u}_1 \rangle, \ldots, \langle \overline{s}_l, \overline{u}_l \rangle, \ldots, \langle \overline{s}_k, \overline{u}_k \rangle) \in \mathfrak{C}$,
  $state(\mathfrak{c}) = (\overline{s}_1, \ldots, \overline{s}_l, \ldots, \overline{s}_k)$,
  $state(\mathfrak{c}(l)) = \overline{s}_l$, and
  $state(\mathfrak{c}(l, i)) = \overline{s}_l(i)$.
- *clock-component*
  $\forall \mathfrak{c} = (\langle \overline{s}_1, \overline{u}_1 \rangle, \ldots, \langle \overline{s}_l, \overline{u}_l \rangle, \ldots, \langle \overline{s}_k, \overline{u}_k \rangle) \in \mathfrak{C}, \forall c \in C_l$,
  $clock(\mathfrak{c}) = (\overline{u}_1, \ldots, \overline{u}_l, \ldots, \overline{u}_k)$,
  $clock(\mathfrak{c}(l)) = \overline{u}_l$,
  $clock(\mathfrak{c}(l, i)) = \overline{u}_l(i)$, thus
  $clock(\mathfrak{c}(l, i))(c) = \overline{u}_l(i)(c)$.
- *time increase*
  $\forall c \in C_l. \forall d \in \mathbb{R}^{\geq 0}. (\overline{u}_l + d)(i)(c) = \overline{u}_l(i)(c) + d$
  $(clock(\mathfrak{c}) + d) = (\overline{u}_1 + d, \ldots, \overline{u}_l + d, \ldots, \overline{u}_k + d)$,
  $(clock(\mathfrak{c}(l)) + d) = (\overline{u}_l + d)$, and
  $(clock(\mathfrak{c}(l, i)) + d) = (\overline{u}_l + d)(i)$.
- *clock reset*
  $\forall c \in C_l \, . \, \forall r \subseteq C_l \, . \, \forall j \, .$

$$\overline{u}_l[(i, r) \mapsto 0](j)(c) = \begin{cases} 0 & \text{if } i = j \text{ and } c \in r \\ \overline{u}_l(j)(c) & \text{otherwise} \end{cases}$$

- *clock constraint evaluation*
  $\overline{u}_l(i) \models g$ *iff the clock values of instance U_l^i denoted by $\overline{u}_l(i)$ satisfy the clock constraint g; the semantics $\models$ is defined as usual by induction on the structure of g;*

- *guard evaluation*

  $state(c) \models \gamma$ *iff* the set of states of $(U_1, \ldots, U_k)^{(n_1, \ldots, n_k)}$ denoted by $state(c)$ satisfies the Boolean guard γ; this predicate as well can be defined by induction on the structure of γ.

Definition 5 (PNTA Transitions). *The transitions among PNTA configurations are governed by the following rules:*

(delay)
$$c \xrightarrow{d} c' \qquad if \quad d \in \mathbb{R}^{\geq 0}$$
$$state(c') = state(c)$$
$$clock(c') = (clock(c) + d)$$
$$\forall l, i, d' \in [0, d].clock(c(l, i)) + d' \models I_l^i(state(c(l, i)))$$

(synchronization)
$$c \xrightarrow{\gamma} c' \qquad if \quad \exists l \in [1, k] . \exists i \in [1, n_l] \ :$$
$$s \xrightarrow{g, r, \gamma} t \in \tau_l^i.$$
$$state(c(l, i)) = s,$$
$$clock(c(l, i)) \models g,$$
$$state(c) \models \gamma,$$
$$c'(h) = c(h) \ \text{for each} \ h \neq l,$$
$$c'(l, j) = c(l, j) \ \text{for each} \ j \neq i,$$
$$c'(l, i) = \langle t, clock(c(l, i))[(r, i) \mapsto 0] \rangle$$
$$clock(c'(l, i)) \models I_l^i(state(c'(l, i)))$$

Let us define what is a *timed-computation* for PNTA.

Definition 6 (Timed Computation). *Let $\hat{c}_0$ be an initial configuration, a timed-computation x is a finite or infinite sequence of pairs:*

$$x = (c_0, t_0) \ldots (c_v, t_v) \ldots$$

s.t. $t_0 = 0$ and $\forall v \geq 0 . (\exists d > 0 . c_v \xrightarrow{d} c_{v+1} \wedge t_{v+1} = t_v + d) \vee (\exists \gamma . c_v \xrightarrow{\gamma} c_{v+1} \wedge t_{v+1} = t_v)$

In other words, a timed computation can be seen as a sequence of *snapshots* of the transition system configurations taken at successive times. It should be noticed that, according to Emerson and Kahlon [15], in this work, it has been adopted the so-called *interleaving semantics*. This means that in a transition between two configurations, only one instance can change its state (see the *synchronization* rule in Definition 5). For the sake of conciseness, let us extend the notion of *projection*, *state-component*, and *clock-component* to timed computations. Let $x = (c_0, t_0) \ldots (c_v, t_v) \ldots$ be a timed computation, let $x_v = (c_v, t_v)$ be the v-th element of x, then

$$
\begin{aligned}
x(l) &= (c_0(l), t_0) \ldots (c_v(l), t_v) \ldots & clock(x_v) &= clock(c_v) \\
x(l, i) &= (c_0(l, i), t_0) \ldots (c_v(l, i), t_v) \ldots & clock(x_v(l)) &= clock(c_v(l)) \\
x_v(l) &= (c_v(l), t_v) & clock(x_v(l, i)) &= clock(c_v(l, i)) \\
x_v(l, i) &= (c_v(l, i), t_v) & & \\
state(x_v) &= state(c_v) & time(x_v) &= t_v \\
state(x_v(l)) &= state(c_v(l)) & time(x_v(l)) &= t_v \\
state(x_v(l, i)) &= state(c_v(l, i)) & time(x_v(l, i)) &= t_v
\end{aligned}
$$

$x(l, i)$ is called the *local computation* of the i-th instance of automaton template l. $time(x_v)$, $time(x_v(l))$, and $time(x_v(l, i))$ are the *time-components* of x_v, $x_v(l)$, and $x_v(l, i)$ respectively.

Definition 7 (Idle Local Computation). *Let* $U_l^i = \langle S_l^i, \hat{s}_l^i, C_l^i, \tau_l^i, I_l^i \rangle$ *be the i-th instance of the timed automaton template* U_l. *An idle local computation* $\hat{s}(l, i)$ *is a timed local computation such that, for all* $v \geq 0$:

$$
\begin{aligned}
\hat{s}(l, i) &= (\langle \hat{s}_l^i, \overline{u}_l(i) \rangle, t_0) \ldots (\langle \hat{s}_l^i, \overline{u}_l(i) + t_v \rangle, t_v) \ldots \\
\hat{s}_v(l, i) &= (\langle \hat{s}_l^i, \overline{u}_l(i) + t_v \rangle, t_v)
\end{aligned}
$$

where $t_0 = 0$ *and for each* $c \in C_l$, $\overline{u}_l(i)(c) = 0$.

It should be noticed that for each v, it must be $\overline{u}_l(i) + t_v \models I_l^i(\hat{s}_l^i)$, since $I_l^i(\hat{s}_l^i) = \top$ according to Definition 1. Intuitively, an idle local computation is an instance of the automaton template U_l that stutters in its initial state.

Definition 8 (Stuttering). *Let* x *and* y *be two timed computations. Let* $x = x_0 \cdot \ldots \cdot x_v \cdot x_{v+1} \ldots$ *The timed computation* y *is a stuttering of the timed computation* x *iff for all* $v \geq 0$, *there exists* $r \geq 0$, *such that*

$$
y = x_0 \cdot \ldots \cdot x_v \cdot x_{v,\delta_1} \cdot x_{v,\delta_2} \cdot \ldots \cdot x_{v,\delta_r} \cdot x_{v+1} \ldots
$$

where $\delta_1, \delta_2, \ldots, \delta_r \in \mathbb{R}^{\geq 0}$, $\delta_1 \leq \delta_2 \leq \cdots \leq \delta_r$, $t_v + \delta_r \leq t_{v+1}$, *and*

$$
\begin{aligned}
x_{v,\delta_1} &= (\langle state(x_v), clock(x_v) + \delta_1 \rangle, t_v + \delta_1) \\
x_{v,\delta_2} &= (\langle state(x_v), clock(x_v) + \delta_2 \rangle, t_v + \delta_2) \\
&\ldots \\
x_{v,\delta_r} &= (\langle state(x_v), clock(x_v) + \delta_r \rangle, t_v + \delta_r)
\end{aligned}
$$

Intuitively, the above definition means that a stuttering of a given timed computation x can be generated by inserting an arbitrary number of *delay transitions* (see Definition 5) short enough to not alter the validity of temporal conditions of the original computation x. It only represents a more detailed view (i.e. a finer sampling) of the interval between a configuration and the next one without changing the original sequence of states.

For the purpose of this work, timed computations conforming to Definition 6 (i.e. each configuration complies with Eq. (1)) can be classified in three different kinds of computation:

- *Infinite Timed Computation*: x is a timed computation of infinite length.
- *Deadlocked Timed Computation*: x is a maximal finite timed computation, i.e. in it reaches a final configuration where all transitions are disabled.
- *Finite Timed Computation*: x is a (not necessarily maximal) final timed computation, i.e. it is either a deadlocked computation or a finite prefix of an infinite one.

4   A Temporal Logic for PNTA

A dedicated logic is needed in order to specify behaviors of a PNTA. This logic, named Indexed-Timed-CTL*, allows to reason about real-time intervals and temporal relations (until, before, after, . . .) in systems of arbitrary size. While its satisfiability problem is undecidable, the problem of model checking a PNTA is proved to be decidable, under certain conditions.

Definition 9 (Indexed-Timed-CTL*). *Let $\{P_l\}_{l\in[1,k]}$ be finite sets of atomic propositions. Let $p(l,i)$ be any atomic proposition such that $l \in [1,k]$, $i \in \mathbb{N}^{>0}$, and $p \in P_l$. Then, the set of ITCTL* formulae is inductively defined as follows:*

$$\phi ::= \top \mid p(l,i) \mid \phi \wedge \phi \mid \neg\phi \mid \bigwedge_{i_l} \phi \mid A\Phi \mid A_{fin}\Phi \mid A_{inf}\Phi$$

$$\Phi ::= \phi \mid \Phi \wedge \Phi \mid \neg\Phi \mid \Phi\,\mathcal{U}_{\sim q}\,\Phi$$

where $\sim\; \in \{<,\leq,\geq,>,=\}$ and $q \in \mathbb{Q}^{\geq 0}$.

As usual for branching-time temporal logics, the terms in ϕ denote *state* formulae, while terms in Φ denote *path* formulae. For the purpose of this work it is enough to assume the set of atomic propositions coincides with the set of states of a given PNTA, i.e. $P_l = S_l$, for every l.

The path quantifier A_{fin} (resp. A_{inf}) is a variant of the usual universal path quantifier A, restricted to paths that are of finite length (resp. infinite length). Such variants are inspired by [15]. Missing Boolean ($\vee, \rightarrow, \dots$) operators, temporal operators ($\mathcal{G}, \mathcal{F}, \mathcal{W}, \dots$), as well as path quantifiers (E, E_{fin}, E_{inf}) can be defined as usual. The semantics of ITCTL* is defined w.r.t. a Kripke Structure integrating the notions of parametric system size and continuous time semantics [12]. The continuous time model requires that between any two configurations it always exists a third state. It is possible, though, introduce *continuous time computation trees* [4]. Let us call *s-path* a function $\rho : \mathbb{R}^{\geq 0} \to \mathfrak{C}$ that intuitively maps a time t with the current system configuration at that time. The mapping $\rho_{\lfloor t'} : [0, t') \to \mathfrak{C}$ is a *prefix* of ρ iff $\forall t < t'.\rho_{\lfloor t'}(t) = \rho(t)$. The mapping $\rho_{\lfloor t'} : [t', \infty) \to \mathfrak{C}$ is a *suffix* of ρ iff $\forall t \geq t'.\rho_{\lfloor t'}(t) = \rho(t)$. Let us take a prefix $\rho_{\lfloor t'}$ and an s-path ρ', then their *concatenation* is defined as:

$$(\rho_{\lfloor t'} \cdot \rho')(t) = \begin{cases} \rho_{\lfloor t'}(t) & \text{if } t < t' \\ \rho'(t - t') & \text{else} \end{cases}$$

Let Π be a set of s-paths, then $\rho_{\downarrow_{t'}} \cdot \Pi = \{\rho_{\downarrow_{t'}} \cdot \rho' : \rho' \in \Pi\}$. A *continuous time computation tree* is a mapping $f : \mathfrak{C} \to 2^{[\mathbb{R}^{\geq 0} \to \mathfrak{C}]}$ such that:

$$\forall \mathfrak{c} \in \mathfrak{C}. \forall \rho \in f(\mathfrak{c}). \forall t \in \mathbb{R}^{\geq 0} . \rho_{\downarrow_t} \cdot f(\rho(t)) \subseteq f(\mathfrak{c}).$$

For the purpose of this work, here only *s-paths* defined over *timed computations* will be considered.

Definition 10 (PNTA s-paths). *For each timed computation* $x = (\mathfrak{c}_0, t_0) \ldots (\mathfrak{c}_v, t_v) \ldots$, *let us call* PNTA s-path *the s-path* $\rho : \mathbb{R}^{\geq 0} \to \mathfrak{C}$ *satisfying:*

$$\forall v. \forall t \in [t_v, t_{v+1}) . \rho(t) = \langle s, c \rangle$$

where $s = state(\mathfrak{c}_v)$ *and* $c = clock(\mathfrak{c}_v) + t - t_v$.

It should be noticed that, according to the above construction, an infinite set of timed computations can generate the same s-path ρ; let us denote such set by $tcomp(\rho)$. As a consequence, for each $y \in tcomp(\rho)$, there exists $x \in tcomp(\rho)$ such that y is a stuttering of x (see Definition 8). The continuous semantics of ITCTL* can be defined as follows.

Definition 11 (Satisfiability of ITCTL*). *Let* $(U_1, \ldots, U_k)^{(n_1, \ldots, n_k)}$ *be a PNTA and* $\mathfrak{c}$ *be the current configuration. Let* ϕ *denote an ITCTL* state formula, then the satisfiability relation* $\mathfrak{c} \models \phi$ *is defined by structural induction as follows:*

$$
\begin{aligned}
\mathfrak{c} &\models \top \\
\mathfrak{c} &\models p(l, i) && \text{iff } p = state(\mathfrak{c}(l, i)) \\
\mathfrak{c} &\models \phi_1 \wedge \phi_2 && \text{iff } \mathfrak{c} \models \phi_1 \text{ and } \mathfrak{c} \models \phi_2 \\
\mathfrak{c} &\models \neg\phi_1 && \text{iff } \mathfrak{c} \,/\!\models \phi_1 \\
\mathfrak{c} &\models A\phi_1 && \text{iff } \rho \models \phi_1, && \text{for all } \rho \in f(\mathfrak{c}) \text{ and} \\
& && && (|\rho| = \omega \text{ or } deadlock(\rho)) \\
\mathfrak{c} &\models A_{inf}\phi_1 && \text{iff } \rho \models \phi_1, && \text{for all } \rho \in f(\mathfrak{c}) \text{ and } |\rho| = \omega \\
\mathfrak{c} &\models A_{fin}\phi_1 && \text{iff } \rho \models \phi_1, && \text{for all } \rho \in f(\mathfrak{c}) \text{ and } |\rho| < \omega \\
\mathfrak{c} &\models \bigwedge_{i_l} \phi(i_l) && \text{iff } \mathfrak{c} \models \phi_1(i_l), && \text{for each } i_l \in [1, n_l]
\end{aligned}
$$

$$
\begin{aligned}
\rho &\models \phi_1 && \text{iff } \rho(0) \models \phi_1 \\
\rho &\models \phi_1 \wedge \phi_2 && \text{iff } \rho \models \phi_1 \text{ and } \rho \models \phi_2 \\
\rho &\models \neg\phi_1 && \text{iff } \rho \,/\!\models \phi_1 \\
\rho &\models \phi_1 \, \mathcal{U}_{\sim q} \, \phi_2 && \text{iff for some } t' \sim q, \text{where } \sim \, \in \{<, \leq, \geq, >, =\} \\
& && \rho_{\downarrow_{t'}} \models \phi_2, \text{ and } \rho_{\downarrow_t} \models \phi_1 \text{ for all } t \in [0, t')
\end{aligned}
$$

where $|\rho| = \omega$ *(resp.* $|\rho| < \omega$, *resp. deadlock(ρ))* denotes that the s-path ρ has infinite length (resp. has finite length, resp. is deadlocked).

Note that a finite s-path is not necessarily deadlocked, since it can be a finite prefix of some infinite s-path. When a given PNTA $(U_1, \ldots, U_k)^{(n_1, \ldots, n_k)}$ satisfies an ITCTL* state-formula ϕ at its initial configuration $\hat{\mathfrak{c}}$, this is denoted by

$$(U_1, \ldots, U_k)^{(n_1, \ldots, n_k)} \models \phi$$

Theorem 1 (Undecidability of ITCTL*). *The satisfiability problem for ITCTL* is undecidable.*

Proof. The satisfiability problem for TCTL is undecidable [4]. TCTL is included in ITCTL*, therefore the latter is undecidable.

In the next section we will call *IMTL* the fragment of ITCTL* having formulae with the following forms: $\bigwedge_{i_l} Qh(i_l)$, where $Q \in \{A, A_{fin}, A_{inf}\}$ and in h only Boolean ($\wedge$ and $\neg$) and temporal ($\mathcal{U}_{\sim q}$) operators are allowed. We will call *IMITL* the subset of IMTL where equality constraints (i.e. $\mathcal{U}_{=q}$) are excluded.

5   Cutoff Theorem for PNTA with Conjunctive Guards

In this section we prove that a cutoff can be computed to make the PMCP of PNTAs with conjunctive guards decidable, for a suitable set of formulae. The system in which every template is instantiated as many times as its cutoff, will be called the *cutoff system*. Given two instantiations $I = (U_1, \ldots, U_k)^{(c_1, \ldots, c_k)}$ and $I' = (U_1, \ldots, U_k)^{(c'_1, \ldots, c'_k)}$, such that all $c'_i \geq c_i$ and at least one $c'_j > c_j$, it can be said that I' is *bigger* than I, written $I' > I$. The cutoff theorem states that given a cutoff system I, for each $I' > I$, both I' and I satisfy the same subset of ITCTL* formulae.

Theorem 2 (Conjunctive Cutoff Theorem). *Let $(U_1, \ldots, U_k)$ be a set of TA templates with conjunctive guards. Let $\phi = \bigwedge_{i_{l_1}, \ldots, i_{l_h}} Q\Phi(i_{l_1}, \ldots, i_{l_h})$ where $Q \in \{A, A_{inf}, A_{fin}, E, E_{inf}, E_{fin}\}$ and Φ is an IMTL formula and $\{l_1, \ldots, l_h\} \subseteq [1, k]$. Then*

$$\forall (n_1, \ldots, n_k).(U_1, \ldots, U_k)^{(n_1, \ldots, n_k)} \models \phi \ \textit{iff}$$
$$\forall (d_1, \ldots, d_k) \preceq (c_1, \ldots, c_k).(U_1, \ldots, U_k)^{(d_1, \ldots, d_k)} \models \phi$$

where the cutoff $(c_1, \ldots, c_k)$ can be computed as follows:

- *In case $Q \in \{A_{inf}, E_{inf}\}$ (i.e., deadlocked or finite timed computations are ignored). Then $c_l = 2$ if $l \in \{l_1, \ldots, l_h\}$, and $c_l = 1$ otherwise (i.e. $l \in [1, k] \setminus \{l_1, \ldots, l_h\}$).*
- *In case $Q \in \{A_{fin}, E_{fin}\}$ (i.e. finite timed computations, either deadlocked or finite prefixes of infinite computations). Then $c_l = 1$ for each l.*
- *In case $Q \in \{A, E\}$ (i.e., infinite and deadlocked). Then $c_l = 2|U_l| + 1$ if $l \in \{l_1, \ldots, l_h\}$; $c_l = 2|U_l|$ otherwise (i.e. $l \in [1, k] \setminus \{l_1, \ldots, l_h\}$).*

The proof of the Cutoff Theorem consists of three steps. The first step (*Conjunctive Monotonicity Lemma*) shows that adding instances to the system does not alter the truth of logic formulae. The second step (*Conjunctive Bounding Lemma*) proves that removing an instance beyond the cutoff number, does not alter the truth of logic formulae either. The third step (*Conjunctive Truncation Lemma*) generalizes the Conjunctive Bounding Lemma to a system that has two automaton templates with an arbitrary number of instances. The given proofs can be generalized to systems with an arbitrary number of templates.

Theorem 3 (Conjunctive Monotonicity Lemma). *Let U_1 and U_2 be two TA templates with conjunctive guards. Let $\Phi(1_l)$ be an IMTL formula, with $l \in \{1,2\}$. Then for any $n \in \mathbb{N}$ such that $n \geq 1$ we have:*

$$(i) \quad (U_1, U_2)^{(1,n)} \models Q\Phi(1_2) \Rightarrow (U_1, U_2)^{(1,n+1)} \models Q\Phi(1_2)$$
$$(ii) \quad (U_1, U_2)^{(1,n)} \models Q\Phi(1_1) \Rightarrow (U_1, U_2)^{(1,n+1)} \models Q\Phi(1_1)$$

where $Q \in \{E, E_{inf}, E_{fin}\}$.

A detailed proof of the theorem is in the extended version of this paper [28]. Intuitively, from any time computation x one can build a new time computation y where each instance behaves as in x, except for a new instance of U_2 that halts in its initial state (remember that by definition the initial states don't falsify any conjunctive guard).

Theorem 4 (Conjunctive Bounding Lemma). *Let U_1 and U_2 be two TA templates with conjunctive guards. Let $\Phi(1_l)$ be an IMTL formula, with $l \in \{1,2\}$. Then for any $n \in \mathbb{N}$ such that $n \geq 1$ we have:*

$$(i) \quad \forall n \geq c_2.(U_1, U_2)^{(1,n)} \models Q\Phi(1_2) \Rightarrow (U_1, U_2)^{(1,c_2)} \models Q\Phi(1_2)$$
$$(ii) \quad \forall n \geq c_1.(U_1, U_2)^{(1,n)} \models Q\Phi(1_1) \Rightarrow (U_1, U_2)^{(1,c_1)} \models Q\Phi(1_1)$$

where $Q \in \{E, E_{inf}, E_{fin}\}$ and:

- $c_1 = 1$ and $c_2 = 2$, when $Q = E_{inf}$;
- $c_1 = c_2 = 1$, when $Q = E_{fin}$;
- $c_1 = 2|U_2|$ and $c_2 = 2|U_2| + 1$, when $Q = E$.

Theorem 5 (Truncation Lemma). *Let U_1 and U_2 be two TA templates with conjunctive guards. Let $\Phi(1_l)$ be an IMTL formula, with $l \in \{1,2\}$, then:*

$$\forall n_1, n_2 \geq 1.(U_1, U_2)^{(n_1,n_2)} \models Q\Phi(1_2) \text{ iff } (U_1, U_2)^{(n_1',n_2')} \models Q\Phi(1_2)$$

where $Q \in \{E, E_{inf}, E_{inf}\}$, $n_1' = min(n_1, c_1)$, $n_2' = min(n_2, c_2)$, and:

- $c_1 = 1$ and $c_2 = 2$, when $Q = E_{inf}$;
- $c_1 = c_2 = 1$, when $Q = E_{fin}$;
- $c_1 = 2|U_2|$ and $c_2 = 2|U_2| + 1$, when $Q = E$.

The detailed proofs of Theorems 4 and 5 are given in the extended version [28]. Thanks to the Truncation Lemma and the duality between operators A and E, the Conjunctive Cutoff Theorem can be easily proved. The Cutoff Theorem together with the known decidability and complexity results of the model checking problems for various timed temporal logics [12] justify the following decidability theorem.

Theorem 6 (Decidability Theorem). *Let $(U_1, \ldots, U_k)$ be a set of TA templates with conjunctive guards and let $\phi = \bigwedge_{i_{l_1}, \ldots, i_{l_h}} Q\Phi(i_{l_1}, \ldots, i_{l_h})$ where $Q \in \{A, A_{inf}, A_{fin}, E, E_{inf}, E_{fin}\}$ and $\{l_1, \ldots, l_h\} \in [1, k]$. The parameterized model checking problem (under the continuous time semantics)*

$$\forall (n_1, \ldots, n_k) \succeq (1, \ldots, 1).(U_1, \ldots, U_k)^{(n_1, \ldots, n_k)} \models \phi$$

is:

- UNDECIDABLE *when Φ is an IMTL formula;*
- DECIDABLE *and* 2-EXPSPACE *when Φ is an IMITL formula;*
- DECIDABLE *and* EXPSPACE *when ϕ is a TCTL formula.*

Proof. For the first two results, consider that the Cutoff Theorem reduces the parameterized model checking problem to an ordinary model checking problem. The latter is undecidable for MTL and is decidable and EXPSPACE-Complete (i.e. DSPACE($2^{O(n)}$), for MITL [12]. Since the model has an exponential number of states (i.e. $n = 2^{|U| |log(|U|)}$, where U is the "biggest" template), the problem is at most 2-EXPSPACE. Concerning the third statement, the TCTL model checking problem is PSPACE-Complete [12]. Again, since the model has an exponential number of states, the parameterized model checking problem is at most EXPSPACE. A more detailed proof can be found in the extended version [28].

6   Case Study

We use the Fischer's protocol for mutual exclusion to show how to model-check a parameterized and timed systems. The protocol uses a single timed automaton template, instantiated an arbitrary number of time. Figure 1 depicts such template, where $inv(b_1) = (c \le k)$ [13]. In Fischer's protocol every process (a) reads and writes a PID from and into a shared variable, and (b) waits a constant amount of time between when it asks to enter the critical section, and when it actually does so. The Fischer's protocol cannot be directly modeled in our framework because of the shared variable. We will first abstract the variable into a finite state system with conjunctive guards, and subsequently we will present the results of our verification.

Abstracting Process Identifier. A variable can be modeled naively as an automaton with the structure of a completely connected graph, whose vertices denote possible assigned values (let us call V such model, see Fig. 2). The state space can thus be infinite or finite, but even in the latter case it is usually too big and makes the verification task unfeasible.

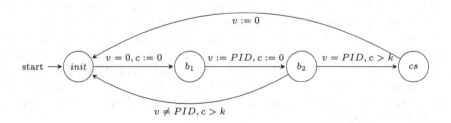

Fig. 1. Process in Fischer's protocol as a Timed Automaton with integer variables

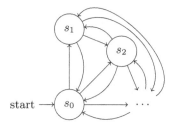

Fig. 2. V: a shared variable

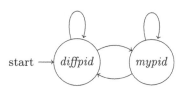

Fig. 3. W: a process-centric view of a shared PID variable

An abstract shared variable for PIDs can be defined, under the assumptions:

- the variable only stores PID values;
- the variable is shared among all processes;
- every PID value overwrites the previous values of the variable itself;
- every process can compare the variable value only with its own PID value.

As in a predicate abstraction, we replace the shared variable with its *process-centric view*. The latter has only two relevant states: it is either the same PID as the process, or it stores a different one. We use W to denote such process (see Fig. 3). Every process P is in a one-to-one relation with its own view of the variable. We introduce a process template $P' = P \times W$ that results from the synchronous product of the P and W. We could then model check a system $P'^{(n)}$. Doing this, we would probably obtain many spurious counter-examples, since two processes could have their copy of W in state *_Mypid. Since no variable can store multiple values, this is impossible. Conjunctive guards, though, allow to constraint the system in such a way that no two processes can be in a state of the *_Mypid group. This solution rules out the undesired spurious behaviors, and is very convenient since it can be applied whenever an algorithm uses a shared variable. We thus define P'' to be the refined version of P' represented in Fig. 4 using the Uppaal notation. It is possible to show that the abstract system simulates the concrete system, namely $(P \times V)^{(1,n)} \preceq (P \times W)^{(1,n)}$, for any positive n.

Figure 4 depicts template P''. Some of the eight states resulting from the product are not reached by any transition, and can thus be removed from the model, implying a smaller cutoff. The model manipulation up to this point can be completely automatized. We notice that it is safe to remove state b2_diff and connect directly state b2_Mypid with Init_Diff, obtaining the reduced system in Fig. 5. Finally, let us remark that variable mypid in Figs. 4 and 5 is added to overcome Uppaal syntax limitations that cannot refer directly to process states in guards and specifications. The reduced system has 4 states, and thus the cutoff is 9.

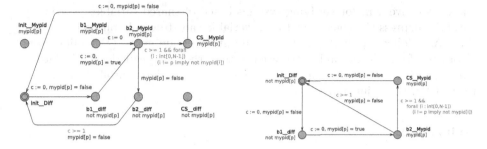

Fig. 4. $P'' = (P \times W) + CG$ template   **Fig. 5.** Reduced P''

Verification Results. Below are the formulae that have been model checked, together with the required time and memory.[2]

Formula	Outcome	Time (s)	Mem. (MB)
(1) $\bigwedge_i EF_{\geq 0}\,(CS\_mypid(i))$	true	0.01	155.2
(2) $\bigwedge_{i \neq j} AG_{\geq 0}!(CS\_mypid(i) \wedge CS\_mypid(j))$	true	30.1	155.2
(3) $\bigwedge_i AF_{\geq 0}\,(CS\_mypid(i))$	false	0.59	155.2

Formula (1) checks that a process can enter its critical section, while (2) checks the actual mutual exclusion property. Finally (3) states that a process will always be able to enter its critical section. It is well known that while the Fischer's protocol ensures the mutual exclusion property (i.e. formulae (1) and (2)), it also suffers from the problem of processes to possibly starve (i.e. formula (3)).

7 Conclusions

In this work we presented the combined study of timed and parameterized systems. We proved that a cutoff exists for PNTA with conjunctive guards and a subset of ITCTL* formulae. Moreover, the cutoff value is equal to the value computed in Emerson and Kahlon's work for untimed systems [15]. This proves that the parameterized model checking problem is decidable for networks of timed automata with disjunctive guards, for a suitable logic. We remark that for timed systems, applying Theorem 2 one obtains a considerably smaller cutoff than applying the (untimed) Emerson and Kahlon's cutoff theorem after reducing the original timed system to a finite state system by means of the traditional region or zone abstractions.

Finally, we used the Fischer's protocol for mutual exclusion as a benchmark for showing how to apply the cutoff theorem. We claim that the use of conjunctive

---

[2] The experiments were run on an Intel Core2 Duo CPU T5870 @ 2.0 Ghz with 4GB RAM, OS Linux 3.13-1-amd64.

guards is convenient for verifying systems based of shared variables, since they naturally express the constraint that a variable can store only one value at any time. As a follow-up of this work, we aim at two main goals: (a) finding more algorithms for real-time and distributed systems that can be model checked using our framework, and (b) extending the Emerson and Kahlon cutoff theorem also to PNTA with Disjunctive Guards.

References

1. Abdulla, P.A., Jonsson, B.: Verifying networks of timed processes (extended abstract). In: Steffen, B. (ed.) TACAS 1998. LNCS, vol. 1384, pp. 298–312. Springer, Heidelberg (1998)
2. Abdulla, P.A., Deneux, J., Mahata, P.: Multi-clock timed networks. In: Proceedings of the 19th IEEE Symposium on Logic in Computer Science, pp. 345–354 (2004)
3. Abdulla, P.A., Jonsson, B.: Model checking of systems with many identical timed processes. Theoret. Comput. Sci. **290**(1), 241–264 (2003)
4. Alur, R., Courcoubetis, C., Dill, D.: Model-checking for real-time systems. In: Proceedings of the Fifth Symposium on Logic in Computer Science, pp. 414–425 (1990)
5. Aminof, B., Jacobs, S., Khalimov, A., Rubin, S.: Parameterized model checking of token-passing systems. In: McMillan, K.L., Rival, X. (eds.) VMCAI 2014. LNCS, vol. 8318, pp. 262–281. Springer, Heidelberg (2014)
6. Apt, K., Kozen, D.: Limits for automatic verification of finite-state concurrent systems. Inf. Process. Lett. **22**, 307–309 (1986)
7. Aminof, B., Kotek, T., Rubin, S., Spegni, F., Veith, H.: Parameterized model checking of rendezvous systems. In: Baldan, P., Gorla, D. (eds.) CONCUR 2014. LNCS, vol. 8704, pp. 109–124. Springer, Heidelberg (2014)
8. Ball, T., Levin, V., Rajamani, S.: A decade of software model checking with SLAM. Commun. ACM **54**(7), 68–76 (2011)
9. Ben-David, S., Eisner, C., Geist, D., Wolfsthal, Y.: Model checking at IBM. Formal Methods Sys. Des. **22**(2), 101–108 (2003)
10. Bengtsson, J., Yi, W.: Timed Automata: Semantics, Algorithms and Tools. Technical report 316, UNU-IIST (2004)
11. Bouajjani, A., Habermehl, P., Vojnar, T.: Verification of parametric concurrent systems with prioritised FIFO resource management. Formal Methods Syst. Des. **32**, 129–172 (2008)
12. Bouyer, P.: Model-checking timed temporal logics. Electron. Notes Theor. Comput. Sci. **231**, 323–341 (2009)
13. Carioni, A., Ghilardi, S., Ranise, S.: MCMT in the land of parameterized timed automata. In: Proceedings of VERIFY@IJCAR 2010, pp. 1–16 (2010)
14. Clarke, E., Grumberg, O., Browne, M.: Reasoning about networks with many identical finite-state processes. In: Proceedings of the 5th Annual ACM Symposium on Principles of Distributed Computing, pp. 240–248 (1986)
15. Emerson, A., Kahlon, V.: Reducing model checking of the many to the few. In: McAllester, D. (ed.) CADE-17. LNCS, vol. 1831, pp. 236–254. Springer, Heidelberg (2000)
16. Emerson, A., Namjoshi, K.: Automatic verification of parameterized synchronous systems. In: Alur, R., Henzinger, T.A. (eds.) CAV 1996. LNCS, vol. 1102, pp. 87–98. Springer, Heidelberg (1996)

17. Emerson, E., Namjoshi, K.: On model checking for non-deterministic infinite-state systems. In: Proceedings of 13th IEEE Symposium on Logic in Computer Science, pp. 70–80 (1998)
18. Emerson, E.A., Namjoshi, K.: On reasoning about rings. Int. J. Found. Comput. Sci. 14(4), 527–550 (2003)
19. German, S.M., Sistla, A.P.: Reasoning about systems with many processes. J. ACM 39(3), 675–735 (1992)
20. Godefroid, P.: Software model checking: The Verisoft approach. Formal Methods Syst. Des. 26(2), 77–101 (2005)
21. Gothel, T., Glesner, S.: Towards the semi-automatic verification of parameterized real-time systems using network invariants. In: 8th IEEE International Conference on Software Engineering and Formal Methods (SEFM), pp. 310–314 (2010)
22. Hanna, Y., Samuelson, D., Basu, S., Rajan, H.: Automating Cut-off for Multi-parameterized systems. In: Dong, J.S., Zhu, H. (eds.) ICFEM 2010. LNCS, vol. 6447, pp. 338–354. Springer, Heidelberg (2010)
23. Johnson, T.T., Mitra, S.: A small model theorem for rectangular hybrid automata networks. In: Giese, H., Rosu, G. (eds.) FORTE/FMOODS 2012. LNCS, vol. 7273, pp. 18–34. Springer, Heidelberg (2012)
24. Kurshan, R., McMillan, K.: A structural induction theorem for processes. In: ACM Symposium on Principles of Distributed Computing, pp. 239–247 (1989)
25. Mansouri-Samani, M., Mehlitz, P., Pasareanu, C., Penix, J., Brat, G., Markosian, L., O'Malley, O., Pressburger, T., Visser, W.: Program model checking-a practitioners guide. Technical report NASA/TM-2008-214577, NASA (2008)
26. Pagliarecci, F., Spalazzi, L., Spegni, F.: Model checking grid security. Future Gener. Comput. Syst. 29(3), 811–827 (2013)
27. RTCA. Software Considerations in Airborne Systems and Equipment Certification. Technical report DO-178C, RTCA Inc. (2011)
28. Spalazzi, L., Spegni, F.: Parameterized model-checking for timed systems with conjunctive guards (extended version) (2014). arxiv:1407.7305[cs.Lo]
29. Yang, Q., Li, M.: A cut-off approach for bounded verification of parameterized systems. In: Proceedings of the International Conference on Software Engineering, pp. 345–354. ACM (2010)
30. Zuck, L., Pnueli, A.: Model checking and abstraction to the aid of parameterized systems (a survey). Comp. Lang. Syst. Struct. 30(3–4), 139–169 (2004)

Timed Refinement for Verification
of Real-Time Object Code Programs

Mohana Asha Latha Dubasi[(✉)], Sudarshan K. Srinivasan,
and Vidura Wijayasekara

North Dakota State University, Fargo, ND, USA
MohanaAshaLatha.Duba@ndsu.edu

Abstract. We introduce a refinement-based notion of correctness for
verification of interrupt driven real-time object code programs, called
timed refinement. The notion of timed refinement is targeted at verification of low-level object code against high-level specification models. For
timed refinement, both the object code (implementation) and the specification are encoded as timed transition systems. Hence, timed refinement
can be construed as a notion of equivalence between two timed transition systems that allows for stuttering between the implementation and
specification, and also allows for the use of refinement maps. Stuttering
is the phenomenon where multiple but finite transitions of the implementation can match a single transition of the specification. Refinement
maps allow low-level implementations to be verified against high-level
specification models. We also present a procedure for checking timed
refinement. The proposed techniques are demonstrated with the verification of object code programs of six case studies from electric motor
control applications.

Keywords: Refinement-based verification · Verification of object code ·
Real-time verification · Stuttering bisimulations · Timed transition
systems

1 Introduction

Safety-critical embedded devices execute object code, and hence verification of
object code is imperative. In industry, verification of object code is primarily
achieved using testing. Interrupt-driven real-time object code programs can often
have behaviors that are very hard to emulate, capture, and analyze using only
testing-based methods. Inadequacy of industry processes to address this problem is evidenced by recent examples of buggy safety-critical embedded devices,
such as the Toyota Camry's electronic throttle system (that could lead to unintended acceleration) [19]. Another example is the medical device industry, which
is plagued with recalls due to software errors that are often deemed to cause
adverse health consequences or death [14,16].

We introduce a notion of refinement for the verification of real-time object
code programs, called timed refinement. The notion of timed-refinement is based

© Springer International Publishing Switzerland 2014
D. Giannakopoulou and D. Kroening (Eds.): VSTTE 2014, LNCS 8471, pp. 252–269, 2014.
DOI: 10.1007/978-3-319-12154-3_16

on the theory of Well Founded Equivalence Bisimulation (WEB) refinement [11]. WEB refinement can be construed as a notion of equivalence between two transitions systems and is applicable for functional verification. However, WEB refinement does not consider timing requirements and properties. Timed refinement is a notion of equivalence between two timed transition systems (TTS) that allows for stuttering between the implementation and specification, and also allows for the use of refinement maps. Stuttering is the phenomenon where multiple but finite transitions of the implementation can match a single transition of the specification. Refinement maps allow low-level implementations to be verified against high-level specification models. The incorporation of stuttering and refinement maps allows for timed refinement to be applicable to the verification of low-level real-time object code against high-level specification models. *For the case studies we verified, abstractions based on stuttering reduce the size of the implementation TTS by at least 4 orders of magnitude* (Sect. 7). Our approach in theory is applicable to the verification of any real-time object code, as long as the specification and object code are expressible as timed transition systems.

The rest of the paper is organized as follows. First, we describe related work in Sect. 2. We use case studies based on stepper motor control to describe and demonstrate timed refinement. Section 3 describes stepper motor control. Background on WEB refinement is presented in Sect. 4. The notion of timed refinement is introduced in Sect. 5. A procedure for checking timed refinement is given in Sect. 6. Verification of case studies based on stepper motor control is described in Sect. 7. Section 8 provides concluding remarks.

2   Related Work

Tools like UPPAAL [9] and Kronos [4] are based on timed automata [2], and have been very successful in verification of real-time system-level models and models of protocols. Another real-time system verification tool is Epsilon [6], which is aimed at verifying communication protocols. Finding bugs in system-level models is very useful in catching design bugs earlier on in the design cycle. However, bugs can be introduced in the synthesis/implementation/compilation process that generates object code. Our work is targeted at bridging the gap between real-time high-level models and real-time object code. We are not aware of prior work in formal techniques for verification of interrupt-driven real-time object code.

Alur et al. have defined Bisimulation based equivalences for TTS [1], and have proposed a method based on language inclusion for checking equivalence of TTS. However, we are not aware of applications of this work for real-time object code verification. Why do we extend the theory of WEB refinement for checking equivalence of TTS? There has been a lot of previous work in developing theory and optimized techniques for WEB refinement-based verification. By extending the theory of WEB refinement to deal with TTS, our motivation is to leverage these techniques and also exploit the properties of WEB refinement in object code verification. The very nice property of WEB refinement is that, it is enough to reason about single steps of the implementation and specification. This can be exploited in object code verification, by reasoning about one instruction at a time. This property significantly reduces the verification burden. Also, our notion of timed refinement is based on the ideas of stuttering segments and stuttering transitions, which provides a natural way to abstract the implementation TTS corresponding to the object code. Without using these abstractions, the number of states and paths would explode (Sect. 7).

David et al. [5] have developed an UPPAAL-based tool to check refinement between specifications of real-time systems. Boudjadar et al. [3] have developed a bisimulation relation for real-time systems with priorities and provide a method for encoding and verifying the problem using UPPAAL. The above refinement approaches for real-time systems are targeted at high-level models and do not consider stuttering and refinement maps. Since we incorporate stuttering and refinement maps, our approach is unique in this regard and applicable to the verification of low-level implementations such as object code.

Ray and Sumners have used a notion of refinement based on stuttering trace containment to verify concurrent programs [15]. Their focus is on functional verification and they do not consider real-time programs.

3   Stepper Motor Control

We use the example of stepper motor control to describe the notion of timed refinement. A stepper motor is a brushless DC electric motor. Stepper motors are widely used in commercial applications such as medical devices, computer peripherals, robotics, machine tools, and process control [8,18], and many of these applications are safety-critical. Current pulse applied to the motor generates discrete rotation of the motor shaft. A stepper motor can have 4 or 6 leads. Consider a motor with 4 leads say a, b, c, and d. Then the following repeating sequence of values to the leads causes the motor to spin: $abcd = 1000, 0100, 0010, 0001, 1000$ etc. There are other such repeating sequences that can cause a 4-lead or 6-lead stepper motor to spin. Every next value in the sequence causes the motor to rotate by a small angle. Thus a stepper motor can be controlled by software (that generates the above sequence of values to the leads), executing on a microcontroller that is interfaced with the motor. The time delay between when each value in the sequence is generated, determines the speed of the motor. The speed also depends on the angle the motor rotates at each step.

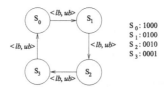

Fig. 1. Stepper motor control specification TTS

Specification

Figure 1 shows a transition system (TS) specification for stepper motor control. The TS has 4 states and captures the repeating sequence of values the software controller must generate. The functionality of the controller is not fully described unless the speed of rotation is specified. The speed is determined by the time delay of each transition. The delay (d) of each transition is given by: $d = \phi/6r$, where, ϕ is the degree of rotation for each step of the motor, and r is the rotational speed of the motor in rpm. In commercial applications, there is typically a tolerance in the speed of the motor. For example, the expected speed is 100 rpm, but it is acceptable for the speed to vary between 96 rpm and 104 rpm. This tolerance results in a lower limit and an upper limit (lb and ub) on the delay of each transition. If $\phi = 1.8°$, then for this example, $lb = 2.884$ ms (corresponding to speed 104 rpm) and $ub = 3.125$ ms (corresponding to speed 96 rpm). However, these timing requirements on the transitions cannot be incorporated in a transition system specification. Therefore, we use timed transition systems for the specification.

Definition 1. *A Timed Transition System (TTS) M is a 3-tuple $\langle S, T, L \rangle$, where S is the set of states, T is the transition relation that defines the state transitions, and L is a labeling function that defines what is visible at each state. T is of the form $\langle w, v, lb, ub \rangle$, where $w, v \in S$ and $lb, ub \in \Re$. lb and ub indicate the lower bound and the upper bound on the time delay of the transition, respectively.*

Figure 1 shows a timed transition system (TTS) specification for stepper motor control. The timing requirements are marked on the transitions with $lb = 2.884$ ms, and $ub = 3.125$ ms.

Implementation

Our target is to verify the stepper motor object code control program. The implementation model is obtained by generating a function for each instruction that describes the effect of the instruction on the state of the microcontroller. The state of a microcontroller includes the registers and memory of the microcontroller. The set of all such functions (one for each instruction) and the initial state of the microcontroller defines the TS model of the implementation. Note that this set includes the instructions in interrupt service routines of the interrupts that the program uses. Each instruction is also associated with a lower bound and an upper bound on the instruction execution time. We note here that there are many techniques and tools for timing analysis, and to determine WCET and BCET [20]. Our goal in this work is not timing analysis, but functional and timing verification. Also, note that on the specification side, the lower and upper delay bounds indicate requirements. On the implementation side, the delay bounds are an estimate of the lower limit and upper limit of the execution time of the instruction/transition. The delay bounds on the implementation side are used to verify if the implementation satisfies the timing requirements of the specification.

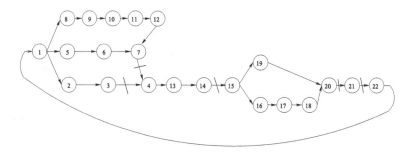

Fig. 2. Implementation TTS

Figure 2 shows an example TTS that is an implementation of the stepper motor specification TTS shown in Fig. 1. Note that times are not shown in the figure due to space limitations. We use this example to introduce the notion of timed refinement. First, we describe the notion of WEB refinement.

4   Background: WEB Refinement

A formal and detailed description of WEB refinement is provided in [10,11]. Here, we give a brief overview of the key features. As stated earlier, in the context of refinement, both the implementation and specification are treated as transition systems. Informally, the implementation behaves correctly as given by the specification, if every behavior of the implementation is matched by a behavior of the specification and vice versa. However, the implementation and specification may not have the same transition behavior. For example, the stepper motor object code control program (the implementation) may take several steps (or transitions) to match a single transition of the stepper motor control specification TS. This phenomenon is known as stuttering. To account for such situations, multiple but finite transitions of the implementation system are allowed to match a single transition of the specification system.

Another issue is that to check equivalence, specification states and implementation states need to be compared. However, these states can look very different. In the stepper motor specification, each state is a four bit value. However, the implementation state in this example includes registers and memory in the microcontroller. WEB refinement employs refinement maps, functions that map implementation states to specification states, to bridge this abstraction gap. Below is the definition of WEB.

Definition 2. *[11] $B \subseteq S \times S$ is a WEB on TS $\mathcal{M} = \langle S, T, L \rangle$ iff:*

(1) B is an equivalence relation on S; and
(2) $\langle \forall s, w \in S :: sBw \ :: \ L(s) = L(w) \rangle$; and

(3) There exist functions $erankl : S \times S \to \mathbb{N}$, $erankt : S \to W$,

   such that $\langle W, < \rangle$ is well-founded, and

   $\langle \forall s, u, w \in S :: sBw \wedge sTu \quad ::$

   (a) $\langle \exists v :: wTv \wedge uBv \rangle \vee$

   (b) $(uBw \wedge erankt(u) < erankt(s)) \vee$

   (c) $\langle \exists v :: wTv \wedge sBv \wedge erankl(v, u) < erankl(w, u) \rangle \rangle$

In the third condition, case (b) denotes stuttering on the specification side and case (c) denotes stuttering on the implementation side. For timed refinement, we ignore stuttering on the specification side (we do not consider case (b)). For object code verification, stuttering rarely occurs on the specification side as the implementation (object code) typically has a much larger number of transitions (millions) when compared with the specification. To check WEB refinement, it is enough to reason about single transitions of the implementation and the specification. Next is the definition of a WEB refinement.

Definition 3. *[11] (WEB Refinement) Let $M = \langle S, T, L \rangle$, $M' = \langle S', T', L' \rangle$, and $r : S \to S'$. We say that M is a WEB refinement of M' with respect to refinement map r, written $M \approx_r M'$, if there exists a relation, B, such that $\langle \forall s \in S :: sBr(s) \rangle$ and B is a WEB on the TS $\langle S \uplus S', T \uplus T', \mathcal{L} \rangle$, where $\mathcal{L}(s) = L'(s)$ for s an S' state and $\mathcal{L}(s) = L'(r(s))$ otherwise.*

Refinement is a compositional notion as given by the following theorem [12]. Below, $M_c \approx_r M_b$ denotes that M_c is a WEB refinement of M_b; and $r; q$ denotes composition, i.e. $(r; q)(s) = q(r(s))$.

Theorem 1. *[12] (Composition for WEB Refinement) If $M_c \approx_r M_b$ and $M_b \approx_q M_a$ then $M_c \approx_{r;q} M_a$.*

5 Timed Refinement

The correct functioning of the stepper motor control program depends also on whether it meets the timing requirements of the specification. The notion of WEB refinement does not consider time. We introduce the notion of timed refinement that accounts for timing requirements in the context of refinement. We define timed refinement in the context of timed transition systems (TTS).

If there is no stuttering between the implementation TTS (M_I) and the specification TTS (M_S), every step of M_I should match a step of M_S, and the delay of an implementation step should "match" the delay of the corresponding specification step. By "match" we mean the following should be satisfied:

$$lb_s \leq lb_i \leq ub_i \leq ub_s$$

where, lb_s, ub_s, lb_i, and ub_i are the lower and upper delay bounds on corresponding specification and implementation steps, respectively. If stuttering is involved, which is the case for the stepper motor example (and would be the case for most real world examples), then the requirements on the relationship between M_I and M_S is more complicated. The reason being that with stuttering, multiple but finite steps of M_I can match a single step of M_S. Also, the number of stuttering steps in each situation is arbitrary and depends on the behavior of the implementation that we want to verify.

Timed refinement is based on the idea that the implementation TTS M_I satisfies the timing requirements of its specification TTS M_S, if in every case, the delay between the previous time that M_I made progress w.r.t. M_S and the next time M_I makes progress w.r.t. M_S, matches the time delay required for M_S to make that progress.

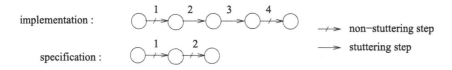

Fig. 3. Example comparing implementation and specification transitions.

We illustrate further with the example in Fig. 3. In the figure, if step 1 of the implementation matches step 1 of the specification, and step 4 of the implementation matches step 2 of the specification, then steps 2 and 3 are stuttering steps of the implementation. Also, steps 1 and 4 of the implementation are non-stuttering steps. Progress on the implementation side corresponds to the non-stuttering steps. For this example, the following should be satisfied.

$$lb_s^2 \leq \sum_{n=2}^{4} lb_i^n \leq \sum_{n=2}^{4} ub_i^n \leq ub_s^2$$

In the above and in the following discussions, in lb^n and ub^n, superscript n indicates transition n. We now formalize the idea of timed refinement. In defining a timed refinement between an M_I and an M_S, we assume that a refinement relationship already exists between the two. In practice, what this means is that verification of timed refinement is preceded by verification of WEB refinement. Since the refinement relationship has been established and a witness refinement map exists, we can then identify the stuttering and non-stuttering transitions of the implementation TTS M_I. This information is captured in a Marked TTS, which is defined below,

Definition 4. *A Marked TTS MM is a TTS where every transition of the TTS is marked with a label s_t or n_t, indicating that the transition is a stuttering transition or a non-stuttering transition, respectively.*

Transitions of a marked TTS are of the form $\langle w, v, lb, ub, m \rangle$ where m $\in$ $\{s_t, n_t\}$. The general theory of WEB refinement allows for stuttering to occur on the implementation side and the specification side. In practice, we rarely encounter situations in which the specification stutters. Therefore, we make the assumption that only the implementation can have stuttering steps. Hence a marked specification TTS MM_S corresponding to a specification TTS M_S, is one in which every transition is a non-stuttering transition and is marked with n_t.

Definition 5. *A marked implementation TTS MM_I of TTS M_I w.r.t a marked specification TTS MM_S is a marked TTS where for every transition of MM_I of the form $\langle w, v, lb, ub, m \rangle$, if $r(w) = r(v)$, then $m = s_t$, else $m = n_t$. r is the refinement map used to establish that M_I is a WEB refinement of M_S.*

MM_I will satisfy the timing requirements of the corresponding MM_S, if every time the implementation makes progress (non-stuttering step), then the sum of the delay of the non-stuttering step and the delays of all preceding stuttering steps matches the delay of the corresponding specification step. Note that there may be many paths in the implementation that lead to a specific non-stuttering step. All these paths individually should satisfy the timing requirements of the corresponding specification step. We call these finite paths as stuttering segments, which are defined below. Note that in the following discussions, we omit the delay bounds from T, if the delay bounds are not relevant for the discussion.

Definition 6. *A stuttering segment (π) of a non-stuttering step $\langle w_a, w_b \rangle$ of an MM_I is a sequence of steps of $MM_I\{\langle w_{n-1}, w_{n-2} \rangle, \langle w_{n-2}, w_{n-3} \rangle, ..., \langle w_2, w_1 \rangle, \langle w_1, w_a \rangle, \langle w_a, w_b \rangle\}$, such that:*

1. *For all i such that $2 \leq i \leq n - 1$, $\langle w_i, w_{i-1} \rangle$ is a stuttering step of MM_I.*
2. *$\langle w_n, w_{n-1} \rangle$ is a non-stuttering step of MM_I.*
3. *$\langle w_1, w_a \rangle$ is a stuttering step of MM_I.*

Fig. 4. Stuttering segment

The above definition is illustrated in Fig. 4. Note that the least length of a stuttering segment is one. This occurs when a non-stuttering step is preceded by another non-stuttering step. The stuttering segment then only consists of one transition which is the non-stuttering step. Also, a non-stuttering step can have many stuttering segments. For the TTS shown in Fig. 2, the stuttering segments of $\langle 7, 4 \rangle$ are:

1. $\{\langle 22, 1 \rangle, \langle 1, 5 \rangle, \langle 5, 6 \rangle, \langle 6, 7 \rangle, \langle 7, 4 \rangle\}$
2. $\{\langle 22, 1 \rangle, \langle 1, 8 \rangle, \langle 8, 9 \rangle, \langle 9, 10 \rangle, \langle 10, 11 \rangle, \langle 11, 12 \rangle, \langle 12, 7 \rangle, \langle 7, 4 \rangle\}$.

The idea of stuttering segments when combined with suitable abstractions for timed refinement verification significantly mitigates the path explosion problem that is often encountered in verification of interrupt driven control programs. The reason being that verification is reduced to analyzing stuttering segments.

Definition 7. *M_I is a timed refinement of M_S if:*

1. *M_I is a WEB refinement of M_S w.r.t. refinement map r.*
2. *Let MM_I be the marked TTS of M_I w.r.t. M_S. Then, for every non-stuttering transition of MM_I $\langle w_a, w_b \rangle$, and for every stuttering segment π of $\langle w_a, w_b \rangle$, the following should be satisfied:*

$$lb_s^{\langle r(w_a), r(w_b) \rangle} \leq \sum_{p \in \pi} lb_i^p \leq \sum_{p \in \pi} ub_i^p \leq ub_s^{\langle r(w_a), r(w_b) \rangle}$$

The notion of timed refinement given above is bisimilar in nature, even though it is not defined in a symmetric manner. If the specification had a behavior that was not matched by the implementation, the implementation would not be a WEB refinement of the specification and hence would not be a timed refinement of the specification. Note that for WEB refinement, an implementation state cannot be related to more than one specification state (as the refinement map is a function used to relate implementation states to specification states). So once we have established WEB refinement, we don't need to check the other direction for timed refinement.

WEB refinement is a compositional notion (see Sect. 4). We derive a similar property for timed refinement. Below, $M_c \unrhd_r M_b$ denotes that M_c is a timed refinement of M_b using refinement map r; and $r; q$ denotes composition, i.e. $(r; q)(s) = q(r(s))$. Let $MM_I^{c \leftarrow b}$ denote the marked M_I of M_c w.r.t. M_b. For the following discussion, let $M_c \unrhd_r M_b$ and $M_b \unrhd_q M_a$.

Lemma 1. *If $\langle w, v \rangle$ is a non-stuttering transition of $MM_I^{c \leftarrow a}$, then $\langle w, v \rangle$ is a non-stuttering transition of $MM_I^{c \leftarrow b}$.*

Proof. If $\langle w, v \rangle$ is a non-stuttering transition of $MM_I^{c \leftarrow a}$, then $q(r(w)) \neq q(r(v))$. This implies that $r(w) \neq r(v)$, which implies that $\langle w, v \rangle$ is a non-stuttering transition of $MM_I^{c \leftarrow b}$. □

Lemma 2. *If $\langle w, v \rangle$ is a stuttering transition of $MM_I^{c \leftarrow a}$, then $\langle r(w), r(v) \rangle$ is a stuttering transition of $MM_I^{b \leftarrow a}$.*

Proof. We have that $M_b \unrhd_q M_a$. Therefore, for $\langle r(w), r(v) \rangle$ to be a stuttering transition of $MM_I^{b \leftarrow a}$, we need $q(r(w)) = q(r(v))$. We have that $\langle w, v \rangle$ is a stuttering transition of $MM_I^{c \leftarrow a}$, which implies that $q(r(w)) = q(r(v))$. □

Lemma 3. *If π is a stuttering segment of $MM_I^{c \leftarrow a}$, then π can be partitioned into m $(m \geq 1)$ segments $\pi_1, \pi_2, ..., \pi_m$, such that $\pi_1, ..., \pi_m$ are stuttering segments of $MM_I^{c \leftarrow b}$.*

Proof. From the definition of stuttering segments, we know that every stuttering segment π is preceded by a non-stuttering transition (say t_p) and the last transition in π is also a non-stuttering transition (say t_l). Since π is a stuttering segment of $MM_I^{c \leftarrow a}$, from Lemma 1, we get that t_p and t_l are non-stuttering transitions of $MM_I^{c \leftarrow b}$. The other transitions of π may or may not be non-stuttering transitions of $MM_I^{c \leftarrow b}$. If m of the transitions in π are non-stuttering w.r.t. $MM_I^{c \leftarrow b}$, then these m non-stuttering transitions and the preceding stuttering transitions will result in m stuttering segments of $MM_I^{c \leftarrow b}$. $\square$

Theorem 2. *(Composition for Timed refinement) If $M_c \trianglerighteq_r M_b$ and $M_b \trianglerighteq_q M_a$ then $M_c \trianglerighteq_{r;q} M_a$.*

Proof. To show that $M_c \trianglerighteq_{r;q} M_a$, there are two conditions. First condition is that $M_c \approx_{r;q} M_a$. Since $M_c \trianglerighteq_r M_b \rightarrow M_c \approx_r M_b$ and $M_b \trianglerighteq_q M_a \rightarrow M_b \approx_q M_a$, from Theorem 1 we get $M_c \approx_{r;q} M_a$.

Proof of second condition (see Definition 7 for second condition): Without loss of generality, consider any non-stuttering transition of $MM_I^{c \leftarrow a}$ say $\langle w_a, w_b \rangle$ and the corresponding stuttering segment π. Every stuttering segment is preceded by a non-stuttering transition (say $\langle w_c, w_d \rangle$). From Lemma 2, we have that π can be partitioned into m stuttering segments of $MM_I^{c \leftarrow b}$: $\pi_1, ..., \pi_m$. Let $t_1, t_2, ..., t_m$ be the non-stuttering transitions of M_b corresponding to the m stuttering segments. Since $M_c \trianglerighteq_r M_b$, each of these m stuttering segments individually will satisfy the timing requirements of the corresponding non-stuttering transitions of M_b. Therefore, π will satisfy the sum of all the timing requirements of $t_1, t_2, ..., t_m$. Note that t_m is $\langle r(w_a), r(w_b) \rangle$. From Lemma 1 $t_m : \langle r(w_a), r(w_b) \rangle$ is a non-stuttering transition of $MM_I^{b \leftarrow a}$. The corresponding non-stuttering transition in M_a is $\langle q; r(w_a), q; r(w_b) \rangle$. Also, from Lemma 2, $t_1, t_2, ..., t_{m-1}$ are stuttering transitions of $MM_I^{b \leftarrow a}$ and $t_1, t_2, ..., t_{m-1}$ is preceded by the non-stuttering transition $\langle r(w_c), r(w_d) \rangle$ of $MM_I^{b \leftarrow a}$. Therefore, $t_1, t_2, ..., t_m$ is a stuttering segment of $MM_I^{b \leftarrow a}$. Since $M_b \trianglerighteq_q M_a$, $t_1, t_2, ..., t_m$ will satisfy the timing requirements of $\langle q; r(w_a), q; r(w_b) \rangle$. Therefore, stuttering segment π of $MM_I^{c \leftarrow a}$ will satisfy timing requirements of $\langle q; r(w_a), q; r(w_b) \rangle$. Second condition is proved, we have: $M_c \trianglerighteq_{r;q} M_a$. $\square$

6   Checking Timed Refinement

Timed refinement verification is performed in three steps. The first step is to verify that the implementation TTS (M_I) is a WEB refinement of the specification TTS (M_S). The second step is to compute Marked M_S (MM_S) and Marked M_I (MM_I) using information from the WEB refinement proof. The third step is to discharge the remaining proof obligations of timed refinement, which is to compute all the stuttering segments of MM_I and check that the stuttering segments satisfy the timing requirements of MM_S.

The proof obligations for the WEB refinement verification were generated manually and discharged using a decision procedure. The details are described in Sect. 7. The second step is straightforward, which is to identify the non-stuttering and stuttering transitions of M_I and mark them as such to get MM_I. However, when computing MM_I, we also abstract the implementation TTS. A brief overview of this abstraction is provided in Sect. 7. We do not delve into the details of the abstraction in this paper. The abstraction is required as otherwise, the number of states and transitions of the implementation TTS will explode.

Algorithm 1. Procedure For Checking Timed refinement

1: **procedure** CHECKTIMEDREF(MM_I, MM_S, r)
2: **for all** $t : \langle w, v, lb, ub, m \rangle \in R_I$ **do**
3:    **if** $m = n_t$ **then**
4:      sseg-list[0] $\leftarrow t$;
5:      sseg-set $\leftarrow \{\langle$FALSE, 0, sseg-list$\rangle\}$;
6:      **repeat**
7:        termination-condition $\leftarrow$ TRUE; sseg-set' $\leftarrow$ sseg-set;
8:        **for all** sseg:$\langle$sseg-complete, sseg-length, sseg-list$\rangle \in$ sseg-set' **do**
9:          **if** $\neg$sseg-complete **then**
10:            $t^p : \langle w^p, v^p, lb^p, ub^p, m^p \rangle \leftarrow$ sseg-list[sseg-length];
11:            sseg-set $\leftarrow$ sseg-set/sseg;
12:            **for all** $t^q : \langle w^q, w^p, lb^q, ub^q, m^q \rangle \in R_I$ **do**
13:              **if** $m^q = n_t$ **then**
14:                sseg-set $\leftarrow$ sseg-set $\cup\{\langle$TRUE, sseg-length, sseg-list$\rangle\}$;
15:              **else**
16:                sseg-list[sseg-length + 1] $\leftarrow t^q$;
17:                sseg-set $\leftarrow$ sseg-set $\cup\{\langle$FALSE, sseg-length+1, sseg-list$\rangle\}$;
18:                termination-condition $\leftarrow$ FALSE;
19:      **until** termination-condition
20:      **for all** $\langle$sseg-complete, sseg-length, sseg-list$\rangle \in$ sseg-set **do**
21:        **for all** $\langle w^s, v^s, lb^s, ub^s, m^s \rangle \in R_{MM_S}$ **do**
22:          **if** $(w^s = r(w))$ & $(v^s = r(v))$ **then**
23:            **if** $\neg(lb^s \leq \sum_{i=0}^{sseg-length} lb^i \leq \sum_{i=0}^{sseg-length} ub^i \leq ub^s)$ **then**
24:              **return** sseg-list;

We have developed a procedure for the third step (given in Algorithm 1), which checks the remaining timed refinement proof obligations. The input to the timed refinement verification procedure is a list of transitions of MM_I, a list of transitions MM_S, and the refinement map used for the WEB refinement proof (which is a list of implementation states and the specification states they map to). Each transition will include information about the delay of the transition (lower bound and upper bound), and whether the transition is a stuttering or non-stuttering transition.

The procedure iterates through the non-stuttering transitions of MM_I (lines 2 and 3). The procedure computes all the stuttering segments for each non-stuttering transition. sseg-set is the set of all stuttering segments corresponding to transition t. A stuttering segment is recorded in the list of transitions sseg-list. The stuttering segments are stored in sseg-set as a three tuple: $\langle$sseg-complete, sseg-length, sseg-list⟩. sseg-complete is a flag that keeps track of whether the computation of the stuttering segment is complete. sseg-length keeps track of the length of the stuttering segment as it is computed. Lines 7–18 are repeated until all the stuttering segments are computed. During the procedure, sseg-set stores the partially computed stuttering segments.

The procedure then iterates through the partially computed stuttering segments (lines 8–9). For each partially computed stuttering segment, the procedure looks at all incoming transitions to the tail of the segment (t^p) in line 12. If there are n incoming transitions, the partially computed stuttering segment will split into n partially computed stuttering segments. Thus the partially computed stuttering segment is removed from sseg-set (line 11). If the incoming transition is a non-stuttering transition, then the stuttering segment is complete as it is (line 14). Then sseg-complete is set to TRUE and the stuttering segment is added to sseg-set. If the incoming transition is a stuttering transition, the transition is added to the tail of the partially computed stuttering segment and added to the sseg-set (lines 16–18).

As an example, the stuttering segments of ⟨7,4⟩ (in Fig. 2) are {⟨7,4⟩, ⟨6,7⟩, ⟨5,6⟩, ⟨1,5⟩, ⟨22,1⟩} and {⟨7,4⟩, ⟨12,7⟩, ⟨11,12⟩, ⟨10,11⟩, ⟨9,10⟩, ⟨8,9⟩, ⟨1,8⟩, ⟨22,1⟩}. The procedure then computes the sum of the lower time delays and upper time delays for each of the stuttering segments in sseg-set. Based on the refinement map, every non-stuttering transition of the implementation maps to a transition of the specification. The procedure then checks that the total of the lower time delays and the total of the upper time delays for each stuttering segment of a non-stuttering transition lie within the lower bound delay and the upper bound delay of the corresponding specification transition (lines 21–22). For example, if the refinement map maps implementation state 7 to specification state s_0 and implementation state 4 to specification state s_1, then the non-stuttering transition ⟨7,4⟩ maps to the specification transition ⟨s_0,s_1⟩. The procedure will check that total delays of every stuttering segment of ⟨7,4⟩ lie within the delay bounds of ⟨s_0,s_1⟩. The stuttering segments that violate this requirement are counter examples. The procedure will output these stuttering segments (line 24). If no violations are found, timed refinement is verified. We now show completeness of the procedure.

Lemma 4. *For all stuttering transitions ⟨w,v⟩ of MM_I, there exists a function* $rank : S_I \to \mathbb{N}$ *such that* $rank(v) < rank(w)$ *iff MM_I does not have stuttering cycles.*

Proof. ⇒: We prove this by contradiction. Consider that MM_I has a stuttering cycle. Then, it is not possible to assign a natural number value to every state in the cycle such that the value decreases for every transition in the cycle. Therefore, there will be at least one transition in the stuttering cycle for which $rank(v) < rank(w)$ is not satisfied.

⇐: Consider the directed graph corresponding to MM_I, where states are the vertices and transitions are the directed edges. We now remove all the non-stuttering transitions from R_I. Since there are no cycles of stuttering transitions, the resulting graph should be a set of DAGs. Natural number values can now be assigned to all the nodes in each DAG such that the value decreases for every transition. This assignment of values is a witness *rank* function that satisfies $rank(v) < rank(w)$ for all stuttering transitions.   □

Theorem 3. (*Completeness*) *If* $M_I \approx_r M_S$, *then Procedure CheckTimedRef will complete for inputs* MM_I, MM_S, *and* r.

Proof. If $M_I \approx_r M_S$, then from the definition of WEB refinement and the definition of Marked M_I (MM_I), we have that there exists a function $rank : S_I \to \mathbb{N}$ such that $rank(v) < rank(w)$ for all stuttering transitions of MM_I. From Lemma 4, MM_I has no stuttering cycles. The repeat loop (lines 6–19) terminates only when all partially computed stuttering segments eventually hit a non-stuttering transition when tracing backward in R_I. Since R_I has no stuttering cycles and is left total, Procedure CheckTimedRef will complete.   □

Theorem 4. *The time complexity of the CheckTimedRef procedure is* $\mathcal{O}(|R_I|^3)$.

Proof. Let n_i, n_s, n_{ss}, and n_{i-ns}, be the number of transitions of MM_I, number of transitions of MM_S, number of stuttering segments of MM_I, and number of non-stuttering transitions of MM_I. The outer for loop starting in line 2 has n_i passes. If initially the transitions of MM_I were classified as stuttering and non-stuttering transitions, the outer loop starting in line 2 can be reduced to n_{i-ns} passes. The initial classification would add an n_i to the running time.

Each run of the repeat loop (line 6) increases the length of the partially computed stuttering segments by 1. Therefore, the repeat loop has as many passes as the maximum length of all stuttering segments of MM_I (max(ss-length)). The deletion in line 10 is (max(ss-length)). The for loop in line 8 has n_{ss} passes and the for loop in line 12 executes n_i times. So the running time of lines 6–19 is max(ss-length)$n_{ss}n_i$.

The loop starting in line 20 executes n_{ss} times and the inner loop in line 21 executes n_s times. Therefore, the complexity of lines 20–24 is $n_{ss}n_s$. Therefore, taking into consideration that the outer loop in line 2 executes n_{i-ns} times and adding up all the components we get the complexity of the procedure to be: $n_i + n_{i-ns}n_{ss}n_i$max(ss-length)$ + n_{i-ns}n_{ss}n_s$. Since we consider only stuttering on the implementation side, the number of transitions of the implementation $n_i >$ the number of transitions of the specification n_s. Therefore, the complexity of the procedure reduces to $n_{i-ns}n_{ss}n_i$max(ss-length). In the worst case, if all transitions are non-stuttering transitions, $n_{i-ns} = n_i$. Also, there would not be any stuttering transitions. Therefore, max(ss-length) $= 1$. Also, number of stuttering segments would be equal to the number of transitions: $n_{ss} = n_i$. $n_i = |R_I|$, therefore, the time complexity of the CheckTimedRef procedure is $\mathcal{O}(|R_I|^3)$.   □

7   Verification of Stepper Motor Control Case Studies

A stepper motor with 4 leads can be stepped in two different ways based on how the leads are energized. When the following four values are applied in a repeating sequence to the leads: $\langle 0001 \rangle$, $\langle 0010 \rangle$, $\langle 0100 \rangle$, $\langle 1000 \rangle$, $\langle 0001 \rangle$, ..., it is known as *full stepping*. Instead if the following eight values are applied in a repeating sequence to the leads: $\langle 0001 \rangle$, $\langle 0011 \rangle$, $\langle 0010 \rangle$, $\langle 0110 \rangle$, $\langle 0100 \rangle$, $\langle 1100 \rangle$, $\langle 1000 \rangle$, $\langle 1001 \rangle$, $\langle 0001 \rangle$, ..., it is known as *half stepping*.

A stepper motor can be controlled by a micro-controller. We used the ARM Cortex-M3 based NXP LPC1768 [7] micro-controller for stepper motor control. Four pins from PORT 2 of the LPC1768 are connected to the stepper motor leads via an electronic circuit. The value of these 4 pins are determined by bits 28–31 of the FIOPIN register.

Case Study 1–Interrupt Driven Full Stepping Stepper Motor Control: Stepper motor control with full stepping is implemented with the Repetitive Interrupt Timer (RIT), which is a timer present in the LPC1768. The controller microcode enables the RIT unit and also a register that RIT has to store a constant value. Then the code enters a while loop. The RIT has a counter which increments every clock cycle. When the counter reaches the value stored in the RIT register, an interrupt is generated. As soon as the interrupt is generated, the counter is reset to 0 and flow of control changes to the RIT interrupt service routine (ISR). In the RIT ISR, the FIOPIN register is updated to the next value of the leads required for full stepping, and then returns control to the main program. The RIT constant register value is initialized such that the delays between consecutive interrupts generated by the RIT matches the delay required between full stepping control states. Also, this delay determines the speed at which the motor runs.

Case Study 2–Interrupt Driven Half Stepping Stepper Motor Control: The control is similar to the mechanism used for case study 1. The RIT unit is employed here also. The ISR is modified to update the FIOPIN register based on half stepping control instead of full stepping control.

Case Study 3–Full Stepping Stepper Motor Control without Interrupts: For this case study, full stepping control is implemented without using interrupts. The delay required between full stepping control states is achieved using for loops with a large number of iterations. The number of iterations of the for loop is determined so that the time required by the microcontroller to execute the for loop matches the delay required between full stepping control states. The drawback with this approach is that if the control program performs other functions and has enabled other interrupts, it may not be possible to guarantee accurate speed of the motor.

Case Study 4–Half Stepping Stepper Motor Control without Interrupts: For this case study, the delay required between half stepping control states is achieved using for loops with a large number of iterations, instead of interrupts.

Case Study 5–Interrupt Driven Variable Speed Full Stepping Stepper Motor Control: The RIT unit is used to implement full stepping control. However, the motor has 3 speed modes and in each mode the motor runs at a different speed. The modes can be changed based on input from a keyboard, which acts as an external interrupt. When any key on the keyboard is pressed, an interrupt is generated (different from the RIT interrupt). The keyboard input is processed to change the speed of the motor. Note that since the control program supports 2 interrupts, the RIT interrupt is given the higher priority.

Case Study 6–Interrupt Driven Variable Speed Half Full Stepping Stepper Motor Control: 3 mode variable speed is implemented using half stepping. The input from keyboard (which acts as an external interrupt) and RIT interrupt are also employed here, with the RIT interrupt having higher priority.

WEB Refinement Verification: For all the six case studies, WEB refinement verification was performed using the Bit-level Analysis Tool (BAT) [13], which is a decision procedure for the theory of bit-vectors with arrays. Note that some of the proof obligations were encoded in SMT-LIB v2 language [17] and discharged using the z3 SMT solver [21]. For the WEB refinement verification, we encoded the specification TTS and the implementation TTS in the input language of the BAT tool. For the WEB refinement proof, timing information is not required and was not included in the descriptions of the implementation and specification TTS. The implementation TTS consisted of the *instruction functions* (see Sect. 3) and the initial state of the micro-controller registers and memory. The next step is to construct a refinement map, which is the function that maps implementation states to specification states. The refinement map for the case studies is the function that extracts bits 28–31 of the FIOPIN register, as these 4 bits are connected to the leads of the stepper motor and directly determine the state of the stepper motor.

Each instruction function corresponds to one or more transitions of the implementation TTS. We verified that each of the instruction functions satisfies the WEB refinement correctness formula (see Sect. 4). The proof obligations were encoded in the BAT language and checked using the BAT decision procedure. Many instructions corresponded to more than one transition. In most cases, all the transitions corresponding to an instruction were similar and could be verified together using symbolic states and symbolic simulation. For some instructions, there is more than one case. An example of this is instructions whose execution could be altered by the RIT or other interrupts. For such situations, we handled the cases separately. We had two verification obligations, one for the case where the interrupt occurs and one for the case where the interrupt does not occur. Note that the non-stuttering transitions corresponded to only those instructions that updated the FIOPIN register. All other instructions corresponded to stuttering transitions. For the proof, we used pre-conditions and post-conditions to propagate the required hypothesis for each of the proof obligations.

Timed Refinement Verification: We implemented the CheckTimedRef procedure (see Sect. 6) as a tool. The tool takes as input, transitions of abstracted MM_I, transitions of MM_S, and the refinement map. The marked implementation TTS of a real-time control program will have a very large number of states

Table 1. Verification statistics

Case study	Model size	Proof size	Refinement verif. time [sec]	# of Transitions of MM_I	# of Transitions of abstract MM_I
1	2,173	10,171	4.30	2.5 million	83
2	3,232	16,018	7.23	4.5 million	135
3	1,151	6,606	2.47	45 million	103
4	1,989	11,861	4.10	81 million	184
5	3,519	17,556	9.73	17.5 million	276
6	5,625	27,854	16.13	32 million	430

and transitions. Hence, this marked TTS cannot be input directly to the timed refinement verification procedure. We use a number of techniques to abstract MM_I. The abstractions are based on the control flow graph of the object code program. Sets of states and sets of transitions corresponding to an instruction are abstracted as symbolic states and symbolic transitions. A basic block consisting of a sequence of stuttering transitions is abstracted as one stuttering transition with a delay which is the sum of the delays of the transitions in the sequence. Loops consisting of only stuttering transitions are replaced with one transition that mimics the delay of the loop. Use of these abstractions resulted in tractable and efficient verification of the stepper motor microcode control case studies. In future work, we plan to formalize and provide correctness proofs for the abstractions used.

Table 1 shows the verification statistics for the 6 case studies. The verification experiments were performed on a Intel(R) Celeron(R) CPU 540 1.86GHz processor with an L2 cache of 1MB. The "Model Size" column gives the number of lines of the implementation model in the input language of the BAT tool. The "Proof Size" column gives the number of lines of BAT code for all the WEB refinement proof obligations (includes the implementation model and the specification model). The refinement verification time column gives the total time required to discharge all the WEB and timed refinement proof obligations. *The table also gives the approximate number of transitions of the implementation TTS MM_I and the number of transitions of the abstracted MM_I. As can be seen from the table, abstractions based on stuttering transitions and stuttering segments significantly reduce the number of transitions of the implementation TTS making object code verification feasible.* We found several bugs both functional and timing. Below we describe one functional bug (found during WEB refinement verification) and one timing bug (found during timed refinement verification).

Functional Bug: The bug was found for case study 1. Bits 28–31 of the 32-bit FIOPIN register control the motor leads. Other bits of FIOPIN can be used for other purposes and should not be updated. The FIOPIN register can only be updated as a whole and individual bits cannot be updated. Therefore, the

FIOPIN is updated by using OR masking to set bits to '1' and AND masking to reset bits to '0'. This was accomplished by first performing the OR mask on the FIOPIN register and then the AND mask. Therefore, the motor state was transitioning from state 0001 to 0011, and then to 0010. This is incorrect as 0011 is not a correct state of the motor when full stepping. The bug was found during WEB refinement verification. If an external interrupt had occurred between the OR mask and the AND mask, then the motor would be stuck in a bad state.

Timing Bug: For both case studies 5 and 6, when switching from a lower speed to a higher speed, we required that the transition take place smoothly with an upper bound for the delay of the transition as the delay for state transitions of the lower speed. However, this timing requirement was not satisfied by the object code in certain states. Specifically, if the value of the RIT counter was close to the compare value when the external interrupt occurred (forcing a change in speed), there was not enough time to update the counter value and the compare value, and still make the transition to the higher speed mode in time.

8   Conclusions

Timed refinement incorporates stuttering and refinement maps and we have shown that hence it can be used for verification of low-level object code against high-level models. We have also provided a procedure for checking timed refinement with complexity $\mathcal{O}(|R_I|^3)$, and used this procedure to verify several interrupt driven motor control object code programs. *For the case studies we verified, abstractions based on stuttering reduce the size of the implementation TTS by at least 4 orders of magnitude.* For future work, we plan to develop a procedure for checking WEB refinement for interrupt driven object code programs, and also automated abstraction techniques for timed refinement verification.

References

1. Alur, R., Courcoubetis, C., Henzinger, T.A.: The observational power of clocks. In: Jonsson, B., Parrow, J. (eds.) CONCUR 1994. LNCS, vol. 836, pp. 162–177. Springer, Heidelberg (1994)
2. Alur, R., Dill, D.L.: A theory of timed automata. Theor. Comput. Sci. **126**(2), 183–235 (1994)
3. Boudjadar, A., Bodeveix, J.-P., Filali, M.: Compositional refinement for real-time systems with priorities. In: Moszkowski, B.C., Reynolds, M., Terenziani, P. (eds.) TIME, pp. 57–64. IEEE Computer Society (2012)
4. Bozga, M., Daws, C., Maler, O., Olivero, A., Tripakis, S., Yovine, S.: KRONOS: a model-checking tool for real-time systems (Tool-presentation for FTRTFT '98). In: Ravn, A.P., Rischel, H. (eds.) FTRTFT 1998. LNCS, vol. 1486, pp. 298–302. Springer, Heidelberg (1998)
5. David, A., Larsen, K.G., Legay, A., Nyman, U., Wasowski, A.: Timed I/O automata: a complete specification theory for real-time systems. In: Johansson, K.H., Yi, W. (eds.) HSCC, pp. 91–100. ACM (2010)

6. Godskesen, J.C., Larsen, K.G., Skou, A.: Automatic verification of real-time systems using epsilon. In: Vuong, S.T., Chanson, S.T. (eds.) PSTV. vol. 1, IFIP Conference Proceedings, pp. 323–330. Chapman & Hall (1994)
7. Keil Cortex-M Evaluation Board Comparison, November 2013. http://www.keil.com/arm/boards/cortexm.asp
8. Kissell, T.E.: Industrial Electronics. Prentice Hall, New Delhi (2006)
9. Larsen, K.G., Pettersson, P., Yi, W.: Uppaal in a nutshell. STTT **1**(1–2), 134–152 (1997)
10. Manolios, P.: Correctness of pipelined machines. In: Johnson, S.D., Hunt Jr., W.A. (eds.) FMCAD 2000. LNCS, vol. 1954, pp. 161–178. Springer, Heidelberg (2000)
11. Manolios, P.: Mechanical verification of reactive systems. Ph.D. thesis, University of Texas at Austin, August 2001. http://www.ccs.neu.edu/home/pete/research/phd-dissertation.html
12. Manolios, P.: A compositional theory of refinement for branching time. In: Geist, D., Tronci, E. (eds.) CHARME 2003. LNCS, vol. 2860, pp. 304–318. Springer, Heidelberg (2003)
13. Manolios, P., Srinivasan, S.K., Vroon, D.: BAT: the bit-level analysis tool. In: Damm, W., Hermanns, H. (eds.) CAV 2007. LNCS, vol. 4590, pp. 303–306. Springer, Heidelberg (2007)
14. List of Device Recalls, U.S. Food and Drug Admin, July 2010
15. Ray, S., Sumners, R.: Specification and verification of concurrent programs through refinements. J. Autom. Reasoning **51**(3), 241–280 (2013)
16. Sandler, K., Ohrstrom, L., Moy, L., McVay, R.: Killed by Code: Software Transparency in Implantable Medical Devices. Software Freedom Law Center (2010)
17. The Satisfiability Modulo Theories Library, November 2013. http://www.smtlib.org/
18. Stepper Motors, January 2014. http://www.telcointercon.com/stepper-motors-10.html
19. Toyota Seeks a Settlement for Sudden Acceleration Cases, December 2013. http://www.nytimes.com/2013/12/14/business/toyota-seeks-settlement-for-lawsuits.html?_r=0
20. Wilhelm, R., Engblom, J.: The worst-case execution-time problem - overview of methods and survey of tools. ACM Trans. Embedded Comput. Syst. **7**(3), 1–53 (2008)
21. z3, November 2013. http://z3.codeplex.com/

What Gives? A Hybrid Algorithm for Error Trace Explanation

Vijayaraghavan Murali[1], Nishant Sinha[2($\boxtimes$)], Emina Torlak[3], and Satish Chandra[4]

[1] National University of Singapore, Singapore, Singapore
m.vijay@comp.nus.edu.sg
[2] IBM Research, Bangalore, India
nishant.sinha@in.ibm.com
[3] University of Washington, Seattle, WA, USA
emina@cs.washington.edu
[4] Samsung Electronics, San Jose, CA, USA
schandra@acm.org

Abstract. When a program fails, the cause of the failure is often buried in a long, hard-to-understand error trace. We present a new technique for automatic error localization, which formally unifies prior approaches based on computing interpolants and minimal unsatisfiable cores of failing executions. Our technique works by automatically reducing an error trace to its essential components—a minimal set of statements that are responsible for the error, together with key predicates that explain how these statements lead to the failure. We prove that our approach is sound, and we show that it is useful for debugging real programs.

1 Introduction

Understanding why a program failed is the first step toward repairing it. But this first step is also time-consuming and tedious. It involves examining the *error trace* of a failing execution (typically generated by print statements), reducing that trace to statements relevant to the error, and figuring out how the relevant statements transform program state to cause the observed failure (e.g., an assertion violation). Although debuggers aid this process by providing watchpoints and breakpoints, it is still a mostly manual task that relies heavily on programmer intuition about the code. In particular, classic debuggers cannot remove irrelevant statements from the error trace to help the programmer.

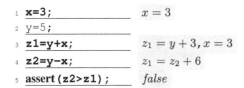

Fig. 1. Explaining error traces using abstract labels after each statement

Dynamic slicing [1,36] was introduced as a way to automatically remove irrelevant statements from the trace. Slicing is done using dependency information (data or control), removing statements that do not impact the violated assertion via any chain of dependence. The main limitation of dynamic slicing is

© Springer International Publishing Switzerland 2014
D. Giannakopoulou and D. Kroening (Eds.): VSTTE 2014, LNCS 8471, pp. 270–286, 2014.
DOI: 10.1007/978-3-319-12154-3_17

that it does not consider the *semantics* of the bug, which can result in irrelevant statement being retained. For example, in the error trace shown in the left column of Fig. 1, dynamic slicing cannot rule out statement 2, whereas at a semantic level, the value of y is irrelevant.

In this paper, we propose a new semantics-aware technique for analyzing error traces and for helping programmers understand the cause of an error. Given an error trace, our algorithm produces a slice of the original trace annotated with abstract labels explaining the failure. For example, our algorithm produces the slice $\{1, 3, 4, 5\}$ for the trace in Fig. 1, along with the explanatory labels highlighted in gray, which show why the assertion z2>z1 fails. We call such an annotated slice an *error explanation*.

Briefly, given an error trace, our technique computes an error explanation in two steps. First, it computes an *interpolant* for each statement in the original trace. An interpolant is a formula that captures the effect of a given statement on the program state (as defined in Sect. 2), and in the context of error explanation, interpolants serve as explanatory labels. Next, the trace is sliced by eliding all statements that are surrounded by identical labels. Throughout this paper, we make use of two conventions: (i) the interpolant before the first statement of a trace is always *true*, which will not be shown, and (ii) if a particular statement does not have a label after it, the previous label is assumed to be present there. In our example (Fig. 1), this approach would elide statement 2, which is semantically correct.

A slice produced by our algorithm is *sound* in that it fails for every binding of its free variables to values (such as the variable y for our example subtrace), and it is *minimal* in that it cannot be reduced any further without loss of soundness. Our technique guarantees both soundness and minimality by exploiting two central results of this paper. The first result is a theorem characterizing a class of interpolant labelings, which we call *inductive interpolant labelings* (IILs), that always lead to sound slices. The second result is a theorem relating slices induced by "maximally stationary" IILs, in which labels remain unchanged over a maximal set of statements (as defined in Sect. 3), to *minimal unsatisfiable cores* (MUC) of the formula that encodes the trace semantics. Informally, a MUC is an unsatisfiable fragment of a formula that becomes satisfiable if any of its constraints are removed. The formula for our example trace (Fig. 1) is shown below, and the constraints comprising its sole MUC are highlighted in gray:

$$x = 3 \,\wedge\, y = 5 \,\wedge\, z_1 = y + x \,\wedge\, z_2 = y - x \,\wedge\, z_2 > z_1$$

1	a[2]=0;	$a[2] = 0$	
2	i=h;	$a[2] = 0, h = 1, i = h$	
3	i++;	$a[2] = 0, h = 1, i = 2$	
4	v=a[i];	$h = 1, i = 2, v = 0, h \leq j, j \leq 1$	
5	j=j-h;	$h = 1, i = 2, v = 0, j = 0$	
6	a[j]=v;	$a[0] = 0$	
7	assert(a[0]==11 $\wedge$ a[1]==14);	*false*	

Our technique uses this MUC to produce the maximally stationary IIL shown in the figure, which leads to the sound and minimal slice $\{1, 3, 4, 5\}$.

Previous work [12] that uses interpolant-based slicing tries to increase stationariness (cf. Sect. 3.2) heuristically, without preserving the inductive

Fig. 2. Error explanation by [12] for shell-sort

property of labeling (see Sect. 2.2 for a quick summary). This can lead to unsound slices. As an example of such unsoundness, consider the faulty shell-sort program from [12], which we will investigate in detail in Sect. 5.1 (Fig. 7). The technique in [12] returns the annotated sliced trace shown in Fig. 2 (taken from Fig. 4 in [12]). Although the slice annotation consists of interpolant labels, the slice itself is unsound because it *does not* violate the assertion on line 7 in the following environment:

$$\{h \mapsto 0, j \mapsto 2, a[0] \mapsto 11, a[1] \mapsto 14\}$$

The unsoundness is due to the omission of several statements that set the variables h and j. These statements are *necessary* for reproducing the failure, and they are included in the sound slice computed by our algorithm (Fig. 7).

This paper makes the following contributions:

1. We formally characterize error explanations using the notion of *inductive interpolant labelings*, which may be viewed as special kind of Hoare proofs.
2. We characterize two key properties of error explanations: *soundness* and *minimality*. We show that IILs form sound error explanations.
3. To characterize minimality, we introduce a new notion of maximally stationary labelings. We show that computing these labelings is equivalent to computing MUCs of the path formula of the failing trace.
4. Finally, we propose a new *hybrid* algorithm for computing sound and minimal error explanation that combines interpolant computation with a black-box MUC extraction procedure. We have implemented this algorithm and applied our prototype to two small case studies.

The rest of the paper is organized as follows. Section 2 reviews the background material on MUCs, interpolants, and the corresponding trace minimization methods. Section 3 establishes formal properties of a restricted, but sound, form of interpolant labeling, and the notion of minimality of slices. These properties are exploited in Sect. 4 to develop our new algorithm for error trace explanation. We evaluate the efficacy of the algorithm in Sect. 5, discuss related work in Sect. 6, and present concluding remarks in Sect. 7.

2   Preliminaries

Our approach draws on two previous techniques for error localization [20] and explanation [12]. We give a brief overview of these techniques and introduce the necessary terminology along the way. Both techniques work on a logical representation of a failing execution path π in a program P, which takes the form of a *path formula* Φ_π. The formula Φ_π is a conjunction $\iota \wedge \Phi \wedge \epsilon$, where ι is the input that triggered the failure of the assertion ϵ in P, and $\Phi = (\phi_1 \wedge \phi_2 \cdots \wedge \phi_n)$ is the SSA encoding of π. Because π violates ϵ, the path formula Φ_π is unsatisfiable. Both of the techniques reviewed in the section, as well as our algorithm, rely on analyzing unsatisfiable path formulas.

2.1 Unsatisfiable Core Based Error Trace Explanation

Every unsatisfiable formula $\Phi = \phi_1 \wedge \ldots \phi_n$ contains one or more *unsatisfiable cores*, which are subsets of Φ whose conjunction is unsatisfiable. When every proper subset of a core is satisfiable, it is called a *minimal unsatisfiable core* (MUC) [32]. An unsatisfiable formula Φ also contains one or more *satisfiable subsets*. When every proper superset in Φ of such a subset is unsatisfiable, we call it a *maximal satisfiable subset* (MSS). The complement of an MSS is called a *minimal correcting subset* (MCS), which denotes a minimal subset of Φ whose removal from Φ will make the remainder satisfiable again. The set of MUCs and the set of MCSs of Φ are duals of each other [21]: one can be obtained by computing the irreducible hitting sets of the other.

Computing MCSs (or, dually, MUCs) of a path formula Φ_π identifies the relevant statements in a trace π [20]. For the example in Fig. 1, this method might first compute an MCS consisting of the statement on line 1, which would be flagged as a possible fix for the error. If the programmer wanted to see another repair candidate, the technique would compute another MCS, consisting of the statement on line 3, and so on. This process eventually flags all MCSs, covering all the statements in each MUC. It would not flag the statement on line 2, because it does not appear in any MUC of the trace.

In cases where multiple MUCs exist for a failing trace, where each MUC explains one aspect of the bug, one may typically employ a ranking heuristic to compare the MUCs, using say, the size of the MUC. In [20], a ranking mechanism highlights statements that occur most frequently in MCSs as having higher likelihood of being the cause. Our experiments, and those in [20], however, suggest that in practice most error traces contain only a small number of MUCs.

2.2 Interpolants-Based Error Trace Explanation

Given a pair of formulas A and B, where $\neg(A \wedge B)$ holds, an *interpolant* of A and B [8], denoted by $Itp(A \mid B)$, is a formula I over the common symbols of A and B such that $A \Rightarrow I$ and $B \Rightarrow \neg I$. Given an indexed set (or sequence) of formulas $\Phi = [A_i]_{i=1}^n$, such that $\bigwedge \Phi = false$, let $\mathcal{A}_i = [A_k]_{k=1}^i$ and $\mathcal{B}_i = [A_k]_{k=i+1}^n$ for some $1 \leq i \leq n$.

An *interpolation sequence* for Φ is a sequence $\mathcal{I} = [I_i]_{i=0}^n$, such that the following holds: (i) $I_0 = true$ and $I_n = false$; (ii) $\bigwedge \mathcal{A}_i \Rightarrow I_i$ and $\bigwedge \mathcal{B}_i \Rightarrow \neg I_i$, where each I_i is an interpolant; and (iii) each I_i is over symbols common to the sets $\mathcal{A}_i$ and $\mathcal{B}_i$. The sequence $\mathcal{I}$ is said to be *inductive* if for each I_i, $I_i \wedge A_{i+1} \Rightarrow I_{i+1}$. An interpolant sequence for a path formula Φ_π (which is itself a sequence $[\iota, \phi_1, \ldots, \phi_n, \epsilon]$, with SSA subscripts dropped), shows the intermediate state abstractions that lead to the error, and hence constitutes an *explanation* for why π failed.

Ermis et al. [12] compute interpolant labelings in the following way. First, they obtain a sequence of *candidate* interpolant labels from a theorem prover for each location along the failing path. This initial set of labels is then *minimized* by a greedy procedure which substitutes an interpolant at a given location, say

I_j, by one from another location, say I_k, and checks if I_k is an interpolant at location j. If this greedy substitution succeeds, then all statements between the two program points are deemed irrelevant and sliced away. We show that this greedy technique may produce *unsound* labelings (defined below) and hence unsound error explanations. (We caution the reader that the term 'inductive' is used in [12] in a different sense than in this paper).

2.3   Labeling and Sound Slices

Given a program trace $\pi = [S_i]_{i=1}^n$, a labeling L for π is the sequence of labels $[I_i]_{i=0}^n$. An *error labeling* L for a failing path π consists of labels that form an interpolant sequence for π. We say that L is *stationary* across S_i, denoted $st(L, i)$ iff $I_{i-1} \equiv I_i$. A labeling L for π induces a *slice* $\rho = \{S_i \in \pi | \neg st(L, i)\}$ that excludes statements in π across which L is stationary.

We say that ρ is a *sound* slice of π iff the path formula for ρ is unsatisfiable. Intuitively, this means that ρ is also a failing path. Instead of saying that the path formula for π is unsatisfiable, for simplicity we say that π is unsatisfiable or that π contains an unsatisfiable core.

3   Desired Properties of Error Explanations

In this section, we discuss two key properties for error explanations: soundness and minimality. We first show that explanations based on unrestricted interpolant labelings are not guaranteed to be sound. We then introduce the defining properties of sound and minimal explanations.

3.1   Sound Error Explanations

Figure 3(a) shows an example of an unsound error explanation, consisting of an error trace with a valid interpolant labeling (i.e., every label is a valid interpolant at its location). According to this explanation, statements 1 and 3 are irrelevant to the error, because both are surrounded by stationary labels (*true* and $z = 1$, respectively). But removing statements 1 and 3 from the trace leaves the variables z and $x1$ unconstrained, which renders the rest of the trace satisfiable.

1 `z=1;`		1 **`z=1;`**	$z = 1$
2 **`x=3;`**	$z = 1$	2 `x=3;`	
3 `x1=x+1;`		3 `x1=x+1;`	
4 **`z1=z+1;`**	$z1 = 2$	4 **`z1=z+1;`**	$z1 = 2$
5 **`assert(x1>5 && z1>5);`**	*false*	5 **`assert(x1>5 && z1>5);`**	*false*
(a)		(b)	

Fig. 3. Problem with interpolants as labels for error explanation

The basic problem of general interpolant labelings is that a labeling as a whole may be unsound, even when the individual labels are valid interpolants. To ensure soundness (Theorem 1), we restrict the space of admissible sequences of interpolant labels to include only *inductive interpolant labelings* (IILs). An IIL is a sequence of interpolants that satisfies the inductive property (cf. Sect. 2)—each interpolant in an IIL must result from the conjunction of the preceding interpolant and the intervening program statement. That is, if I_1 and I_2 are the interpolant labels before and after a statement S, then $I_1 \land S \implies I_2$.

It is easy to see that the inductive property forbids the labeling sequence in Fig. 3(a), as $true \land x = 3 \;\not\!\!\!\implies\; z = 1$. A possible IIL for this trace is given in Fig. 3(b), and it is the labeling computed by our method (Sect. 4). To the best of our knowledge, none of the previous methods for interpolant-based error explanation (including [12,31]) guarantee the inductive property, nor any alternative soundness condition (see Sect. 6).

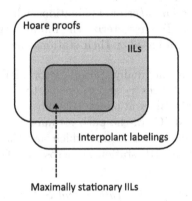

Fig. 4. Relating Hoare proofs, Interpolant labelings and IILs.

Remark. IILs correspond to a Hoare proof for a failing path π. In particular, $\{I_{j-1}\}S_j\{I_j\}$ is a valid Hoare triple for each $1 \le j \le n$. In an arbitrary Hoare proof for failure of π (with $true$ and $false$ as the first and last labels respectively), the assertion labels are inductive but they are not necessarily interpolants, i.e., they may contain symbols local to either the prefix or the suffix. Similarly, arbitrary interpolant error labelings do not form a Hoare proof, because they may not be inductive. IILs are restricted Hoare proofs that contain labels only over symbols common to the prefix and the suffix. Figure 4 shows the general relationship between Hoare proofs, interpolant labelings and IILs visually (maximally stationary IILs are explained in Sect. 3.2).

Theorem 1 (Sound Error Labelings)
If an error labeling L for π is an inductive interpolant labeling (IIL) then the sliced error path π' induced by L is sound.

Proof. Without loss of generality, assume that exactly two statements S_j and S_k ($j < k$) are elided from the error path π to obtain π'. We then know the following:

(1) I_j is the same as I_{j-1} and I_k is the same as I_{k-1}, because S_j and S_k are sliced away
(2) $\bigwedge\{S_1, \ldots, S_{j-1}\} \implies I_{j-1}$ (Interpolant property)
(3) $I_k \land \bigwedge\{S_{k+1}, \ldots S_n\}$ is unsatisfiable   (Interpolant property)
    This means $I_{k-1} \land \bigwedge\{S_{k+1}, \ldots S_n\}$ is unsatisfiable   (1)

(4) $I_j \wedge \bigwedge\{S_{j+1}, \ldots, S_{k-1}\} \implies I_{k-1}$ (Inductive property)
This means $I_{j-1} \wedge \bigwedge\{S_{j+1}, \ldots, S_{k-1}\} \implies I_{k-1}$ (1)

From (2) and (4), we have
(5) $\bigwedge\{S_1, \ldots, S_{j-1}, S_{j+1}, \ldots, S_{k-1}\} \implies I_{k-1}$

From (3) and (5), we have
(6) $\bigwedge\{S_1, \ldots, S_{j-1}, S_{j+1}, \ldots, S_{k-1}, S_{k+1}, \ldots, S_n\}$ is unsatisfiable.

This set contains all statements in the error path π except S_j and S_k and so represents the sliced error path π'. Hence, the path formula for π' is unsatisfiable, and π' is sound (cf. Sect. 2). The proof can be directly extended to an arbitrary number of elided statements.   □

3.2   Minimal Error Explanations

Our goal is to compute not only sound but also *minimal* error explanations, which succinctly explain the fault to the programmer. To characterize the minimality of explanations, we propose a new formal criterion based on their stationariness.

Maximally Stationary Labeling. An IIL L is maximally stationary for a failing path π iff there exists no IIL L' (with induced slices π_L and $\pi_{L'}$ respectively), such that $\pi_L \subset \pi'_L$. In order to compute maximally-stationary IILs efficiently, we show that they correspond exactly to the MUCs of the path formula for π (Theorem 2). To prove this result, we need the following lemma which says that for *any* unsatisfiable core M of π, there exists an IIL stationary across all the statements S excluded from the core.

Lemma 1. *Let M be an unsatisfiable core for a failing path π and $S \subset \pi$. If $S \cap M = \emptyset$, then there exists an IIL L which is stationary across each statement in S.*

Proof. Let $|M| = l$. Let $\pi' = [S_{i_k}]_{k=1}^l$ be the *projection* of $\pi = [S_j]_{j=1}^n$ on to M such that each $S_{i_k} \in M$ and $1 \le i_1 < i_2 \cdots < i_l \le n$. Because M is unsatisfiable, there exists an IIL $L' = [I_{i_k}]_{k=1}^{l+1}$ for π', where for each i_k, (1) $I_{i_k} \wedge S_{i_k} \Rightarrow I_{i_{k+1}}$ (2) $I_{i_k} = Itp(\iota \wedge S_{i_1} \wedge \ldots \wedge S_{i_{k-1}} \mid S_{i_k} \wedge \ldots \wedge S_{i_l} \wedge \epsilon)$. Given a statement $S \in S$, we will show how L' can be extended to an IIL for $M \cup \{S\}$. Assuming S occurs at position p in π, where $i_{k-1} < p < i_k$, we extend L' to L'' by copying I_{i_k} across S: $(I_{i_1})S_{i_1} \ldots S_{i_{k-1}}(I_{i_k})S(I_{i_k})S_{i_k}(I_{i_{k+1}}) \ldots S_{i_l}(I_{i_{l+1}})$.

It follows from (1) and $I_{i_k} \wedge S \Rightarrow I_{i_k}$ that L'' is inductive. To prove that each label is an interpolant, consider labels I_{i_m} where $m < p$. It follows from (2) that $(\iota \wedge S_{i_1} \wedge \ldots \wedge S_{i_{m-1}}) \Rightarrow I_{i_m}$. Also, $(S_{i_m} \wedge \ldots S_{i_l} \wedge \epsilon) \Rightarrow \neg I_{i_m}$. Hence, $(S \wedge S_{i_m} \wedge \ldots S_{i_l} \wedge \epsilon) \Rightarrow \neg I_{i_m}$. Also, each I_{i_m} is defined only over the shared symbols at position m in L''. The proof is similar for $m > p$. By extending L' for each $S \in S$ iteratively, we obtain an IIL for π.   □

Using Lemma 1, we can now prove our main theorem.

Theorem 2. *An IIL L for a failing trace π is maximally stationary iff the induced slice of L forms a MUC.*

Proof. We show that ($\Rightarrow$) the slice induced by a maximally stationary IIL forms a MUC, and that ($\Leftarrow$) for every MUC M of π, there exists a maximally stationary IIL whose induced slice is equivalent to M. Both proofs are by contradiction.

($\Rightarrow$) Suppose the slice M induced by L is not a MUC. Then there exists an $S \in M$, such that $M \setminus \{S\}$ is unsatisfiable. So, by Lemma 1, there is an L' whose induced slice is $M \setminus \{S\} \subset M$. So, L is not maximally stationary.

($\Leftarrow$) By Lemma 1, there exists an IIL L whose induced slice is exactly M. Suppose L is not maximal. So there exists IIL L' with induced slice $M' \subset M$. Because L' is an IIL, it follows from Theorem 1 that the slice M' is sound, i.e., M' is also unsatisfiable. So M is not a MUC. $\square$

In the next section, we exploit Theorem 2 to propose a new error explanation algorithm that computes maximally stationary IILs by using a MUC computation engine as a black-box. Our algorithm thus benefits directly from the advances in techniques for computing MUCs.

4   A Hybrid Algorithm for Error Trace Explanation

We now present a new algorithm for error trace understanding that combines the benefits of MUCs and interpolants. Figure 5 shows the pseudocode for GEN-LABELS, the main procedure of our algorithm, to which the error path $\pi \equiv \{S_1, S_2, \ldots, S_n\}$ is provided. Without loss of generality, we assume that the input ι and the violated assertion ϵ are included in π. GENLABELS computes an IIL L for the failing trace π.

GENLABELS ($\pi \equiv S_1, S_2 \ldots, S_n$)
1:     **let** $C := \text{GETCORE}(\pi)$ be $\{S_{c_1}, S_{c_2} \ldots, S_{c_m}\}$ s.t. $c_1 < c_2 \ldots < c_m$
2:     $I_0 := \textit{true}$
3:     **for** i := 1 **to** n **do**
4:         **if** S_i occurs in C **then**
5:             **let** k be such that $c_k == i$
6:             $\mathcal{V} := \text{vars}(I_{i-1} \wedge S_i)$
7:             $\mathcal{V}' := \text{vars}(S_{c_{k+1}} \wedge S_{c_{k+2}} \ldots \wedge S_{c_m})$
8:             $I_i := \exists \overline{(\mathcal{V} \cap \mathcal{V}')}.(I_{i-1} \wedge S_i)$ (eliminate irrelevant variables)
9:         **else**
10:             $I_i := I_{i-1}$
11:     **endfor**
12:     **return** $\{I_0, I_1 \ldots, I_n\}$

Fig. 5. Generating IILs from unsatisfiable cores

GENLABELS starts by obtaining an unsatisfiable core of π by calling GET-CORE (line 1). GETCORE is a procedure that returns an unsatisfiable core of the given formula, while maintaining the relative ordering of constraints (statements) in the formula. Our algorithm then computes an IIL for C, which induces a sound slice of π (by Theorem 1). If $\mathcal{C}$ is a MUC, the resulting IIL is maximally stationary (by Theorem 2), and the corresponding slice is minimal.

Line 2 initializes I_0 to true, the first label for any error trace. Then, for each statement S_i, GENLABELS performs the following steps. If S_i occurs in the core $\mathcal{C}$ (line 4), it computes the set $\mathcal{V}$ of variables that appear in the conjunction of the previous label I_{i-1} and the current statement S_i (line 6). It also computes the set $\mathcal{V}'$ of variables that appear in the core statements following S_i (line 7). The set $\mathcal{V} \cap \mathcal{V}'$ consists of variables that appear in both $I_{i-1} \wedge S_i$ and in the core statements following S_i. Its complement, $\overline{\mathcal{V} \cap \mathcal{V}'}$, represents the variables that are *not* common to $I_{i-1} \wedge S_i$ and the core statements following S_i.

On line 8, all variables in the set $\overline{\mathcal{V} \cap \mathcal{V}'}$ are existentially quantified and eliminated from the formula $I_{i-1} \wedge S_i$. The resulting formula is the label I_i after S_i. This step results in I_i being the "projection" of $I_{i-1} \wedge S_i$ onto the variables of the statements in $\mathcal{C}$ that follow S_i—that is, I_i is a formula only over the variables in $\mathcal{V} \cap \mathcal{V}'$. Finally, if the current statement S_i is not in the core $\mathcal{C}$, line 10 sets I_i to be the same as I_{i-1}. In Sect. 4.2, we prove that the labels generated in this way form an IIL for π.

As an example, consider the trace in Fig. 1. Given $\pi \equiv \{x = 3, y = 5, z1 = y + x, z2 = y - x, z2 > z1\}$, assume that GETCORE returns the MUC $\mathcal{C} \equiv \{x = 3, z1 = y + x, z2 = y - x, z2 > z1\}$. Our algorithm first initializes I_0 to true. For the first statement $S_1 \equiv x = 3$, it sets $\mathcal{V}$ to be the variables in $I_0 \wedge S_1$, i.e., $\{x\}$, and $\mathcal{V}'$ to be the variables in $S_3 \wedge \ldots \wedge S_5$, i.e., $\{x, y, z1, z2\}$. Now, I_1 is the formula $\exists\{y, z1, z2\}.(true \wedge x = 3)$, which yields $x = 3$ after quantifier elimination. The second statement, y=5, is not in $\mathcal{C}$ so we generate the same label $x = 3$ after it. For $S_3 \equiv z1 = y + x$, the sets $\mathcal{V}$ and $\mathcal{V}'$ would be $\{x, y, z1\}$ and $\{x, y, z1, z2\}$ respectively. Thus I_3 is the formula $\exists\{z2\}(x = 3 \wedge z1 = y + x)$, which is equivalent to the quantifier-free $x = 3 \wedge z1 = y + 3$.

The final label I_4 is interesting: $\mathcal{V}$ is the set of variables in $I_3 \wedge S_4$, i.e., $\{x, y, z1, z2\}$, and $\mathcal{V}'$ is the set $\{z1, z2\}$. Therefore I_4 is $\exists\{x, y\}(z1 = y + 3 \wedge x = 3 \wedge z2 = y - x)$. Eliminating the quantifier yields $z1 = z2 + 6$, a predicate that is not obvious from the program. This shows that regardless of the value of y, z1 is 6 more than z2, which is why the assertion $z2 > z1$ failed. It can be seen that each label is indeed an interpolant and the sequence is inductive, as we will formally prove in Sect. 4.2.

4.1   Discussion of the Algorithm

Our algorithm is a variation on the strongest postcondition (SP) and weakest precondition (WP) computation [9]. In general, SP and WP labels may not be interpolants—particularly, they may carry variables not common to the prefix and suffix at a program point—because they only utilize information from "one direction" (forward for SP and backward for WP). Our algorithm fixes this by using MUCs to obtain, in the forward direction, the set of relevant statements so far and, in the backward direction, the set of variables to project away. With this knowledge, our algorithm is able to combine the benefits of forward and backward reasoning.

Nevertheless, even if the restriction of interpolants to be only on common variables is relaxed, SP and WP rarely keep the labels stationary. Figure 6 shows the same example from Fig. 3 but labeled with (a) WP and (b) SP. It can be seen that neither is stationary at any point along the trace, hence no statement is removed from their induced slices.

1	`z=1;`	*true*	1	`z=1;`	$z = 1$
2	`x=3;`	$x \leq 4 \vee z \leq 4$	2	`x=3;`	$z = 1, x = 3$
3	`x1=x+1;`	$x1 \leq 5 \vee z \leq 4$	3	`x1=x+1;`	$z = 1, x1 = 4$
4	`z1=z+1;`	$x1 \leq 5 \vee z1 \leq 5$	4	`z1=z+1;`	$z1 = 2, x1 = 4$
5	`assert(x1>5 && z1>5);`	*false*	5	`assert(x1>5 && z1>5);`	*false*
	(a)			(b)	

Fig. 6. WP and SP may keep irrelevant statements in the explanation

Our algorithm uses the GETCORE procedure to project out variables unnecessary to *an* explanation that corresponds to an unsatisfiable core (for which we typically use a MUC). In Fig. 3(b), having prior knowledge of a particular MUC that excludes the constraint $x = 3$ allows our algorithm to project away x, keeping the interpolant stationary across the statement x=3.[1] Without the knowledge of such a core—e.g., if GETCORE were to return the entire trace—the algorithm would have no basis to project away x. It is this lack of "global knowledge" that makes explanations based purely on an interpolant computation (using WPs, SPs, or similar methods) less powerful than those seeded with a MUC.

We remark that we made the design choice of using quantifier-elimination in our algorithm for two reasons. First, we do not need to depend on an interpolating theorem prover or construct a refutation proof of the formula. Second, this approach exposes an interesting connection to SP and WP, as seen above. Having said that, our algorithm can be easily extended to use proof-based interpolation procedures [11,24] by first obtaining the refutation proof p corresponding to an unsatisfiable core of π and then computing inductive interpolants from p.

4.2 Properties of the Algorithm

We present formal proofs that our algorithm generates IILs for every error trace π, thus inducing sound slices (Theorem 1).

Lemma 2. (Labels are inductive)
If I_{i-1} and I_i are the labels generated by our algorithm before and after a statement S_i respectively, then $I_{i-1} \wedge S_i \Rightarrow I_i$

---

[1] We could have also produced another IIL corresponding to the other MUC, removing the statement z=1 in that case.

Proof. Assume that GETCORE returned some unsatisfiable core $\mathcal{C}$ of the error path. If S_i did not appear in $\mathcal{C}$, then according to the algorithm (line 10), I_i is the same as I_{i-1}, and we are done since $I_{i-1} \wedge S_i \Rightarrow I_{i-1}$.

If S_i did appear in $\mathcal{C}$, then $I_i \equiv \exists \mathcal{V}''.(I_{i-1} \wedge S_i)$ where $\mathcal{V}''$ is as defined in the algorithm (lines 6–8). Assuming the theory of $I_{i-1} \wedge S_i$ supports quantifier elimination, $I_{i-1} \wedge S \Rightarrow \exists \mathcal{V}''.(I_{i-1} \wedge S_i)$ since quantifier elimination from a formula entails abstraction. Therefore $I_{i-1} \wedge S_i \Rightarrow I_i$. □

Note that by transitive closure of the inductive property for a sequence $S_i \ldots S_j$ of statements, we have that $I_{i-1} \wedge \bigwedge \{S_i, S_{i+1} \ldots S_j\} \Rightarrow I_j$.

Lemma 3 (Labels are interpolants). *Let the error path* $\pi \equiv S_1, S_2 \ldots, S_i,$ $\ldots, S_n$. *If* I_i *is the label generated by our algorithm after* S_i, *then* I_i *is an interpolant. That is,*

(a) $\bigwedge \{S_1, \ldots, S_i\} \Rightarrow I_i$
(b) $I_i \wedge \bigwedge \{S_{i+1}, \ldots, S_n\}$ *is unsatisfiable*
(c) I_i *is a formula only on the common variables of* $\{S_1, \ldots, S_i\}$ *and* $\{S_{i+1}, \ldots, S_n\}$

Proof. Base case: *true* is an interpolant before S_1 (or after an implicit empty S_0) since it satisfies (a), (b) and (c).

Assume that I_{i-1} is an interpolant after S_{i-1}.

(a) $\bigwedge \{S_1, \ldots, S_{i-1}\} \Rightarrow I_{i-1}$ (hypothesis), and $I_{i-1} \wedge S_i \Rightarrow I_i$ (Lemma 2). Therefore, $\bigwedge \{S_1, \ldots, S_i\} \Rightarrow I_i$
(b) $I_{i-1} \wedge \bigwedge \{S_i, \ldots, S_n\}$ is unsatisfiable (hypothesis).

> Consider the case S_i not occurring in $\mathcal{C}$. Then, $I_{i-1} \wedge \bigwedge \{S_{i+1}, \ldots, S_n\}$ is unsatisfiable (from hypothesis). The algorithm in this case sets I_i to be I_{i-1}. Therefore, $I_i \wedge \bigwedge \{S_{i+1}, \ldots, S_n\}$ is unsatisfiable.
> Consider the case S_i occurring in $\mathcal{C}$. Then, $I_{i-1} \wedge \bigwedge \{S_{c_k}, S_{c_{k+1}}, \ldots, S_{c_m}\}$ is unsatisfiable, where $i = c_k$ and $\{S_{c_{k+1}}, S_{c_{k+2}}, \ldots, S_{c_m}\}$ is a subset of $\{S_{i+1}, \ldots, S_n\}$. We assume that the quantifier elimination is such that $I_i \equiv \exists \overline{\mathcal{V} \cap \mathcal{V}'}(I_{i-1} \wedge S_i)$ is the strongest formula implied by $I_{i-1} \wedge S_i$ on the variables $\mathcal{V} \cap \mathcal{V}'$. That is, I_i is *equivalent* to $I_{i-1} \wedge S_i$ on $\mathcal{V}$ and $\mathcal{V}'$. We also know that $\mathcal{V}' \equiv$ vars $(S_{c_{k+1}} \wedge S_{c_{k+2}} \ldots \wedge S_{c_m})$. This entails $I_i \wedge \bigwedge \{S_{c_{k+1}}, S_{c_{k+2}}, \ldots, S_{c_m}\}$ is unsatisfiable. Therefore, $I_i \wedge \bigwedge \{S_{i+1}, S_{i+2}, \ldots, S_n\}$ is unsatisfiable.
(c) We in fact prove a stronger version of (c): that I_i is only on the common variables of $\{S_{c_1}, S_{c_2}, \ldots, S_{c_k}\}$ and $\{S_{c_{k+1}}, S_{c_{k+2}}, \ldots, S_{c_m}\}$ for some k where the former is a subset of $\{S_1, S_2, \ldots, S_i\}$ and the latter is a subset of $\{S_{i+1}, S_{i+2}, \ldots, S_n\}$. The induction hypothesis here is that I_{i-1} is only on the common variables of $\{S_{c_1}, S_{c_2}, \ldots, S_{c_{k-1}}\}$ and $\{S_{c_k}, S_{c_{k+1}}, \ldots, S_{c_m}\}$ where the former is a subset of $\{S_1, S_2, \ldots, S_{i-1}\}$ and the latter is a subset of $\{S_i, S_{i+1}, \ldots, S_n\}$.

Consider the case S_i not occurring in $\mathcal{C}$, which implies $i \neq c_k$. Let $j = k - 1$. Then, I_i (the same as I_{i-1}, as set by the algorithm) is only on the common variables of $\{S_{c_1}, S_{c_2}, \ldots, S_{c_j}\}$ and $\{S_{c_{j+1}}, S_{c_{j+2}}, \ldots, S_{c_m}\}$. From the hypothesis, the former is a subset of $\{S_1, S_2, \ldots, S_{i-1}, S_i\}$ and the latter is a subset of $\{S_{i+1}, S_{i+2}, \ldots, S_n\}$, since $i \neq c_k$ (or $i \neq c_{j+1}$).

Consider the case S_i occurring in $\mathcal{C}$, which implies $i = c_k$. Then, $I_{i-1} \wedge S_i$ will be on $\mathsf{vars}(I_{i-1}) \cup \mathsf{vars}(S_i)$. Now, if all variables in $\mathsf{vars}(S_i)$ occur in $S_{c_{k+1}}, \ldots, S_{c_m}$ then $\mathcal{V} \cap \mathcal{V}'$ is simply $\mathsf{vars}(I_{i-1}) \cup \mathsf{vars}(S_i)$. Hence I_i is on the common variables of $\{S_{c_1}, \ldots, S_{c_k}\}$ and $\{S_{c_{k+1}}, \ldots S_{c_m}\}$. If there is a variable $v \in \mathsf{vars}(S_i)$ not occurring in $S_{c_{k+1}} \ldots S_{c_m}$, then v will not appear in $\mathcal{V} \cap \mathcal{V}'$. Hence it will appear in $\overline{\mathcal{V} \cap \mathcal{V}'}$ and will be quantified and eliminated from I_i. Thus, I_i is an interpolant after S_i. □

5 Experimental Evaluation

We implemented our algorithm on the TRACER [17] framework for symbolic execution. The GETCORE procedure was implemented to return a MUC. We computed all MUCs using the method presented in [2], and generated an IIL for each MUC. We found that the method scales poorly for large programs, so one can also implement algorithms such as [4, 21, 26]. Our target programming language was C.

We provided input traces manually for our case studies, but they were automatically converted to SSA form by TRACER. The underlying constraint solver is CLP($\mathcal{R}$) [16], which uses the Fourier-Motzkin procedure for quantifier elimination over reals. We modeled program variables in the theory of linear real arithmetic due to our choice of solver, but any theory with quantifier elimination would work. Arrays were modeled using uninterpreted functions, and the McCarthy axioms [23] were applied to obtain a symbolic expression for each array reference. The heap was modeled as an array.

We now describe two case studies that serve as proof-of-concept that our algorithm works well in practice. The first case study uses the faulty sorting example from [12], and the second case study uses a more realistic program from the SIR repository [33]. We emphasize that the goal of this paper is mainly to provide a formal unification of MUC-based and interpolant-based error explanation, and so user studies regarding which approach is more "intuitive" for debugging are out of scope of this paper.

5.1 Shell Sort

Figure 7(a) shows the faulty program from [12], which is supposed to sort a given array of integers. When applied to the already sorted input [11,14], it returns [0,11] instead of the input itself. Our safety property therefore asserts that the output should be [11,14]. The corresponding error trace is shown in Fig. 7(b), annotated with the labels computed by our algorithm, where bolded statements constitute the slice. We do not show the assume statements as they

1	*a[0]=11*	
2	*a[1]=14*	*true*
3	*a[2]=0*	$a[2] = 0$
4	*size=3*	

```
shell_sort (int a[], int size)
    int h=1, i, j;
    do
        h=h*3;
    while (h <= size);
    do {
        h /= 3;
        for (i=h; i<size; i++) {
            int v = a[i];
            for (j=i; j>=h &&
                a[j-h]>v; j-=h)
                a[j] = a[j-h];
            if (i != j)
                a[j] = v;
        }
    } while (h != 1);
```

(a)

5	**h=1;**	$a[2] = 0, h = 1$
6	**i=h;**	$a[2] = 0, h = 1, i = 1$
7	v=a[i];	
8	j=i;	
9	**i++;**	$a[2] = 0, h = 1, i = 2$
10	**v=a[i];**	$v = 0, h = 1, i = 2$
11	**j=i;**	$v = 0, h = 1, j = 2$
12	a[j]=a[j-h];	
13	**j=j-h;**	$v = 0, h = 1, j = 1$
14	a[j]=a[j-h];	
15	**j=j-h;**	$v = 0, j = 0$
16	**a[j]=v;**	$a[0] = 0$
17	i++;	
18	**assert(a[0]==11);** $\wedge$	
	assert(a[1]==14); *false*	

(b)

Fig. 7. (a) The faulty shell sort program and (b) its error trace for input [11, 14] with labels

do not change the program state, and hence do not affect the interpolants. Note that we have "grounded" h to 1 instead of executing h=h*3 and h=h/3 because our underlying solver does not reason about integer arithmetic.

The initial label $a[2] = 0$ immediately suggests that there is a problem, because we are only sorting an array of two integers and should not be accessing a[2]. The rest of the labels capture how the value in a[2] gets propagated to a[0]. The variables h and i are initialized to 1. Then, i is incremented to 2, causing a[i] (now 0) to be stored in v (line 10). Next, j is initialized to i, and decremented by h twice to result in j being 0. Finally, line 16 stores v (which is 0) into a[0], causing the violation. Our algorithm computed these labels within 2–3 s.

The inductiveness of labels is key to the quality of the explanation. Each label is implied by the conjunction of the previous label and the intermediate (bolded) statement, enabling local reasoning about the bug flow. Since each label is an interpolant, it only captures variables that are relevant to the bug at each point (see, e.g., line 10, where a[2] stops being relevant to the bug and v becomes relevant).

30 `prio=1;`	$prio = 1$
31 `prio`$_{new\_job}$`=prio;`	$prio_{new\_job} = 1$
37 `new_process=malloc(sizeof(struct process));`	
	$prio_{new\_job} = 1, new\_process \neq$ NULL
41 `prio`$_{enqueue}$`=prio`$_{new\_job}$`;`	$prio_{enqueue} = 1, new\_process \neq$ NULL
42 `prio`$_{put\_end}$`=prio`$_{enqueue}$`;`	$prio_{put\_end} = 1, new\_process \neq$ NULL
43 `process`$_{put\_end}$`=new_process;`	$prio_{put\_end} = 1, process_{put\_end} \neq$ NULL
44 `prio_queue[prio`$_{put\_end}$`].head=process`$_{put\_end}$`;`	$prio\_queue[1].head \neq$ NULL
45 `prio`$_{get\_current}$`=3;`	$prio_{get\_current} = 3, prio\_queue[1].head \neq$ NULL
46 `prio`$_{get\_current}$`=prio`$_{get\_current}$`-1;`	$prio_{get\_current} = 2, prio\_queue[1].head \neq$ NULL
47 `prio`$_{get\_current}$`=prio`$_{get\_current}$`-1;`	$prio_{get\_current} = 1, prio\_queue[1].head \neq$ NULL
48 `prio`$_{get\_process}$`=prio`$_{get\_current}$`;`	$prio_{get\_process} = 1, prio\_queue[1].head \neq$ NULL
49 `job`$_{get\_process}$`=&current_job;`	
	$job_{get\_process} = \&current\_job, prio_{get\_process} = 1, prio\_queue[1].head \neq$ NULL
50 `next`$_{get\_process}$`=&prio_queue[prio`$_{get\_process}$`].head;`	
	$job_{get\_process} = \&current\_job, *next_{get\_process} \neq$ NULL
51 `*job`$_{get\_process}$`=*next`$_{get\_process}$`;`	$current\_job \neq$ NULL
54 `job`$_{finish}$`=current_job;`	$job_{finish} \neq$ NULL
58 `assert(job`$_{finish}$`==NULL);`	$false$

Fig. 8. Inductive interpolant labeling computed by our algorithm for schedule2

5.2   Schedule2

For our second case study, we used the schedule2 program from the SIR repository [33]. It implements a priority scheduler for a given sequence of processes and their priorities (1, 2, or 3). The program's distributors seeded a bug, which sets the default priority (`prio`) of a process with no priority to be 1 (instead of -1). The error trace for an input of one process with no priority is shown in Fig. 8.

We do not show the entire trace for space reasons. However, it is worth noting that we applied dynamic slicing [27] on the original trace, which reduced its size from 129 to 58 statements, on which we applied our algorithm. In Fig. 8, the initial statement `prio=1` is the seeded bug which our labeling has captured. At line 37, a new process is created, which is captured by the label $new\_process \neq$ NULL.

At line 44, the process is added to the priority queue data structure, as shown by the label $prio\_queue[1].head \neq$ NULL. This indicates to the programmer that something is wrong, because the process should not have been added to the queue. At line 50, the process is retrieved from the head of the queue and set as the current job to be executed, as captured by the label $current\_job \neq$ NULL at line 51. The assertion states that when the `finish` function is called to execute the processes, there should be no jobs available, but there is one due to the bug, and therefore the assertion is violated. Our algorithm computed these labels in about 2–3 s.

Ultimately the dynamically sliced trace of 58 statements was reduced to just 16 statements through our algorithm. Together with the explanatory labels, it presents a much better explanation of the trace compared to dynamic slicing.

6   Related Work

BugAssist [20] analyzes proofs of unsatisfiability of the path formula to localize errors; a minimal set of statements which, on removal, makes the formula satisfiable again is marked as containing potential causes of the error. Instead, our approach computes error-explaining labels on the trace and exploits MUCs to compute a path slice relevant to the error. Ermis et al. [12] proposed the idea of computing error-explaining labels using interpolants. Because they compute individual labels independently, followed by a post-processing step to improve stationariness, the resulting sequence of labels may be unsound (cf. Sect. 3).

Popular methods for fault localization include Delta debugging [7, 35] and Darwin [28], which compare failing and successful program states and executions; DIDUCE [14], which computes likely invariants from good runs and checks for their violations on other runs; statistical methods [19], which compute suspiciousness of statements based on the frequency of their occurrences in passing and failing runs; and methods based on dynamic slicing [1, 36], which consider dependency flows in failing runs. Other approaches use symbolic techniques to explain counterexamples obtained by model checking [3, 13]. Symbolic techniques have also been used for program repair [6, 22]. Sahoo et al. [30] combine likely invariants, delta debugging and dynamic slicing techniques for scalable root cause analysis on real-world programs. Error-explaining labels may be viewed as likely invariants along the failing path; they assist the developer in pinpointing the root cause.

Interpolant computation [24] is widely used to enable convergence of SAT/ SMT-based bounded model checking of both hardware [24] and software [15, 25]. Interpolants of different strengths may be derived from the same proof of unsatisfiability; D'Silva et al. [11] present a unified lattice-based framework for ordering the interpolants computed by different methods. Like our method, CEGAR-based software verification techniques [5, 15], which use interpolants for refinement, also require that the interpolant sequence is inductive [18, 29, 34]. Dillig et al. use abductive inference for assisting developers in classifying erroneous analysis reports [10].

7   Conclusion

Interpolant-based error explanations are attractive in their ability to convey the essence of an error trace to a programmer. In this paper, we examined their ability to filter out statements that are guaranteed to be irrelevant to the error. Since the goal of minimal unsatisfiable core computation is also similar, we examined whether the two techniques have any formal relationship. We found that, in general, interpolant-based error explanations are weaker than minimal cores in their ability to exclude irrelevant statements. More importantly, we identified sufficient conditions on interpolant sequences so that statements are not unsoundly ruled out as irrelevant; previous work is vulnerable to this pitfall. We also pinpoint reasons why it is difficult to arrive at sound interpolant labeling that matches minimal unsatisfiable cores in their power to exclude irrelevant statements.

References

1. Agrawal, H., Horgan, J.R.: Dynamic program slicing. In: PLDI '90, pp. 246–256 (1990)
2. Bailey, J., Stuckey, P.J.: Discovery of minimal unsatisfiable subsets of constraints using hitting set dualization. In: Hermenegildo, M.V., Cabeza, D. (eds.) PADL 2004. LNCS, vol. 3350, pp. 174–186. Springer, Heidelberg (2005)
3. Ball, T., Naik, M., Rajamani, S.K.: From symptom to cause: localizing errors in counterexample traces. In: POPL '03, pp. 97–105 (2003)
4. Belov, A., Marques-Silva, J.: MUSer2: An efficient MUS extractor. JSAT **8**, 123–128 (2012)
5. Beyer, D., Henzinger, T.A., Jhala, R., Majumdar, R.: The software model checker BLAST: Applications to software engineering. Int. J. Softw. Tools Technol. Transf. **9**(5), 505–525 (2007)
6. Chandra, S., Torlak, E., Barman, S., Bodik, R.: Angelic debugging. In: ICSE (2011)
7. Cleve, H., Zeller, A.: Locating causes of program failures. In: ICSE, pp. 342–351 (2005)
8. Craig, W.: Three uses of Herbrand-Gentzen theorem in relating model theory and proof theory. J. Symb. Comput. **22**, 250–268 (1957)
9. Dijkstra, E.W.: A Discipline of Programming, 1st edn. Prentice Hall PTR, Upper Saddle River, NJ, USA (1997)
10. Dillig, I., Dillig, T., Aiken, A.: Automated error diagnosis using abductive inference. In: PLDI (2012)
11. D'Silva, V., Kroening, D., Purandare, M., Weissenbacher, G.: Interpolant strength. In: Barthe, G., Hermenegildo, M. (eds.) VMCAI 2010. LNCS, vol. 5944, pp. 129–145. Springer, Heidelberg (2010)
12. Ermis, E., Schäf, M., Wies, T.: Error invariants. In: Giannakopoulou, D., Méry, D. (eds.) FM 2012. LNCS, vol. 7436, pp. 187–201. Springer, Heidelberg (2012)
13. Groce, A., Chaki, S., Kroening, D., Strichman, O.: Error explanation with distance metrics. Softw. Tools Technol. Transf. (STTT) **8**, 229–247 (2006)
14. Hangal, S., Lam, M.S.: Tracking down software bugs using automatic anomaly detection. In: ICSE '02 (2002)
15. Henzinger, T.A., Jhala, R., Majumdar, R., McMillan, K.L.: Abstractions from proofs. In: POPL (2004)
16. Jaffar, J., Michaylov, S., Stuckey, P.J., Yap, R.H.C.: The CLP($\mathcal{R}$) language and system. ACM Trans. Program. Lang. Syst. **14**(3), 339–395 (1992)
17. Jaffar, J., Murali, V., Navas, J.A., Santosa, A.E.: TRACER: A Symbolic execution tool for verification. In: Madhusudan, P., Seshia, S.A. (eds.) CAV 2012. LNCS, vol. 7358, pp. 758–766. Springer, Heidelberg (2012)

18. Jhala, R., McMillan, K.L.: A practical and complete approach to predicate refinement. In: Hermanns, H., Palsberg, J. (eds.) TACAS 2006. LNCS, vol. 3920, pp. 459–473. Springer, Heidelberg (2006)

19. Jones, J.A., Harrold, M.J., Stasko, J.: Visualization of test information to assist fault localization. In: ICSE '02, pp. 467–477 (2002)

20. Jose, M., Majumdar, R.: Cause clue clauses: Error localization using maximum satisfiability. SIGPLAN Not. **46**(6), 437–446 (2011)

21. Liffiton, M.H., Sakallah, K.A.: Algorithms for computing minimal unsatisfiable subsets of constraints. J. Autom. Reason. **40**(1), 1–33 (2008)

22. Logozzo, F., Ball, T.: Modular and verified automatic program repair. In: OOPSLA (2012)

23. McCarthy, J.: A basis for a mathematical theory of computation. In: Braffort, P., Hirshberg, D. (eds.) Computer Programming and Formal Systems, pp. 33–70. North-Holland, Amsterdam (1963)

24. McMillan, K.L.: Interpolation and SAT-Based model checking. In: Hunt Jr., W.A., Somenzi, F. (eds.) CAV 2003. LNCS, vol. 2725, pp. 1–13. Springer, Heidelberg (2003)

25. McMillan, K.L.: Applications of Craig interpolants in model checking. In: Halbwachs, N., Zuck, L.D. (eds.) TACAS 2005. LNCS, vol. 3440, pp. 1–12. Springer, Heidelberg (2005)

26. Nadel, A.: Boosting minimal unsatisfiable core extraction. In: FMCAD (2010)

27. Necula, G.C., McPeak, S., Rahul, S.P., Weimer, W.: CIL: Intermediate language and tools for analysis and transformation of C programs. In: Nigel Horspool, R. (ed.) CC 2002. LNCS, vol. 2304, pp. 213–228. Springer, Heidelberg (2002)

28. Qi, D., Roychoudhury, A., Liang, Z., Vaswani, K.: Darwin: An approach to debugging evolving programs. ACM Trans. Softw. Eng. Methodol. **21**(3), 19 (2012)

29. Rollini, S.F., Sery, O., Sharygina, N.: Leveraging interpolant strength in model checking. In: Madhusudan, P., Seshia, S.A. (eds.) CAV 2012. LNCS, vol. 7358, pp. 193–209. Springer, Heidelberg (2012)

30. Sahoo, S.K., Criswell, J., Geigle, C., Adve, V.: Using likely invariants for automated software fault localization. In: ASPLOS (2013)

31. Schäf, M., Schwartz-Narbonne, D., Wies, T.: Explaining inconsistent code. In: ESEC/SIGSOFT FSE, pp. 521–531 (2013)

32. Silva, J.P.M.: Minimal unsatisfiability: Models, algorithms and applications (invited paper). In: ISMVL (2010)

33. Software-artifact infrastructure repository (SIR), August 2010. http://sir.unl.edu/portal/index.html

34. Vizel, Y., Grumberg, O.: Interpolation-sequence based model checking. In: FMCAD (2009)

35. Zeller, A.: Isolating cause-effect chains from computer programs. In: FSE '02, pp. 1–10 (2002)

36. Zhang, X., Gupta, N., Gupta, R.: A study of effectiveness of dynamic slicing in locating real faults. Empir. Softw. Engg. **12**(2), 143–160 (2007)

Author Index